ERASMUS ON THE NEW TESTAMENT

Edited by Robert D. Sider

When Erasmus, at Cambridge in 1512, began to mark up his copy of the Vulgate Bible with a few alternative Latin translations and a biting comment here and there in Latin, he could not have guessed that his work would grow over the next twenty-three years into the twenty volumes currently being produced as annotated translations in *The Collected Works of Erasmus*. His *Paraphrases* vastly expanded the text of the New Testament books and brought dynamic and controversial interpretations to the traditional reading of the Latin texts. A new translation based on the Greek text, the first ever to be published by a printing firm, became the basis for ever-expanding notes that explained the Greek, measured the contemporary church against the truth revealed by the Greek, taunted critics and opponents, and revealed the mind of a humanist at work on the Scriptures. The sheer vastness of the work that finally accumulated is almost beyond the reach of a single individual. Through excerpts chosen from the entire extent of Erasmus' New Testament work, this book hopes to reduce that immensity to manageable size, and bring the rich, virtually unlimited treasure of the Erasmian mind on the Scriptures within the comfortable reach of every interested individual.

(Erasmus Studies)

ROBERT D. SIDER is the Charles A. Dana professor emeritus of Classical Languages at Dickinson College and adjunct professor of History at University of Saskatchewan.

EDITED BY ROBERT D. SIDER

Erasmus on the New Testament

Selections from the *Paraphrases*, the *Annotations*, and the Writings on Biblical Interpretation

UNIVERSITY OF TORONTO PRESS
Toronto Buffalo London

Toronto Buffalo London
utorontopress.com
Printed in Canada

ISBN 978-1-4875-0610-0 (cloth) ISBN 978-1-4875-3330-4 (ePUB)
ISBN 978 1-4875-2410-4 (paper) ISBN 978-1-4875-3325-0 (PDF)

Library and Archives Canada Cataloguing in Publication

Title: Erasmus on the New Testament : selections from the Paraphrases, the Annotations, and the writings on biblical interpretation / edited by Robert Sider.
Names: Erasmus, Desiderius, –1536, author. | Sider, Robert D. (Robert Dick), editor. | Container of (work): Erasmus, Desiderius, –1536. Annotationes in Novum Testamentum. Selections. | Container of (work): Erasmus, Desiderius, –1536. Paraphrases in Novum Testamentum. Selections.
Series: Erasmus studies.
Description: Series statement: Erasmus studies | Includes bibliographical references and index.
Identifiers: Canadiana (print) 20190227206 | Canadiana (ebook) 20190227907 | ISBN 9781487506100 (cloth) | ISBN 9781487524104 (paper) | ISBN 9781487533304 (EPUB) | ISBN 9781487533250 (PDF)
Subjects: LCSH: Erasmus, Desiderius, –1536. Paraphrases in Novum Testamentum. | LCSH: Erasmus, Desiderius, –1536. Annotationes in Novum Testamentum. | LCSH: Bible. New Testament – Paraphrases, Latin. | LCSH: Bible. New Testament – Criticism, interpretation, etc. | LCSH: Bible. New Testament – Commentaries.
Classification: LCC BS2335 .E73 2020 | DDC 225.4/7 – dc23

University of Toronto Press acknowledges the financial assistance to its publishing program of the Canada Council for the Arts and the Ontario Arts Council, an agency of the Government of Ontario.

Canada Council for the Arts Conseil des Arts du Canada

Funded by the Government of Canada Financé par le gouvernement du Canada | Canada

For Lura Mae,
inseparable companion of my labours

Contents

Preface

Erasmus, a man of the Renaissance, continues in our century to tease, challenge, and provoke. In spite of the distance in time and the transformation of his texts from Latin into English, the modern reader will be immediately responsive to the issues Erasmus raises in his New Testament scholarship: the place of Scripture in the life of the individual and the church, the authority of the primitive church in the decisions of Christians who live in very different times, the validity of historic interpretations of dogmatic formulations tested by a philological reading of Scripture, the ethics of the Gospels, the theological vision of Paul. When we read the *Paraphrases* Erasmus will challenge us with his provocative interpretations of Scripture, and he will delight, perhaps amuse, us by the imaginative heights to which he sometimes endeavours to soar. Beyond their theological interest Erasmus' writings on the New Testament command our attention by their persistent interest in problems of historical verification, by their manifest love of language, their charming reflection of the alacrity of their author's mind, and by their colourful portrait of the world around him and the people who inhabit it. Considerations of this sort have guided me in preparing this book of selections from the vast expanse of Erasmus' New Testament scholarship.

The selections have been determined by the definition of 'Erasmus' New Testament Scholarship' that underlies the contents of the twenty volumes of the Collected Works of Erasmus dedicated to Erasmus' work on the New Testament (vols 41–60). The only exception is a set of selections from the Correspondence of Erasmus and a few excerpts from the controversy with Alberto Pio, both providing a revealing insight into the nature and purpose of his New Testament scholarship. The vast extent of Erasmus' work on the New Testament seemed to justify the assumption that a book of selections from this almost limitless and certainly varied material could best reflect the mind of Erasmus if it followed a pattern of organization primarily thematic. In order to provide points of reference and to facilitate for the reader a sense of cohesion among selections placed with necessarily minimal respect to chronology, I have in the Introduction made a brief chronological sketch of the development of Erasmus' New Testament scholarship. Following the introduction, I present in chapter 2 Erasmus' stimulating exposition of the 'philosophy of Christ,' the *Paraclesis*. Exceptionally, we print it in full because of its abiding popularity, its perennial importance and its winsome, indeed, almost lyrical, summons to all Christian readers to discover this life-giving evangelical philosophy in the Holy Scriptures. I turn in chapter 3 to Erasmus' important hermeneutical essay, the *Ratio verae theologiae*, a richly exemplified if somewhat prosaic set of guidelines for the proper, intelligent reading of Scripture, which was developed from the short *Methodus* of 1516 and vastly enlarged over several editions. Its diffuse train of thought and abundant illustration lends itself to abbreviation with some advantage for the reader seeking to grasp its main lines of argument. Chapters 4, 5, and 6 are devoted to the *Paraphrases*: chapter 4 on the Gospels and Acts, chapter 5 on the Pauline Epistles, and chapter 6 on the Catholic Epistles. Following the pattern established in the volumes of CWE I have placed the selections from the *Paraphrases* before those from the *Annotations* though the relationship between the two is somewhat ambiguous.[1] Although Erasmus completed the *Paraphrases* on the Epistles before he began those on the Gospels (the order, consequently, in which they appear in CWE), I have adopted the more familiar canonical order in presenting through the *Paraphrases* first the life of Jesus, then the life and thought of Paul. The selections in both cases have been chosen to accommodate the theme without regard to the chronological order in which they were originally published. The Catholic Epistles, so varied in attributed authorship and provenance, invite selections in paraphrase based on interest rather than on a common theme; the paraphrases on these, therefore, appear in the chronological order in which they were written and published.

Chapter 7 includes selections from the *Annotations*. The annotations were designed to explain and justify Erasmus' translation of the New Testament. Originally, therefore, they were predominantly concerned with the considerations of text, translation and semantics. But even in

1 Publication of the *Paraphrases* generally followed that of the editions of the New Testament, and yet Erasmus noted on more than one occasion that his annotations profited from what he had discovered when he was writing the *Paraphrases*.

the first edition, and much more so in later editions, the annotations went far beyond the straightforward defence of translation and text to include discussions of doctrinal issues as well as attacks, sometimes vicious, on the contemporary state of affairs in church and society. Erasmus also found a place in them to commend friends whom he named explicitly and to excoriate enemies who, ostentatiously anonymous, are, with few exceptions, all too easily identified. All of these various facets of Erasmus' annotations are sampled in this volume. A final section (chapter 8) makes available to the reader selections from Erasmus' correspondence and elsewhere that shed much light on his New Testament labours.

For the selections from the *Paraphrases* I have followed closely the text found in the CWE volumes. I have attempted, particularly in the sections 'The Life of Jesus' and 'Images of Paul,' to create as far as possible a coherent narrative, occasionally adapting the translation in CWE to achieve this goal. I have also sought to make the paraphrases readily comprehensible and have therefore consistently omitted from the text the repetition and the meandering that make the paraphrases of Erasmus so extensive. Thus the texts provided here (the *Paraclesis* apart) are abbreviations of a wide selection of Erasmian texts rather than a narrow selection of a few complete and exemplary examples of Erasmus' work. This is, of course, to offer an Erasmus that is not quite Erasmian, but this procedure will, I hope, provide a more instructive avenue to our readers for the further exploration of Erasmus in the undocked text of CWE. I have attempted to keep my own commentary minimal. The Life of Jesus is readily constructed in the biblical sequence from the Gospels, and required very little introductory comment. The life and thought of Paul come before us in the Epistles in a much more eclectic manner so that more explanation seemed necessary for context and continuity. I have provided the most essential notes; for more extensive annotation the reader may consult the volumes of CWE.

During the preparation of this book only the annotations on Romans had been published in the Collected Works of Erasmus, though the annotations on Galatians and Ephesians appeared before the preparation was completed. Hence, except in the case of the selections from CWE 56 and 58 the translation of the annotations is largely mine. I owe particular thanks, however, to Mark Vessey, who shared with me his unpublished translation of the annotations on Luke. His translation will appear in the Collected Works of Erasmus as volume 53. For the annotations the texts selected in this book have been identified in the manner customary in CWE, that is, by cue-phrase and Vulgate text, so that they can easily be matched with the texts as they appear in the published volumes of CWE. I have translated the annotations freely, at times cautiously paraphrasing. As with the selections from the *Paraphrases* I have omitted portions that deterred the straightforward movement of the argument or narrative. For my translations I have followed the text of ASD series VI vols 5–10 and have gleaned much from the excellent notes in these volumes. The translation of the annotations presupposes the text as it appeared in 1535. However, since most annotations are the result of an original note (1516 edition) with further comments added in subsequent editions I have generally attempted to identify in some manner by date or edition the components of the excerpts selected from each annotation. For the *Paraclesis*, and the selections from the *Ratio verae theologiae* and the *Contra morosos* I had available the translations that will appear in CWE 41.

I wish to express my gratitude to the Editorial Board of the Collected Works of Erasmus for its encouragement of this publication, and to the University of Toronto Press for its financial support. It has been a pleasure to work under the benign and efficient editorial guidance of Suzanne Rancourt, while the skills and patience of the copy-editors have, as usual, been most impressive, especially Evelyn Mackie. I have been very fortunate to be able to enjoy and profit from the encouragement and collegiality of the Department of History at the University of Saskatchewan as well as the unstinting cooperation of the University's Librarians. To no one do I owe more than to my wife, Lura Mae, whose enduring patience over the many years I have devoted to the study of Erasmus' New Testament has, among her friends, won her the sympathetic epithet 'Erasmus widow.' To her I dedicate this book.

ERASMUS ON THE NEW TESTAMENT

CHAPTER ONE

Introduction: Erasmus' New Testament Scholarship: Its Origin and Development

Erasmus' New Testament scholarship constituted an endeavour that stretched across more than twenty years. During this time Erasmus published five editions of his New Testament, several editions of his *Paraphrases*, and numerous editions of his two popular works on reading the Bible, the *Paraclesis* and the *Ratio verae theologiae*. With the exception of the *Paraclesis*, all of these publications underwent considerable change due to authorial revision throughout the years, though the fundamental form, once established, remained fairly stable. The New Testament editions were published with prefaces followed by the biblical text, then annotations (notes), and concluding matter such as indexes.[1] While there were revisions in text and annotations – corrections and improvements – the kind of change in the notes was essentially a vast expansion, each succeeding edition providing both new notes and additions to old ones. The conceptualization of the *Paraphrases* as a nearly exhaustive exposition of the biblical text, bringing into view its underlying presuppositions, its implicit allusions, and its homiletical applicability controlled the form of the paraphrase throughout. While the text of the *Paraphrases* saw relatively little expansion after the first edition, in subsequent years occasional significant revisions appeared. For the most part, such changes, whether in annotation or paraphrase, reflect little development in Erasmus' theological understanding of or approach to theological and ecclesiastical issues and the revolutionary events of his day. This stability and coherence of his thought facilitates the topical approach to his work taken generally in this book. The reader will,

1 The first edition and the edition of 1522 provided no subject index.

however, wish to know the temporal context of the selections below, if only as a point of reference, so I trace out briefly in this introductory chapter the developments in Erasmus' New Testament scholarship in their chronological sequence.

Erasmus was almost fifty years of age when he published his first edition of the New Testament in March 1516.[2] From his correspondence, we may conclude that he had begun work four years previously on what became his New Testament when he was at Cambridge University where he had held an appointment since 1511 as lecturer in Greek. There were, of course antecedents to his work at Cambridge on the New Testament. In 1501 he had attempted to write a commentary on the Epistles of Paul and, he tells us, had completed four volumes before he finally abandoned the effort, since at that time he lacked sufficient knowledge of Greek for the task. A few years later, in 1504, he discovered a manuscript by the Italian humanist Lorenzo Valla (1403–57), who had collated several Greek and Latin manuscripts of the New Testament against his Latin text of the Vulgate, noting passages where the Vulgate text failed to represent adequately the Greek. Erasmus published Valla's notes in 1505 under a title that designated the work as 'annotations.' But in general, Erasmus' interests in the first decade of the sixteenth century were focused elsewhere: mastering Greek, which he needed for his work on an edition of the letters of Jerome, translating the Greek classics, publishing magnificent volumes of proverbs, preparing textbooks for the education of the young, and writing the *Praise of Folly*, that immortal critique of the sixteenth century church and society.

Even in his first letters from Cambridge, Erasmus indicates that his interests are in the classics and the Fathers, though he tells John Colet, Dean of St Paul's and a lover of St Paul, that he may lecture on the Apostle. In May of 1512 we find a Paris printer, Josse Bade, negotiating with him for the publication of some work he is preparing; the letter makes no mention of work on the New Testament. Then, suddenly, in the autumn of that year he writes to a friend that he 'intends to finish the revision of the New Testament.' About a year later, he says that he has 'finished a collation of the New Testament.' In July of the following year (1514) he claims to have 'revised the whole of the New Testament from a collation of Greek and ancient [Latin] manuscripts and annotated over a thousand places with some benefit to theologians.'[3] By that

2 Erasmus was born in Rotterdam during the night of 28/29 October. The year of his birth is somewhat problematical; I believe the evidence points persuasively to 1466.

3 For the citations see Epp 264:17, 270:67 and 296:164–6.

time he had left Cambridge and was on his way to Basel to negotiate with John Froben the publication of several texts by the Froben Press.

It seems likely that the negotiations with Froben had a significant impact on the conception of Erasmus' New Testament. During the two years of preliminary work at Cambridge, Erasmus evidently had in mind a project somewhat like the one undertaken by Valla: ample notes explaining the results of the collation of Latin and Greek manuscripts against the Latin text of the Vulgate Bible, the text in common use in the early sixteenth century. Erasmus tells us quite explicitly how he had prepared his second edition of the New Testament and we may suppose that at Cambridge he had worked in much the same way: his notes and 'corrected' translations of Vulgate expressions crammed into his copy of the Vulgate Bible, some written perhaps in the margins, some perhaps in the interlinear space, some jotted down on pages appropriately inserted between the pages of his Bible. It seems to have been only after he had arrived in Basel and had talked with Froben and others that the design of the publication was perfected: a Bible that would present on every page in parallel columns a Greek text and Erasmus' revision of the Latin Vulgate, so that every reader could check the revision of the Latin against the Greek. The notes would be collected and placed at the end of the volume, after the Greek and Latin texts.

The preparation for publication of the full text of the New Testament demanded much further work, going well beyond what he had done in the materials brought from Cambridge to Basel. Greek manuscripts available in the Library of the University of Basel had to be collated. Erasmus' revisions of the Latin Vulgate already prepared had to be extended to cover the entire New Testament and had to match the Greek in the parallel column. More extensive annotation was required to justify the additional changes Erasmus was making to the Vulgate and to further illuminate the biblical text. As the Vulgate was regarded by many as fully inspired, there was a need not only to justify and defend specific revisions, but also the project itself, as well as to issue an urgent summons to the reader to participate in the benefit offered by the endeavour. Erasmus sought to satisfy these latter desiderata by a set of prefaces, chiefly essays, introducing the edition he was to publish. He had arrived in Basel in August 1514; the New Testament was not published until March 1516.

Erasmus' New Testament reflected the humanism that had become prominent in Europe since the thirteenth century. In southern Europe, humanism had found its inspiration in classical antiquity. Its devotees professed to find in classical literature an intimacy that brought its authors into the presence of the reader, their narratives providing a record of life that seemed capable of reaching across the ages to be absorbed by those who lived more than a millennium later. Not surprisingly, for these people classical antiquity established a standard of propriety for literature and the arts, encouraging a hope for the restoration of what was best in an ancient golden age. Hence classical Latin became a widely accepted standard for polished Latin speech in the Renaissance. After the fall of Constantinople to the Turks in 1453, Greek scholars brought to Italy some of the literary treasures of Greece and Byzantium. The new literary wealth invited the publication of editions, encouraged the translation of the Greek classics into polished Latin, and motivated a continuing search for yet other manuscripts. In northern Europe, some scholars were particularly eager to bring these prominent features of humanism into the service of Christian faith. In this endeavour perhaps no one stands out more visibly than Erasmus, above all in the editions of his New Testament. His search for and reliance upon Greek manuscripts, his insistence on a polished translation of the Bible, a translation that educated people could read with pleasure, his persistent, occasionally harsh criticism of the sometimes crude Latin of the Vulgate, his confidence that in the pages of the New Testament one could personally encounter Christ – all these features were in some measure influenced by the humanism he espoused.

The essays and other introductory material with which Erasmus prefaced his New Testament emphasized the humanist orientation of the project. An elaborate title explained that the work was a revision and correction, in effect, a restoration of the Vulgate Bible, a restoration based on the collation of ancient Greek and Latin manuscripts. The edition, dedicated to Pope Leo X, recalled in the dedicatory letter the magnanimous contribution of Leo's family, the Medici of Florence, to literature and the arts. The three essays that followed were carefully designed to promote and justify the new Bible. The *Paraclesis* was a winsome 'summons' (the meaning of this Greek word) to every Christian to read the Scriptures and to confront in them a Christ still living and reaching across the centuries to speak to the people of 'today.' The *Methodus*, later to be developed into the much more extensive *Ratio verae theologiae*, provided a guide to the reading and interpretation of Scripture and for this purpose advocated an education in the humanities. The last essay of the three, the *Apologia*, defended on humanist principles this bold undertaking. Only after this explanation and defence did the text of the New Testament in Latin and Greek appear, followed by the notes.

Criticism quickly emerged. Indeed Erasmus' project, already known to some scholars while his work was in preparation, had received fairly severe criticism even before the New Testament was published. The Vulgate was, after all, a sacred and authoritative text, while Greek manuscripts, it was said, could not be reliable since the Greek church was 'schismatic,' even 'heretical.' In countering such criticism Erasmus had remarked to a friend just a few months after the New Testament had appeared, 'Suppose I had expounded all the sacred books by way of a paraphrase, and made it possible to keep the sense inviolate and yet to read them without stumbling and understand them more easily? Would they quarrel with me then?'[4] Within a year Erasmus would be hard at work writing his first *Paraphrase*, the *Paraphrase on Romans*. It was published in November 1517, only a couple of weeks after Martin Luther had posted his Ninety-five Theses in Wittenberg. In fact it would not be long before a relationship between Erasmus and Luther would be established, a connection to be severed, however, only a few years later.

If in its conception the *Paraphrase on Romans* was in some sense a response to Erasmus' critics for his bold attempt at a translation of the Bible, it was rather in the second edition of the New Testament that Erasmus spoke specifically and decisively to the criticism of the first edition. Already in the first edition Erasmus had promised a second edition. He was in many ways dissatisfied with the first edition as a publication: it had been hastily thrown together and Erasmus himself has preserved for us a vivid literary image of the chaos in the shop during the printing.[5] The new edition offered an opportunity to enhance the physical properties of the book, to refine the translation, enlarge the annotations, and respond forcefully to his critics.

The second edition was published in March 1519. It was a handsome two-volume set, the second volume devoted to the annotations newly expanded and providing at the end an elaborate, detailed (and still useful) subject index of fifty-two columns (twenty-six pages). In the first volume the prefatory materials were increased from twenty-eight pages in the first edition to one hundred and twenty pages in the second. The increase was due primarily to four notable features: 1/ a letter from Pope Leo X commending the work, 2/ the transformation of the *Methodus* (nine pages) into the *Ratio verae theologiae* (fifty pages), 3/ twenty pages that provided for the reader a system facilitating the

4 Ep 456:93–6 (Aug 1516) to Henry Bullock, the 'closest of Erasmus' friends in Cambridge' [Ep 449 introduction]).

5 Cf Ep 421:50–76 and CWE 41 56–7 with nn239 and 240.

identification of parallel passages in the Gospels,[6] 4/ one hundred and eleven paragraphs gathered together under an incriminating title[7] and responding in precise detail to objections that had been raised to the first edition. While these objections might posture as theological principles, they grew out of Erasmus' claim to have found in the Vulgate various kinds of textual, linguistic, and literary faults. He therefore added seven lists of the various kinds of errors in the Vulgate[8] as demonstrable proof that his claim was justified. The first of the two volumes was, moreover, embellished with elaborately decorated borders framing the text of the letters to and from Pope Leo and the first page of the main sections of the text, thus the first page of each of the Gospels and of Acts, the first page of the Pauline Epistles (Romans), of the Catholic Epistles (James), and of Revelation. The second edition of Erasmus' New Testament was indeed a proud achievement in the making of books!

Erasmus continued to work on his translation as he prepared his second edition. While the first edition could be regarded as a fairly radical revision of the Vulgate, Erasmus recognized that it was far from finished. He tells us that he did not have time during the preparation of the first edition to work much on Luke, that elsewhere some passages had undoubtedly been overlooked, and that at some points he had thought it indiscreet to change the Vulgate, but now for the second edition he was emboldened to do so.[9] The annotations were vastly enlarged by inserting additions to those already established in the first edition, but also by adding many new annotations.[10] The new material kept to the purpose and direction of the annotations of the first edition, continuing to defend, explain, and illuminate the translation. The

6 Gospel parallels are easily identified today by reference to chapter and verse numbers often signalled in the text itself or in the margins of each page. But the present verse system did not come into use until 1551; previously from the fourth century parallels were identified by the application of the 'Eusebian canons,' ten rather complicated but in fact effective tables frequently presented in the front of Bibles. It was these tables that Erasmus included in the introductory material to his second edition (and the three subsequent editions).

7 'The Chief Points in the Arguments Answering Some Crabby and Ignorant Critics,' generally cited in this book as *Contra morosos* 'Crabby Critics.' Excerpts are included below.

8 These are translated under the title 'Errors in the Vulgate' and appear after the *Contra morosos* in CWE 41.

9 Cf CWE 41 46 with n202 and 123–6.

10 While Erasmus added new annotations in each edition subsequent to that of 1516, the growth of the annotations arose largely from additions inserted into existing annotations, often seamlessly. In the excerpts selected below, I have attempted to alert the reader to the date/edition of the major additions to the text.

response to objectors, however, was now frequently vigorous, sharp, and sustained, while criticism of church and society was extensive, passionate, sometimes bitter. Erasmus added fifty-six paragraphs to his annotation on Hebrews 2:7 ('You have made him a little lower than the angels' [AV])[11] in defence of his *1516* interpretation that had been severely criticized by his fellow humanist, Jacques Lefèvre d'Étaples; he added more than a page to defend his translation of Acts 10:38 ('how he anointed him'), in which he had claimed the apostles spoke faulty Greek; he wrote a ten-page critique of the church's position on divorce;[12] and in his annotation on Luke 22:36 ('but now whoever has a bag') he elaborated his views on the Christian in relation to warfare by adding a full page to an annotation that was already uncommonly long in the 1516 edition. The freedom of expression he thus indulged in the annotations of *1519* became the norm for the three editions that would follow (1522, 1527 and 1535). The first edition had been highly creative in establishing the general structure and methodology for Erasmus' New Testament; the second edition was equally creative in shaping what had been established in 1516 into an instrument of refined scholarship and a provocative vehicle for ecclesiastical reform and the renewal of the Christian faith.

Erasmus had been pleased with the success of his *Paraphrase on Romans*. In general it had been received not only warmly but with much praise. Within a month of its publication Erasmus had sent to the prince-bishop of Liège, Erard de la Marck, a copy of the *Paraphrase*. One of the bishop's retinue reported that the prince had 'raised [the *Paraphrase*] to his lips several times and uttered the name of Erasmus with delight.'[13] No wonder, then, that as soon as Erasmus had completed work on the second edition of the New Testament (late October 1518), he began at once to compose another *Paraphrase*, the *Paraphrase on the Two Epistles of Paul to the Corinthians*, completed by January 1519 – he seems to have required remarkably little time to write a *Paraphrase*! Throughout 1519 and into early 1520 he continued to paraphrase the Pauline Epistles: after Corinthians came Galatians, then (breaking the sequence of the canonical order) in a single publication the Pastoral Epistles (Timothy to Philemon), and finally, and again in a single publication, the Epistles from Ephesians to Thessalonians. Thinking it appropriate to do for St

11 In RSV, NRSV 'for a little while lower' – as Erasmus wished to understand.

12 Cf the annotation (excerpted below) on 1 Cor 7:39 (*liberata est a lege, cui autem vult, nubat* 'she is free from the law and may marry whomever she wishes').

13 Ep 748:24–5.

Peter what he had done for St Paul, in the earlier part of 1520 he paraphrased the two Epistles of Peter and Jude. Later he was persuaded to paraphrase the remaining Catholic Epistles: James in 1520, followed last of all by the three Johns and Hebrews completed in early 1521. The Apocalypse alone remained, which Erasmus never found suitable for paraphrase. Each publication was preceded by a letter of dedication to a distinguished churchman and with only two exceptions (Galatians and Hebrews) these letters were always published with the *Paraphrase* or set of *Paraphrases* they originally prefaced. None became more noted than the dedication of the *Paraphrase on the Two Epistles of Paul to the Corinthians* to Erard de la Marck. It is a very long letter, spread over seventeen pages in CWE 43. The letter is distinguished, first, by its extensive comparison between the primitive church and the church of the sixteenth century, with an implicit call for reform; the implications of this study in sharp contrasts could not be missed and the letter eventually became a focus of attack by Erasmus' critics. The letter is distinguished, second, by its brilliant characterization of Paul in a paragraph that is included in the selections below.

The second edition of the New Testament had done nothing to allay criticism; in fact Erasmus felt the criticism so keenly that he determined to make the third edition his last[14] – 'not,' he says, 'because there is no need to say anything further, but because I must give way before the slanderers who are everywhere in control now, and excessive labour in an enterprise so lowly and unembellished is properly regarded as reprehensible!'[15] Some of his critics were in high places and influential, for example, a bishop in England (Henry Standish) and an assistant inquisitor, professor at the University of Louvain (Nicolaas Baechem), who insisted on associating Erasmus with Luther, characterizing both as heretics. But two other critics played a very particular role in the preparation of the third edition: Edward Lee, a relatively young Englishman and Franciscan at Louvain University, and Diego Lopéz Zúñiga, a Spaniard who had moved to Rome in 1520. Lee was angry because he felt that in his second edition Erasmus had ignored the 'helpful criticism' of the first edition he had offered him in casual notes on sheets of paper on which Erasmus had scribbled responses in the autumn of 1517. His criticisms, enshrined in a book published in 1520, formalized the notes scribbled in 1517, and so were directed at Erasmus' annotations particularly as they appeared in the first edition, though a few

14 He made the same comment in his fourth and fifth editions!

15 Preface to the annotations on the Gospel of Mark.

'new notes' took account of annotations in the second edition. Zúñiga, a Greek and Hebrew scholar who disdained Erasmus' lack of Hebrew and (as he thought) inadequate Greek, attacked his translation, also as it appeared in the first edition. Erasmus published responses specific to each.[16] The text of the annotations of the third edition is in numerous instances closely related to these responses, sometimes identical, word for word. The edition was published in February 1522.

As we have seen, the first and second editions were each in its own way highly creative productions. Much less so the third edition. There were two major changes in format: the *Ratio verae theologiae*, now a highly successful publication circulating apart from the New Testament, was omitted from the prefaces, and though the second edition had provided an excellent subject index none was offered in the third. Otherwise, the edition closely followed the pattern established in 1519. It was a two-volume set with borders as in the second edition, while the text of the New Testament followed the second volume so closely that except for the last few pages the pagination was identical in the two editions. In the second edition the *Contra morosos* had been followed by fifteen pages listing hundreds of examples of the faults of the Vulgate and appropriately keyed to the pagination of that volume; curiously, the list appeared again in the third edition but keyed to the pagination of the annotations of the second edition – useless for anyone who did not have both editions at hand! The edition seems to have been rather carelessly slung together, its primary motivation the response to critics.

Nowhere is the response to critics more striking (or better known!) than in the text of 1 John 5:7–8. Today it is widely acknowledged that the 'heavenly witnesses' are an interpolation into the text, so that the text originally read, 'There are three who give witness, the Spirit, the water and the blood, and these three agree.' This was the reading of all the Greek manuscripts Erasmus had seen. It was not, however, the text of the Vulgate, which read, 'There are three who give witness in heaven, the Father, the Word and the Holy Spirit, and these three are one, and there are three who give witness on earth, the Spirit, the water and the blood, and these three agree in one.' In the first two editions Erasmus omitted the 'heavenly witnesses,' and explained that if he had found these words in a single Greek manuscript he would have added them. He was severely criticized for the omission because it seemed to remove

16 *An Apologia in Response to the Two Invectives of Edward Lee* and *A Response to the Annotations of Edward Lee*, both in CWE 72; *Apologia contra Stunicam* (ie Zúñiga) translation forthcoming in CWE 74.

a strong witness to the traditional doctrine of the Trinity. Conveniently, while Erasmus was preparing his third edition someone did find the 'heavenly witnesses' in a manuscript now in the Library of Trinity College, Dublin; Erasmus obligingly inserted them in the text of the third edition (and the two subsequent editions). It is commonly believed, though not authoritatively proven, that the manuscript was produced deliberately to force Erasmus to restore the 'heavenly witnesses' to his text! A selection from the annotation is given below.

Erasmus continued in the third edition to tamper with his revision of the Vulgate translation. He added new annotations and inserted many additions into the old ones, often with the same acerbic comments as earlier on the state of affairs in church and society. He was also now able to add new and important witnesses to the text. From the first edition Erasmus had recognized the importance of biblical citations in the commentaries of the Fathers as valuable evidence for the original biblical text. While he was preparing this third edition he found a commentary of the Venerable Bede on the Catholic Epistles. He discovered also a magnificent Latin manuscript of the Gospels in the Royal Library in Mechelen, all its letters written in gold – the codex aureus (golden codex), a truly striking manuscript now displayed in the library of the Escorial adjacent to the town of S. Lorenzo de El Escorial, Spain. Finally, in the summer of 1521, as he was finishing his work on this third edition, he found in the library of St Donatian in Bruges several more Latin manuscripts of the New Testament. In the third edition he frequently appeals to these as authorities for the true text of Scripture.

In the summer of 1521, while Erasmus was intently engaged in the preparation of the third edition of his New Testament, Matthäus Schiner, Cardinal of Sion (in Switzerland), an international diplomat, came to Brussels where he met Erasmus, and encouraged him to 'do for Matthew's Gospel what he had done for the apostolic Epistles.'[17] Erasmus hesitated: was it permissible to put in the mouth of the incarnate God words other than what the Lord had spoken? In some passages Jesus had seemed to speak obscurely, as though he wished not to be understood; some passages had always been and still remained inexplicable. The paraphrast did not have the commentator's freedom to qualify his interpretation; and was it not a sort of audacity to clarify what was intended to be obscure? Moreover, if a *Paraphrase on Matthew* should be warmly welcomed, there might well be a demand for paraphrases on the other Gospels, which could mean an unproductive repetition in

17 Ep 1255:30.

parallel passages in the Synoptic Gospels.[18] But Erasmus overcame his reticence, and shortly after he had moved to Basel (15 November 1521) to assist at the printing of the third edition of the New Testament, he was busily engaged in paraphrasing the Gospel of Matthew. While this *Paraphrase* bears the date of March 1522, Erasmus had, in fact, completed it in time to be included as the first *Paraphrase* in a new 'collected edition' in folio of the *Paraphrases* on the apostolic Epistles, published in February 1522.

Paraphrases on the other Gospels soon followed, John in February 1523 and Luke in August of the same year. Erasmus had undertaken to paraphrase these Gospels on the urging of others; he then realized that unless he took action someone else would fill in the gap that remained by paraphrasing Mark, and would do so in a style that might well be discordant with his own in the *Paraphrases* on the other Gospels. Hence the *Paraphrase on Mark*, completed by the end of 1523 – truly a banner year for the *Paraphrases*. By that time Froben had decided to publish in two volumes an edition of the 'Collected *Paraphrases*.' The second volume, the *Paraphrases on the Apostolic Epistles*, was, of course, ready for publication and appeared in late 1523. The first volume still needed Acts, the *Paraphrase* which Erasmus hastened to complete. It was published in February 1524, and appeared again along with the Gospels as volume one of the complete *Paraphrases* published in the spring of the same year.

I noted above that letters of dedication normally prefaced the *Paraphrases*. If we consider the political station of the dedicatees, we can detect an interesting pattern in these dedications. After Romans (dedicated to Cardinal Grimani) Erasmus turned to regional prince-bishops: Erard de la Marck, Liège (1 and 2 Corinthians), Philip of Burgundy, Utrecht, Erasmus' own bishop, (the Pastoral Epistles), then to international diplomats: Cardinal Campeggi (Ephesians – 2 Thessalonians), Cardinal Wolsey (1 and 2 Peter, Jude), Cardinal Schiner (James, 1–3 John), Bishop Sylvester Gigli (Hebrews). The Gospels Erasmus dedicated to kings: Charles V (Spain, also emperor from 1520), Ferdinand, Charles' brother (the Austrian duchies), Henry VIII (England), and Francis 1 (France) – respectively Matthew, John, Luke, and Mark. Acts alone remained and this Erasmus dedicated to Pope Clement VII, God's vicegerent on earth! The kings were at war at this time, and Erasmus used the occasion of the letters to the kings and the pope to call the

18 Cf Ep 1255:32–79. The letter is excerpted below.

world's rulers to peace: the gospel of Christ expressed in the Gospels is a gospel of peace. The theme is expressed beautifully in the letter to King Francis, written in anticipation of volume 1 of the Collected *Paraphrase* in which the four Gospels would be published together: 'I offer my most fervent prayers ... that as the four Gospels in one volume now unite your names, so may we soon see the gospel spirit unite your hearts together in enduring concord.'[19]

We observed above Erasmus' intention stated so clearly in the third edition of his New Testament that 'because of the slanderers' he would publish no further editions of the New Testament. Nevertheless, in the very month that saw the finishing touches placed on the last of the *Paraphrases* to be written (Acts, February 1524) he noted in a letter to Cardinal Campeggi that a fourth edition of his New Testament was in preparation. Six months later he claimed that his fourth edition was ready – undoubtedly an anticipatory over-statement, as Erasmus continued to work on the edition for two more years.

Erasmus himself suggests that he was motivated to prepare a fourth edition by his work on the *Paraphrases* for he had 'discovered while writing the *Paraphrases* that many things had escaped him.'[20] But there were undoubtedly other significant factors. Erasmus had become increasingly devoted to editing the church Fathers. As early as 1517 he had negotiated with Froben an edition of Augustine (completed only in 1529). In 1520 he published an edition of Cyprian, in 1523 one of Hilary, in 1524–6 a new edition of Jerome, in 1526 also an edition of the Latin Irenaeus. But he had become especially interested in the Greek Chrysostom, and by 1525 was publishing editions of the Greek texts of the 'golden-mouth.' Some years before, in responding to Lee (1520), he had managed to receive from friends scraps of Chrysostom's *Homilies on Acts* that he had been able to use in his third edition. As a Greek speaker Chrysostom would cite in his *Homilies* the Greek text of Scripture; accordingly, Erasmus believed that he should thus be a reliable witness to the original biblical text. Copyists had, to be sure, in some cases accommodated the biblical text to the Vulgate reading, but Chrysostom's comments on the texts would generally reflect the Greek text he was using, and thus in spite of copyists' occasional accommodation of the Latin text to the Greek the reading of Chrysostom should reveal the true text of Scripture. By the time of publication of the fourth edition

19 Ep 1403:14–17.

20 Ep 1341A:493–5.

Erasmus had at hand Greek manuscripts of Chrysostom's *Homilies* on Acts, Romans, and 2 Corinthians, and two *Homilies* on Philippians.

Yet another reason for a new edition was Erasmus' perceived need to respond to critics. Although the *Paraphrases* had at first been generally well received, by 1525 new and deadly criticism had begun to arise, in particular from the theologians at the University of Paris, above all from Noël Béda. By 1524 Béda had worked through Erasmus' *Paraphrase on Luke* (published August 1523), and had found numerous problems – errors of fact as well as questionable theology. He then proceeded to do the same with Erasmus' other *Paraphrases* and reported the results of his work to the faculty of theology at the University, then published his findings which reflected the central focus of his attack: the charge of Lutheranism. Another French theologian, Pierre Cousturier, a friend of Béda, published in 1525 an attack on Erasmus' translation, ie, his revision of the Vulgate, attacking in fact the very idea of a translation. He maintained that the Vulgate translation was inspired – every word – by the Holy Spirit, and any alteration of the Vulgate was thus a sin against the Holy Spirit. Erasmus wrote fitting responses to both men, but he felt it was important in addition to clarify his position in his New Testament annotations where the criticism affected his biblical scholarship.

There were other critics as well. Zúñiga continued to write against Erasmus' 'blasphemies.' Some of the scholarly elite of Rome mocked Erasmus' style, a vivid, forceful style no doubt, but for all that lacking genuinely Ciceronian polish. In 1524 or 1525 Girolamo Aleandro, once a friend of Erasmus but apparently a determined and astute self-seeker who had become a powerful figure in the Vatican, wrote and circulated a scathing attack on Erasmus' annotations on 'Racha' in Matthew 5:22 and on 'Gehenna' ('Tophet') in Matthew 10:28.[21] All of these considerations would have been in Erasmus' mind as he prepared the fourth edition.

The new edition, published in March 1527, was marked by some changes in format. Most important was the decision to include in the text the Vulgate translation. In this edition, therefore, each page of text was divided into three columns, on the left the Greek, on the right the Vulgate, and between the two, Erasmus' revision of the Vulgate. Every reader could now see at a glance the difference between Erasmus' revision and the text of the Vulgate and could compare both with the Greek. The decorative borders that embellished the two previous editions were

21 An excerpt from Erasmus' response in the *Annotations* is included below.

omitted; this was in general a less handsome edition than those of 1519 and 1522.

The *Paraclesis* was no longer included among the prefaces – it had for some time circulated successfully as a publication separate from the New Testament. Thus of the three major essays that prefaced the edition of 1516 only the *Apologia* now remained. It was followed by the *Contra morosos* as in *1519* and *1522*.[22] In both of these Erasmus added further discussion about the respective roles of the Holy Spirit and the translator in producing the text of Scripture. The issue had been forcefully raised by Pierre Cousturier. In these additions Erasmus insisted on an incarnational theology: the Holy Spirit works through a fallible human instrument, whose fallibility leaves its mark on the sacred word without destroying the authority of that word. It is, after all, in the church that the truth lies, and there it remains secure.

As we have noted, the manuscripts of Chrysostom which Erasmus had edited, translated, and published offered important new evidence for the text of the New Testament. Some new Latin texts also became available through the good services of his friend John Botzheim, a canon of the cathedral in Constance, Switzerland. Erasmus found that these manuscripts tended generally to confirm the Greek text he had printed in previous editions. He consulted the new Spanish Polyglot Bible published about 1522, and though he adopted a number of its readings few made a major difference in his translation. In fact, by now his translation was firmly in place; the number of substantive changes to the translation in the 1527 edition amounted to just over a dozen in the Gospels and Acts, and half of these were reversions to the Vulgate.

Much was added to the annotations. Erasmus addressed with noticeable pique Aleandro's criticisms of his comments on 'Racha' and 'Gehenna,' drawing in his annotation on the latter an ugly portrait of his critic (excerpted below). Nor did he did spare those knife-like jabs at church and society familiar from the earlier editions: 'Now the world has innumerable celibates, practically none of them chaste'; 'Now [bishops] call it hospitality when they receive satraps and kings and send them on their way with gifts'; 'Now when there is need of force [bishops] have swords and gunpowder, but where the front line of vices is to be attacked by the sword of the divine word, they have

22 The illustrative lists of errors (cf 8 with nn7 and 8 above) was, however, separated from the *Contra morosos* and placed after the *Annotations* at the end of the second volume, where they would be less obvious and therefore less offensive. They were omitted entirely in the edition of 1535.

neither tongue nor hand.'[23] The 1527 edition is notable for Erasmus' frank avowal of a version of the just war theory as a corrective to prior statements that seemed to endorse a pacifist position. Although Erasmus had often commented on the style of the biblical authors, in *1527* he explored at length the prose style of Paul in three impressive passages in Romans: 8:29–35, 12:6–21, and 13:12–14. He concluded his analysis of the first passage by observing that the speech was 'elevated because Paul, breathed upon as it were by the divine power, says nothing in the low style,' and he asks, 'What did Cicero ever say that effected more the grand style?'

The 1527 edition compels our interest also by Erasmus' attempts to address issues with important theological implications. Béda thought his charges of Lutheranism found substance in Erasmus' paraphrases on Luke 1 and 2 where Mary is a central figure. In particular, Erasmus defended the claim implicit in his *Paraphrase* that Mary was chosen as the *theotokos* not because of her merits but because of God's grace. Nowhere else does Erasmus state his position on grace and merits more clearly than in an addition to the annotation on Eph 1:6: '[Paul] everywhere extols grace, minimizing trust in human works. There are those who err in either direction. The safest way is in the middle, but if one must move to one side or the other, it is safer to turn to the side of grace where Christ is glorified than to works wherein human beings are glorified.' Moreover, the 1527 edition is distinguished by an entirely new annotation on faith. Though the Lutheran emphasis on faith may have given the annotation a certain relevance at this time, the annotation would seem to refer more specifically to comments made by both Lee and Zúñiga objecting to Erasmus' assertion that the famous statement in Hebrews 11:1, 'Faith is the substance of things hoped for,' was not a definition. Notably, Erasmus' long attempt at definition proceeds philologically; though it has theological significance it is not a theological response.

After the edition of March 1527 Erasmus looked upon a world that seemed to him to be growing ever darker. He had lost friends, some to death, among them his publisher, John Froben. In Basel the Reformation came to a climax in February 1529 with the savage destruction of religious images and an absolute ban on the Mass within the city's boundaries. Erasmus felt afraid and, as a distinguished Catholic whose

---

23 For the citations see the annotations on 1 Tim 3:2 (first two) and 2 Cor 10:4 (third), also CWE 41 305.

continuing presence might suggest complicity, felt obligated to leave. He moved to Freiburg im Breisgau and returned to Basel only in 1535, about a year before his death. His New Testament had come under attack again from several quarters, but, of particular note, from a relatively young Louvain scholar, Frans Titelmans, whose youthful pretensions and egregious piety, evident in his *Discussions on Romans*, Erasmus found especially annoying.[24] Béda had managed to get support for his criticisms of Erasmus' *Paraphrases* and a few other works, and in 1531 the 'Censures' of the faculty of theology were published. Erasmus himself suffered increasingly from sickness, and became pathologically suspicious even of friends. Anticipating death he expected to be able to produce no further editions of either the *Paraphrases* or the New Testament, and consequently he issued in 1529 a few corrections to his New Testament publications. In fact, he had seven more years of productive literary activity, during which he was able to revise his *Paraphrases* (*1532, 1534, 1535*), and produce a fifth and final edition of his New Testament (1535).

The immediate impetus for the revision in 1532 of the *Paraphrases* on the apostolic Epistles seems to have been the publication of the Censures of the University of Paris in 1531. There are significant revisions in this edition of the *Paraphrases* that qualify previous statements construed as casting the Mosaic law in a negative light; there are some small changes that reflected Erasmus' understanding of faith and charity as an inseparable pair, and, as we shall see below, further significant revisions addressing questions of the relationship between free will and divine grace that had been raised by critics even before 1520. All of these, it would seem, were in response primarily to the 'Censures.' But Erasmus attempted also to perfect the work simply as a literary artifact: to embellish the language, to give the sentence structure more rhetorical polish, to give greater illumination in the paraphrastic expression of the biblical text. An edition in 1534 of all the *Paraphrases* saw some important revisions in the Gospels, especially in the *Paraphrase on Matthew*, but the edition in 1535 of the Gospels and Acts offered very little that was new.

The New Testament of 1535 gave Erasmus an opportunity to perfect the annotations and to respond once again to critics, especially Titelmans and the Paris theologians. Here, too, as in the *Paraphrases*, one can see the perfecting touch in the corrections and in the completion of

24 *Five Discussions on the Epistle to the Romans*; cf CWE 41 265–6 with n1109.

the cue-phrases, some of which in previous editions had been sharply abbreviated. By extending the lemma (cue-phrase) in *1535* Erasmus gave the reader easier access to the point of the annotation. Two very large annotations on 1 Corinthians 13 worked out in detail Erasmus' views on 'faith' and its relation to 'charity.' But no one influenced the annotations of *1535* more than Titelmans. Indeed many of the annotations on Romans in *1535* are directed quite specifically to Titelmans' concerns, none more than the massive addition to the annotation on Romans 5:12, where Erasmus defends himself against the charge of Pelagianism. An entirely new annotation of two and a half pages attacked monastic pretensions to poverty.[25]

The final edition provided Erasmus with yet one further opportunity. We have seen that Erasmus increasingly sought to verify his New Testament text by appeal to the text found in the *Homilies* of Chrysostom. In spite of heroic efforts to find manuscripts of the *Homilies* there still remained a noticeable gap in his references to the text of this Greek bishop in the annotations on the Epistles from Galatians to 2 Thessalonians. But in 1529 Gian Matteo Giberti published in three volumes (in Greek) the *Homilies* of Chrysostom on the Pauline Epistles. By 1532, if not before, Erasmus had become aware of this publication. He was thus enabled now to bring the authority of this Greek Father to the text of all the Pauline Epistles.

The edition was published once again by the Froben Press, but under the management of Jerome Froben (John's son) and Nicolaus Episcopius (Jerome's brother-in-law). Again the work appeared in two volumes, the first accommodated the text, the second the annotations. The text of the New Testament returned to the format of the first three editions, with two columns only, one for Erasmus' revision of the Vulgate and one for the Greek text. Although on Erasmus' recommendation a new and attractive font was used, the decorative features that had made the editions of 1519 and 1522 so pleasing were absent. Erasmus retained the *Contra morosos*, but completely eliminated the list of 'Errors' that in the three preceding editions had witnessed lavishly and loudly to the embarrassing faults of the Vulgate; this was an act, he affirmed, of indulgent irenicism: he omitted these pages because readers had found them simply too offensive!

---

25 Selections from the two annotations on 1 Corinthians, and the annotations on Romans 5 and on monastic poverty (Mark 6) are included below.

PARAPHRASE AND ANNOTATION: GENERAL CHARACTERISTICS[26]

Paraphrase

Erasmus intended his paraphrases to be an *explanatio*, that is, a 'clarification' of the text. By *explanatio* he seems to have meant a narrative that brought to the surface the assumptions that underlay the explicit language of the text, thus placing the assumptions on a level with the text. In this way the language of the paraphrase becomes a creative combination of the explicit language of the biblical text and that of Erasmus as he works into the narrative the ideas he finds implicit in the biblical text. This entailed a vast expansion of the biblical text. Clarification also meant elucidating the connotation of the biblical words, sharpening the outlines of the biblical narrative through summaries, occasional recapitulation of the thought, and the use of sometimes elaborate connectives to mark the relationship of ideas as the biblical text moves forward.[27]

It is evident, however, from the *Paraphrases* that Erasmus wished not only to clarify and enlarge upon the text of Scripture but also to enrich it. He did so by incorporating the interpretations he found in the commentaries of the Fathers, sometimes their actual language. He bestowed upon the text in hand a certain resonance that expands its sense by inviting through suggestive allusion the recollection of other biblical texts. He understood the power of both drama and rhetoric to embellish a text that may in itself be plain. Though he strove for a middle style he frequently adorned a passage with effective rhythms and beautiful images. It is also evident that in the very act of clarifying the original historic text he made it speak to his own generation. Here and there key words point, if sometimes slyly, to contemporary issues: baptism, ceremonies, superstitious practices. Personal pronouns in the original text (you, we) can be generalized to refer to the contemporary reader, while temporal phrases like 'today,' 'now,' obscure the distinction between past and present and link ambiguously the addressee of ancient times with the reader of Erasmus' (and our) contemporary world.

---

26 In this account I have followed closely the narrative in the introductory essay (chapter 1) in CWE 41; for paraphrase see CWE 41 88–90, for annotation 49–58.

27 See the description of the Erasmian paraphrase in CWE 42 xi–xix. For an excellent account of the paraphrase in classical antiquity and its relationship to the classical articulation of the theory of the paraphrase see Michael Roberts *Biblical Epic and Rhetorical Paraphrase in Late Antiquity* ARCA Classical and Medieval Texts, Papers, and Monographs 16 (Liverpool 1985).

Annotation

In adopting the annotation as a form of commentary Erasmus followed a genre employed in both pagan and Christian antiquity and that continued in the Renaissance. The genre was understood as a vehicle for short notes on interesting topics, 'jottings' as it were, informal and unmethodical, normally structured with little formal design, where the serendipitous and the desultory could find an unembarrassed place. Erasmus' annotations seem also to follow a long tradition of philological commentary designed to facilitate and enrich the reading of a literary text. In this tradition the commentary addressed problems of textual authenticity and the construction of the text. It enriched the reading of a text with observations on the language, distinguishing words in respect to their proper domicile and connotation, noting figures of speech, with an occasional comment on the elegance and propriety of a word in its context. In bringing together these two traditions ('jottings' and philological commentary) Erasmus moved his annotations beyond purely mundane notes to achieve a certain level of literary interest arising from several features: the annotations reflect a critical instinct indicative of an engaged and engaging mind; they move repeatedly and often unexpectedly to probe critical points of theological concern and to challenge existing ecclesiastical practices; they pause, however briefly, for story-telling, incorporating Erasmus' superb instinct for drama in the delineation of setting and action and in the portrayal of character; they become in places pungent with satire that emerges sometimes from a brief remark, pithy, unexpected, apparently spontaneous, sometimes from comments more studied and sustained, the satire sometimes genial and Horatian, sometimes savage and Juvenalian.

We should note briefly the format of Erasmus' annotations. Each annotation was introduced by a *lemma*, that is, a cue-phrase, usually a short expression taken from the Vulgate, followed by Erasmus' comment. In the first edition the comments were often (but not always) brief. Over time, however, Erasmus acquired new manuscripts witnessing to the text of the Bible, and he read ever more broadly and deeply in the Fathers; he also felt the need to answer a growing raft of critics, and he responded, usually rather critically, to the remarkable developments in the contemporary world of ecclesiastical affairs, all of which provided new material for his annotations. To accommodate his comments Erasmus often added new annotations, but in many cases he simply added to existing annotations, dexterously fitting the new into the old. Thus a majority of the annotations are comprised of comments from two or more editions, combined so carefully that normally one cannot distinguish the different editions without a critical text such as that of the ASD or the translations of CWE. As I have noted in the Preface, in the selections below I have provided some indication of the stages of growth in the annotations over the various editions.

CHAPTER TWO

The Philosophy of Christ

THE *PARACLESIS*: LIVING WITH THE SCRIPTURES

[Few of the many works of Erasmus have enjoyed a wider appeal than the *Paraclesis*. The *Paraclesis* is perhaps most often cited for its bold advocacy of vernacular translations of the Bible, but its appeal lies rather more deeply in its winsome summons to all Christians to understand and to live the marvellous and transforming 'philosophy of Christ.' I noted above that the *Paraclesis* began as a preface to Erasmus' first edition of the New Testament. As such it was placed first in a set of three essays, which included the *Methodus* and the *Apologia*; these essays were intended as a group to set out the rationale for the publication of the New Testament in a Latin version that could activate the potential of the biblical narrative to transform the life of the individual Christian and of Christian society. However, the significance of the *Paraclesis* as a distinct work of 'religious instruction' was almost immediately recognized; hence, it soon began to circulate apart from the New Testament, and after 1522 was no longer included among the prefaces to the New Testament.

The *Paraclesis,* as its title indicates, is a summons, in this case a summons to the reading of the Scriptures, and through the Scriptures to the philosophy of Christ. It is written against the background of contemporary theological education, or at least Erasmus' conception of it, an education he regarded as grounded in Aristotelian philosophical presuppositions, and thus a challenge even for the few who could master its complexity; an education strictly intellectual, arid, and powerless to touch the heart and redirect the will (cf Ep 64). Erasmus will show in the *Paraclesis* that the philosophy of Christ contrasts in every way with the assumptions underlying theological studies then offered at the universities. Hence the development of his essay. He believes that the philosophy of Christ originates not in the schools of pagan Greece or in Egypt or Babylon; rather it has its origin in heaven. Its founder is not a pagan philosopher, but Christ the incarnate God, a philosophy conveyed to us perennially by the Spirit. Its devotees – its students – are not the select few who can boast a lengthy university training, but 'everyman' – men, women, children, sailors, professors. Its fundamental principles are not based on an obscure text of Aristotelian philosophy but are articulated with provocative clarity in the Sermon on the Mount and in the ethical teaching of the apostles. Its effect is conversion and transformation. And where do we find access to it? Not in Aristotle but in the Gospels of the evangelists and the Epistles of the apostles. If this philosophy transforms the reader into a 'Christian,' it is because Christ is in the pages of the Bible and we meet him there as a living person. As we read those pages we absorb his presence, we become one with him.

One may be surprised that though Aristotelian philosophy generally provides a negative backdrop for the portrait of the philosophy of Christ, at one point pagan philosophy is represented in positive terms. But Erasmus explains: the transformation of which he speaks is essentially simply a 'restoration of nature.' Although the light of Christ has been obscured among pagans, pagan philosophers have been able to deduce some truth from the 'pages' of nature. Where their discoveries coincide with the revelation of Scripture they too may play a part in the process of our transformation back into the original, that is, the natural state in which humanity was created.

To read the *Paraclesis* in its literary and historical context enables us to place in proper perspective Erasmus' enthusiastic promotion of vernacular translations of the Bible. A philosophy based so completely in Scripture and intended for all must be accessible to all and therefore available to all in a language every person can understand. In his preface to the *Paraphrase on Matthew* (1522) Erasmus will again speak in favour of vernacular translations: 'Why does it seem inappropriate if someone sounds forth the gospel in his native language? ... I share the view of St Jerome that … it should be proclaimed in every language … If it be the ploughman guiding his plough, let him chant in his own language something from the mystic Psalms. If it be the weaver sitting at his loom, let him ease his labour by reciting in rhythm something from a Gospel. From the same let the skipper as he steers his boat give voice' (CWE 45 18). We should note, however, that Erasmus would come to hedge this unqualified support for vernacular translations. In 1525 he told Pierre Cousturier that he 'had never said that anyone at all should translate the sacred books into the vernacular … In fact, I frankly confess that it is better that the common people learn through the spoken word' (LB IX 783). Late in life he actually wrote a short preface for a little book that attempted to persuade James IV of Scotland to suppress attempts at providing vernacular translations for the people of his realm (Allen Ep 2886).

As noted in the Preface, the text of the *Paraclesis* that follows, taken from CWE 41, is printed in full.]

When,[1] excellent reader, the distinguished writer Firmianus Lactantius, whose style Jerome particularly admired, was beginning his defence of the Christian religion against the pagans, he wished first of all to be given eloquence similar to that of Cicero, thinking it impertinent, I suppose, to desire its equal.[2] But as long as I am engaged in exhorting all mortals to the holy and healing study of the philosophy of Christ and in summoning them as with a clarion call, I would wish with all my heart – if anything is accomplished by wishes of this kind, – to be granted a much different eloquence from that of Cicero; perhaps not so colourful as his, but certainly more effective. Indeed I would wish – if this has ever been granted to anyone – to have such a forceful style as the stories of the ancient poets ascribed, not altogether without reason, to Mercury who, as with a magic staff and divine lyre, imposes sleep when he wishes and takes it away, forces to the Realm of the Dead whomsoever he wishes and recalls from it again; or such power as they noted in Amphion and Orpheus, of whom the one is said to have moved solid rocks, the other to have drawn oak and ash trees with his lyre; or such as the Gauls ascribed to their Ogmius, who led everyone about wherever he wished by means of fine chains fastened from his tongue to their ears; or such as mythical antiquity ascribed to Marsyas; or lest we linger too long among fables, certainly such as Alcibiades attributed to Socrates, the Old Comedy to Pericles: an eloquence that does not simply charm the ears by a pleasure soon to die, but that leaves barbs clinging in the hearts of those who hear; an eloquence that seizes, transforms, and sends the listener

1 The work appeared as a preface in the first three editions of Erasmus' New Testament (1516, 1519, 1522) with the title, 'A Summons [*ie paraclesis*] to the Pious Reader by Erasmus of Rotterdam.' Later editions sometimes employed a more revealing title, for example, '*Paraclesis*, that is, a summons to the holy and health-giving study of the philosophy of Christ so that, if not our only care, at least our first care be given to the reading of the Gospels and the letters of the apostles.'

2 Jerome (357–420) is known for his translation of and commentaries on the Bible (cf 43 n12 and 46 n19); Lactantius (240–c320) was a rhetorician and apologist for the Christian faith, whose brilliant style has won him the title of 'the Christian Cicero'; Cicero (106 BC–46 BC), Roman orator and politician, is famous for his eloquence.

away a much different person from the one it received. We read that the celebrated musician Timotheus often inflamed Alexander the Great to zeal for war by singing songs in the Dorian mode.[3] Nor were people lacking long ago who believed that nothing was more effective than the prayers which the Greeks call 'epodes.' But if there exists anywhere any such incantation and any power of harmony filled with true inspiration, any Peitho who is truly persuasive, I would desire her to help me now, that I may persuade all people of that most beneficial of all beliefs. Yet this, rather, should be my prayer: that Christ himself, whose business is in hand, will so tune the strings of my lyre that this song will affect and move all hearts to their very core; and for this to take place, there is no need for the arguments and ornaments of the rhetoricians. My wish is that nothing stand out with greater certainty than truth herself, for the effectiveness of her style increases in proportion to its simplicity.[4]

To begin, then: I do not wish at present to reopen the complaint, by no means new but alas! all too just, and perhaps never more just than at this time when everyone is so passionately devoted to his own interests – that the philosophy of Christ, and this philosophy alone, is scoffed at even by some Christians, neglected by most, and discussed by few, although without enthusiasm (for I will not say without sincerity). In all the other branches of knowledge that human industry has produced, there is nothing so hidden, so recondite that keen minds have not investigated it, nothing so difficult that unremitting labour has not conquered it. How is it then that this philosophy is the only one that is not embraced with the enthusiasm that is its due by all of us who even in the title by which we are known confess the name of Christ?

3 The text moves from 'fables,' ie mythological and legendary figures, to historical persons. Of the former, Erasmus describes those characteristics appropriate to his theme, but note further that Mercury was the messenger of the gods, Amphion moved stones for building the walls of Thebes by the music of his lyre, Ogmius was a Gallic god, and Marsyas a satyr famous for his dexterity with the flute. After Marsyas, allusions to historical figures follow. In Plato's *Symposium* (215 BC) Alcibiades says that Socrates, using only his voice, is able to charm the souls of men. 'Old Comedy,' best known from the plays of Aristophanes (fifth century BC), flourished during the period of the Greek independent states (fifth and fourth centuries BC), and is distinguished by the term from the subsequent 'Middle' and 'New' Comedy. The Greeks recognized 'musical modes,' Ionian, Phrygian, and Dorian, and thought the last especially suited for the conduct of war. Alexander the Great (356–323 BC) had conquered much of the then-known world by the time he was thirty-three. Pericles, imperialist and popular Athenian statesman (450–429 BC), was said to have Peitho, Greek goddess of persuasion, on his lips.

4 The appeal to a divine being for aid in telling a story is characteristic of epic poetry.

Platonists, Pythagoreans, Academicians, Stoics, Cynics, Peripatetics, Epicureans[5] have all learned thoroughly the teachings of their schools, know them by heart, fight for them, are even prepared to die for them sooner than give up the defence of their founder. Why are we not more ready to show such enthusiasm for Christ, the founder of our faith and our Lord? Who would not think it deeply shocking if someone who professed the philosophy of Aristotle did not know what he thought about the origin of thunderbolts, about prime matter, about the infinite, matters that do not make one happy if known or unhappy if unknown?[6] Yet we who are consecrated to Christ in so many ways, bound to him by so many sacraments, do we not think it shocking and shameful to be ignorant of his teachings, which offer sure and certain happiness to all?

But what purpose is served here by piling up arguments, when it is a kind of impious madness to compare Christ to Zeno or Aristotle, and Christ's doctrine to their petty pronouncements, to choose the mildest term. Let their adherents claim for the leaders of their sects whatever credit they can or wish. Certain it is that our teacher alone was sent from heaven; that he alone could teach unchanging truth since he is eternal wisdom; that he alone, the only author of our salvation, taught the means of salvation; that he alone exemplified completely all that he ever taught; that he alone is able to fulfil all that he has promised. If something comes from the Chaldeans or Egyptians[7] our desire to know it is keener simply because it has been imported from a distant land, and its value derives in part from the fact that it has come from far away.

---

5 These schools of philosophy are listed without regard to the chronological order of their origin. Platonists emerged with Plato (429–347 BC); Pythagoreans were a quasi-religious society founded by Pythagoras (540–510 BC); Academicians, third–second century BC with roots in Platonism, tended toward skepticism; Stoics looked to Zeno (335–263 BC) as their founder, and, taking their name from the Stoa (a painted porch in Athens) in which Zeno lectured, they developed controversial epistemological theories; Cynics, founded by Antisthenes (fifth century BC), who taught in a gymnasium called 'cynosarges' outside the city of Athens, were known for their severe and uncouth criticism of men and manners; the followers of Aristotle (384–322 BC) were called Peripatetics from Aristotle's habit of walking (Greek, *peripateo*) rather than sitting while he lectured; Epicureans, named after their founder Epicurus (342–270 BC), believed in happiness as the ultimate goal of life.

6 Aristotle's many compositions included works on meteorology and physics.

7 Apparently a reference to the Hermetic Corpus, a body of Greek works emanating from Egypt, attributed to Hermes Trismegistus, and to the Chaldaic Oracles, attributed to Zoroaster, together with commentaries written on them by the eleventh-century Byzantine scholar Michael Psellus. These works had been translated into Latin by Marsilio Ficino (1433–99) and the Florentine Platonists.

Often we torment ourselves with the fantasies of some nonentity – I will not say imposter – not simply without benefit, but with a great waste of time, to mention no more serious consequence, although the lack of benefit is serious enough.

But how does it come about that a similar desire does not stimulate the minds of Christians, since they have been persuaded, as is in fact true, that this doctrine has come not from Egypt or Syria, but from heaven itself? Why do we not all think as follows: What a new and wonderful kind of philosophy this must be! For in order to transmit it to mortals, he who was God became man, he who was immortal became mortal, he who was in the heart of the Father came down to earth. Whatever it is that the wonderful founder of our faith came to teach, it must be something great, something by no means commonplace, since there had already been so many schools of excellent philosophers, so many distinguished prophets. Why do we not study it here point by point, investigate it, examine it with reverent curiosity? especially since this kind of wisdom, so remarkable that it has rendered foolish once and for all the entire wisdom of this world,[8] can be drunk from these few books as from the clearest streams with far less trouble than the teaching of Aristotle, preserved in so many thorny volumes, with all the long and contradictory commentaries of his interpreters? And, need I add, with greater profit? It is unnecessary for you to approach this philosophy furnished with such a load of burdensome knowledge. Provision for the way is simple and available to everyone. Only see that you bring to it a pious and ready mind and one that is, above all, endowed with a sincere and pure faith. Only be willing to learn and you have advanced far in this philosophy. It supplies as its teacher the Spirit that is imparted to none so freely as to the sincere of heart. The systems of the philosophers, apart from their promise of a false happiness, rebuff the inquiring minds of many through the sheer difficulty of their concepts. This philosophy accommodates itself equally to all. It lowers itself to infants, adjusting to their need. It nourishes them with milk, carries them, cherishes and supports them, does everything necessary until we grow strong in Christ.[9] Again, while it does not fail the lowest, the highest also find it worthy of admiration. Indeed, the farther you have advanced into the riches of this philosophy, the farther you withdraw yourself from the splendour of other philosophers. For the inexperienced, it is perfectly simple; for the experienced, it is utterly demanding. This philosophy rejects no age, no

8 Cf 1 Cor 1:20 and 3:19.

9 Cf 1 Cor 3:1–2.

sex, no rank, no condition. The sun above is not so universal and accessible to all as is the teaching of Christ. It keeps no one at a distance except the person who distances himself, to his own detriment.

I disagree entirely with those who do not want divine literature to be translated into the vernacular tongues and read by ordinary people, as if Christ taught such convoluted doctrine that it could be understood only by a handful of theologians and then with difficulty; or as if the defence of the Christian religion were contingent on this, that it remain unknown. Perhaps it is expedient to conceal the secrets of kings, but Christ desires his mysteries to be known as widely as possible. I would like every woman to read the Gospel, to read the Epistles of Paul. And oh, that these books were translated into every tongue of every land so that not only the Scots and the Irish, but Turks and Saracens too could read and get to know them. The first stage, unquestionably, is to get to know them – somehow or other. Granted that many people would laugh; yet some would be won over. How I wish that the farmer at his plough would chant some passage from these books, that the weaver at his shuttles would sing something from them; that the traveller would relieve the tedium of his journey with stories of this kind; that all the discussions of all Christians would start from these books,[10] for our daily conversation reflects in large measure what we are. Let each person understand what he can; let each express what he can. Let the one who comes after not envy the one who goes before; and let the one who is ahead encourage the one who follows, not despair of him. Why do we restrict to a few a profession of faith that is common to all? Since baptism, in which we make the first profession of our Christian faith, is the common possession of all Christians alike, and since the other sacraments and the reward of eternal life belong to all alike, it is illogical to believe that dogma alone should be reserved for those few whom the people today call monks and theologians. These men are a tiny fraction of the people of Christ; I only wish they were more worthy of the names by which they are called. For I am afraid that you will find among theologians those who are far from deserving the title of their office, men who talk of earthly, not heavenly things;[11] and that among monks who profess to follow the poverty of Christ and to despise the world you will find an excess of worldliness.

10 The practice of such conversations is well illustrated in Erasmus' colloquy 'The Godly Feast' CWE 39 175–207.

11 An allusion to the word 'theologian,' from the Greek, *theos* 'God' and *logos* 'word,' thus discourse about God, ie 'heavenly things.'

In my opinion, a man is truly a theologian who teaches, not by convoluted syllogisms, but by his disposition, by the expression on his face and in his eyes, and by his way of life,[12] that wealth is to be scorned, that a Christian must not trust in worldly supports but must depend solely on heaven, that he must not avenge a wrong, that he must bless them that curse him, do good to them that abuse him; that all good people are to be loved and cherished equally as members of the same body; that the wicked are to be tolerated if they cannot be corrected; that those who are despoiled of their goods, those who are deprived of their possessions, those who mourn, are to be counted happy, not to be pitied; that death is to be desired by the godly for it is none other than the passage to immortality. If anyone filled with the spirit of Christ preaches and inculcates these precepts and others like them, if he urges, invites, and inspires others to accept them, he is indeed a true theologian even though a ditch-digger or weaver. Also, if anyone exemplifies these teachings by his own conduct, he is indeed a great teacher. Perhaps some other person, a non-Christian even, may dispute with greater subtlety how angels understand;[13] but to persuade human beings that in this world we should live like angels, pure from all stain of sin, that alone is the duty of a Christian theologian.

But if anyone should object that these precepts are somewhat crude and unsophisticated, I would answer simply that it was these crude precepts above all that Christ taught, that the apostles inculcate; and however unsophisticated they may be, they have resulted in our having so many true Christians, such multitudes of glorious martyrs. It is this philosophy, I say, unlettered as they see it, that has drawn the mightiest princes of the world, many realms and many nations, to endorse its laws, something which neither the power of tyrants nor the learning of philosophers was able to do. But I do not oppose the discussion of that kind of philosophy among them that are perfect[14] if

---

12 Erasmus frequently portrays with irony and sarcasm contemporary theological education; cf Epistle 64 and the *Praise of Folly* CWE 27 126–30, 133. One hears the sarcasm here in the expression 'convoluted syllogisms,' and notes the contrast with the simple ethical principles of the New Testament, which now are listed. For the ethical principles listed see Matt 6:19–21 (wealth, worldly supports), Rom 12:19, 14, Luke 6:28 (revenge, blessing/cursing) 1 Cor 12:27–14:1 (cherish the members), Matt 13:24–30 (tolerate the wicked), Matt 5:3–10 (spoliation, deprivation, mourning), 2 Cor 5:1 (death/immortality).

13 For discussions on the angelic mode of cognition see the article 'angel' in the *Oxford Dictionary of the Christian Church* ed F.L. Cross 3rd ed rev E.A. Livingstone (Oxford 2005).

14 For the expression see 1 Cor 2:6.

such discussions seem to be good. But the humble mass of Christians may confidently take comfort from the fact that the apostles certainly did not teach those subtle arguments;[15] whether they knew them or not, let others decide. If princes promoted this commonplace doctrine as a responsibility of their position, if priests taught it in their sermons, if schoolmasters instilled it in their pupils instead of that erudite doctrine drawn from the wellsprings of Aristotle and Averroës,[16] Christendom would not everywhere be in an almost constant state of war, the world would not seethe with such an insane desire to heap up wealth by fair means or foul, sacred and profane alike would not echo with clamorous disputes. In a word, not in name and ritual only would we differ from those who do not profess the philosophy of Christ. For the responsibility of renewing and enhancing the Christian religion rests principally with these three groups: with rulers, and the magistrates who govern in their stead, with bishops and the priests who represent them, and with those who instruct children in their earliest years when they respond eagerly to everything. If it should happen that these people set aside their own interests and joined together wholeheartedly in Christ, we would undoubtedly see within a few years a genuine and, as Paul says, a 'legitimate'[17] breed of Christians emerging everywhere who would transmit the philosophy of Christ not only by ceremonies and logical propositions, but with heart and soul in every aspect of their lives. The enemies of Christianity would be won over to faith in Christ far more quickly by these weapons than by threats and arms. Were we to combine all our defences, there is nothing more powerful than truth itself.

No one is a Platonist who has not read the books of Plato. Is he a theologian, let alone a Christian, who has not read the literature of Christ? 'He who loves me,' he said, 'keeps my words' [John 14:15]. He himself set down this distinguishing mark. Therefore, if we are Christians truly and sincerely, if we truly believe that he was sent from heaven to

---

15 Ie the arguments employed in the debates required for academic advancement in contemporary theological education. Duns Scotus, one of the great scholastics, was named the 'subtle doctor'; cf n28 below.

16 Averroës (Ibn Rushd 1126–98), born into a Muslim family of Cordova, venerated Aristotle on whose works he wrote commentaries. The church recognized in his theories a danger to Catholic truth. Although his theories were condemned, Averroism continued to have influence in the Universities until the time of the Renaissance.

17 Erasmus uses here the Greek word *gnesion* found in 2 Cor 8:8 and 1 Tim 1:2 where RSV translates '*genuine* love' and '*true* son' respectively. Expressions like 'true Christian,' 'truly Christian' are found frequently in Erasmus' works.

teach us things that the wisdom of philosophers could not teach, if we truly expect to receive from him what no princes can give however rich they may be, why is anything more important to us than the literature of Christ? Why does anything seem even faintly learned that departs from his teaching? Why, with respect to these writings that deserve our adoration, do we allow ourselves as much – I might almost say 'more' – liberty than secular commentators allow themselves when dealing with civil law or medical texts, so that we say whatever comes into our heads, we tangle them, we distort them, just as if we were dealing with trivial matter? We shape the heavenly teachings to our way of life as if they were a Lydian rule;[18] and while we avoid by every means the appearance of ignorance and bring to this endeavour the whole range of secular learning, I will not say we destroy what is truly distinctive in the Christian philosophy, but it cannot be denied that we confine to a small number of people what Christ particularly wished to be available to all. The philosophy of Christ lies more in the inclinations and intentions of the heart than in syllogisms. It is a way of life rather than a form of argument. It is inspiration rather than erudition. It is transformation rather than argumentation. To be learned falls to the lot of very few, but no one is prevented from being a Christian, no one is prevented from being godly; and, I shall boldly add, no one is prevented from being a theologian.

Now whatever is in complete accord with nature sinks readily into the minds of all. And what else is the philosophy of Christ, which he himself calls a 'rebirth,' than the 'restoration' of nature, which was created whole and sound?[19] So although no one has taught this philosophy more completely, more effectively than Christ, yet one may find many statements in the books of the pagans that agree with his doctrine. There has never been a school of philosophy so crude as to teach that money makes a man happy; never one so shameless as to determine that our chief good is the attainment of commonplace honours and pleasures. The Stoics perceived that no one is wise unless he is good; they perceived that nothing is truly good or honourable except true virtue, that nothing is to be feared or is bad except only what is morally wrong. In the works of Plato Socrates teaches in many ways that wrong is not to be

18 Erasmus probably means the Lesbian rule: a ruler that could be used by masons to fit the shape of any stone; cf *Adages* I iv 93.

19 'Rebirth,' Latin *renascentia* (cf 'born again'), 'restoration,' Latin *instauratio*; see respectively John 3:3 and Eph 1:10. In his translation of *1516* Erasmus used the analogous verb forms to give the same sense. However, from *1519* he translated the Greek of John 3:3 'born from above' rather than 'born again.'

repaid with wrong. Also, that since the soul is immortal, one must not mourn for those who pass from this life to a happier one, confident of having lived life well. Further, that the soul must be led by all possible means away from inclinations of the body and towards those things that truly exist although they are not seen. Aristotle wrote in his *Politics* that nothing can be pleasurable to us which is not in some measure despised, virtue alone excepted. Epicurus also says that nothing in life can be pleasant to a person unless he knows that his conscience is clear; and then true pleasure bubbles forth as from a spring of water.[20] What of the fact that numerous philosophers have presented much of this teaching, notably Socrates, Diogenes and Epictetus?[21] Yet since Christ has both taught and exemplified the same teaching so much more fully, is it not monstrous that it is ignored and neglected and even ridiculed by Christians? If there are doctrines that pertain more closely to Christianity than his, let us reject his and follow those. But if his alone are the doctrines which are able to make a person truly Christian, why do we treat them as almost more obsolete and invalid than the books of Moses? The first requirement is to know what Christ taught, the second is to do it. For I do not think that anyone should count himself a Christian because he argues with a thorny, baffling tangle of words about instances, relativities, quiddities and formalities,[22] but rather because he observes and imitates what Christ taught and did.

I do not condemn the work of those who have exercised their intellectual powers and achieved renown in subtle arguments of this kind, for I do not wish anyone to be offended; but I think, and unless I am mistaken I think correctly, that there is no richer source for the pure and genuine philosophy of Christ than the Gospels and the apostolic letters,

20 For the views ascribed here to the Stoics see Cicero *De finibus* 3.33, 70–6, 106. The views attributed to Socrates are variously expressed in, for example, the *Apology*, the *Phaedo* and the *Republic*. Plato spoke of 'forms' or 'patterns' that exist independently of our minds. They are reflected in objects of this world but to see them we must turn away from the reflection of the objects to the 'intelligible' patterns. See, eg, the *Phaedo* 64A–67c 114D–115A and the *Republic* VI and VII. The passage in Aristotle has not been satisfactorily identified. For Epicurus see Cicero *De finibus* 1.52–4.

21 Diogenes (412–323 BC) was a follower of Antisthenes, but the reference here is probably to Diogenes Laertius (second century BC) who wrote *The Lives of the Philosophers*, an uncritical but valuable record of ancient philosophy. Epictetus (first–second century AD), a freedman, was a Stoic philosopher to whom is attributed a short manual, the *Enchiridion*.

22 Technical terms of scholastic philosophy; for definitions see in CWE 41 *Paraclesis* n74 and *Methodus* n55.

and if anyone applies himself to these studies with a pious mind, praying rather than disputing, and desiring to be transformed rather than to be armed, he will undoubtedly discover that there is nothing that pertains to human happiness, nothing that pertains to any aspect of this life, that has not been taught, examined and resolved in these writings. If we want to learn something, why does another authority please us more than Christ himself? If we are searching for a pattern of life, why do we give another model precedence over Christ himself, who is the archetype? If we desire a remedy against distressing passions of the mind, why do we suppose that we can find more immediate help elsewhere? If we wish to rouse a listless and languid mind by reading, where, I ask, will you find intellectual sparks so lively and effective? If it seems good to distract the mind from the troubles of this life, why are other pleasures more delightful? Why do we unhesitatingly prefer to learn the wisdom of Christ from the writings of human beings rather than from Christ himself, who in these books especially fulfills what he promised, that he would be with us always, even unto the end of the world;[23] for in them he lives even now, breathes and speaks to us, I might almost say more effectively than when he lived among men. The Jews saw less and heard less than you see and hear[24] in the Gospel writings, provided you bring eyes and ears by which he can be seen and heard.

What kind of behaviour, I ask you, is this? We preserve the letters written by a dear friend, we admire them greatly, we carry them about; we read them over and over again; yet there are thousands and thousands of Christians who, although learned in other respects, have never even read the Gospels and Epistles in their whole life. Mohammedans uphold their doctrines. Jews even to-day study their Moses from the cradle. Why do we not do the same for Christ? Those who profess the Rule of Benedict learn, study, and master a rule written by a man, a fairly ordinary man, and for ordinary men. Members of the Augustinian Order know the rule of their founder. Franciscans reverence the precious teachings of their Francis; they embrace them and take them with them into whatever part of the world they go; they do not believe they are safe unless the little book is near their hearts.[25] Why do the men of those orders accord more respect to a

23 Cf Matt 28:20.

24 Cf Luke 10:24.

25 The 'little book' is the *Regula bullata* ie the 'Second Rule' of St Francis. On the two 'Rules' see CWE 40 1026–8.

rule written by a man than Christians universally accord to their rule, which Christ gave to all, which all have professed equally at baptism, and which is more holy than any other even if you listed another six hundred such rules? Just as Paul wrote that the Law of Moses lost its glory when compared to the glory of the gospel that succeeded it,[26] so I wish that the Gospels and the Epistles of the apostles would come to be regarded by all Christians as so holy that these other writings would not even appear to be holy in comparison with them. As far as I am concerned, others are free to show whatever respect they like to Albertus Magnus, to Alexander, to Thomas, Aegidius, Richard and Occam,[27] for I would not wish to diminish the glory of anyone or to contend with studies now well established. However learned the works of those men may be, however 'subtle' and, if it please them, however 'seraphic,'[28] it must still be admitted that the Gospels and Epistles are the supreme authority. Paul wants the spirits of the prophets to be judged, whether they are from God.[29] Augustine, who read critically all the works of all the authors, asks no greater respect for his own works.[30] In the Gospels and Epistles alone, I venerate even what I do not understand. Not a school of theologians, but the heavenly Father himself has approved this authority for us by the testimony of his divine voice, and has done so on two occasions, first at his baptism in Jordan and then at his transfiguration on Mt Tabor.[31] 'This,'

26 2 Cor 3:7–11.

27 The theologians named here were all students of Aristotelian philosophy or of Peter Lombard's *Sentences*, a standard textbook of Catholic theology established as orthodox in 1215 at the Fourth Lateran Council. Short biographies of each may be found in the *Oxford Dictionary of the Christian Church*. Each came to be characterized by an epithet: Albertus Magnus (universal doctor), a German Dominican (1200–80); Alexander of Hales (unshakeable doctor), English Franciscan (1186–1245); Thomas Aquinas (angelic doctor), Italian Dominican whose theological endeavours, strongly influenced by Aristotle, culminated in his great *Summa theologica* (1225–74); Aegidius (Giles) of Rome (most foundational doctor), Italian Augustinian (1245–1316); Richard of Middleton (sound doctor), a Franciscan of English or French origin (1249–?); William of Occam (invincible doctor) English Franciscan (1285–1347).

28 Allusions respectively to Duns Scotus (subtle doctor), a Scottish Franciscan (1266–1308) and St Bonaventure (seraphic doctor), an Italian Franciscan (1217–74), who wrote a biography of St Francis.

29 Cf 1 Cor 14:32 and 1 John 4:1.

30 Augustine's *Retractationes* (completed 427) is a reconsideration, with criticisms, of his previous writings. See also the treatise *Against Faustus the Manichaean* (*Contra Faustum Manichaeum*) 11.5.

31 Cf Matt 3:17 (baptism) and 17:5 (transfiguration). Mt Tabor is the site traditionally assigned for the transfiguration, though not mentioned as such in Scripture; cf CWE 44 114n24.

he said, 'is my beloved Son, in whom I am well pleased; hear ye him' [Matt 17:5]. Here is a 'sound' authority, and, to use their word, a truly 'unshakeable' one. What is the meaning of 'Hear ye him'? It is, 'This is the one and only Doctor. Be ye disciples of Him alone.' Each man may honour his own authority in his studies as much as he wishes; but this statement was made of one only without exception, of Christ. On Him first the dove descended in confirmation of his Father's testimony.[32] It is his spirit that Peter recalls most closely to whom that great shepherd committed his sheep once, twice and a third time to be fed, fed without doubt on the food of the teaching of Christ.[33] It was Christ who was born again, as it were, in Paul, whom he called a chosen instrument and illustrious herald of his name.[34] John set down in his writings what he had learned from the sacred fountain of his breast.[35] What, I ask you, is like this in Scotus? (I would not wish this to be taken as an insult.) What is like this in Thomas? To be sure, I do indeed marvel at the ability of the former and even reverence the sanctity of the latter, but why do we not all learn our philosophy from the writings of those incomparable authorities, the Gospels and Epistles? Why do we not carry these books near our hearts, have these books always in our hands? Why do we not hunt through these books, examine and discuss them constantly? Why devote a greater part of life to Averroës than to the Gospels? Why spend almost all our allotted time on the decisions of mortal men and on contradictory opinions? I grant, if you like, that these books are the works of sublime theologians; but let us be sure that the basic training of the great theologian of the future is by way of the Gospels and Epistles.

May all of us who swore allegiance to Christ at baptism, if indeed we made the vow sincerely, be filled with the teaching of Christ early amid the embraces of our parents and the caresses of our nurses, for whatever the little unglazed storage-pot of the mind first soaks up, penetrates most deeply and adheres most tenaciously. Let the first halting word be 'Christ,' let earliest infancy be formed by His Gospels; and above all may Christ be taught in such a way that he is loved even by children. For just as the severity of certain teachers causes children to hate reading while they are still learning to read, so there are teachers who make the philosophy of Christ disagreeable and tedious, although

32 Cf Matt 3:16.
33 Cf John 21:15–17.
34 Cf Acts 9:15.
35 Cf John 13:25 and 1 John 1:1–3.

nothing is more sweet.[36] Let the children, then, be occupied in these studies until they grow imperceptibly to strong manhood in Christ. The writings of others are such that many have regretted the effort spent on them; and it often happens that those who have battled right up to the approach of death in defence of the tenets of their philosophers, withdraw from the school of their master at the very hour of death. But happy is that man whom death catches while he is meditating on the gospel of Christ.

Therefore, let us all desire these books eagerly; let us embrace them; let us live with them constantly; let us admire them greatly; let us die in them; let us be transformed into them, since our preoccupations affect our character. Whoever cannot pursue this course – but who cannot if only he so desires? – let him at least honour those writings as the repository of the divine mind. If someone exhibited a print made by the feet of Christ, how we Christians would prostrate ourselves, how we would adore! Why, then, do we not rather venerate his living and breathing image, preserved in these books? If someone displayed the tunic of Christ, would we not fly to the ends of the earth to kiss it? But even if you were to produce every possession he owned, there is nothing that would show Christ more clearly and more truly than the Gospel writings. Through our love of Christ we enrich a statue of wood or stone with jewels and gold. Why do we not rather adorn these books with gold and jewels and anything more precious, for they recall Christ to us more vividly than any little statue. A statue shows only the appearance of his body – if indeed it shows anything of that – but these books show you the living image of his holy mind and Christ himself, speaking, healing, dying, rising to life again. In short, they restore Christ to us so completely and so vividly that you would see him less clearly should you behold him standing before your very eyes.

36 Perhaps an allusion to Matt 11:28–30.

CHAPTER THREE

The Interpretation of Scripture

THE *RATIO VERAE THEOLOGIAE*

[In the 1516 edition of the New Testament the *Paraclesis* was followed immediately by the *Methodus* – appropriately, as Erasmus noted: if the summons to the philosophy of Christ had inspired the reader to open his Bible, how was he to read and understand this precious book? 'Show us the way,' he cries, and Erasmus supplied a response by the *Methodus*. The *Methodus* was followed by an *apologia*, a response to the criticism he anticipated would arise from the new edition of the New Testament. The three pieces together formed a coherent preparation for the reader to appreciate Erasmus' endeavour, hence a suitable preface to the text of the New Testament and to the annotations that followed.

As Erasmus noted, for the second edition of 1519 he virtually 'remade' his book of 1516. Nowhere was the remaking more evident than in the transformation of the *Methodus* into the *Ratio verae theologiae*, virtually a book in itself. While it incorporated much of the *Methodus* into its beginning and end the central part was almost entirely new. It was in this central part that Erasmus radically extended the fundamental principles of biblical interpretation articulated in the *Methodus*, and in the course of doing so drew the images of the time-periods and the circles so central to the method he was propounding for understanding and applying the Scriptures. It was also in the central part that he placed an entirely new emphasis on the significance of the moral life and the spiritual resources of the interpreter. In its beginning and end, where the *Ratio* incorporated the *Methodus* it went far beyond the *Methodus* in amplifying its themes, for example, the place of the humanistic disciplines in the preparation of the interpreter, and the exemplification of grammatical and rhetorical principles, the figures of thought and speech, for which anyone who wishes to read the Bible intelligently must carefully watch.

In the elaboration of these themes the centre of attention in the *Ratio* – the nature of biblical interpretation – comes forcefully into focus. In the *Paraclesis* the contrast between the complex philosophy taught in the schools and the simple philosophy of Christ provided an obvious base for the declaration of what might be framed in the terms of a slogan, 'The Bible for Everyone.' But Erasmus himself did not produce his New Testament for 'everyone'; his prefaces are written for the educated classes, and specifically those who could read Latin. Hence in the *Ratio* he turns to elaborate a system of education that will enable the future clergy – he calls them 'tyros' – to deliver the philosophy of Christ to the members of their future congregations. The backdrop against which he develops his system of education is the same as in the *Paraclesis* – the scholastic system of education in the Universities. This he will replace with a system of education that enables one to read, not Aristotle, but the Bible, and to read it not as a source of doctrinal syllogisms but as literature, inviting an appreciation of context, an awareness of thematic continuity and contrast, fostering sensitivity to images, developing a capacity for emotional response, and stimulating the transformation of the instructor into a living and exemplary image of the philosophy of Christ. To read the Bible in this way is to become an effective interpreter of Scripture.

The *Ratio verae theologiae* appeared as a preface to the New Testament in *1519* only. Thereafter it circulated as an independent work, often coupled with another comparable work such as the *Paraclesis* or the *Paraphrase on Romans*. Indeed, even before it was published as a preface to the 1519 New Testament, it appeared (in November 1518) as an independent publication along with a set of *Arguments* Erasmus had prepared to use as an introduction to each of the apostolic Epistles, both as the Epistles would appear in paraphrase and as they appeared in Erasmus' translation of the New Testament. In fact, as an enormous amplification of the *Methodus* it had become really too large to serve as a preface. Moreover, it was further enlarged in the editions of 1520, 1522, and 1523. With the 1520 edition came major additions. In particular, to the extensive review of Gospel literature included in *1519* an impressive review of the epistolary and especially Pauline literature was added in *1520*. Criticism of church and society with an implied demand for reform was both more extensive and intensive, and crucial theological themes like faith and charity, well established in the work in *1519*, were probed more deeply in *1520*. The additions of *1522* and *1523* each only modestly enlarged the text of its preceding edition. The additions were chiefly illustrative and explanatory, reiterating and emphasizing points already made. But one very significant addition of *1523* is readily noted, an extensive discussion on the validity of the tenets on indissoluble marriage, a response to discussion on Erasmus' proposal for the reconsideration of divorce, a proposal put forward with lengthy and determined argumentation in the *1519* annotation on 1 Corinthians 7:39 (*liberata est a lege, cui autem vult, nubat*) (excerpts included below).

In the independent publication of 1518 the work appeared under the title *Ratio seu methodus compendio perveniendi ad veram theologiam per Erasmum Roterodamum 'A System or Method of Arriving by a Short-Cut at True Theology by Erasmus of Rotterdam.'* It was, however, frequently published under a shortened title, *Ratio seu compendium verae theologiae 'A System or Short-Cut to True Theology.'* Even so, the upper margins of the text sometimes carried the still shorter title of *Ratio verae theologiae 'A System of true Theology.'* In the selection offered here it is generally referred to simply as the *Ratio*, and *ratio* is variously translated as 'system,' 'principles,' 'method.'

In the translation presented here much has been omitted from the full text of the *Ratio*. The selections included are designed to clarify the movement of the argument and to highlight the continuity of thought, which in the full text of the *Ratio* often seems interrupted by the amplitude of exemplification and the occasional apparent diversion. The selections are taken from the latest authorized edition (1523); only exceptionally do I call attention to the other editions. The full text is available in CWE 41 and in Mark Vessey, ed *Erasmus on Literature* (Toronto forthcoming).

I have divided the work as selected here into six sections with captions. Neither the divisions nor the captions form part of Erasmus' text.]

(1) Introduction

[**CWE** 489] It is a great thing to arouse in human hearts a burning desire for the study of theology, but it takes a more expert practitioner to expound the way and the method of this heavenly study.[1] Not that I do

1 The sentence establishes the connection between the *Paraclesis*, which sought to inflame the desire for the philosophy of Christ, a philosophy rooted in the Scriptures, and the *Ratio verae theologiae*, which makes an attempt to show the way to read the Scriptures effectively, that is, in such a way that the philosophy of Christ will be realized in the life of the individual and society.

so in a manner worthy of the subject – for what can human effort do to match the divine realities – but in such a way that this labour of mine might offer some small advantage to candidates of a most venerable theology. [490] St Augustine in *On Christian Doctrine* has, it is true, discussed this subject both fully and with exacting care.[2] [491] All the more reason why I shall treat it more succinctly but also in a plainer fashion, for I am not preparing this for distinguished persons; rather I am striving with such industry as I have to bring help to unsophisticated folk and to ordinary intellects of a lower order.

(2) The Proper Approach to the Study of Scripture

Accordingly, what in the first place should have been taught is extremely easy and can be told, as they say, like ABC; but in practical experience it is by far the first and greatest thing of all, and just as it requires only the slightest effort to teach, so it takes an enormous effort to manifest in practice. What I mean is this: that to this philosophy [of Christ], which is neither Platonic nor Stoic nor Peripatetic,[3] but entirely of heaven, we bring a mind worthy of it, one that is not only free from all the stains of sin (as far as possible), but at peace and rest from every tumult of the passions, so that the image of that truth may be reflected more distinctly in us, as in a peaceful river. For if the ancient worshippers of the [492] demons would not receive anyone into their profane mysteries unless they had first been cleansed by many observances,[4] how much more is it right for us to approach the school – or, more truly, the temple – of this divine wisdom with minds completely cleansed.

[493] For this, therefore, you should prepare your heart, so that you also may deserve to be called by the prophetic term 'taught by God.'[5] Let there be in you an eye of faith that is sound and like that of the dove, an eye that sees nothing but the heavenly things. Add to this a most ardent desire for learning. This incomparable pearl does not deign either to

2 The *De doctrina christiana* is a textbook on the interpretation and exposition of Scripture written by Augustine in two stages, begun in 396 and completed in 426/427. In the *Ratio* Erasmus draws heavily from this work. Augustine (354–430) was bishop of Hippo Regius in North Africa, and a prolific writer whose works are often cited by Erasmus.

3 These philosophical schools are briefly identified in 27 n5 above.

4 Those preparing for initiation into the ancient mysteries, most famously the Eleusinian mysteries in honour of Demeter, were required to undergo preparatory rites of purification.

5 Cf 1 Thess 4:9 and John 6:45, where Isa 54:13 is quoted.

be loved in any ordinary way, or to be cherished along with others; it demands a thirsting soul, and a soul thirsting for nothing else.[6] Let all pride now be far away, all arrogance be far away from those about to approach this sacred threshold.[7] From things of this sort that Spirit at once recoils, for it takes delight in souls that are gentle and meek. The palace of this queen is majestic if you go all the way into its innermost chambers, but access lies through an extremely low portal; you must bend your neck if you want admittance.[8] Let the appetite for glory be far away, that plague most pernicious to the truth and customary companion of indomitable natures; far away obstinacy, the breeder of brawls, and even more, blind temerity. [494] Let this be your first and only goal, this your prayer, attend to this alone, that you be changed, be swept away, be inspired, be transformed into what you are learning. The food [495] of the soul is useful not if it remains in the memory as in the stomach, but only if it penetrates into the very affections and into the very viscera of the mind. You may conclude that you have made progress if you sense that little by little you are becoming a different person, less proud, less irascible, less fond of money or pleasures or of life; if every day some vice disappears and some growth in godliness occurs. Let prayer or thanksgiving frequently interrupt the reading – prayer that seeks the help of the sacred Spirit; thanksgiving that acknowledges the favour whenever you feel that you have made progress.

(3) Preparation for the Study of Scripture

[496] Now, in regard to that literature by whose support we more easily attain this [fruitful reading of Scripture], without question our first concern should be to learn well the three languages – Latin, Greek, and Hebrew – since it is clear that all of mystic Scripture has been handed down in these. Of these languages St Augustine was genuinely skilled only in Latin, had some small acquaintance with Greek, but neither

---

6 Biblical allusions abound: 'sound eye' (Matt 6:22), 'eye of the dove' (Song of Solomon 1:15, 4:1), 'incomparable pearl' (Matt 13:46), 'thirsting soul' (Ps 42:2, 63:1).

7 Erasmus alludes to the traditional formula ('stay far away') used to keep the uninitiated away from holy things (cf Virgil *Aeneid* 6.258–9). The language here and just below reflects Erasmus' negative view of contemporary theological education marked by the arrogance of professors and by quarrelsome public debates that encourage intellectual displays for self-glorification; cf 30 n12 and 31 n15 above.

8 'Queen' suggests the common designation of theology as the queen of the sciences; for the palace with the low doorway as a symbol of appropriate humility see the image in Virgil *Aeneid* 8. 359–68.

knew nor hoped to know Hebrew; nevertheless, in the second book *On Christian Doctrine* he does not hesitate to declare that the knowledge of these languages is essential whether to understand the sacred books or to restore them.[9] [497] He does not demand that you advance in Hebrew and Greek literature to prodigious fluency; it is enough if you get as far as neatness and propriety of expression, that is, if you achieve some modest skill such as suffices for making judgments. For, to pass over all the other disciplines of humane learning, it is in no way possible to understand what is written if you are ignorant of the language in which it is written – unless, perhaps, sitting idly by we prefer to wait with the apostles for this as some gift from heaven.[10]

[498] To disregard for the moment the fact that it matters very much whether you draw from the originating springs of Scripture or from any sort of pool whatever, what of the fact that certain things, because of idioms peculiar to the languages, cannot even be transferred to a foreign language without losing their original clarity, their native grace, their special nuance? What of the fact that some things are too small to be translated at all, as Jerome everywhere cries out and complains?[11] What of the fact that many things restored by Jerome have perished due to the ravages of time – for example, his New Testament.[12] What of the fact that either through the error or the indiscretion of the scribes the sacred codices were long ago corrupted and today at many points are being corrupted?

[501] Now, if some rare felicity, 'some exceptional natural gift,' as we say, seems to give promise of a distinguished theologian, I am not averse to something Augustine welcomed in the book *On Christian Doctrine*,[13] that such natural abilities be trained suitably to one's age and equipped through a modest and guarded acquaintance with the

---

9 Cf *De doctrina christiana* 2.11.16.

10 An allusion to the gift of tongues at Pentecost, Acts 1:4–5, 2:1–4. See the annotation on Acts 10:38 (*quomodo unxit eum*) for an extensive discussion on the Apostles' knowledge of languages (excerpted below).

11 Notably in Jerome's preface to his translation of Eusebius' *Chronicle* (available in the PL 2 33–7).

12 Jerome (347–420), at the request (382) of Pope Damasus revised the old Latin translations of the Gospels but did little with the Epistles. His translations (cf n19 below) were the base for what became the Vulgate Bible, the Latin text of the Bible regarded as standard throughout the medieval period and officially authorized at the Council of Trent in the mid-sixteenth century. Erasmus always insisted that the Vulgate Bibles of the sixteenth century had suffered so many changes subsequent to Jerome's work that they were no longer really 'Jerome's Bible.'

13 Cf *De doctrina christiana* 2.16–18, 28–31.

more liberal disciplines, namely, dialectic, rhetoric, arithmetic, music; above all, however, through a knowledge of the objects of nature, for example, stars, animals, trees, jewels, and, in addition, places – especially those that divine literature mentions. For it is the case that when territories are recognized from cosmography,[14] we follow the narrative in our thought as it passes before us, and we are, as it were, completely carried away with it, having a sense of pleasure, so that we seem not to read about but to look upon the events narrated; at the same time what you have thus read sticks much more firmly. Further, if we will learn from historical literature not only the setting, but also the origin, customs, institutions, culture and character of the peoples whose history is being narrated or to whom the apostles write, it is remarkable how much more light and, if I may use the expression, life will come to the reading. The reading has to be quite boring and lifeless, whenever not only such things but also the terms for almost everything are unknown. The result is that, either shamelessly guessing or consulting absolutely wretched dictionaries, they[15] make a quadruped out of a tree, a fish out of a jewel, a river out of a musician, a shrub out of a town, a bird out of a star, pants out of plants. It seems to them profoundly learned if only they add 'It is the name of a [502] jewel,' or, 'It is a species of tree,' or, 'It is a kind of animal,' or whatever you prefer. But often the understanding of the mystery hangs upon the very nature of the thing.

[505] I also think that it will be useful for the young man destined for theology to be carefully practised in the figures and tropes of the grammarians and rhetoricians, which are learned with little effort; also to acquire preliminary experience in [506] the allegorical explanation of stories, especially those that look toward good conduct. And since the theological profession rests rather on emotions than on clever arguments, which even in pagan philosophers the pagans themselves ridicule, and Paul denounces in a Christian – and in more than one place[16] – it will be well to be vigorously practised in this field throughout youth,

---

14 'Cosmography,' the study of the system of concentric spheres, included, in the early sixteenth century, the study of geography.

15 'They' is undefined; perhaps a reference to medieval commentaries or to professors of scholastic theology. Erasmus, like other humanists, had a horror of many 'dictionaries' in contemporary use that revealed, he thought, more ignorance than knowledge; he mentions perhaps none with more scorn than the *Catholicon*.

16 For the denunciation of clever arguments in Paul see 1 Cor 1:17–29, 3:18–21, 1 Tim 1:4; for the ridicule of pagans see Aristophanes *Clouds* 877–1112 and Lucian *Philosophers for Sale* especially 20–5.

so that later you might be able to engage more skilfully in discussing theological allegories and commonplaces.

[507] Augustine, in the first book *On Order*, saw this, if I am not mistaken, when he bids his Licentius to return to his liberal studies from which he was then preparing to depart, because studies of that sort make the intellect more vigorous and lively in approaching as well other subjects.[17] At the same time, Augustine counts a knowledge of poetry among the liberal arts. But it will be better, I think, because of those disposed to dispute, to add the words of Augustine himself. He says, 'You must return to those verses. For education in the liberal arts – at least if it is modest and limited – makes its lovers keener, more persistent, more prepared to embrace the truth, so that they seek it more passionately, follow it more faithfully, and, finally, cling to it more dearly.' Otherwise, if anyone is imbued only with those silly, troublesome and jejune little rules – those, say, of dialectic, or, more truly, as it is now generally taught, of sophistry, one turns out, indeed, to be unconquered in debate, but in treating divine literature, in preaching the sacred word, God immortal! how flat we see they are, how frigid, indeed, how lifeless!

[510] I could show with innumerable examples how insipid, not to say ridiculous, are the trifles and absurdities uttered by certain people. For the present, however, it is not my concern to ridicule anyone's ignorance, but to invite young men to the best system of study. Only, I shall say this in general: if anyone seeks some ready proof of this,[18] let him place those ancient theologians, Origen, Basil, Chrysostom, Jerome beside these more recent ones and let him compare them.[19] He will see there a sort of golden river flowing, here some shallow streams, neither very pure nor much like their source. There, the oracles of eternal truth thunder forth, here, you hear the trifling fabrications of men, which, the

17 Augustine *De ordine* 1.8.21–4. In this dialogue, when Augustine's friend Licentius confesses that he is ready to abandon the poets to pursue his love of philosophy and the vision of the truth, Augustine points out to him the value of the liberal arts as a preparation for his quest for truth.

18 'This,' that is, the advantage of approaching the Scriptures from the imaginative perspective of poetry rather than from the application of the petty rules of logic and propositional reasoning that characterizes, as Erasmus contends, contemporary theological education.

19 Origen (c185–c251), perhaps the most prolific theologian of the ancient Greek-speaking world, was born in Alexandria, later (c233) moved to Jerusalem and Caesarea in Palestine. He suffered (251) in the persecution under the emperor Decius. Basil, known as the 'Great,' bishop of Caesarea in Cappadocia, was admired by sixteenth century humanists for his apparent advocacy of classical literature in his *Address*

more closely you investigate the more they vanish like dreams. [513] Do those early Christian writers discourse with less wit because they do not dissect everything into corollaries and conclusions? But it is precisely such things – the very dullest – that seem to us erudite!

(4) Principles of Interpretation

[517] It would be to the point, in my opinion, to hand down to our young tyro doctrines reduced to a compendium and to their chief particulars, and this above all from the Gospel sources, then from the apostolic Epistles, so that everywhere he might have clearly defined target points[20] with which to set in line his reading. As examples of such teachings I note the following few: that Christ, the heavenly teacher, established in the world a new sort of people that depended entirely upon heaven, and distrusting all the supports of this world, was rich in a different sort of way, was wise, noble, powerful, happy in some different way, and that found its happiness by despising all the things the common crowd admires.[21] These were a people who did not know envy or spite – no doubt because their eye was sound; who did not know impure desire inasmuch as they were of their own accord castrated, practising in the flesh the life of angels;[22] who did not know divorce, evidently either bearing or correcting every evil; who did not know

---

to Young Men. Jerome translated the Old Testament into Latin and wrote extensive commentaries on various books of the Bible. After he had revised the Gospels (cf n12, above), he left Rome, established a monastic community near Bethlehem where most of his biblical work was completed. John Chrysostom (c342–407), was a distinguished preacher, first as a priest in Antioch (ancient Syria), then as bishop of Constantinople, where his preaching offended the empress, Eudoxia, in consequence of which he died in exile. He is the author of many homilies on numerous books of the New Testament, and acquired the epithet, 'golden-mouth' (Greek 'chrysostomos') on account of his eloquence. He is often found in indexes under his name 'John.' By 'more recent ones' Erasmus refers to the medieval theologians, especially the scholastics, whom he often calls the *neoterici* (a transliteration from the Greek) ie 'the newer ones.'

20 'Target points,' for the Latin *scopus;* cf the Greek *skopos*, found in the New Testament only in Phil 3:14, but an important word for Erasmus' hermeneutic. Erasmus sets out here a fundamental principle of biblical interpretation: trustworthy interpretation will be 'in line with,' 'accommodate itself to' the portrait drawn here of the ideal Christian community. The portrait is composed of a tissue of biblical images.

21 For the characterization here of the 'new people' see Matt 6:25–34. For a similar characterization see 30 with n12.

22 Cf Matt 6:22 (sound eye), Matt 19:12 (castrated), 22:30 (like angels).

the taking of oaths, as people who neither distrusted anyone nor [518] deceived anyone; who did not know the love of money, as their treasure had been laid up in heaven;[23] who were not titillated by vainglory, as people who referred all things to the glory of Christ alone; who did not know ambition inasmuch as they were people who, the greater anyone was, the more he submitted himself to all on account of Christ;[24] who, not even when provoked knew how to become angry or to curse, much less to take revenge – in fact, they strove to do well even to those who had harmed them;[25] whose manner of life was so innocent that it was approved even by the pagans;[26] who had been, as it were, born again, refashioned into the purity and the simplicity of babes; who, like the birds and the lilies, lived from day to day;[27] among whom there was the greatest harmony, exactly like that among the members of the body in whom mutual charity made all things common, so that when some good befell it came to the assistance of those in need, and when anything evil arose it was either [519] removed or at least alleviated by the obligations of kindness.[28] These were people who, as the heavenly spirit was their teacher, were so wise, who so lived according to the example of Christ, that they were the salt and light of the world, a city set on a hill and visible to all around;[29] who, whatever they were able to do, this they were able to do in the interest of helping all; for whom this life was of no consequence, while death was to be desired because of their longing for immortality;[30] who feared neither tyranny nor death, nor even Satan himself, relying on the help of Christ alone; who in every respect conducted themselves in such a way that they were always girded, as it

---

23 Cf Matt 5:31–2, 1 Cor 13:7 (divorce), Matt 5:33–7 (oaths), 1 Tim 6:10, Matt 6:19–21 (love of money and treasure).

24 Cf 1 Cor 10:31 (all to the glory of Christ), Matt 20:20–8, John 13:12–15 (vain glory and ambition).

25 Cf Rom 12:14–21, Matt 5:21–2, 38–44 (anger and revenge).

26 Perhaps an allusion to Matt 5:16, but Erasmus may have in mind early non-canonical literature, eg Tertullian *Apology* 3.1–3, or even Pliny *Epistles* 10.96: Pliny, the Roman governor of Bithynia-Pontus (111–13 AD) after examination found no impropriety in the lives of Christians except their 'superstition'; cf Robert Wilkin *The Christians as the Romans Saw Them* (New Haven 1984) 79–81.

27 Cf 1 Pet 1:23–2:2, Mark 10:13–16 (babes), Matt 6:25–34 (birds and lilies).

28 Cf 1 Cor 12:12–26, Acts 2:44–5, 4:32. Erasmus' very first adage develops the theme 'Between friends all is common'; cf William Barker *The Adages of Erasmus* (Toronto 2001) 28–30.

29 Cf John 14:26 (heavenly spirit), Matt 10:16 (wisdom), Matt 5:13–14 (salt and light).

30 Cf Phil 1:21-3, 2 Cor 5:1–4.

were, and ready for that final day.[31] [I note] that this is the target-point set out by Christ to which all the affairs of Christians must be directed – granted, meanwhile, that we must bear with and encourage the weak, until they make progress and in gradual stages unobserved grow into the measure of the fullness of Christ.[32]

These are the new teachings of our founder, teachings that no company of philosophers has handed down. This was the new wine that was to be poured only into new skins. These are the teachings through which we are born again from above – hence also Paul calls anyone who is in Christ a new creature.[33]

[520] But in these teachings there is some variety, because of the differences in persons and circumstances. Certain things our founder plainly forbids. The following belong to this category: among us there should not be divorce, jealousy, ambition, love of money, revenge, mistrust, disparagement. Certain things he plainly prescribes for everyone. In this category are the precepts about mutual love, about forgiving the faults of our brothers, about each one taking up his cross, about faith, which he demands everywhere, about kindness to all.[34] Certain things he commends but does not require, enticing with a reward those who can fulfill them, without threatening punishment if they cannot. [521] Perhaps to this class belongs Christ's word to the young man, 'If you wish to be perfect, go, sell all that you possess, and come, follow me' [Matt 19:21]. In some cases Christ dissimulates, as it were, as though the matters do not pertain to him, or as though he is indifferent to them. A case in point is found in Matthew, the seventeenth chapter. He asks Peter, 'Who owes tribute to kings, sons or strangers?' [17:25] – as though he were unskilled and inexperienced in these things, since they were things that pertained to the base condition of this world.

[523] For understanding the sense of Scripture some light will be shed from another source also, that is, if we consider not only what is said, but also the words used, by whom and to whom they are spoken, the time, the occasion, what precedes and what follows. For one type of

31 Cf Phil 4:13 (relying on Christ), Matt 10: 17–26, Rom 8:38–9, (Christians fearless), Luke 12:35–7, 1 Cor 1:8 (girded, ready for final day). In this portrait of the Christian Erasmus lists first the vices avoided, then the virtues practised.

32 Cf Rom 14–15:1 (bear with the weak), Eph 4:13–16 (stages of growth).

33 Cf Matt 9:17 (new wine), 2 Cor 5:17 (new creature). 'Born again from above': Erasmus joins two possible meanings of John 3:3, 'born again,' and 'born from above'; cf 32 n19.

34 The 'things forbidden' correspond closely to the list just above of vices avoided (cf n31); for 'things prescribed' see: n28 above (mutual love), Matt 18:15–35 (forgiveness), Matt 16:24–7 (the cross), Matt 21:18–22 (faith), Matt 5:43–8 (kindness).

discourse befits John the Baptist, another Christ. The untrained populace is taught one thing, the apostles are taught another. Again, one thing is taught to the apostles while they are still untrained, another when they have now become formed and educated. One sort of reply is given to those who interrogate with an insidious design, another to those who inquire with sincere intent. Finally, the very sequence of the narrative discloses on thorough investigation the thought that is otherwise obscure. Many times a comparison of passages unravels the knot of a problem, when what is said somewhat obscurely at one point is repeated at another point quite clearly.

And since in almost all his discourse Christ speaks obliquely through figures and tropes, the candidate for theology will search out with a keen nose what role the speaker sustains – whether he speaks as head or members, shepherd or flock. For when Christ on the cross cries out to the Father, 'My God, my God, why have you forsaken me? Far from my salvation are [524] the words of my transgressions,' he speaks with the voice not of the head but of the members – this on the authority of Augustine.[35] Again when Christ, plaiting a whip, drives the crowd of money-changers out of the temple, he plays the part of the chief pastor.[36] [525] When he asks his disciples, 'Who do you say that I am? [Matt 16:15] he plays the role of the head. Peter replies with the voice of, and in the place of, the whole Christian people, 'You are the Christ, the Son of the living God,' for there is no one in the body of Christ from whom this confession – 'You are the Christ, the Son of the living God' – is not required. In like manner, the words spoken to Peter, 'You are Peter, and upon this rock I will build my church, and I will give to you the keys of the kingdom of heaven' [Matt 16:18–19], extend, according to the interpretation of certain people, to the entire body of Christian people.[37] It is different when he says to Peter, who [526] had thrice declared his

35 Matt 27:46 cites Ps 22:1a; Erasmus extends the citation to 22:1b, which he quotes from the Vulgate according to the Septuagint (cf 204 n15]. In Erasmus' view to recognize correctly the role assumed by the speaker in a biblical passage or by the narrator is to find an important clue to its interpretation. He refers to the speaker in the assumed role as the *persona* (plural *personae*). Sometimes the audience may be referred to as the *persona*. For the Augustine reference see Augustine *Enarratio in psalmum* 37.6 (on Ps 38.3).

36 Cf Matt 21:12–13, and for the whip see John 2:15.

37 In his annotation on Matt 16:18 (*quia tu es*) Erasmus cites Origen, Cyprian, and Augustine as representative of this interpretation. This passage in the *Ratio* was severely criticized; for the criticism of Alberto Pio see CWE 84 299 with n1126. Cf the interpretation of Peter's Confession 105 with n82.

love, 'Feed my sheep' [John 21:15-19]. Here Christ represents himself as the chief shepherd, that is, as the head, while Peter is a type of each and every bishop. Similarly, Paul does not in my opinion speak in his own voice in Romans 7, when after a long lament about his own flesh rebelling against the Spirit, he at last cries out, 'Wretched man that I am, who will deliver me from the body of this death?' [7:24]; he speaks rather with the voice of some other person, someone who was still weak, still no match for his own desires. Certain things, however, are put forward in such a way that they do indeed pertain to all, but not without distinction. For example, when Christ, speaking to the apostles, says, 'You are the salt of the earth; you are the light of the world' [Matt 5:13–14], this pertains to all who profess the religion of Christ, but chiefly to bishops and magistrates. Likewise, when he says, 'Be perfect, as also your Father in heaven is perfect' [Matt 5:48], he shows to all his people the end to which they must strive; yet those who are in charge of the church of Christ must especially manifest this.

The Time Periods

[527] By taking into account the difference of times, like the difference of persons, one dispels the obscurity in arcane literature. For not every command, prohibition, or permission given to the Jews should be accommodated to the life of Christians. Not that there is anything in the books of the Old Testament that does not pertain to us, but because many things that were handed down on a temporary basis as a type and dim outline of things to come are destructive unless they are allegorized – like circumcision, the Sabbath, choice of foods, sacrifices, hatred of an enemy, wars undertaken and waged in this spirit, a multitude of wives. These are things that in part are no longer permitted, in part have utterly vanished like shadows in the gleaming light of the gospel. However, with respect to the choice that one must consider – whether to adapt these rules and customs in a straightforward manner to our conduct, or to give them an allegorical interpretation – it is not my purpose to pursue the subject here, since Augustine has discussed this quite fully in the books *On Christian Doctrine*.[38]

38 Augustine *De doctrina christiana* 3.10.14–25.35. 'Adapt ... to conduct' ie give a 'tropological' interpretation, that is, a moral or ethical interpretation, which was sometimes regarded as an allegorical interpretation. Cf 67 with n93 below, where Erasmus defines the four modes of scriptural interpretation commonly acknowledged in his day.

Let the **first time-period**, then, if you will, be that which preceded the life of Christ; the **second**, when the shadows of the former law were fading as the light of the gospel was near at hand and now approaching though it had not yet, in fact, arisen – as the sky gradually grows light when the sun, not yet risen, hastens to arise. Then it was still enough to be baptized with the baptism of John, to be invited to repent of one's former life. It was enough that the tax collectors be admonished to demand nothing beyond [528] what had been set for them; it was enough that the soldiers be admonished to do violence to no one, to rob and pillage no one, but to be content with their wages. Not that these things made them good men or truly Christians, but that they caused them to be less evil and prepared them for the preaching of Christ that was soon to follow. For John nowhere taught that one must not swear, must not divorce his wife, must take up his cross, must be kind to an enemy.[39] These doctrines that made people Christians in the proper sense were being reserved for Christ. Perhaps to this period of time belongs also the first preaching of the apostles, when, with the example of John before them, they are bidden to call to repentance, to announce that the kingdom of heaven is near, to say nothing about Christ.[40] Perhaps also the baptism with which they were at that time baptizing was of this sort, for the apostles were also then baptizing, as John bears witness, though Christ himself baptized no one[41] – nor is it related at all in canonical literature that anyone had been baptized by Christ.

[529] Let the **third period**, if you like, be the time when Christ was now becoming widely manifest to the world through miracles and teaching, and the evangelical doctrine was being proclaimed – without, however, forbidding the observance of the Law. This time-period includes also the beginnings of the nascent and still unformed church after the Holy Spirit had been given. Certain things, however, seem to belong specifically to this period – for example, all those parables about the cultivators of the vineyard who had killed the owner's son, about the wedding and the invitees who excused themselves; likewise Christ's predictions about the sufferings and the afflictions of preachers, and perhaps his admonitions to take up the cross, to shake off the dust from the feet, to greet no one on the way, to flee from city to city, to leave father and mother and wife, his precepts about the happiness

39 For the preaching of John the Baptist see Luke 3:10–14.

40 Cf Matt 10:5–15 and Mark 6:7–13. In these narratives nothing is said about preaching Christ; Erasmus evidently infers from the silence that the apostles were told 'to say nothing about Christ.'

41 Cf John 4:1–2.

of those who castrate themselves on account of the kingdom of heaven, about selling possessions and renouncing all affections, about frequently changing place; finally, his words about the signs that would follow those who believed – otherwise we would not be Christians today, for it is clear that these [530] signs have not followed us.[42] And yet, from the above this much applies to us, that we are commanded to possess what we hold dear in such a spirit that we are ready to give it up for the glory of Christ whenever the need arises.

To this same period of time belongs also the decision taken through Peter and James in the Acts of the Apostles that gentiles who had come to Christ should abstain from eating anything that had been strangled, and from blood, neither of which we regard as forbidden.[43] This concession was made to the unconquerable obstinacy of the Jews, who would not have been able to associate with the gentiles if these had had nothing at all of Judaism. Perhaps we should view in the same manner the stumbling block before which the apostles with godly intent gave way at a time when the gospel was still of a tender age, when Judaism and paganism held sway. Today, would one not be a laughing stock who abstained from pork in the presence of Jews to avoid giving them offence? But the apostles continued to do so for some time.[44]

[531] There are many other things of this kind that were instituted for use in those times but have later been consigned to oblivion or changed, for example, many sacramental ceremonies. Many rites were then not observed that we are now told to observe, for example, feast days and perhaps the private confession of sins – would that at the present time we might use it as profitably as we use it indiscriminately![45] [532] For

---

42 For these allusions see, in the sequence cited, Matt 21:33–43 (vineyard), Matt 22:1–10 (wedding), Matt 10:16–23 (afflictions), Matt 10:38, 16:24 (taking up the cross), Matt 10:14 (shaking off the dust), Luke 10:4 (greeting no one), Matt 10:23 (fleeing), Luke 14:26 (leaving family including wife), Matt 19:12 (the self-castrated), Matt 19:16–29 (possessions/affections), Luke 10:7 (changing place, but cf also Matt 10:23), Mark 16:15–18 (signs). Erasmus believed that the great signs recorded in Acts were given to the primitive church to induce belief in the gospel in the particular situation of that time, and were not expected to continue, though he recognized that such signs were known to have occurred well into the second century; cf Ep 1738:39–45.

43 Cf Acts 15:19–29.

44 Apparently a reference to Gal 2:1–14 (Peter and Barnabas withdrew from eating with gentiles) and Acts 16:1–3 (Paul circumcised Timothy). Cf also 1 Cor 8:13, Rom 14:20–1.

45 Erasmus' comments on private confession became very controversial; cf CWE 72 362–77 and CWE 39 103 n53. He also frequently complained about the many feast days Christians of the sixteenth century were asked to observe; cf CWE 40 750 n256.

the religion of Christ had by then spread throughout the entire world and become established. The emperors were not persecuting it with military arms, but were protecting it. They were not plundering but augmenting the resources of the church – for here we have, if you will, the **fourth time-period**. New laws were introduced to match the transformation in the state of affairs. A few of these laws would seem to conflict with the tenets of Christ, unless we bring the Scriptures into harmony by observing the distinction of time-periods.

We can make a **fifth time-period** now of the church falling away and degenerating from the pristine vigor of the Christian spirit. To this period, I think, belongs the Lord's saying in the Gospel that as iniquity abounds the love of many will grow cold;[46] also, that there would be those who would say, 'Lo! here is the Christ; lo! there' [Mark 13:21]. Paul, writing to Timothy, seems to have designated this time: 'In the last days shall come on dangerous times, men shall be lovers of themselves … having an appearance indeed of godliness, but denying the power thereof' [2 Tim 3:1–5].

The Circles

But to prevent such a great variety of times, persons, and things from overwhelming the reader, it might be of some value to distribute the whole [533] people of Christ into three circles, all of which, however, have a single centre, Jesus Christ, toward whose absolutely unstained purity all must strive with all the power each person has. For we must never move the target from its place; rather all the actions of mortals must be directed toward the goal.[47]

Let those occupy the **first circle**, then, who, because they have, as it were, succeeded to the place of Christ, are closest to Christ, always cleaving to and following the Lamb wherever he goes.[48] These are such persons as priests, abbots, bishops, cardinals, and popes. These must be as free as possible from the contamination of worldly things, such as the love of pleasures, the pursuit of money, ambition, the appetite for life. It is the responsibility of these to transfuse into the second

46 Matt 24:12.

47 The image of the circles as represented here has a very close parallel in a letter to Paul Volz, Ep 858:225–365, dated 14 Aug 1518. A few months later (Nov 1518), the images of time-periods and the circles appeared in the first edition of the *Ratio* to be published.

48 For the expression see Rev 14:4.

circle the purity and light of Christ they have derived from nearby. The **second circle** contains the secular leaders. Though secular, their arms and their laws in some way serve Christ, whether by overthrowing the enemy in necessary and just wars and keeping the public peace, or by curbing criminals with lawful punishments. We may [534] allot the **third circle** to the undiscriminated crowd as the most stolid and untutored part of this orb we are constructing, remembering that though it is the most stolid and untutored part, it nevertheless belongs to the body of Christ.

Within the individual circles we may picture to ourselves a sort of differentiating order. For when priests offer sacrifices to God, when they feed the people with the food of the evangelical word, when they converse with God in pure prayers, and when they intercede for the welfare of the flock, or when they meditate at home in private study to make the people better, they are no doubt dwelling in the purest part of their own circle. But when they comply with the inclinations of princes to prevent the latter from becoming provoked and arousing a worse commotion, when they unwillingly concede much to the frailty of the weak to prevent them from falling into things still worse, they are moving on the outside boundary of their circle, a boundary to which they proceed, however, only to draw others to themselves, not to become worse themselves. [535] The borders serve to transform into the better, not into the worse. So also Christ would frequently accommodate himself to the frailties of the disciples; so Paul used to indulge the Corinthians in many things, though he distinguished sometimes what he set forth in the name of the Lord for the perfect and what in his own name he pardoned in the weak with the hope nevertheless that they would progress.[49] Accordingly, when popes with their pardons and indulgences foster and encourage those who are slothful or close to despair until they progress to better things, they are not moving in the highest part of their circle. When they also pass laws [536] about defending the patrimony of Peter, about subduing the Turks in war,[50] about innumerable other things – however necessary or at least useful to our common life – no

49 For the 'accommodation' of Christ see John 16:12; for the allusions to Paul see 1 Cor 3:1–2 (indulge the weak), and 1 Cor 7:8–16, 25–31, 39–40 (distinguish precepts).

50 Both very relevant allusions: Pope Julius II (d1513) was a notorious defender of the 'patrimony of Peter' ie the Papal States; he is satirized in *Julius Excluded* CWE 27 168–97. In 1517 the Fifth Lateran Council voted to call a crusade against the Turks; in the letter to Paul Volz (cf n47 above) Erasmus discussed at some length the issue of war with the Turks; cf Ep 858:85–165.

one would say they are engaged in what is peculiar to the heavenly philosophy. And indeed perhaps popes, even if they particularly wished, could not regulate their laws – the laws they publish for the common life of human beings – in such a way that these would correspond in every respect to the precepts of Christ. Christ, as that purest source of all light and innocence, teaches things that taste of heaven. Popes are men and prescribe according to circumstances what seems helpful for people who are weak, and weak in so many different ways.

[537] I have said these things so that we might not taint the celestial philosophy of Christ with either the laws or the doctrines of human beings. Let that target remain intact; let that one unparalleled spring be unpolluted; let that truly sacred anchor of gospel teaching be preserved; in it one can take refuge amidst such dark mists of human affairs. May that cynosure[51] never become obscured for us, lest there be no sure constellation by which we might be put back once again on the right course when we have been enveloped in such great billows of error. May this pillar not be moved,[52] in order that with its support we may withstand the force of this world, which always both sinks toward and carries one off to the worse. May that foundation remain solid, and ready to give way before no blasts of opinion or storm winds of persecution – a secure foundation on which the good architect might place a structure of gold, silver, and precious stones, and when the hay and straw of the studied opinions of human beings have been consumed by fire, the [538] foundation itself might remain for a better edifice.[53] Men can make mistakes; Christ does not know how to err. Do not reject forthwith what human beings prescribe, but consider carefully who prescribes, to whom he prescribes, at what time, on what occasion, and, finally, with what intent the prescription is given; but above all whether a prescription agrees with gospel teaching, whether it has the taste of the life of Christ and reflects his life.

[550] It would perhaps not be unreasonable to establish some order of authority among the sacred writings as Augustine did not scruple to do.[54] First [551] place is owed to those books about which the ancients

51 'Cynosure,' the constellation of the Little Bear, by which, as Cicero reports, the Phoenicians steered their ships (*Academica* 2.20.66).

52 Cf 1 Tim 3:15.

53 Cf 1 Cor 3:12. The interpretation of this biblical passage was highly controversial; cf CWE 72 278–80.

54 Augustine *De doctrina christiana* 2.8.13, where, however, Augustine merely reflects a traditional order of the biblical books. This paragraph (CWE 550–2) has been relocated to precede the paragraph that immediately follows here (CWE 546).

never had any doubt. For me, at least, Isaiah has more weight than Judith or Esther, the Gospel of Matthew more than the Apocalypse attributed to John, the Epistles of Paul to the Romans and the Corinthians more than the Epistle to the Hebrews. Next place after these is held by certain things that have been handed down to us by hand, as it were, and have reached to us either from the apostles themselves or from those who lived close to the time of the apostles. Among these I place first of all the creed known as the 'Apostles,' produced, if I mistake not, at the council of Nicaea.[55] I believe it derives [552] its name from the fact that it manifests the weight, the moderation and also the brevity of apostolic speech – and would that our eagerness to believe had been satisfied with that one creed! When there began to be less faith among Christians both the number and the size of the creeds grew.[56] And yet even the apostles, while they resemble Christ, do not rise to his majestic grandeur.

[546] In addition, we will enjoy an important advantage [in interpreting Scripture] if we diligently read through the books of both Testaments and consider closely that wonderful circle and harmony of the entire drama of Christ (if I may use the expression), a drama acted out for our sake by the one who was made man. If we do so we shall not only understand more correctly what we read, but we shall also read with a more certain confidence. For no lie is so skilfully fabricated that it is at all points consistent. Collect from the books of the Old Testament the types, and the oracles of the prophets: the types sketch out and represent in outline the Christ; the oracles point as though with the eyes of faith to his coming. Those divine seers portrayed almost everything Christ did. There is nothing in his teaching that does not find a correspondence in some passage in the Old Testament.

[552] Nor, in truth, does the diversity in Christ bring this harmony into disorder. Rather, just as in song the sweetest harmony arises from different voices aptly ordered, so the diversity of Christ produces a fuller harmony. He became all things to all people[57] but without ever compromising himself. Sometimes he manifests the signs of divinity – when he commands the winds and the sea, when he forgives sins, when on the

55 Erasmus 'is disposed to date [the Apostle's Creed] from the first council of Nicaea' (325), CWE 39 432 n16.

56 Erasmus may be thinking of the Nicene Creed (325), the Constantinopolitan Creed (381/2), and the Athanasian Creed (date uncertain, probably originating in the early medieval period). Cf CWE 70 252–3 n21 and 249 n146 below.

57 Cf 1 Cor 9:22.

mountain he presents to his disciples a new appearance.[58] At other times he plays the part of a human being, concealing his divinity – when he is hungry, thirsty, tired out from work, when he mourns, when he is afflicted and killed.[59]

[557] But we [may be inclined to] stumble over passages that at first glance seem contradictory. Cases of this are the following: in [558] the Gospel of John Christ denies that John the Baptist is the light, though later he declares of the same John, 'He was a burning, shining light' [John 5:35]; and when he says to the still unformed apostles, 'You are the light of the world' [Matt 5:14], likewise when he says, 'My teaching is not mine' [John 7:16], if anyone pays attention only to the surface meaning of the words, there seem to be inconsistencies. Moreover, in certain narratives the apparent variation lay open to the slander of the ungodly. For example, Matthew reports one blind man healed though Luke affirms that two were healed.[60] Likewise when sometimes one name seems to be substituted for another; when Stephen, in Acts the seventh chapter, seems to tell the story somewhat differently from the way it is found in Genesis – in the twelfth chapter, that is.[61] [559] If difficulties of this sort sometimes arise one should not be offended or doubt the trustworthiness of what is written, but should consider carefully all the details and then look for a way to resolve the problem. Our predecessors toiled with sweat in this very task; their assiduous efforts will help us if we do not find an answer that satisfies the mind.

(5) Spiritual Resources of the Interpreter

[579] We must also notice in what ways and how carefully [Christ] prepares those who are about to go out to preach the gospel. Our observation will enable those who today undertake the ministry of preaching Christ to understand the preparation they ought to acquire. The kingdom of heaven is being summoned; it is fitting that from this heavenly kingdom the earthly passions that hold sway in those who love the world be far removed. Accordingly, it is [580] worthwhile to consider with what great zeal Christ banished all such passions from the hearts

---

58 Cf Matt 8:23–7 (commands winds), Matt 9:2 (forgives sins), Matt 17:1–8 (transfiguration).

59 Cf John 4:6–7 (weariness, thirst), Matt 21:18 (hunger), John 11:35 (mourns).

60 Cf Matt 9:27–31, 20:29–34 and Luke 18:35–43, where, however, one blind man is found in Luke's account, two in Matthew's, but cf Matt 12:22 where one man both blind and deaf was healed.

61 Compare Acts 7:2–4 with Gen 12:1–6.

of his disciples. He took away luxury and the love of sensual pleasures with the parable of the rich reveller and the beggar Lazarus.[62] Again, he removes the pursuit of wealth when he prohibits us from being concerned about tomorrow; when he asks that treasures, subject to neither moths nor thieves, be laid up eternal in the heavens; when he enjoins us to live from day to day, like lilies and little sparrows, relying on the goodness and the providential care of the heavenly Father.[63]

[582] Now in regard to the love of honour and the disease of ambition, which is usually innate in noble and lofty natures, in how many ways does he root this out of the hearts of the disciples, knowing full well that this would be the chief bane of ecclesiastical princes. He allowed his disciples to feel this emotion so that he could more effectively eradicate it. It was from ambition that the sons of Zebedee request (through their mother whom they had secretly directed to this end) that they sit next to Christ in the kingdom of heaven. It was from ambition that the disciples disputed among themselves who would be first in the kingdom of heaven.[64] Accordingly they hear from the Lord: 'The princes of the gentiles lord it over them, and those who have power exercise it over their own. It shall not be so among you; rather, whoever will be greater among you, let him be your minister, and he that will be first among you shall be your servant [Matt 20:25–7].

[584] He banishes utterly the evil of rage, inviting us with so many parables to be clement and ready to forgive. So it is, in Matthew the eighteenth chapter, with the parable of the slave who would not pardon a fellow slave, though he himself had experienced the mercy of their common master.[65] [585] There is also another affection that lies in wait even for good men in the very midst of their good deeds, if they are not careful: trust in ourselves.[66] Christ does not tolerate this disposition in his disciples. One who thinks he is godly is not godly enough. Christ scorns the Pharisee who stood by and proclaimed his merits; he acknowledges the publican who was standing far off, displeased with himself.[67] [589] In the ninth chapter of the Epistle to the Romans he

62 Luke 16:19–31.

63 Cf Matt 6:19–20, 25–33, though for 'sparrows' see Matt 10:29–31.

64 Cf Matt 20:20–8 and Luke 22:24–7.

65 Matt 18:23–35.

66 In the Latin, *fiducia nostri*, which may also be rendered 'self-confidence.' In Erasmus' theological vocabulary the word *fiducia* characteristically invites, as here, a contrast between reliance upon merits achieved through our own efforts and reliance upon the freely given grace of God for salvation; cf CWE 44 243 n1.

67 Cf Luke 18:9–14. To be displeased, dissatisfied, with oneself was regarded as the first of three stages in true repentance; cf CWE 44 13 n5.

shows that salvation comes to us only through the righteousness that is from faith. Furthermore, what he calls the 'righteousness from faith' is this: when we attribute absolutely nothing to our own deeds, but acknowledge that whatever success we have as we try for the best with all our might is the result of his gift freely given.[68]

[594] Since, however, the goal of all of Christ's teaching is that we should live our lives in a godly and holy manner, it will be fitting to track [595] down in the divine books the example and pattern for all the actions of our lives. [596] There are two things especially that Christ constantly inculcates – faith and love. Faith ensures that we cease to trust ourselves and we place all our trust in God; love urges us to do good to all. In Matthew, the ninth chapter, he imputes to the paralytic the faith even of others: 'And Jesus seeing their faith' [9:2]. [597] On the matter of love, how does it help to specify? For what else does Christ teach, what else does he inculcate by his whole life except the most consummate love? This was the one thing he had come to teach us. [598] Love alone is the token by which he wanted his disciples to be distinguished from others when he said: 'By this all will know that you are my disciples, if you have love for one another' [John 13:35]. [599] Go through the whole New Testament: nowhere will you find any precept relating to ceremonies. Where is there a single word about food or clothes? Where is there any mention of abstaining from food or the like? Love alone he calls his commandment. Discord arises from ceremonies, peace comes from love.

[602] Consider how the teaching and character of the apostles conform to this pattern, and above all, that of Paul, for no one resembled the preceptor Christ more than he. Would that those who have succeeded to the apostolic office and boast that they are called the vicars of Christ could deservedly apply to themselves the words with which Paul exhorts the Corinthians to true piety when he says, 'I ask you, be ye followers of me, as I also am of Christ' [1 Cor 4:16 Vulgate]. He repeats this in as many words in the eleventh chapter of the same Epistle.[69] It is therefore important to observe how there is not a page in Paul that does not abound in the frequent mention of faith and love, which

68 Cf Rom 9:30. The sentence reflects the complexity in Erasmus' understanding of the relationship between free will and the divine initiative. See below 181–4. Note in the selection from the *Paraphrase* on Romans 9 the contrasting statements in the editions of 1517 and 1532. Erasmus debated the problem at length in his controversy with Martin Luther; see his lengthy statement of his views in *On the Freedom of the Will* and *Hyperaspistes* I and II, translated in CWE 76 and 77.

69 Cf 1 Cor 11:1.

he commends sometimes separately, sometimes jointly to his people. [613] I judge it superfluous to adduce testimonies from the Epistle of John since he speaks of nothing but love and concord. Let us hear Peter, prince of [614] our profession. In the fourth chapter of the First Epistle he says, 'Above all have mutual love among yourselves,' and 'love will cover a multitude of sins' [4:7–8].

Now just as a resolute mind and true godliness are the companions of faith and love, so when the latter languish or are absent superstition thrives. And just as unalloyed godliness rests upon purity of mind, superstition commends itself by ceremonies. [615] Godliness of the mind has a place everywhere, but nothing is more deadly than a counterfeit holiness, and there is no mask through which this more deceives than that of ceremonies.

(6) The Language of Scripture: Significance for the Interpreter

[632] For the interpreter of Scripture considerable difficulty lies in the very character of the speech in which sacred literature has been handed down to us. For Scripture generally speaks indirectly and under the cover of tropes and allegories, and of comparisons or parallels, sometimes to the point of obscurity in a riddle.[70] Perhaps Christ thought it fitting to reproduce the speech of the prophets to [633] which Jewish ears had grown accustomed, or he wanted to stimulate our sluggishness with this difficulty, so that fruit sought with effort might later be more pleasing, or through this design he wanted his mysteries to be covered and concealed from the profane and the ungodly without at the same time cutting off hope of understanding from godly investigators. Or perhaps he particularly liked the mode of expression that is most effectively persuasive, and, likewise, accessible to learned and unlearned alike, and familiar and completely natural, especially if similitudes are drawn from things best known to the common crowd; we read that Socratic comparisons were generally of this kind.[71]

A parable is effectual not only for teaching and persuading, but also for stirring the emotions, for alluring with its charm, for bringing clarity, for implanting one central idea deep within the mind, beyond the possibility of escape. The mind is quite extraordinarily moved by the

---

70 'Riddle' (Latin *aenigma*) is a key term in the Erasmian hermeneutic; see CWE 43 161 n18 (and the reference there to CWE 44 236); see also CWE 48 14 n38.

71 Cf eg in Plato's *Republic* the allegories of the metals, the line and the cave as well as the myth of Er, respectively 414B–416B, 509D–511E, 514A–517E and 614B–621B.

parable that is introduced concerning the prodigal son, who came to his senses and repented.[72] [634] The images in this story strike the mind more sharply than if, without a parable, one should say that God willingly receives a sinner provided the sinner sincerely repents of his former life, and God does not hold the sin against one who profoundly hates his transgressions. Just as this idea steals into the minds of hearers more effectively through the allurement of this similitude, so it is etched more deeply when it is restated through the image of the wandering sheep that is brought back home on the shoulders of the shepherd after a long search.[73]

Again, there is the mystic parable from Genesis: Abraham everywhere digs wells, the Philistines fill up the pits by throwing earth in them, Isaac digs the same wells again and adds several more besides that have veins of living water. When you introduce this parable will you not be heard with greater pleasure than if you should simply say that one must seek in the divine books instruction for good living – that those who are devoted to earthly [635] goods have no taste for these?[74]

[640] Christ sometimes deceives his disciples temporarily through riddles of an allegorical nature so that what he wanted them to understand would stick more deeply later on. For example, in the sixteenth chapter of Matthew, when Christ warns the disciples to beware of the leaven of the Pharisees, it is the loaves they had forgotten that come to their minds, though he was speaking about avoiding the hypocrisy of the Pharisees.[75] Again, in Luke he bids them sell their tunics and buy a sword; they reply that two swords are at hand, and he says, 'It is enough.' When the opportunity arose, the words added incentive to Peter to set about the matter with a sword, though Christ was trying to pluck out of their hearts from its very roots this desire to protect themselves by force against their persecutors.[76]

[636] These examples show that there are things that appear in a more pleasing way through crystal or amber than if they are looked upon alone and bare. And somehow sacred things have more majesty

72 Luke 15:11–32.

73 Luke 15:3–7.

74 For the story see Gen 26:15–22, for the interpretation Origen *Homilies on Genesis* 13 in Ronald Heine trans *Origen. Homilies on Genesis and Exodus* FOTC 71 (Washington 1982) 185–95.

75 Matt 16:5–12. This paragraph has been relocated to precede the paragraph that follows here.

76 Cf Luke 22:35–8, 47–51.

if they are brought before the eyes under a cover than if they are seen absolutely bare. Thus truth that has tormented us first under cover of a riddle is more pleasing once grasped – we who are the animal that walks first on four feet, then two, finally three.[77]

[637] Moreover, just as Christ imitated the speech of the prophets, so Paul and the other apostles reflect the speech of Christ, projecting a theme visually, through parables, and, by frequent repetition, fastening it upon the mind. Thus Paul repeatedly calls us temples dedicated to God, and temples of the Holy Spirit, which it is forbidden to desecrate. Thus it is with the parable of the olive tree and the wild olive, the root and the branches that concludes that whole discussion about the rejection of Israel and the adoption of the gentiles.[78] [641] Again, imitating Christ he refers everything from its normal meaning to its inner meaning. According to the general opinion a Jew is one who has a little bit of foreskin cut off. According to Paul's interpretation a Jew is a person who has a mind cleansed from earthly desires, [642] while the uncircumcised is one who is led by base affections. [641] Thus, by whatever design, it pleased the eternal wisdom both to insinuate itself into the minds of the godly, and, if I may use the expression, to deceive the minds of the profane through images sketched in outline only.

[644] There are, however, tropes that belong to the idiomatic character of speech; if an idiom is misunderstood the reader will frequently either be deceived or delayed. The Greek language has, in fact, many idiomatic expressions in common with Latin, some peculiar to itself. But Hebrew has many forms of expression different from both. We use the same idiom as the Greeks when we say that one who 'deserves well of another' 'does a kindness.' But we do not share in common with them the fact that their expression *eupathein*, that is, 'to be fortunate' [*bene pati*, literally, 'suffer well'], is used idiomatically to mean 'to receive a kindness.'[79] We share with them a common idiom for 'I am grateful' *habeo gratiam*, [*echo charin*] [literally, 'I have thanks']; we do not share with them an idiom that expresses the same idea [*oida charin*, literally, 'I know thanks']. [645] Further, although the apostles wrote in

77 An allusion to the famous riddle of the sphinx; cf Sophocles *King Oedipus* 390–8.

78 Cf 1 Cor 3:16–17, 6:19, 2 Cor 6:16 (temples), Rom 11:16–24 (olive trees, root/branches).

79 Ie whereas the Greek word *eupathein*, literally 'to suffer well,' is used in Greek to mean both 'to be fortunate' and 'to receive a kindness,' Latin speakers wishing to express the latter idea would not use *bene pati* the literal equivalent of the Greek, but *beneficio affici*, literally 'to be affected with a kindness.'

Greek they retain in no small measure the idiom of Hebrew speech. As a result, one who has little proficiency in Hebrew, even if very skilled in Greek, sometimes does not follow the thought of the speaker. Examples of this kind are: 'who swears in heaven,' for the expression 'he swears by heaven';[80] and 'he believes in him' for the expression 'he trusts in him'; [646] likewise, 'all flesh' for 'all people,' 'many souls' for 'many persons.'

[648] Now a problem is frequently solved through other kinds of tropes also. For example: Matthew and Mark reported that the robbers who were crucified with Christ reviled him, though Luke tells us that only one did so. Augustine unravels the knot by saying that this is a case of the rhetorical figure of *heterosis*, a change of number, where 'robbers' is used for 'a robber.'[81] Again, he explains by *synechdoche* the statement that Christ was in the tomb for a period of three days, as also the passage written in Mark that he would rise again after three days, although he rose at daybreak on the third day.[82] How many times, moreover, do Chrysostom and Jerome and Augustine scatter the obscurity of meaning by unravelling the intricacies of a *hyperbaton*.[83] [649] Indeed, we frequently encounter *hyperbole* also, as in this passage: 'They mount up to heaven, they go down to the depths' [Ps 107:26], where the Psalmist wanted us to picture the violent surging of storm-driven waves. A statement that goes beyond demonstrable reality is not necessarily a lie, but a trope is applied to make discourse more pungent and passionate. And no one should think it absurd to point out hyperboles in the divine books, for Origen does so, as does Chrysostom, and so do Augustine and Jerome.

[654] But you might perhaps be inclined to doubt whether one is permitted to find irony in the literature of the apostles and of the Gospels – though [655] there can be no doubt that it is found in the Old Testament. Certainly in the eighteenth chapter of the third book of Kings Elijah mocking the prophets of Baal says: 'Cry out with a louder voice, for he is a god, and perhaps he is talking, or he is at an inn, or is on a journey,

80 In expressions like this, Biblical Greek, influenced by Hebrew idiom, often writes 'in' with the sense of 'by.'

81 Cf Matt 27:44, Mark 15:32, Luke 23:39, Augustine *De consensu evangelistarum* 3.16.53. For *heterosis*, referring to a variation in the form of a word, see CWE 56 119 n10, and cf English, 'the book' as an abstract reference to books in general.

82 Cf Matt 12:40, Mark 8:31 and Matt 16:1 ('on the third day'), Augustine *De consensu evangelistarum* 3.24.66.

83 For *hyperbaton*, a transposition of words from their natural order, see CWE 56 25 n21; also 306 with n38 below.

or surely he is asleep, and must be awakened' [1 Kings 18:27]. Again, in Paul, the sixth chapter of the first Epistle to the Corinthians 'Those who are the more despised, set them to judge' [6:4] – this can be seen to have been said with irony, especially since there follows, 'I speak to your shame' [6:5].[84] Perhaps also those words of Christ are not very far from irony, 'I came not to call the righteous but sinners' [Matt 9:13], for he did not truly believe [656] that they were righteous, but he reproaches them because they thought they were righteous.

Now, ambiguity is without question a fault in discourse, but one that often cannot be avoided. [658] The special use of a word sometimes makes the discourse ambiguous, but this is peculiar not so much to the language as to the writer, inasmuch as among authors each has language that is peculiar to himself. Thus Paul at one time calls kindred or blood-relationship 'flesh,' at another time he designates the whole person as flesh; sometimes the grosser part of a person or of another thing of any sort at all is said to be flesh; occasionally, he designates as flesh the affection of a person that entices one to the vices. Similarly, he often calls 'body' that which consists of limbs; sometimes 'body' has for him the same force as 'flesh.'[85] [659] Of the same kind are these expressions, too: when they say *fides* for *fiducia* [trust], since in Latin *fides* is used of the one who promises, as in the expression *dare fidem* [to give a pledge], or of one who does or does not fulfil a promise, as in the expression *solvere fidem* [to fulfil a promise']. *Praestare fidem* [to keep faith] does not designate the action of the one who trusts or believes, except when we say, 'I have confidence in you' [*habeo tibi fidem*].[86]

The special significance attached to words will also have to be noted. For this, a knowledge of the different languages is especially useful. There is a case in point [660] in the Epistle to the Corinthians, where Paul calls the apostles *hyperetas*, that is, ministers of Christ and *oikonomous*,

---

84 The Greek verb permits the sentence to be read as either a command (DV, AV and Erasmus) or a question (RSV, NRSV). In his annotation on the verse (*illos constituite ad iudicandum*) Erasmus says, 'Paul does not really mean that [the Corinthians] should do so.'

85 For the various, ie ambiguous ways Paul uses the word 'flesh' see: Rom 11:14 (kindred), Rom 3:20 (person), Rom 7:18 (grosser part), Rom 7:5 (affection); for 'body' see 1 Cor 12:14 (limbs), Rom 7:17–24 (equivalent to flesh).

86 For a notable attempt to define *fides* 'faith' see the annotation on Rom 1:17 ('from faith unto faith') CWE 56 42–5 (excerpted below, 219–21). *Praestare fidem* is best expressed by our idiom 'to keep faith,' and as such is used of the one who makes a promise, but the Latin also conveys the meaning of 'offer faith,' hence in this sense can be used of one who is giving his trust.

that is, stewards of the mysteries of God.[87] A minister is an administrator and steward of someone else's property, not his own, and dispenses at his lord's will, not his own, what and how much each needs, according to circumstances. Thus bishops do not seek their own interests, they do not teach their own doctrines, but what belongs to Christ. They do not propound the same things to everyone, but attune their discourse to the receptivity of each. This *emphasis* is most properly observed in the original language in which the author wrote. [656] There are many other figures of speech and figures of thought that contribute to the artistic arrangement or the weight or the pleasure of discourse. Though the sense of mystic Scripture stands firm without them, through these figures the Scriptures steal into our minds more effectually and more pleasurably.[88]

[661] But to return to allegories. Special care must be devoted to these, since almost all divine Scripture, through which the eternal wisdom speaks with us in a stammering tongue, as it were, rests upon allegories. Unless these come to our attention, especially in the books of the Old Testament, the reader will lose a large part of the fruit. If a passage were taken in a [662] straightforward way, the sense of the words would sometimes be manifestly untrue, occasionally even ridiculous and absurd. And[89] by a salutary plan the divine wisdom has taken precaution lest, if no obstacle appeared in the historical text, we should suppose there was not any more meaning there. Accordingly the divine wisdom breaks up the course of the biblical reading with certain rough bogs, chasms, and similar obstacles, mixing in things either that cannot have happened or could not happen, or that, if they happened, they would be absurd. In this way, the mind, barred by such obstacles from understanding the passage in the ordinary manner, might wander through more hidden by-ways and at length arrive at the place where the riches of a more recondite understanding are spread out. This pattern occurs not only in narratives, but in prophecies and precepts.

And yet we must not remove all the historical sense in the divine books just because, for the reasons mentioned, certain passages are found through which the divine providence wished to compel, as it were, our mental powers to explore the spiritual meaning. Generally

87 Cf 1 Cor 4:1. 'Special significance' translates the technical rhetorical term *emphasis*.

88 'There … pleasurably': These two sentences from CWE 41 656 have been relocated to conclude the discussion on tropes found in CWE 41 656–61.

89 From this point most of the discussion on allegories presented here was added to the *Ratio* in the edition of 1523.

both senses stand together. For I believe that God's precept, 'You shall not muzzle an ox when it treads out the grain' [Deut 25:4] had long ago been observed among the Hebrews also according to the historical sense. And yet Paul writes, "Does God take care for oxen? Or does he not speak especially for our sake? For this was written for our sake, because one who ploughs should plough in hope, and one who threshes in the hope of receiving' [1 Cor 9:9–10].

[663] But if anyone should look for an example of an incongruous narrative, many are encountered straight off in Genesis itself. For how is it consistent that the first day of the created world, the second, and the third, for which both evening and morning are mentioned, were without sun, moon, stars, the first day, moreover, even without sky? Next, how incongruous to understand according to the historical sense that God, like some farmer, planted trees in Paradise, in Eden toward the East, and there he planted a certain tree of life, that is, a real tree that could be seen and touched; to understand that this tree had such power that whoever had eaten of its fruit with his physical teeth would receive life, that he planted also another tree from which, if anyone ate, such a person would understand the distinction between good and evil. The narratives that follow are almost as feeble, where it is said that God walks in Paradise in the cool afternoon air, that Adam hides under a tree, that Cain withdrew from the face of the Lord; finally, where it is written that God completed some portion of his work on each day and at last on the seventh day rested from his work, as though he was worn out.[90]

Inasmuch as the exterior form of this sort of story offends the reader at first blush, it advises him that under this covering their lies hidden some more recondite sense, so that he should ask what an allegorical day is, what is the division of days, what is the rest from work, what the planting, the tree of life, the tree giving knowledge of good and evil, what is the 'afternoon,' what is 'God walking in the cool air,' Adam lying hidden, what is the face of the Lord, what is 'departing from him?' But whoever will examine the books of the Old Testament, which abounds in tropes of this kind, will find many examples like these.

The same thing is somewhat more rare in the New Testament; nevertheless, we may even here, perhaps, find narrative that is absurd according to the historical sense. For example, we read that the Lord was led away into [664] a high mountain, from where he looked upon all the kingdoms of the world and their glory.[91] How would anyone be

90 The stories are found in Gen 1–2; for the two trees see Gen 2:9.

91 Cf Matt 4:8.

able to show to corporeal eyes from a single mountain, no matter how high, the kingdom of the Persians, Scythians, Indians, Spaniards, Gauls, Britons, and to show in what ways each particular nation does homage to its king? [666] In the apostolic Epistles, [667] too, certain things are found that bar us from the ordinary sense, and compel us to turn up, with the help of tropology, a sense worthy of the Holy Spirit. For example, it would be impious to want to keep, according to the literal sense, this precept of Paul, 'For doing this, you will heap coals of fire upon his head' [Rom 12:20].

[671] Whoever wishes to treat sacred literature seriously will observe moderation in interpretation of this sort. Moreover, it would be safest in tracing out allegories to follow the sources many of which the Lord himself opened up for us; Paul also some.[92] But if anyone permits himself sometimes to indulge in allegories, he will be [672] granted more forbearance when he does so in exhortation, in consolation, in rebuke than in asserting the truth. [677] Meanwhile, I shall add this one comment. It is not enough to observe how in diverse things the eternal truth shines out in different ways – according to the historical sense, which is straightforward, according to the tropological sense, which is concerned with morals and our life together, according to the allegorical sense, which investigates the hidden things of the head and the whole mystical body, according to the anagogical sense, which touches upon the celestial hierarchy (for I see that certain people make such a division).[93] One must also consider in each of these individually what levels there are, what differences, what method of treatment is there. This is not to mention [678] that a type receives a different shape, as it were, according to the variety of things, the diversity of times, to which it is accommodated. For example, the husks the swine feed upon, with which in desperation the prodigal son is eager to fill his starving belly,[94] can be made to fit riches, pleasures, honours, worldly erudition, and yet you are still engaged in tropology. Further, that whole parable can be applied to the Jewish people and the gentiles of that time. The gentiles

92 For the allegorizing parables of Jesus see eg Matt 21:33–46 (the wicked tenants); of Paul Gal 4:21–31 (Hagar and Sarah).

93 The historical development of biblical interpretation according to the various senses of Scripture is described succinctly but effectively in CWE 63 xxiv–xxx. Cf Erasmus' 'Commentary on Psalm 2' CWE 63 78: 'In many psalms the theme is twofold: the historical, which underlies it … and the allegorical, or anagogical, which, beneath the cloak of historical events, conceals, or rather reveals, the gospel story, instruction in true piety, or an image of eternal bliss.'

94 Cf Luke 15:11–32.

come to their senses, repent and are welcomed, the Jews murmur; and their common father soothes both. And now from the variation in persons and times to which the parable is being accommodated, a virtually new face is put upon the discourse.

(7) Concluding Admonitions

Moreover, the theological candidate must especially be advised of this also, that he learn to cite appropriately the testimonies of sacred Scripture, not from little summas[95] or review-lists or cheap and trifling homiletical texts, or other excerpt-collections of this sort that have been poured back and forth and mingled together already an infinite number of times, one deriving from another, but from the sources themselves. He should not imitate certain people who are not ashamed to twist forcibly the oracles of the divine wisdom to a sense foreign to them, sometimes even to the opposite sense. [679] There are certain men who bring their own doctrinal formulations with them, and imbued with popular opinions, compel arcane Scripture to serve these, though one's own judgments should rather be sought from Scripture. There are some who drag Scripture to the support of public moods and mores, and since it suits to adopt this rule when they are considering the course that should be followed, it is with the patronage of Scripture that they defend popular behaviour.

[684] I think the right way is to treat the sacred words appropriately and without violation. If you take care at first to do this as well as you can, later you will do so with ease besides. Though I should like this principle to be maintained everywhere, it is, nevertheless, especially appropriate to maintain it when we are dealing with an opponent of our religion, or when falsehood is being refuted and the truth affirmed, or when the sense of mystic Scripture is being expounded. Otherwise, the effect is that we not only fail to carry the point we are establishing, but we become a laughing stock to our own adversary.

[690] What I am now about to say will perhaps offer an advantage of the highest importance to anyone who applies the principle with skill. It is this: either prepare for yourself or take over from someone else a number of theological headings under which you put everything you have read, placing them into something like little pigeon-holes so

95 'Little summas' were compendious collections of materials useful in various endeavours, eg teaching or preaching.

that you might the more readily produce or store away what you wish, when you please – I note by way of example the subject of faith, of fasting, of enduring evils, helping the weak, enduring ungodly magistrates, avoiding offence to the simple, the study of sacred literature, godly devotion to parents or children, Christian charity, honoring the leading people, envy, disparagement, chastity, and other things of this kind (for countless categories can be imagined). Arrange these in order according to opposites or similarities. Whatever is noteworthy anywhere in all the books of the Old Testament, in the Gospels, in Acts, in the apostolic Epistles, that either agrees or disagrees should be listed under the appropriate category. In fact, if anyone likes, he can bring to these topics what he deems will be of use from the [691] ancient commentators; likewise, lastly, from the books of the pagans. I rather think I notice from Jerome's own writings that he used this method.[96] If something has to be discussed, materials will be ready at hand; if something is to be clarified, a comparison of passages will be easy.

[693] And now, furnished with these things, let our theological tyro engage in constant meditation on divine literature, let him 'take care to turn by night, by day' its pages.[97] Let him have the Scriptures always in hand, always in pocket; from Scripture let something always sound in his ears, or meet his eyes or hover within his mind. What has been fixed deep within through constant use will become a part of one's nature. In my opinion it will not be ill-advised to learn the divine books word for word even though they are not understood. For this opinion Augustine is my authority; by the words, 'even though not understood,' I take him to mean, 'even if you do not yet catch the mystic sense.'[98]

[695] But meanwhile someone asks, 'Well, surely for your part you don't think divine Scripture so easy and accessible that it can be understood apart from commentaries?' Why not to some extent, that is, to the degree sufficient not for theatrical display, but for sound teaching, if its teachings have been learned first, and that comparison of passages, as I have described, has been applied. In any case, what else have they done who were the first to publish commentaries on divine Scripture? Chief among these is Origen, who so began to weave this lovely web that no one after him dared to put a hand to it. Then Tertullian, earlier than Origen, and a man so prodigiously learned in divine Scripture that Cyprian

96 Erasmus describes Jerome's method in his *Life of Jerome* CWE 61 33.

97 Adapted from Horace *Ars poetica* 269.

98 Cf Augustine *De doctrina christiana* 2.9: 'Our first concern is to know these books even though they are not understood.'

with good reason used to call him his master.[99] What prevents others from arriving at the same goal as these if they proceed by the same path.

I do not say these things because I want to give authority to anyone to pass over the commentaries of the ancients, and to claim or even hunt for himself a knowledge of divine Scripture. Rather let the labour of the ancients save us from part of the work, let us find assistance in their commentaries, provided, [696] first, that we choose the best of them, for example, Origen, who is so far ahead that no one else can be compared to him; after him, Basil, Nazianzus, Athanasius, Cyril, Chrysostom, Jerome, Ambrose, Hilary, Augustine;[100] second, that we read even these with judgment and discrimination, though I want them to be read with respect. They were men: certain things they did not know, at points their minds wandered, sometimes they were nodding, they conceded some things to the heretics in order to overcome them in any way at all (for at that time all things were seething with the contentions of the heretics), certain things they imparted for the ears of those to whom they were then speaking.

[711] This, at least, cannot be denied, that the teaching of Christ has been defended and illuminated by those ancient theologians, whom I should allow to be set aside only if it were clear that by the cunning ever so cunning and the subtleties ever so subtle in which the scholastics engage either a single pagan has been converted to faith in Christ or a single heretic has been refuted and changed. For if we are willing to admit the truth, the fact that fewer heresies today exist, or at least are obvious, we owe to the stake more truly than to syllogisms. Is there any kind of knot that can be tied with dialectical subtlety that the same subtlety may not untie if both sides are [712] free to make whatever assumptions they wish?[101] But those simple writings, effective through

---

99 Tertullian was active as a prolific Christian author in Carthage between 197 and 213 (or possibly a decade later). The famous statement of Cyprian, bishop of Carthage (250–8) is recorded in Jerome *On Illustrious Men* 53.

100 Gregory of Nazianzus (c329–90), briefly bishop of Constantinople (381) and thereafter of Nazianzus (in Cappadocia) was famous for his *Theological Orations*; Athanasius (c300–73) was bishop of Alexandria (328–73) and a central figure on the 'orthodox' side in the Arian controversy; Cyril (375–444), bishop of Alexandria, was intimately involved in the Christological controversies of the early fifth century; Ambrose (c339–93) as bishop of Milan (374–97) dramatically confronted the imperial power to force the establishment of orthodox Christianity in the Roman empire; Erasmus attributed the commentaries of Ambrosiaster to Ambrose. Hilary (315–c367), elected bishop of Poitiers (France) in 353 was one of the first to attempt in Latin the defence of orthodox Trinitarianism. For the others listed here see n19 above.

101 Cf the excerpt from the annotation on 1 Tim 1:6 275–8 below.

their truth, not their subtlety, were able in the course of a few small years to make new the peoples of the whole world.

So then if anyone wishes to be trained for godliness he should occupy himself at once and above all with the sources, should occupy himself with those writers who have drunk most nearly from the sources. If any uncertainty arises with regard to matters that pertain to godliness, a sound and prudent person will not lack a wholesome response from the divine oracles. Paul has trustworthy advice even when he does not have a command from the Lord. Ultimately you will be a superior theologian if you succumb to no vice, yield to no desires. Whoever teaches Christ purely is an exceedingly great teacher.

[713] The End of the *System of True Theology* by Desiderius Erasmus of Rotterdam.

CHAPTER FOUR

Paraphrases on the Gospels and Acts

[Erasmus undertook to paraphrase the Gospels after he had paraphrased the Epistles; he did so at the urging of Cardinal Schiner, but with reluctance. The synoptic Gospels presented among other problems a special difficulty: how could he suitably vary his paraphrase from Gospel to Gospel when all three evangelists told the same story? Erasmus was able to overcome this problem in part by presenting a paraphrase on each of the three Gospels in its own unique light. Matthew presented Jesus as the Master Teacher, hence the Sermon on the Mount assumes a place in the *Paraphrase* proportionately larger than it does in the Gospel. Luke was a physician and historian, and as historian invited the reader to look for evidence and historical reliability and to recognize as a historical phenomenon the hand of divine providence in passing events. Erasmus regarded Mark as an abbreviator of Matthew; as Matthew's story-line had already received a cautious interpretation in the *Paraphrase* on that Gospel, Mark offered an opportunity for a *Paraphrase* with a more imaginative interpretation, for a fuller exploitation of allegory and for homiletical appeal.

The succinct character of the Gospel stories invited the paraphrast to expand the narrative by filling in details of place, time and culture, elucidating aspects of character and suggesting motivations, points of interest given little or, indeed, no elaboration by the authors of the Gospels. In addition, theologians for centuries had noted the implications of the narratives for theology in general and for Christology in particular; this too encouraged the paraphrast to expand the Gospel text by articulating its significance for theology.

Taken together, the Gospels offer a reasonably broad if limited account of the life of Jesus. The selections that follow reveal Erasmus as paraphrast interpreting the Scriptural narrative of that life at its nodal points of birth and youth, adult ministry, death, resurrection, and ascension. They also reflect Erasmus' view of Jesus as master teacher, who challenges the values of society, who affirms the agreement of special (ie divine) and natural revelation, who, perhaps surprisingly, is not reluctant to echo the thought of pagans where they have come to a knowledge of the truth through natural revelation; finally a teacher who knows the persuasive appeal of parables as simple but moving analogies from the common life of his hearers. In the selections that follow, the paraphrast creates a very attractive and comprehensible narrative of the life of Jesus; the text proceeds therefore without introductory notes (cf Preface xv).]

I. THE LIFE OF JESUS

(1) Nativity and Childhood (from the paraphrase on Luke 1 and 2, CWE 47 22–47 and 67–101)

[**Luke 1**] [22] Now the time was at hand that had been established in the divine purpose, foretold by various sayings of the prophets, and for so many generations longed for by holy and devout mortals: the time for the Son of God to take human nature upon himself, when he would redeem the human race by his death, instruct us by his teaching and actions in knowledge of the truth and zeal for gospel godliness, and ultimately raise us by his promises to the hope of a heavenly life. [23] Since this whole undertaking was a strange affair, never heard of in any age, no kind of proof was overlooked, the divine wisdom directing everything that might win among mortals faith in an event in itself not likely to be believed. But the chief requisite for our salvation was that everyone be persuaded that Jesus was the Messiah whose coming had been promised by all the predictions of the prophets, the Messiah whom the whole law of Moses had foreshadowed, and from whom alone salvation might be hoped for by all. Hence in the divine purpose a man was prepared to be the forerunner of the heavenly offspring of a virgin, being himself born in a marvellous way; one who would, by the nobility of his family, by the unheard-of holiness of his way of life, and by his rare endowments, win the first attention and trust among sceptical Jews before Jesus was known.

[25] So this was the time: Herod, a godless man and polluted by many murders, held power among the Jews. The religion of the Jewish temple, which consisted in bodily figures and ceremonies, [26] was in its greatest flowering among humankind, while under a cloak of religion the height of godlessness ruled among the scribes, Pharisees, elders,

and priests. It was at such a time that the coming of our Lord Jesus first began to be known in the world.

There was under the godless king a godly priest, the remnant of an ancient order not yet corrupted by so many vices. His name was Zechariah, and at that time the lots and the regular rotation summoned him to the administration of the rites. [27] Zechariah had a wife, Elizabeth, not so much commendable for the nobility of her family (though in fact she was descended from Aaron) as revered for the uprightness of her character. Zechariah and Elizabeth wholeheartedly observed everything that the Lord had instructed in the Law so that they gave people no handle for reproach, and, indeed, commended themselves even to God by the purity of their lives. This, too, was an arrangement of the divine purpose, [28] so that he who would bear witness to the coming Christ would be commended to the Jewish people in every respect, first by the nobility of his family, then by the blameless life of both his father and mother, further by his own rare and admirable virtues, and finally by his glorious death on behalf of truth.[1]

It had even been arranged by divine providence that the strange circumstances of John's birth would rouse people's minds to admiration for him as one who was born by a gracious act of heaven. For in one regard the godliness of Zechariah and Elizabeth seemed hardly blessed, since the two of them had grown old together childless. Now among the Jews just as marital fecundity was regarded as a special good, so barrenness was counted as among the chief evils of life. [29] The situation was a grievous torment to them both, but especially to Elizabeth, who was commonly called by the reproachful label 'barren.'

It happened that Zechariah was carrying out the duties of the priesthood in the order of his turn. [30] Though he had at one time wearied God with many prayers to free his wife from the reproach of barrenness, on the present occasion, already despairing of offspring, in ardent prayer he asked for the general redemption of his people, expected for many generations now. And the incense rose from the altar and spread through the air as the prayer of the devout priest reached all the way to God, carried there by angels whose part it is to carry the prayers of the devout to the heavenly presence, and then bring down to us God's gracious gifts.[2] So an angel was sent from heaven and stood at the right

1 Cf John 1:7–8 (the Baptist as witness), Matt 14:1–12 (death of the Baptist).

2 Cf Rev 8:3–4, where angels convey the prayers of the saints; for a similar observation see CWE 70 175–6.

side of the altar where the incense was burning, as if poised to announce glad tidings.

When Zechariah unexpectedly saw this angel gleaming with heavenly light he was thrown into a state of confusion and was seized with fear. But the angel greeting Zechariah with a mild look said in a mild voice, [31] 'There is no reason to be afraid, Zechariah, rather there is reason to be glad, for I bring happy news to you and to the entire people for whom you pray. God has smiled on your devout prayers. The Messiah long promised and expected now for many generations is going to come, the liberator and saviour of his people. Moreover, the divine goodness adds to your prayers the thing you did not dare to ask for: you asked for a redeemer; you will receive also the redeemer's herald. The fruitfulness for which you had lost all hope will serve a specific purpose, namely, that everyone will understand that this is no ordinary birth but that the child to be born will be born because God made it possible. Your wife will indeed bear you a child, but not for you alone; she will bear it for all the people, and she will bear it for God, by whose providence the whole business is being directed. She will bear not just any son but the great herald and forerunner of the great Messiah.[3] He has been chosen for so high a duty by the freely granted favour of God, and therefore you shall call his name 'John,' so that even by the name the people will be informed that he will be most pleasing to God and have divine gifts liberally heaped upon him.[4]

[36] When the regular time of his service was complete Zechariah went back to his home. There relying on the angel's promises, he embraced his barren old Elizabeth. Chaste are the embraces of husband and wife whom a divine promise, not sexual indulgence, links. Sacred is the intercourse that seeks nothing but offspring. [37] As soon as she knew by definite signs that she was pregnant, she took joy in her happy state. Then she hid herself from public view for five months as befits a modest uprightness, a little embarrassed that, old woman though she was, she could seem still to be making time for sexual indulgence.

---

3 'Herald and forerunner': 'herald' (cf the Greek *keryx*, Latin *praeco* because John is described as 'heralding,' ie preaching [Greek *kerysso*], Matt 3:1, Luke 3:3); 'forerunner' [*praecursor* rather than the frequently used *prodromus*]). In the full text Erasmus adds to the paraphrase an explanation of the two words: 'as though an *anteambulo* and a *viator*,' images suggesting the ancient Roman 'pathbreaker'(*anteambulo*) who cleared the path through crowds for his master and the summoner (*viator*) who summoned persons to a magistrate; cf Luke 1:17 and CWE 47 31 n37.

4 'Most pleasing to God': the definition given by Jerome *De nominibus hebraicis* 91 (PL 23 841).

Matters having reached this state, it remained for the more sacred and greater part of this mystery to be arranged through the angel: that is, that the Son of God, himself God immortal, would be born a mortal human being from a human virgin. So when the time drew near, the time established from eternity, the time when God through his Son would free the whole world from the tyranny of death and sin, he [38] sent the same angel, Gabriel, as a sort of groomsman and matchmaker for the divine union with the virgin.[5] This took place in the sixth month after Elizabeth had conceived.

[39] A young maiden, whose name was Mary, had been chosen for this celestial business; she was recommended not by wealth or by a brilliant family name, or by other things that this world generally admires, but by the remarkable spiritual gifts with which she was endowed and that recommend a person in God's sight: purity, modesty, godliness. She lived in a small and unremarkable city, Nazareth in Galilee (a people despised among the Jews). She was a virgin engaged to a man, Joseph by name, in no way noteworthy according to worldly standards, but of a spirit commendable to God in its virtues, a carpenter by trade. God had chosen humble people so that the world could not claim anything for itself in this matter. [40] He had chosen Joseph so that there would be no lack of a suitable witness to an otherwise unbelievable fact: that a virgin had given birth without union with a man.

When this girl was in her chamber spending her time in contemplation of heavenly things, the angel Gabriel came to her and spoke in a strange form of address: 'Hail and rejoice, maiden uniquely dear and favoured; [41] you have a Lord favourable and propitious to you, and for this reason you shall be uniquely famous and of a name that shall be much praised among all women.' But at the sudden sight of an angel and the strange and unheard-of form of greeting that she heard, since she herself had no particularly high opinion of herself, [42] the maiden was rather perturbed in spirit. For it was natural to her virginal and tender shyness that she was alarmed at the unexpected entry of a young male person. She did not answer immediately but silently turned over in her mind what so novel and grand a greeting might mean.

Now since what she was debating within herself did not escape the angel, he did not leave her in uncertainty any longer, but took away her

5 The language here, which suggests romantic love, courtship and marriage, reflects Erasmus' interpretation of Luke 1:28 expressed in his annotation on the verse (*gratia plena*), for which he was severely criticized by Edward Lee; cf CWE 72 131–7 and the selection from the annotation below 225 with n74.

dread by his gentle speech and explained the reason for his unusual greeting. 'There is no reason,' he said, 'for you to be afraid, Mary; your treasured virginity is safe. Nor am I trying to soften you with a meaningless greeting. I have come to you as the messenger of a very great and happy matter. Do not weigh your merits against it. What is offered is the result of divine favour, not of your merit.'[6] You are pleasing to the Lord exactly because you are not over-pleased with yourself. [43] Let it be enough for you that you have met with grace and favour from God. Listen to a thing unheard-of but true.

'You will conceive a child in your womb and you will bear a son, and call his name Jesus, because he will bring salvation to his people.[7] Though born of lowly origins and of a lowly girl, by his divine powers he will be great in every way, so much so that after he becomes known to the world he is to be called not a prophet but Son of the Most High. In him the Lord God will make good what a prophecy not unknown to you has promised: a son born of David's stock shall sit upon his forefather's throne. He will not use his earthly resources to seize a temporary kingdom on earth as his own. His heavenly Father will give him David's heavenly kingdom, and he will reign over Israel forever. His kingdom will be without end, as the prophet Isaiah foretold.'[8]

The virgin did not grow presumptuous from the angel's promises, nor did she become distrustful from the elevated subject-matter. She did not suppose that she too would reign with her son in his reign. She was only anxious about her dearly treasured virginity, and sought modestly and sensibly to learn from the angel the manner of doing the thing: 'How will it happen that I shall bear a son since, while I am espoused to a man and am now living with him, he and I do not have marital relations? [44] For chastity pleases us both, and we would wish, if this were possible, this blessed state to be permanent.' The angel then explained the method and took away the Virgin's anxiety about her virginity. 'Nothing here, maiden,' he said, 'will be done in the common course of nature. The birth will be heavenly and will be accomplished by way of the heavenly Workman. You will continue to honour your spouse

---

6 The Paris theologians censured this statement as 'derogating from the honour of the most holy Virgin,' and by implication reflecting a negative view of the doctrine of merits; cf CWE 82 233–4. See the selections below from the annotation on Luke 1:48 (*humilitatem ancillae*) 227 with n82. Cf also the introductory note to 'faith' 219–20 below).

7 Cf Matt 1:21.

8 Cf Isa 9:6–7.

with a chaste love, for a spouse has not been given to you to make you a mother, but because it is God's will that there be a most reliable witness to the unusual birth. Moreover, he did not want you to be without someone devoted in chaste companionship and loyal services to you and the child who will be born.

[45] 'This holy union of the divine nature with the human will not violate but consecrate your chastity. The heavenly Father has determined to beget his Son again, in a new way,[9] from you. There will be no necessity for the seed of a mortal man to effect the divine conception. The Holy Spirit will glide into you from heaven above and in your womb as in a celestial workshop will carry out the construction of the sacred infant, and in place of the physical embrace of a husband the Most High will overshadow you, so moderating his immeasurable power to the limits of human nature that it can endure the congress.[10] When lust interferes with intercourse, what is born is born impure and in bondage to sin. But as for what will be born from you since it will be conceived from the most holy embrace of the Most High, from the workmanship of the Holy Spirit, who makes all things holy, and from a most pure virgin whom, alone free from every stain of sin,[11] God chose for this very purpose, it will immediately be holy, just as it will be conceived.

'And because of his human body, derived from the substance of your body, he will rightly be called Son of a virgin and Son of Man; [46] but once the mystery of his birth is known he will be called not son of Joseph but Son of God – not indeed in the ordinary way, as righteous people are called sons of God by adoption.[12] But in a unique sense he will be called Son of God, from whom he is truly twice born: once from the beginning, eternal from eternal, and now in time, mortal from a mortal mother, human from a human being. Just as in this union the divine nature will be bonded together with the human nature, so the child will reflect the nature of each parent.'[13]

9 For the 'double generation of the Son' (eternally begotten by the Father and begotten in time as the son of Mary) see the paraphrase on John 1:1–4 CWE 46 17. Erasmus refers to the double generation again in the next paragraph.

10 Compare the similar account of the conception by the Virgin in the paraphrase on Matt 1:20 CWE 45 43–4. In the *Praise of Folly* Erasmus' satirizes theologians' absurd rationalizing of the conception and gestation of Mary; cf CWE 27 126 with n405; similarly in the *Ratio* CWE 41 539–40 (passage omitted above).

11 On Mary's sinlessness see the selections from the annotations 228–32, and especially the selection from the annotation on Matt 12:46 (*quaerentes te*) 231–2 with n101.

12 Cf Rom 8:15–17 (sons by adoption).

13 Cf the *Ratio* 56–7 above where Erasmus cites the evidence for the divine and human nature in the adult Christ.

When Gabriel finished saying this, the maiden replied in a few words: 'I have no doubt that God can do everything he wishes, and will not fail in his promises. But if he thought it best to choose me to serve this mystery, [47] there is no reason why I should claim either merit or special favour from it. I only offer myself as a handmaiden to the Lord to whom I have been once and for all dedicated, ready for every obedience.' And with that statement the heavenly conception was imperceptibly carried out: Mary had the Son of God in her womb, she was filled with the Holy Spirit. And soon the angel left her.

[**Luke 2**] [67] It was arranged in the divine plan that under Augustus Caesar, who controlled a considerable part of the world, all the provinces that acknowledged Roman power should be assessed. [68] So on the authority of Caesar and by decree of the senate, Quirinus, governor of the province, was sent to carry out the registration in Syria. [69] In obedience to Caesar's edict, which Quirinus had caused to be published, everyone set out, each to his own tribe and city to make his declaration in the customary way. Joseph, therefore, left his home, and with him the Virgin Mary, who was pregnant and close to her time. Together they set out for a small city that king David had built up, Bethlehem by name,[14] because Joseph and the Virgin not only belonged to the tribe of Judah but also traced their descent from the line and stock of David. The Lord of heaven and earth had chosen for himself a humble little town and humble parents. [70] He chose to be born away from home so that we would be ashamed of both our pride and our greed, and learn from his example that a person's happiness is not to be measured by ordinary goods.

In Bethlehem, then, which means 'house of bread,' the holy young virgin brought forth for us the heavenly bread; whoever eats of this bread will never die.[15] And this was the one and only virgin birth. To his mother he was an only child; to us he was the first-born, for he would bring many brothers with him to share eternal salvation.[16] When the

---

14 Bethlehem of Judah was in fact a very ancient city, and is mentioned in Judges (cf 17:7–13); in Ruth it is represented as the home of Boaz and Ruth, great-grandparents of David. It was the home of David (1 Sam 16:1–5), and was fortified (RSV 'built') by Rehoboam, David's grandson (2 Chron 11:6).

15 For the interpretation of Bethlehem as 'house of bread' see Jerome's commentary on Micah 5:2 (PL 25 1197B). For the interpretation's association with John 6:50 (heavenly bread) see CWE 45 57 with nn 40, 41.

16 Cf Rom 8:29, Heb 2:10–11. 'An only child' – an allusion to the perpetual virginity of Mary; a common tradition interpreted the brothers mentioned in Matt 12:46 as cousins; cf the paraphrase on the Matthaean verse CWE 45 207 with n56.

wee babe was born his mother did not hand him over to nurses, but she herself wrapped him in swaddling bands. [71] And since there was no other place for a new mother in the public inn because of the crowd of visitors, she laid her child in a manger. Listen, proud rich man, you who construct houses, manors, palaces everywhere: he who is both Lord and creator of heaven and earth, and with whom you registered in your baptism, is born far from home and has not even a place in an inn! If you recognize your prince, do not be embarrassed to imitate his example.

Now hear how the complete lowliness of his birth is full of grandeur. There were in that region shepherds who were keeping night watches over their flocks – our Lord preferred to become known first to the lowly, to shepherds as himself a shepherd,[17] [72] rather than to emperors, kings, governors, Pharisees, scribes, and high priests. Suddenly, the angel Gabriel from on high hovered over their heads and a strange light at once shone around the shepherds. At the unusual and unexpected marvel the shepherds were seized with great alarm. But the angel soon took away the fear with his soothing address: 'Lay aside your alarm,' he said, 'there is no reason for you to be anxious. I am the messenger of a very happy event, and I bring a joy unheard of until now.[18] The Israelite people have long since been looking for the promised Messiah. [73] He has been born this night in Bethlehem, the city of David, born prince and Lord of all, both priest and king, anointed from on high.[19] Go and seek him out. I will give you a sign by which he can be recognized. Go to the inn, and you will find the wee babe all wrapped in swaddling bands and laid in a manger.'

When Gabriel finished his announcement at once there was the sound of a vast multitude of the heavenly host, that is, of the angels who are the servants of the Lord mighty in battle and who do battle for us against the princes of this world.[20] In an inexpressible heavenly chant they sang praises to God, declaring his indescribable love for the human race and rejoicing with humankind, on whom so great a blessing had fallen by

---

17 Cf John 10:11.

18 The expression here in the paraphrase on Luke 2:10 reflects Erasmus' understanding of the Greek words *evangelizomai* 'to preach the gospel,' 'to proclaim good news' and *evangelion* 'gospel' (Mark 1:1), both related to the word *angelos* 'angel,' 'messenger,' hence here 'messenger of a very happy event' and 'bring a joy unheard of.' Cf the paraphrase on Mark 1:1 CWE 49 13–14.

19 'Anointed': the meaning of the Greek '*Christos*,' here in Luke 2:11, the equivalent of the Hebrew 'Messiah.'

20 For 'heavenly host' see Ps 24:8–10, for the military role of angels Rev 12:7, for the expression, 'princes of this world,' 1 Cor 2:6–8, also John 12:31 and 14:30.

reason of the favour of the divine power. The hymn the angelic choir sang was this: 'Glory to God in the highest and on earth peace, good will among men.' [74] For us the angels' song means that no glory in this affair is owed to angels or mortals, but all the glory is owed to the goodness that God in his marvellous purpose provides from heaven for us, also that on earth nothing else is to be wished for but the peace that takes away sins and reconciles to God, the peace that cements us together in mutual love. Such peace is not the world's peace but God's peace, the peace that is offered freely through the mediator of God and men, not by the intervention of our merits but from the loving-kindness of God towards us.[21]

When the angels had sung this birthday song with happy voices[22] to the shepherds they withdrew into heaven. In response the simple group of shepherds formed a plan. 'Let us,' they said, 'set out from here for Bethlehem, so we can see with our own eyes that what we have heard with our ears has happened. And then we can tell others more confidently [75] what the Lord has condescended to announce to us through his angels.' So the shepherds made haste. They arrived in Bethlehem, got to the inn, and there, just as the angels had said, they found Mary, the new mother, and Joseph the witness to the virgin birth, and the child, too, encased in swaddling bands and settled down in a manger. The shepherds were encouraged by these circumstances to a firmer readiness of belief when they discovered with their own eyes as witnesses that what the angel had reported was no empty fiction. Only when they had ascertained its truth were they not afraid to declare to others also what they had been told.[23]

[77] When the eighth day after Jesus' birth had come, the law of Moses requiring circumcision was satisfied. [78] On the fifth day after the circumcision three wise men arrived,[24] roused in a distant land by

21 Biblical allusions on 'peace': Rom 5:1 (reconciles), 2 Cor 13:11 (cements), John 14:27 (peace not of the world), Rom 15:33 (peace freely offered), 1 Tim 2:4–6 (mediator).

22 In his response to the Paris theologians who had censured his comments on church music, Erasmus noted the contrast between the distasteful singing in the liturgy of his day and the 'heavenly music sung by the angels with the greatest gladness' (CWE 82 206). Cf the excerpts below 265–7 from the annotation on 1 Cor 14:19 (*quam decem milia*).

23 Appropriate to a paraphrase on the Gospel of Luke the historian, Erasmus emphasizes the significance of historical probability and the need to establish the grounds of belief.

24 Exegetical tradition had established the thirteenth day after the birth as the day of the Magi's visit, hence five days after the circumcision on the eighth day. Thus the visit took place on the Feast of Epiphany; cf CWE 47 78 n29. Erasmus inserts here the story from Matthew 2.

the sign of a star to come and see the child. They worshipped the new Prince of the world and honoured him with mystic gifts.

[90] King Herod, alerted by the wise men that a new king had been born, had ordered all infants who had been born within the last two years in Bethlehem and the surrounding territory to be killed. Warned by an angel as he slept, Joseph took the baby and his mother away into Egypt, and there they stayed until the death of the godless king. Then, again at the prompting of the angel, they returned – not to Bethlehem, so as not to give an opportunity for savagery to Herod's son, who had succeeded to his father's kingdom, but to Galilee, to the city of Nazareth, where the child had been conceived. He wanted to lie low for the time being; and by living in Nazareth he could easily escape the cruelty of those who feared the appearance of a new king.

Here the boy's increasing age gradually brought size and strength to his body, in which an amazing quality shone out, [91] displaying something more than human. His strength of spirit grew also,[25] day by day showing itself more fully in his face, carriage, speech, actions: in them everything breathed modesty, chastity, sweet temper, godliness. For he was not subject to the faults under which that time of life usually labours, silliness, playfulness, fickleness, foolishness. Instead the divine wisdom with which he was filled showed itself already then so that he who had been recommended by the testimony of others was now rendered both admirable and lovable to everyone.[26] Wisdom, holiness, integrity, maturity such as you would find in no old man made him admirable. Then the sweetness of his character, his friendliness, his modesty made him lovable to all. It was no ordinary or temporary popularity, which that age sometimes garners for itself through human endowments, such as a pleasing appearance or precocious aptitude for learning, but in him a divine and wonderful grace shone forth, drawing everyone to the love of virtue.

[98] Thus it seemed best to the Lord Jesus to govern all his words and deeds so as to let out on occasion some flashes, as it were, of his divine power, and then again to lower himself to a human humbleness. This

---

25 The majority of texts read in 2:40, 'The child grew and became strong' (RSV, Vulgate); Erasmus followed a textual tradition that read, 'He grew and became strong in spirit' (AV).

26 'Testimony of others': perhaps above all, the testimony of Simeon and Anna (Luke 2:25–35), the paraphrase on which has been omitted here; but in the paraphrase their story is prefaced by a summary statement of those who in the account thus far provide a testimony or witness to the birth of Jesus as prince and redeemer: the angel, Mary, Joseph, John still in the womb, etc.

of course was to our benefit, so that in every way humankind might be persuaded that his human nature and his divine nature, each genuine and complete, were joined to form a perfect unity. His sharing our human nature was a kind of enticement for us to form a love for our Lord Jesus, but from that point we progress toward love of his divine nature. Hence whether he lowers himself to our weakness or raises himself to his own sublimity, he is doing the work of our salvation.

[99] Jesus did nothing particularly noteworthy until about his thirtieth year, except that in a manner more than human, as he progressed in physical stature, strength, and years, that heavenly wisdom and the rest of his divine gifts likewise evidenced themselves more abundantly in him; and just as in those things he was completely pleasing to God, [100] so every day he was more and more pleasing to mortals. Indeed, it contributed not only to the salvation of the human race in a novel and unheard-of plan of redemption, but also to the formation of our life that Jesus, gradually and by particular stages, brought his divine gifts (with which he was full)[27] to the knowledge of humankind, to teach us from those first elements of righteousness how we must drink deeply right from infancy, and must in unending progress press on to more perfect things. For just as the body has its stages of growth up to its rightful limit of stature and its rightful strength, proceeding from infancy to adolescence and from young manhood to maturity, so godliness too has its stages, until we grow up to the perfect vigour of the fullness of Christ.[28] [101] Thus those who have once put on Jesus Christ[29] ought always, on his model, to strive for improvement, so that they may commend themselves to the eyes of God by their purity of spirit, and by the uprightness of their life get themselves an honourable reputation among humankind.

(2) The Ministry of John the Baptist (from the paraphrase on Mark 1 CWE 49 14–19)

[**Mark 1**] [14] When the time was at hand for Jesus Christ the Son of God [15] to begin the task for which he had been sent from heaven to earth, John, according to the prophets' oracles, was playing the role of the precursor, baptizing with water in the wilderness. His purpose was not to wash away men's sins himself, but to invite them to repent of their

27 Cf John 1:14.
28 Cf Eph 4:13.
29 Cf Rom 13:14, Gal 3:27.

former life, to acknowledge their disease, and to desire the coming of him who alone baptizes with fire and the Spirit.[30] John was not the light that would shine upon every person coming into the world, but was a messenger of the light that was soon to arise.[31] He was not the bridegroom, but the bridegroom's forerunner who was to awaken everyone that they might go and meet the bridegroom on his arrival.[32] John, on the borderline between Law and grace, like a mixture of both, had some of the old law in him, for he threatened everyone with destruction unless they came to their senses soon; he also had something in him of the new law, for he did not call for victims or burnt offerings, for vows or fasting, but for baptism and repentance of one's former life, and he announced that the most merciful Messiah was now present and would freely forgive everyone all their sins if they placed their faith in him.

[16] Nor was John's cry in vain. Indeed many, terrified on account of his preaching, left their homes and hurried to the Jordan, and however many came were received and taught by John without respect of persons. He baptized those who felt dissatisfaction with themselves and confessed their sins – as if he were by some image alluding to the pattern in the gospel.[33] For the first task is instruction; through instruction the catechumen begins to recognize both his own baseness and God's goodness and is wholly displeased with himself. Then, realizing that hope of salvation is obtained from no other source, he takes refuge in the gratuitous kindness of God.[34] John's preaching foreshadows the catechism of the gospel; his baptism represents the baptism of Christ. John's readiness to receive anyone tells us that just as all stand in need of evangelical grace, so no one ought to be kept away. The Pharisees had their own ablutions: they washed their hands; they washed their bodies; they washed their cups, as if a little water used by the Pharisees could make a man purer in the eyes of God.[35] Such forms of baptism do

---

30 Cf Matt 3:11. Throughout his paraphrase on the baptism of Jesus as recorded in Mark, Erasmus has drawn upon elements of the story found in the other Gospels.

31 Cf John 1:7–9.

32 Cf Mark 2:18–20, Matt 25:6–13. For 'precursor' and 'forerunner' (here *anteambulo*) see 75 n3.

33 Cf Matt 28:19. In his annotation on Mark 1:4 (*in remissionem*) Erasmus notes that the apostles are commanded first to instruct, then to baptize – the pattern established from the earliest Christian period; cf the paraphrases on Acts 2:41 and 8:36 CWE 50 24 with n114 and 62–3.

34 Recognition and regret are the first two steps in a three-stage process of repentance; cf CWE 44 13 n5 and 177 n13.

35 Cf Mark 7:2–4.

not make a man purer; they make him prouder. Blessed are those who have left Mosaic and Pharisaical ablutions behind and are hurrying to Jordan's cleansing waters. Here is that purifying stream gushing forth from two sources: the acknowledgement of one's own injustice and the remembrance of God's goodness. Here is that baptism of penitence, that river of tears, bringing forth from the heart's innermost veins a bitter stream – saltpetre removing all the soul's stains.[36]

[17] John, then, who preceded Christ's first coming just as Elijah is to precede his final coming according to Malachi's testimony, lived in the wilderness, the more to resemble Elijah.[37] He utterly avoided the sinful company of men; he dressed in garments, not of silk or wool, but woven of camel's hair. His food – locusts and wild honey – was supplied by the land itself. Such a life was fitting indeed for the preacher of repentance who led an austere life lest his preaching lack weight if his conduct did not match his doctrine. By these means he had gained such authority and recognition among the Jews that many thought he was the Messiah. John, however, preached openly before all, saying: 'I am not who you think I am. My teaching is humble and weak, my baptism ineffectual. I am nothing but a messenger of him who will come soon to confer salvation on all. Him you must worship, him seek out with all your zeal. I teach about the things on earth, he will teach you about the things in heaven.'[38]

[18] After John had with such words roused the hearts of many to hope for the coming of the Messiah, Jesus appeared. He came from a small, humble village, from Galilee, a region most despised among the Jewish people. He went forth, a humble man without retinue, like one of the people, walking in the midst of sinners, soldiers, prostitutes, and tax collectors. He came to the baptism of penitence, he who purified everything. It was not enough for him to have been circumcised according to the Law's commandment, to have been purified according to the Mosaic tradition – he also sought John's baptism.[39] Thus he instructed and taught us that he who would prepare himself for the task of teaching the gospel must omit nothing pertaining to any increase in piety and must avoid everything that could give even the slightest offence to the weak. Our Lord Jesus' whole intention was this: that the world should recognize him as the one and only source of salvation; that he

36 Saltpetre (sodium nitrate) was used as a cleanser, cf Pliny *Naturalis historia* 31. 115.

37 Cf Mal 4:5; for Elijah see 1 Kings 17:1–6, 19:4–18.

38 Cf John 3:12.

39 For circumcision and purification see Luke 2:21–2.

should represent to us the type of the true and evangelical piety. [19] He therefore came to John like a penitent man, sought and obtained baptism. He was baptized in the Jordan, where tanners, tax collectors, and soldiers (no other kind of man is more sinful than they) were baptized as well. He was baptized like one of the people, but the heavenly Father set him apart from the others by a special and unusual sign. For as soon as Jesus had left the Jordan and had returned to dry ground, John saw the heavens part and the Holy Spirit fly down from it and rest on the sacred head of the Lord. A visible sign was displayed before our eyes so that we might learn that the heavenly Spirit loves modest, meek, and peaceful minds. For nothing is simpler than a dove, nothing more removed from war and rapine. In the Lord was expressed in corporeal form what happens spiritually to all people who in sincere faith receive the evangelical baptism. The body is bathed with water, and the spirit is anointed with invisible grace. Moreover, the fact that the dove remained on the Lord's head meant that there was a perennial fountain of all heavenly grace in Christ. For the dove did not at that time confer on him a new kind of grace; it revealed the fullness of grace in him. It showed from what source all grace flows to us.[40]

(3) The Temptation of Jesus (from the paraphrase on Matthew 4 CWE 45 71–5)

[**Matthew 4**] [71] Even after making such a start, Jesus did not jump straight into preaching. Rather, he removed himself suddenly from the eyes of the crowd and withdrew to a solitary place, because a retreat from interaction with people both increases authority and sharpens desire. [72] And since the devil is particularly accustomed to setting snares for those who are striving after the lofty and angelic life, Christ himself, like a master teacher, entered the palaestra and taught his own athletes how that malicious, crafty old fox must be overcome, and how little he can do against those who are sober and vigilant, and who trust in divine Scripture with all their heart.[41] [73] At the same time Christ impresses upon us that no one is fit to preach the Gospel except the person who, having made trial of himself, is steady and strong against

40 Cf John 1:14–16.

41 The theme of Christ the master teacher is dominant in the *Paraphrase on Matthew*. *Palaestra* is the Greek term for 'gymnasium,' or more particularly, for a wrestling school. For the biblical allusions see eg 2 Tim 4:7 (athlete), 1 Peter 5:8 (sober and vigilant, where the devil is represented as a lion rather than a fox).

all worldly desires, against excess and things that go along with it – lust, ambition, greed – and against similar diseases of the mind.

When Christ, therefore, had fasted for forty days, eventually, in order to give obvious proof of human weakness, he did not conceal that he was feeling the pain of hunger. When the scheming tempter sensed this, and now supposing him to be hardly anything other than a man, however remarkable, he cast forth a hook baited with the enticement of vainglory, because it is by this that those who aspire to the heights are especially caught. He said: 'If you are the Son of God,[42] what need is there for you to be tortured with hunger? [74] Rather, tell these stones to be turned into loaves of bread. With a nod you can furnish yourself with what you want.' You may recognize this as the same ambusher who lured that first Adam into death by the enticement of food; but Christ, the later Adam, heavenly in spirit, did not decline the appellation 'Son of God,' and at the same time showed that he could not be overcome by hunger like an ordinary man. Indeed, to avoid any claim of personal authority for his reply, he cast before the devil a very well-known passage of Scripture, saying: 'It has been written in Deuteronomy that "man will not be nourished by bread alone, but by every word that proceeds from the mouth of God"' [8:3].

Outsmarted by this elusive answer, the devil now used the words of Holy Scripture to do harm, and just as he had deceived the first parent of the human race using ambition as bait, promising him honour and immortality equal with the gods,[43] he attacked the Lord with a similar stratagem: he took him to the holy city and set him on the highest pinnacle of the temple. He urged him to hurl himself headlong from the height if he truly were the Son of God, since he would suffer no harm, seeing that God himself had made this promise in the mystical Psalm: 'He will give his angels charge of you,' and 'On their hands they will bear you up, lest by chance you strike your foot against a stone' [91:11–12]. But setting forth an opposing scripture, the Lord Jesus showed without further words how the devil perversely twisted the meaning of Holy Scripture. He said: 'On the contrary, it is written in Deuteronomy, "You shall not tempt the Lord your God"' [6:16]. For Scripture exhorts us to be of good hope when the inescapable falls upon us, relying on divine aid, but not to throw ourselves headlong into danger without good cause.

42 Erasmus interprets the two hypothetical clauses 'If you are the Son of God' (Matt 4:3, 6) as implying that Satan is uncertain about the status of Jesus.

43 Cf Gen 3:5–6.

[75] Now in order to teach his followers that they should not yield to a sense of security after one or two victories, for a third time Christ endured the wickedness of the tempter. And just as the tempter had entrapped that first Adam with the bait of curiosity and greed, promising him knowledge of good and evil, so he set upon the second Adam, and carrying him from the pinnacle of the temple brought him to some very high mountain from where a free prospect, lying open far and wide, placed before his eyes all the kingdoms of the world and the amazing glory and pomp of each one. No doubt he had learned in his dealings with other men that there was nothing so ungodly and nefarious that men will not dare for the sake of power. Moreover, although God is the author and creator of all things that are in heaven and earth, nevertheless, just as though he were the master of all things, the wicked one dared speak thus to the Christ: 'All these things will I give you if you will fall down and worship me.' O blind impiety! That wicked spirit promised what belonged to another, and sought a reward befitting God alone. But Jesus, who to this point bore calmly the insult to himself, did not bear the insult to his Father. He said: 'Depart from me, Satan; divine Scripture teaches something far removed from what you are prompting. It says: "You shall worship the Lord your God and him only shall you serve"' [Deut 6:13]. And when the devil had tempted him in these and other ways, and found that the athlete was invincible against all his contrivances, at last he left him, twice frustrated in his hopes: first, because he had realized that Christ could not be defeated; second, because, although he had come to find out if he was the Son of God, he left somewhat more uncertain than when he had come.

(4) Jesus, Successor to John the Baptist (from the paraphrase on Matthew 4 CWE 45 76–9)

[**Matthew 4**] [76] Now that Christ had acquired authority and esteem, especially after John, as if entrusting Jesus and commending him to his own disciples, had pointed to him and said, 'Behold the Lamb of God' [John 1:29], and now that he had overcome the devil and was wholly filled with the Holy Spirit,[44] nothing remained but to choose the time and place to begin his preaching. [77] And in fact, Jesus began this work only after the report had been spread abroad that Herod the tetrarch had thrown John into prison,[45] reaping the reward those usually receive

44 Cf Luke 4:14.
45 For the story see Matt 14:1–12.

who dare to admonish too frankly the princes of this world. When Jesus heard this report he left Nazareth [78] and withdrew to Galilee of the gentiles. He went to the city of Capernaum, called 'Capernaum by the sea' because it is bounded by the lake of Gennesaret and there he began to preach.

[79] Let us hear, then, the beginning of his preaching. Christ, when he succeeded John, began the undertaking with John's known and familiar teaching. His preaching, however, was not only milder than John's (for there was no mention of an axe or of a winnowing fork or of fire that can never be put out),[46] but was also commended by the many kindnesses bestowed without discrimination on all who were hastening to him. Therefore Jesus also cried, as if imitating John: 'Come back to your senses, repent of your former lives, for the kingdom of heaven is now at hand. And although the kingdom of heaven must be closed to no one, nevertheless it will lie open to none but those who are pure and seeking heavenly things and who cut away all their earthly desires.'[47] What is simpler than this philosophy? Let everyone lament his wicked deeds, and heavenly goods are present to all freely.

(5) Jesus with His Disciples in Ministry (from the paraphrases on Mark 1, 2 and 3, and 6 CWE 49 23–9, 30–45 and 46–51, and 70–83)

[**Mark 1**] [23] When the Lord Jesus had roused the hearts of the Jews with words of this kind and had won them over to the philosophy of the gospel, he too, after the example of John, began to gather some disciples – but only a few, and they were humble and unlearned men, so that when all nations of the world had been converted by them it would be truly evident that the kingdom was of God, not of this world. Accordingly, when he was passing along Lake Galilee one day, he saw Simon and his brother Andrew working together, casting their nets into the lake – for they were fishermen and made their living by this craft. The lowliness of their craft brought them glory. The concord of the brothers denoted the consensus of the church. Their fishing was a type of the evangelical task. Those catchers of fish, then, Jesus caught first. 'Come,' he said, 'and follow me, for I shall turn you into fishers of men.' Hearing his words,

---

46 Cf Matt 3:10–12 (John's axe, the winnowing fork, the unquenchable fire).

47 Cf the paraphrase on the parallel passage in Mark (1:15). 'Behold the kingdom of God is here! Instead of shadows truth will shine forth, spirit will take the place of flesh, instead of carnal ceremonies true piety will rule.'

the two brothers left their nets at once, and without hesitation followed the Lord Jesus. For the voice of Jesus held a heavenly charm.[48] And when the Lord had gone a little farther he saw two other men, James, the son of Zebedee, and John, his brother. They too were in a boat, mending their nets in preparation for fishing. They too were occupied with other things as Jesus addressed them suddenly with his call and bade them follow him. And this is the sign by which you may recognize the young men's evangelical faith: they did not hesitate, but left their father Zebedee and his hired hands in the boat and immediately followed Jesus' call.[49] [24] From such beginnings the Lord Jesus gathered the princes of his church, scorning the scornful priests and Pharisees of Jerusalem.

Accompanied by this retinue Jesus came to Capernaum, a community as proud and impious as it was wealthy and flourishing.[50] Here he began right away the task of the evangelist. For on the Sabbath he entered the synagogue and publicly taught the Jews, offering them not the empty figments of the Pharisees, but explaining the true meaning of the Law, which was spiritual, not carnal. Immediately the people sensed that there was among them a new teacher and a new kind of teaching. They saw a humble man surrounded by a small and humble retinue, but they admired his speech, which had an aura of divine power. For he did not teach insipid and petty rules in the manner of the scribes nor old wives' tales about genealogies;[51] his words had authority, and the greatness of his miracles added faith in the truth of his speech.

Immediately an opportunity to work a miracle presented itself. There was in this assembly someone possessed by an unclean spirit. The unclean spirit began to rail against the heavenly doctrine, crying out and saying: 'What business do you have with us, Jesus of Nazareth? Have you come to ruin us before our day? I know who you are. Indeed you are that holy one promised a long time ago by the prophet Daniel,[52] whom God has uniquely blest before all others.' The Lord, however, was not pleased with testimony that was true but extorted by

48 Erasmus frequently observes the powerful effect of Jesus' voice, glance, and touch.

49 For Erasmus a distinguishing mark of evangelical faith is a trust that does not pause to calculate probabilities or consequences; cf the annotations on Rom 4:20 ('indeed, in the counter-promise of God' and 'he did not hesitate') CWE 56 123–4, and the colourful portrait of Abraham in the paraphrase on Rom 4:18–22 CWE 42 31.

50 A typical characterization of maritime cities; cf the Argument to the *Paraphrase on 1 Corinthians* CWE 43 19, also CWE 50 112 with n3. For Capernaum in particular see Matt 20:23 and the paraphrase on the verse CWE 45 188.

51 Cf Matt 15:1–3 (petty rules), and 1 Tim 1:4 and 4:7 (old wives tales).

52 Cf Dan 9:24.

fear and coming from a wicked spirit who was himself a liar and liked to deceive the human race. Jesus therefore reproached him, saying: 'Be still and leave the man. Thus you will better declare who I am.' And without delay the unclean spirit obeyed the voice of the commanding Lord and left the man, but convulsing him and crying out with a loud voice, showing that he was taking flight compelled by divine force.

[25] On account of this marvellous deed Jesus' fame spread through the whole region of Galilee, and miracle followed upon miracle. Soon after they had left the synagogue, they went to the house of Simon and Andrew. James and John were with them. Now the mother-in-law of Simon was lying sick, gravely ill with fever. As soon as they had informed Jesus of this, he went to her bedside, took the woman's hand and raised her up; and at once the fever left her. And her return to health was as complete as it was unexpected. For the woman's strength had returned suddenly, to the point where she could do her usual chores, and she ministered to Jesus and his disciples.

Anyone who rages with a passion for carnal pleasures, who lives in luxury, leading an indolent life, is dangerously ill. Once the first woman, lured by a tempting apple, began to labour under that fever. Our flesh, which has desires contrary to the spirit, is our Eve.[53] Blessed are those, on the other hand, whom Jesus raises up to the love of heavenly things[54] by the touch of his Spirit, so that he who before was a slave to indolence, luxury, and filthy desires suddenly gains strength and, a new man, becomes a servant to chastity, purity, and sobriety. Now imagine the house of Simon to be the church, where it is not fitting to show a slack spirit, but rather to be fervent with evangelical strength. [26] And yet sometimes the mother-in-law of Peter – the synagogue – is lying ill there. For he belongs to the synagogue who still likes the taste of the insipid letter, still likes to savour the water of Pharisaical meaning and does not yet savour the wine of the evangelical spirit. As soon as they were in the house they asked the Lord Jesus to raise up the bedridden woman. Let us who are in the church also ask him to consider those worthy of his outstretched hand who are full of fear, clinging to the letter of the law, addicted to ceremonies, and to raise them up to the freedom of the gospel.[55]

---

53 Cf Gal 5:17 and Erasmus' exposition of the war between the flesh and the spirit in the paraphrase on that verse CWE 42 125.

54 Cf Eph 2:6.

55 Cf John 2:1–11, in the paraphrase on which Erasmus contrasts the 'wine of the Gospel' with the 'tasteless and watered-down letter of the law of Moses.' The contrast between letter and spirit is Pauline; cf Rom 2:29, 7:6.

It was already late at night, and the sun had set, so that it could seem impudent to call on the physician at this hour, but the desire to be healed overcame the feeling of embarrassment. People had brought a great multitude suffering from all kinds of disease, and among them also men possessed by unclean spirits. To see this sight, the whole community of Capernaum had come together at the doorstep of the house. Jesus, nevertheless, uncomplainingly healed a great many people afflicted with diseases of every sort and cast out many demons. Now this happened according to the historical sense. But today also we see many crowded together at the house of Simon Peter (which represents the church, while Capernaum is a simile for the whole world). The sunset alludes to Christ's death; the door of the house is baptism; it is sought by repentance of one's former life and faith in obtaining salvation at the hands of Jesus. The sick besiege the doors[56] desiring to be received into the fellowship of the church.

[27] The following day Jesus rose at dawn and, as if desiring rest, fled the crowd. Leaving Capernaum and going into the wilderness, he prayed there, thanking the Father for the benefactions he had decided to lavish on mankind through him. When Simon Peter and the other disciples realized that Jesus had secretly gone away, they went after him until they found out where he was. The multitude also followed him into the wilderness. The disciples announced to the Lord that a great number of people from Capernaum were present and asking for him.

The Lord said to them: 'It is sufficient at present to have laid these foundations in the community of Capernaum; it is time to go forth also into the neighbouring towns and villages to preach the kingdom of God there as well. For I have not come to preach in one community, but to proclaim salvation to all.' Thus the Lord Jesus travelled throughout the towns and villages in all of Galilee, preaching in their synagogues, dislodging diseases, and casting out demons, so that by his mighty deeds he would give the simple people confidence in his teaching.

One day, on a mountainside, Jesus had taught the people many noteworthy things about the perfect conduct belonging to the profession of the gospel. As he descended, it happened that he met with a leper infected with a disease both loathsome and incurable. The leper hated his disease and had conceived complete faith in Jesus: you see in him the penitent sinner close to being healed. [28] He was not afraid of the crowd, even though he knew that he was hateful to them. He had before his eyes only the goodness of Jesus. He ran up to him, therefore, and fell

56 Cf Matt 11:12, Luke 16:16.

down at his feet. What would a proud Pharisee have done in this case? He would have shouted: 'Remove this detestable creature, that he may not give offence even to my eyes.' And he would have asked for a wash-basin to wash away the man's breath. But what did our most kind Lord do? He did not remove him as he was lying at his feet. He knew what the man wanted but wished his extraordinary faith to be an example to all. Those who are in the grasp of lust, avarice, hatred, envy, and the other shameful desires, are covered with abominable leprous growth. Let such persons hear the voice of the leper that they may imitate him: 'If it is your will,' he said, 'you can make me clean.' He acknowledges his disease, he does not doubt the power and goodness of the Lord. He leaves it to the Lord's judgment whether or not he is worthy of so great a favour.

Such great faith joined with the most abject humility won him the mercy of Jesus. Displaying compassion even in his countenance to show us how we must feel towards sinners, Jesus stretched out his hand, touched the leper, and said: 'It is my will. Be made clean.' Genuine faith is not wordy, and evangelical love confers favour willingly.[57] As soon as he had said 'be made clean,' all disease left the man so completely that no trace of the evil remained. Let us pray that he may touch our hearts with his word to cleanse them of impurity. You, too, must hurry to Jesus, whatever your sin – whether you are a fornicator, adulterer, or defiled by other diseases – for he is coming to meet you. Fall at his feet, prostrate yourself, conscious of your sinfulness. Call out to him, [29] but call with deep faith in your heart: 'Lord, if it be your will, you can make me clean.' Soon you will hear the voice of mercy: 'It is my will. Be made clean.'

[**Mark 2**] [30] Jesus returned to Capernaum almost in secret, hiding in a house before his arrival [31] could become known to the people. But the rumour that Jesus was in the house had already spread through the whole town. At once such a crowd of people came together there that not only was the whole house filled, but neither the courtyard nor the area in front of the gate was large enough to hold the multitude. Blessed is the house to which Jesus has come and which he never leaves. That house is the church. The kingdom of God suffers violence at the hands of the gentiles[58] and with a certain violence the common crowd

57 In the paraphrase on Gal 5:14 Erasmus contrasts the 'wordiness' of the Law and the simplicity of evangelical love CWE 42 124–5. On the relation between faith and love see selections from the two annotations on 1 Corinthians 13 242–7 below.

58 Cf Matt 11:12 and Luke 16:16.

rushes in. Catechumens besiege the doors, greatly desiring to be let into the house of the Lord, 'thirsting and hungering after the justice' [Matt 5:6] of the heavenly kingdom. Jesus, however, does not exclude anyone from this house, neither the poor man nor the rich, neither the healthy man nor the sick, as long as he has a strong desire to hear Jesus. The Lord, therefore, teaching us that we must always think first of our spirit, then of our body, first shared with them the word of the gospel to heal their spirits of disease. Thus they do well who, when they are about to give alms to beggars, first give them a word of advice to improve their souls and then present them with their contribution.

While Jesus was still teaching and attending to the healing of spirits, some people came bringing with them a paralysed man so weakened by the disease that he was tied to his bed and carried by four bearers. Here you have the simile of a mind so undone and weakened by earthly desires that it cannot rise to any pious deeds or heavenly thoughts. Since the thronging multitude that besieged the doors and the courtyard blocked their way, they could not bring him within sight of Jesus. They lifted their burden up to the roof, which they had opened up by pulling off some tiles, lowered it by ropes and set the man, together with his bed, down at Jesus' feet. They had no doubt that the merciful Lord would come to the aid of the wretched man as soon as he laid those eyes of his on the paralysed man lying there like a living corpse. Jesus had seen the wretched man earlier and was not unaware of the faith of his bearers. [32] When Jesus had seen their uncommon faith, he felt the greater pity for the man as he saw him labour more in spirit than in body, for his spirit was a slave to vices. Nothing more was expected than that bodily health be restored to the wretch. But Jesus, delighted by such uncommon faith and wishing to heal the whole man, turned to the paralytic and said: 'Son, your sins are forgiven.'

There were in that assembly some scribes whom instruction in Holy Writ had made no better, but rather more inclined to slander. They had learnt from the books of the prophets and Moses that it was up to God alone to forgive sins. For a priest did not remit sins, he only acted as an intermediary before God, interceding for other men's sins and that not without offering sacrifice.[59] As the scribes knew this very well they

59 For the role of the priest in the books of the prophets see Ezek 45:18–25, in the books of Moses (ie the Pentateuch) Lev 4:32–5; cf also Heb 5:1–4. Among the prophets God is said to be the one who forgives sins in Isa 43:25; in the Pentateuch it is God who does not forgive in Exod 32:30–4 (implying that God alone can forgive), but cf 1 Kings 8:33–53.

thought in their hearts: 'What novel words does this man utter? Neither Moses nor Aaron nor any of the prophets of old dared to speak in this manner. Indeed, this man insults God by claiming for himself divine authority. Only God can fulfil what this man promises.' Indeed, the weakness of his human body that met the eye kept them from thinking of Jesus as more than human in any way.

[33] But Jesus, who wished to prove his divine nature by deeds rather than by preaching in words, turned to the scribes to show that nothing was so deeply hidden in the hearts of even the most astute men that it could escape his mind, which searches everything and perceives everything.[60] He turned to them as if they had addressed him with the thoughts they had turned over in their minds and said to them: 'Why do you ponder those slanderous thoughts in your minds? Why do you judge me by my weak body rather than by the facts themselves? Why do you not rather recognize from those things you see with your eyes that those things are true also which cannot be seen with the eyes?[61] You are offended by the words "Your sins are forgiven"; you believe that they were said in vain, for you cannot see their efficacy, which is displayed in the mind. As for yourselves, while you have healthy corporeal eyes, the eyes of your mind are diseased.[62] Judge me by the facts. Anyone is able to say to a man in the grip of sin: "Your sins are forgiven"; it is equally easy to say to a paralytic in the grip of disease: "Rise, take your bed, and walk." You have heard one command and have slandered me, now hear the other, which you cannot slanderously misrepresent when you see clearly that deed follows upon word. This I shall do, not to display my power, but that you may realize that God has given to the Son of man, who now appears before you humble and weak, the power to remit sins with a word, a power that your priests never had. And this power he has not only in Judaea, but everywhere on earth. Thus, whatever he forgives on earth is forgiven in heaven, whatever he has not loosened on earth, remains bound in heaven.[63]

[34] Thus Jesus spoke and as they watched intently what he would do, he turned to the paralytic and said: 'I say to you, rise, take your bed, and go away to your house.' He had hardly spoken, when the power instantly manifested itself; for the paralytic did not improve gradually, but at Jesus' word he rose joyfully, as if he had never suffered from paralysis and, taking the bed upon his shoulders, walked out through

60 'Searches and perceives': cf 1 Chron 28:9, Rom 8:27, 1 Cor 2:10–12.

61 Cf Rom 1:19–20 and the paraphrase on those verses CWE 42 17–18.

62 For the 'diseased eye' see Matt 6:23, Luke 11:34 (literally, 'eye not sound').

63 Cf Matt 28:18 (all power given), John 20:23 (sins forgiven), Matt 18:18 (sins loosed).

the throng of men, displaying before all a strange sight never seen before: a man who just a little while ago had been tied to his bed like a lifeless corpse now moved about in a lively manner and had strength enough to carry so great a weight by himself.

Now sometimes, when we step back from the works of sculptors and painters, contemplating the several parts of their work, we keep noticing new points that escaped our eyes before; thus I think that it will certainly be appropriate to pause a while at this remarkable sight, examining its individual aspects with pious curiosity. Indeed, everything the Lord wrought on earth he did so that we might meditate upon it and choose for ourselves whatever is conducive to a pious life.

[35] Let us first consider the force and magnitude of the disease. Paralysis seizes and lames the body's muscles so that the man who suffers from this evil appears almost like a living corpse. It is one of the diseases from which the physicians' art likes to keep at a distance as being incurable. The hopelessness of this man's illness is indicated by the fact that he was tied to his bed, no different from a lifeless corpse, carried by four bearers: indeed, the illness often takes away the use of the tongue and weakens the mind's strength. It appears that this is what had happened to our man, who asked nothing from the Lord.

And now apply your spiritual eyes for a while and consider how much more wretched is the paralysis of a mind whose entire power has been seized by useless concerns for fleeting things to such an extent that he is completely numb to all moral duty, that he has no hands to help the needs of the poor, no feet to approach Jesus, no tongue to implore the help of the Saviour; who, like one dead to justice, is carried hither and thither by the verdict of his desires as if they were his bearers? What would this unhappy spirit do who is so enervated by excesses, indulgence in pleasure, and desire for fame and money, that he has no strength left in him to raise himself from his sordid cares to the love of heavenly things? Certainly there is no human power that can help him; only Jesus, with his almighty command, can rid him of the full force of the disease. This, then, is the physician we must approach, but we must approach him with great faith, which carries so much weight with the Lord Jesus that he came to the aid of this paralytic even on the strength of other men's faith. Even though they asked nothing in words, they nevertheless urgently implored him by their deed. That imploring faith is what is primarily efficacious with Christ; [36] God requires from sinners neither burnt offerings nor gifts.[64] Simply acknowledge your

64 Cf Ps 40:6, Heb 10:5–6.

disease and have faith in the physician – yet even this ability is given to you by no one but God.

Now consider that reverend irreverence. What man affected by a grave physical ailment is mindful of modesty and shame? Does he not uncover even the most private parts of the body and allow the physician to treat them? In the same position is the man who begins to acknowledge the shameful disease of his spirit. For what is more outrageous than to climb on the roof of another's house, make an aperture, and offer from above a repulsive and abominable sight for all to see? The proud Pharisee would have cried: 'Shame! Shame!' He would have reproached their impudence: the porters had acted against common law, had dug through the roof, broken into the private residence of a stranger, and with that spectacle of death had defiled the eyes of the listeners. He would have ordered the cadaverous paralytic to be carried away and would have washed himself from top to toe with water.

Yet those same men who were bound to offend the ostentatious [37] follower of Mosaic justice delighted the Lord Jesus because they displayed uncommon faith in him, so much so that he gave the wretched man his health without waiting for his prayer. First he takes away the diseases of the spirit, that is, the sins; then he frees the body of paralysis. Here we must consider how great was the generosity of Jesus in forgiving the man's sins. For when he said: 'Your sins are forgiven,' he remitted all of them. There is no mention of past merits, no demand for sacrifices or satisfaction. There is only mention of faith. It was sufficient that the man fell down at Jesus' feet. He has sacrificed enough who shows himself to Jesus in complete faith: no burnt offerings can be more acceptable to him.[65]

What did the paralytic do? He took his bed upon his shoulders in a turnabout of things: indeed, he was now master of his desires whereas before he had been their slave. This is what carrying the cross means; this is what 'crucifying the flesh with its vices and desires' [Gal 5:24] means. Now there is no more need for the four bearers. He walks about on his own legs wherever Christ's spirit takes him.

[38] I shall dismiss you from this scene after first pointing out to you the persons in the drama. The paralytic and his bearers are emboldened by faith and obtain what they desire. Jesus, delighted with their faith,

65 Statements like this appeared to the Paris theologians to support the 'Lutheran heresy.' Erasmus explained that his statements do not imply that faith is all-sufficient for they do not deny the need for meritorious works of charity after baptism. It is, however, with faith alone that we come to Christ; cf CWE 82 165–71.

even without being asked, freely doubles his favour. The simple and unlearned people discern nothing special in him whom they believe to be a man; they merely marvel at the divine power. Only the scribes mutter secretly to themselves. Let us avoid the example of the scribes. Let us be one of the simple crowd, glorifying God.

[43] One day the disciples happened to walk through a cornfield and it was the Sabbath, when it was forbidden to Jews to do any work. The disciples were going ahead; Jesus was following behind. And when hunger prompted them, they began to pluck the ears of corn, shook out the grain by rubbing it between their hands, and ate it. [44] The Pharisees who accompanied Jesus, thinking themselves most just and seeing what his disciples were doing, accused the Lord on account of the actions of his disciples, as if they were doing something unlawful, violating the Sabbath. The Lord, however, protected his disciples in a manner that rebuffed the experts in Mosaic law.

'How dare you,' he said, 'accuse my disciples of wrongdoing when they are obliged by hunger to pluck for their sustenance a few ears of corn they happened to find, when the Law itself, whose teachers you profess to be, records that David, when he found himself in like need, committed an act that appears to be a greater violation of the Law. Indeed, when he was endangered by famine he took refuge in the house of God and was not afraid, though he was a layman, to ask Abiathar, who was then the high priest,[66] to give him the singularly holy bread called 'showbread' the eating of which was unlawful to anyone except priests. If you do not know that this is written or do not remember it, how can you profess knowledge of the Law? The Law also taught us this: that we must "love our neighbour as we each love ourselves" [Lev 19:18]. Since this is of all commandments in the Law the first and foremost, why do you in your wrong judgment violate the greatest and eternal law on account of things that are petty and will not endure forever? There was once a time when there was no holy Sabbath. And there will be a time when each and every day will be equally holy to pious men.

[45] Jesus had set out these things in clear arguments, but since the Pharisees were devout to a fault, he added this general statement: 'The Sabbath was made for man, not man for the Sabbath. And the Son of

66 The story is told in 1 Sam 21:1–6; Erasmus uses the term 'Law' here to include the historical books. Lev 24:5–9 implies that the 'showbread' is for the priests alone. Erasmus keeps the text of Mark, which names the priest 'Abiathar,' though the priest in the story is Ahimelech, father of Abiathar (1 Sam 21:1–6, 23:6).

man has come, not to ruin men, but to save them; therefore he has power even to abrogate the Sabbath whenever man's salvation requires it. What I have said about the Sabbath must be extended to all other regulations of this kind. They were instituted for the time being so that a rebellious people should gradually become accustomed to obey God's commandments, that they might be led by the hand, as it were, through corporeal figures to an understanding of spiritual things. The man who, free from the tumult of evil passions, violates the Sabbath from a desire to help his neighbour, violates it in a pious fashion. Fasting is a pious practice, but it becomes impious if what has been instituted for the salvation of man is turned into a means of destroying mind and body. To make vows is a pious act, but it becomes impious whenever a man, through his superstitious wish to keep them, is called away from things that are more closely related to true piety. A man who offers a gift at the altar is acting in a saintly manner, but the proffered gift is unholy if he has not been reconciled with his neighbour.[67] It is lawful to eat any kind of food when human need requires it. Indeed all those bodily things in which you place perfect justice – temple, victims, food, dress, feast days, fasting, vows, gifts – are observed in an unholy fashion if the welfare of your neighbour is harmed. Moses was the steward, not the author of such laws; the servant, not the master. Those who adhere to the Son of man, who is the master of all law and teaches us to observe spiritually the regulations which have been prefigured by those carnal forms, are free from such Judaic ceremonies.'

[**Mark 3**] [46] From the following we may clearly learn that nothing is more slanderous than the mistaken belief that one is godly. When Jesus entered the synagogue to teach the people there according to his custom, another occasion arose for the Lord to do good and for the Pharisees to utter false accusations, because there was present in the crowd someone who presented to all a pitiful sight, for he had a stiff and withered hand, and he was the more unfortunate because he used to support himself and his poor destitute family by the work of his hands.

O Pharisaical malice, keen-eyed when it comes to slandering the good deeds of Christ, blind when it comes to understanding the heavenly doctrine! From what they saw with their corporeal eyes they discerned his human nature; in his actions they did not see his divine power. They saw the wretched man and knew the merciful Jesus, and therefore guessed what was to follow; immediately they got ready to slander. To make everyone more attentive to the spectacle about to ensue, the Lord called

67 Cf Matt 5:23–4, and 131 with n146 for a more expansive treatment of the image.

the man whose hand was withered: 'Rise up,' he said, 'and stand in the middle of the crowd.' Hopeful, he stood up. Then Jesus turned to the Pharisees, and said to them: 'Since you profess knowledge of the Law, what is your opinion – which is a violation of the Sabbath: doing good deeds or bad? Saving or ruining a man's life?' The purpose of this thorny question did not escape them. If they had replied that, for the sake of observing the Sabbath, it was better to let one's neighbour perish than to help him who was in danger, the people would not have tolerated such an absurd reply, one that was contrary to natural common sense. If they had answered that it was allowed, they would have deprived themselves of the right to criticize him. Therefore they decided to keep silent. [47] To make their answer easier Jesus proposed a question drawn from a parable: Who among them would observe the Sabbath so religiously as to allow a sheep to perish that on the Sabbath had fallen into a ditch? There was not a single man in that crowd who did not realize how much more important it was to care for a man's welfare than for a sheep's. And so to teach us that one must not refrain from helping one's neighbour on account of the hopeless wrongheadedness of evil men, our most gracious Lord disregarded the Pharisees, turned to the man, and said to him: 'Stretch forth your hand.' As soon as his voice had been heard, the man stretched out his hand, which had suddenly been changed and could do any task as well as his other hand, which had never been withered. All of this merely provoked the Pharisees to more nefarious schemes, infected as they were with the leaven of envy.

[48] Indeed, even though the Pharisees did not dare to grumble before the people, they plotted among themselves and made secret plans; they even called upon the Herodians to make their conspiracy more powerful, and deliberated how they could destroy Jesus. Yet to teach us by his example that one must on occasion yield for a time to the incurable stubbornness of evil men, the Lord withdrew, lest they should be provoked to greater crimes, and once again retired to the lake. And now a numerous throng of people came together there from all directions to see him, not only from Galilee but also from Judaea and even from Jerusalem itself; also from Idumaea and from the regions beyond the Jordan, as well as from the places around Tyre and Sidon. So great was the eagerness of the multitude in their desire for health [49] that one pushed against the other just to touch Jesus, since even the touch of his garment could drive out sickness.[68] There was no distinction of persons or disease before the powerful and benign physician. Anyone

68 The 'garment' is a detail taken from Mark 5:25–34.

possessed by any evil was immediately freed even if he was only able to draw near to Jesus.

When the multitude surged against Jesus, he gave instructions to his disciples to obtain a small vessel so that he could be safe from the disorderly and tumultuous crowd, who thirsted more for corporeal than for spiritual health and smothered rather than touched Jesus. Immediately the disciples prepared for him the vessel of a purer church; for Jesus is more pleased with a few pure and placid souls than with a turbulent multitude. Yet he withdraws in such a manner that he nevertheless teaches the multitude from on board ship. When you see Jesus teaching on board a small vessel think of him as a bishop preaching to a mixed crowd comprised of men instructed in the faith, men possessed by evil spirits, Jews, and pagans. Blessed are those who spiritually touch Christ. But they cannot touch him unless they are first touched by him. For all whom he has touched are delivered of all vices. They are changed from tumultuous to tranquil men and will be admitted to the ship of the church to enjoy Jesus' company in perpetuity, always to sit at his table. The Lord had refused to be proclaimed by demons and yet here was evidence that the kingdom of God had come, for worthy and unworthy men alike tried to enter it violently.[69]

[50] Accordingly, he obtained some prefects to be his helpers in claiming the heavenly kingdom, sufficient in number for the many nations that were soon to flock to the philosophy of the gospel from all over the world. For this is what the monarchs of this world usually do: they choose reliable prefects through whom they can secure, expand, administer, and safeguard their dominions. These prefects must be especially faithful, prudent, and industrious, but most of all, they must be acquainted with the king's wishes. Here, then, that 'King of kings, that Lord of lords' [1 Tim 6:15] chose twelve prefects who, like faithful attendants, would never leave his side – but when the business of the gospel required it, he would dispatch them like personal envoys to preach what they had learnt from their king and to promulgate the edicts of their prince all over the world.

The first of the apostles was Simon, whose name Jesus changed to Cephas, that is, Peter, or rock, that we might learn from the very name that the chief principle of evangelical philosophy is immovable, constant faith.[70] Next was James, the son of Zebedee, together with his

---

69 Once again, a reference to Matt 11:12, Luke 16:16.

70 On Peter as the rock, here 'immovable faith,' see 105, 'The Confession of Peter,' with n80 below.

brother John: to them he gave surnames that they might be called Boanerges, which, in Aramaic, means 'sons of thunder' declaring by their names that they would send forth the thunder of evangelical preaching throughout the whole world. Just as the sound of thunder comes from high above, so the voice of the evangelical preacher utters nothing lowly or carnal, but speaks of all heavenly things. [51] 'Repent, the heavenly kingdom is near' [Matt 3:2], says the voice of thunder. Fear of lightning seizes everyone at this sound, but a shower follows: 'Believe in the gospel and you shall be saved.'[71] Andrew, the brother of Peter, was the fourth apostle; Philip the fifth; Bartholomew the sixth; Matthew the seventh; Thomas, called Didymus,[72] the eighth; James, the son of Alphaeus, the ninth; Thaddaeus the tenth; Simon the Canaanite the eleventh. The twelfth was Judas Iscariot, who betrayed the Lord. Through these few obscure, illiterate, and powerless men it pleased the Lord to renew the whole world, lest human wisdom or power claim for itself a part of the merit in this heavenly business.

[**Mark 6**] [76] Now the time had come for the apostles whom he had destined for the evangelical task and who had now been for some time the constant companions of Jesus to rehearse their future task, and to give the leader a sample of their diligence and loyalty. He therefore assembled the twelve whom he had selected for this task [77] and addressed them with one speech, so that there should not be any disagreement among those who were bound by the same commandments. To make their enterprise more fruitful, he sent them out in pairs, designating a province to each pair jointly as though to prefects. He dispatched them naked and unarmed, so that human resources should not claim any stake in this heavenly business. Moreover, lest the authority of fishermen and private individuals be too light, he added a gift that the monarchs of this world cannot give to their envoys and prefects. For he gave them the power of taking away diseases and casting out demons.

That they should be better equipped for a task that requires an energetic and tireless administrator, he instructed them to bring only a staff on this journey and to carry no baggage, provisions, or arms: no bag in which to keep provisions, not so much as a piece of bread that might be carried without a bag, no belts laden with money. He instructed them not to guard their shins with pads, but to wear only sandals to protect the soles of their feet against injury from stones and thorns. They were

71 Cf Mark 16:16.

72 Ie 'the twin,' cf John 20:24.

to content themselves with simple clothing. Jesus' purpose in giving these instructions was to teach his disciples that the man who has taken on the evangelical office must be free and unencumbered by any care for corporeal things, lest there be an obstacle slowing down the progress of the heavenly doctrine. [78] The Lord did not utter these words in the sense that it would never be right for those who carried on the business of the gospel to bring along the essentials, a small satchel or some money, which the apostles would not hesitate to do even today. Indeed, perhaps the man who teaches the gospel at his own expense merits greater praise. But with this kind of hyperbole Jesus wished to free his disciples completely from all care of those things that often hold the mind back when it goes about some heavenly business. Moreover, his figurative manner of speech has the effect of implanting what is taught more deeply in simple minds. For the evangelical teacher would not commit a sin if he used boots or two cloaks among the Getes,[73] or if he set out for some inhospitable tribe and brought along some provisions and money. But whatever delays the progress of the gospel must be rejected. Now think how great a burden weighs those down who set out on behalf of the gospel, carrying around royal wealth and bringing with them the titles and desires of this world and a thirst for revenge if anything grievous should happen to them.

[79] When the Lord Jesus had carefully instructed his apostles with these and many other words of this kind, [80] the twelve captains of the heavenly kingdom set out, and matters proceeded in order: they proclaimed to all that they must repent of their former evil deeds, that they must not trust in their own deeds but only in the promise of the gospel. The kingdom of God was at hand; it would bring perfect justice to all through faith in the gospel. This is the first principle of the evangelical doctrine: to believe what you hear and to have faith in what is promised.[74] And they found people who received their teaching with willing ears. Nor was a large number of miracles lacking to lend credibility to the words of men, however humble and unknown. They anointed the sick, and they were healed. They commanded evil spirits to leave in the name of Jesus, and they left. This was the power of the heavenly kingdom. What could be more humble or despised than the apostles? But the less power they had, the more readily their actions could be ascribed to divine power. They had no wealth, no learning, no office, no

73 The Getes were a tribal people living along the Danube in ancient Thrace; the name was used to signify a cold climate.

74 This and the previous sentence have been relocated from the previous paragraph.

entourage, no famous lineage, no renown, no authority. They had nothing but simple faith in Jesus, whom they did not as yet know perfectly.

[83] When their mission had been completed, the apostles returned, and at once congregated around Jesus, giving an account of their mission, recounting individual points with great alacrity: what they had taught, what they had done, and how things had gone according to their wishes. The Lord commended their faith but restrained their triumph, leading them to a solitary place that they might be restored and recover from such great labours. This sojourn was granted them, not to relax the mind with pleasures, but to nourish and renew the vigour of the spirit through private prayer, since they would soon have to hurry back to their work. Men who undertake the apostolic task are obliged to have dealings with strong people and weak, the learned and the unlearned, good and bad alike, so that losing some of that perfect composure is at times unavoidable. When that happens they must turn their minds to concentrated, private prayer, to the pure contemplation of heavenly things, so that they may regain their spiritual strength and soon return to aid their brothers.[75]

(6) The Confession of Peter (from the paraphrase on Matthew 16 CWE 45 244–7)

[**Matthew 16**] [244] When he had now come into the region of the city of Caesarea, which the tetrarch Philip had so named in honour of Caesar,[76] Jesus wanted to make trial of his disciples to find out how much progress they had made as a result of the many words they had heard and the miracles they had seen, and to learn whether they had a more elevated understanding of him than did the common person. Therefore he questioned them, saying: 'Who do men say the Son of man is?' They said, 'Some say "John the Baptist"' for so the Herodians had supposed,[77] [245] 'some "Elijah"' because he had been carried away, and for

75 Cf in the paraphrase on John 6:1–3 the similar advice extrapolated from Jesus' retreat, with some details, however, rather more graphic than here: '"Vicars of Christ" are not to retreat for drinking-parties, sexual indulgence, gambling, hunting or similar pleasures' CWE 46 76.

76 Hence the name 'Caesarea Philippi.'

77 'Herodians,' an interpretation of 'some' (Matt 16:14), appears to be a conjecture based perhaps on the story of the Baptist's death in Matt 14:1–12. Erasmus was uncertain about the identity of the Herodians, which indeed remains a matter of debate. Here he may be thinking of them simply as 'followers of Herod'; cf CWE 45 244 n17.

this reason they now were supposing that he would appear according to the prophecy of Malachi,[78] 'some "Jeremiah"' because he was a type of Christ.[79] When Jesus heard this response, in order to elicit a more certain and more elevated confession he said: 'As for you who ought to know me better, who do you say I am?' Here Simon Peter, as the one who was most loving of Jesus, responded on behalf of all, inasmuch as he would be head of the apostolic order:[80] 'You are the Christ, the Son of the living God,' confessing with certain and undoubted knowledge that he was the Messiah promised by the prophets, in some unique way[81] the Son of God.

[246] Jesus was delighted by a confession so ready and assured, and said: 'You are blessed, Simon, son of John. This declaration did not come to you from a human impulse or impression, but the heavenly Father by secret inspiration brought it to your mind. And that you might not bestow on me gratuitously the honour of such splendid testimony, I in turn affirm that you are in truth Peter, that is, a solid rock, not wavering this way and that according to the various opinions of the crowd; and upon the rock of your confession[82] I will build my church, which I will so fortify that no force will be able to take it by storm. Satan will [247] rouse against you a cohort of ungodly spirits, but with my protection my building will stand unassailable, only let this confession of yours remain firm. The church is the heavenly kingdom, the world is the kingdom of the devil. To you, Peter, I will hand over the keys of this heavenly kingdom, for it is fitting that he who is first in profession of faith and in love should there be first in authority. In the meantime, that kingdom of heaven is indeed on earth, but in communion with heaven, on which it depends. Accordingly, whoever is still bound by sins belongs to the kingdom of the lower world and cannot enter into

78 Cf 2 Kings 2:1–12 (Elijah carried away) and Mal 4:5–6 (Elijah returned).

79 Jeremiah was regarded by some as an exemplar of patient endurance in adversity.

80 Likewise in the paraphrase on John 21:15 CWE 46 223 Erasmus associates Peter 'the most loving' and Peter's primacy. In general, however, Erasmus' representation of Peter's primacy is somewhat ambiguous; cf the *Ratio* in CWE 41 605 n613.

81 In *1522* and *1524* this passage read: 'He was the Messiah promised by the prophets *through a certain unique love the Son of God.*' Béda and the Paris theologians suspected that the expression (italicized here) compromised orthodox Trinitarianism. Hence in paraphrasing Matt 16:16 in *1534* and *1535* Erasmus clarified by substituting the expression 'in some unique way.' Cf CWE 82 239–40.

82 In his annotation on Matt 16:18 (*quia tu es*) Erasmus explains that the rock on which the church is founded is Peter's confession (rather than Peter himself); cf *Ratio* 49 with n37. On Erasmus' representation of Peter's primacy see n80 above, and the short essay by Craig Thompson in CWE 40 734 n98.

the kingdom of heaven.[83] But he will enter if, having confessed before you what you have confessed, he is freed from his sins by baptism. This is my particular power, to forgive sins, but I will impart this power to you in some measure so that, since you have received my keys, what you loose on the earth before men will be loosed also in heaven before God. On the other hand, what you bind on the earth will be bound also in heaven. For God will approve your judgment, as it has originated from his Spirit.'

(7) The Transfiguration (from the paraphrase on Mark 9 CWE 49 109–10)

[**Mark 9**] [109] To keep the disciples from doubting that he would make good in the future his promise about the majesty of the second coming, Jesus wished to reveal to them even before his death a taste of his future majesty. And so after six days Jesus took with him three of the chosen twelve, to indicate that those to whom he was to entrust this vision were the most distinguished and were to keep silent until the time of speaking out had come. These were Peter, James, and John. These only he led to a very high mountain.[84] For those whom Jesus considers worthy of this vision must be far above caring for lowly things.

When they came to the mountaintop, they first spent time in prayer. For this most of all prepared the eyes of the spirit for such a vision. As they were praying, Jesus' appearance was suddenly changed. His face, which before had seemed nothing out of the ordinary, had the splendour of the sun. His garments, too, shone with a whiteness more dazzling than snow, a whiteness no fuller can give to fabrics by applying his art. And they saw not only Jesus in this manner, but also Elijah and Moses in conversation with Jesus. Their conversation with Jesus manifestly signifies the consensus between the Law and the prophets. For the Law had outlined Christ in mystical figures, the prophets had predicted in their prophecies that Christ would come in the form in which he did. The conversation was about the glorious death he was shortly to suffer on the cross in Jerusalem, so that in this case, too, the mention of death would temper the intensity of the pleasure, of which no human mind was capable. Peter, carried away by this ineffable vision and no longer in control of himself, interrupted the conversation they

83 Cf John 3:5.

84 Identified in the *Paraclesis* as Mt Tabor in Galilee; cf 35 n31. Erasmus gives this traditional site in none of the paraphrases on the story in the Synoptic Gospels.

had begun about Jesus' death, and said: 'Teacher, let Jerusalem be,[85] it is good for us to be here. Let us forthwith build here three tents, one for you, one for Moses, and a third one for Elijah.'

Peter's words had their source partly in a deep-seated horror of death, partly in the pleasure of the vision, which had inebriated him, so to speak. For he spoke like a man who was beside himself and did not know what he was saying.

[110] Then, lest the apostles be overcome by the greatness of this splendour, a cloud rose up and enveloped them, shielding them from the intolerable brightness. Here a taste of the majesty was given to corporeal eyes, and a little also to the ears. For the voice of the Father himself, full of majesty, [2 Pet 1:17] rose from the cloud, saying: 'This is my most beloved Son. Hear him.' After the Father's voice had been heard, the scene suddenly changed, and a different vision returned. For when they looked around as if awakened from sleep, they saw nothing of the things that they had seen before, only Jesus, who was once more among his disciples in his usual appearance. He had shown them his greatness only through a cloud, and they could not comprehend it. What would they have done if he had opened up to them his true, sublime glory?

(8) The Road to Jerusalem and the Triumphal Procession (from the paraphrases on Mark 10 and 11 CWE 49 121–31 and 135–8)

[**Mark 10**] [121] Jesus now left Galilee and [128] prepared to go up to Jerusalem. He called the twelve to him and impressed on their minds what he had previously taught in a covert manner and recently predicted openly.[86]

'Behold now comes the time about which I have already spoken to you. We are going up to Jerusalem so that you may understand that I am suffering willingly and knowingly what I shall suffer. The Son of man will be given over into the hands of those who are first among the priests, scribes, Pharisees, and elders of the people. They will condemn him as being guilty and impious and, after accusing him of various crimes, will condemn him to death. [129] He will be scourged and slain, but he will rise from the dead on the third day.'

85 Cf Matt 16:21–3; after Peter's 'Confession' Jesus told the disciples that he 'must go to Jerusalem,' where he would suffer and die.

86 'Recently,' ie the prediction after the Transfiguration of Christ's death; cf Mark 9:12, 31.

Then two of the disciples, James and John, the sons of Zebedee, approached Jesus privately. They had conceived good hope from his mention of resurrection, thinking that the kingdom which Christ had promised so many times would come soon. 'Lord,' they said, 'we ask for this honour in your kingdom: let us be the ones to sit next to you, one on your right hand, the other on your left.' Jesus revealed their ignorance by a question. For they were still dreaming of a material kingdom, still thinking of first rank.[87] Jesus, however, did not reproach them, but recalled to their minds the mention of death from which they recoiled:[88] 'Because you do not understand the nature of God's kingdom you also do not know what you are asking for. You are asking for vain glory and you are not considering how to arrive at true glory in my kingdom, for true glory is not the one you are dreaming of now. Are you able to drink from the cup from which I am now preparing to drink? Are you able to receive the baptism which I am about to receive?' In their eagerness to obtain their wish they made promises as rash as their demand had been foolish, for they did not yet sufficiently know themselves: 'Yes, we are able,' they said.

In his kindness the Lord did not rebuke the folly of his disciples, for the time had not yet come for them to comprehend such things. [130] Instead, Jesus adapted his speech to their weakness. It had been the voice of ambition that made them say: 'Let us sit next to you in your kingdom.' It had been the voice of rashness that made them say: 'Yes, we can.' But an error that has its origin not in wickedness but in simplicity has to be either healed or endured for the time being. Thus Jesus replied: 'You will indeed drink from my cup and receive the baptism that I shall receive, but in the future. For you cannot yet do what you are so confident of doing: for this you must prepare your minds. As for your reward, leave all judgment to God the Father – let your only endeavour be to emulate me. He has a reward ready for each person and distributes it according to his judgment, as it seems good to him.'

When the rest of the disciples found out what the two had sought from the Lord, they were angry with them for not sufficiently acknowledging their mediocrity and for daring to ask for first place, which was more rightly deserved by others. There was no one who did not hold out hopes for himself, and each fancied his own gifts and merits. These are indeed the feelings of men who live in the courts of princes. Each is pleased with himself, each promises himself the foremost honours and

87 Cf Acts 1:8 (earthly kingdom), Matt 18:1 (first place).

88 Cf Matt 16:21–3.

envies others who are preferred, except that malice is mixed in with the ambition of courtiers – the ambition of the disciples was merely simplicity.

[131] Jesus realized that the foolish petition of the two and the indignation of the others derived from the same source, and called them all together to give them all a dose of the same medicine. 'Whenever you hear about the kingdom of heaven being completely spiritual,' he said, 'and as different from the kingdom of the world as earth is from heaven, do not think of the shape of things as they appear to you in earthly kingdoms. For you know that those who are seen to rule over the heathen people of this world lord it over their subjects; and those who are chiefs among them exercise their authority over their underlings – beware lest the same happen to you. In this kingdom the desire to help aggrandizes you, not ambition. And, as I have taught you before,[89] anyone among you who wishes to be truly great must be your servant. Let him not be eager for power, but let him lower himself to be of service to all. This is the rule of the gospel. Let him who will, strive for it after my example. It would be impudent to seek honours according to the example of earthly princes and to seek a reward from the heavenly Father.'

[**Mark 11**] [135] The disciples were thus still dreaming of the kingdom of this world. To impress more deeply on their minds that those who seek to follow Jesus must not strive for this kingdom, the Lord displayed before their eyes a spectacle to ridicule the glory of this world as being a fleeting thing and soon to perish. He had now advanced closer to Jerusalem, indeed close to Bethphage and Bethany, two small towns on the mountain called the Mount of Olives, whence one could see Jerusalem. From there he dispatched two disciples with the following instructions: 'Go,' he said, 'into that village which you see on the other side. When you enter the gate you will find tied there a young donkey, as yet unbroken, on whom no man has ever sat. Untie him and bring him to me. And if anyone should ask you why you untie the colt, say: "The Lord needs it, and he will send it back here to you at once." The disciples left as they were told, came to the village, found the colt tied by the gate at the fork of the road, and untied him. At that some among the bystanders, seeing the colt being untied by strangers, said to them: 'What are you doing? Why are you untying the colt?' The disciples answered exactly as they had been bidden by the Lord: 'The Lord needs it.' Since they did not understand whom the disciples were

89 Cf Mark 9:35.

calling 'Lord,' they asked no further questions and let the colt go. Having untied the animal, the disciples brought him to Jesus.

Here I want you to take note, dear reader, that none of this was done by chance but rather by a divine plan and for the instruction of mankind. For there is nothing [in the life of Jesus] that does not have an exemplary character displaying godliness for us, nothing that does not reflect ancient prophecy [136] or express a figure by which, in a dark manner, the Law had designated Christ, or does not have a meaning forecasting future events. While this must be studied in all Jesus' deeds, they are the more filled with sacred mystery the closer the day of his death came, by which he was chiefly to carry out the business of our salvation. Thus the young unbroken colt on whom no man had yet sat is the nation of gentiles, neither obeying the law of nature, nor yet serving the Mosaic law; for Moses had weighed down the back of the ass, that is the synagogue, and so had the prophets.[90] In order to summon the gentiles, however, some of the new disciples were dispatched to call them, not to Moses, but to Jesus. The Jews cried out: 'This salvation was promised to us. How is it that we share it with gentiles and worshippers of idols?' They were told that he who is the Lord of all needs such colts. He was weary now of his vain labours among the Jews and wished to repose quietly on a young and unbroken colt. A new rider must have a new beast of burden.

The apostles played a supporting role in this act. They covered the colt with their own cloaks, so that Jesus should not sit on its bare back. Imitate the disciples' concern, you who are a teacher of the gospel. Whenever you see an unbroken young colt tied down by the wayside, ignorant of the gospel law, subject to many vices, untie him, bring him to Jesus, and cover him with the cloak of salutary doctrine. Then the Lord of all, Jesus, will consider him worthy of riding.

Compare this sight, dear reader, with one of those who hold first place [137] among the Jewish priests. With the dignity of the Son of God, ruler and Saviour of the whole world, compare the high priest of a single temple who has bought the priesthood for a year's duration from an impious ruler at a shameful price. Compare the bare head of Jesus with the priest's tiara, sparkling with gold and gems. Compare

90 Mark speaks only of a colt, but Matthew (21:1–10), following Zechariah 9:9, has both a colt and an ass. Erasmus adopts the traditional allegorical interpretation that understood the colt to represent the gentiles, the ass, its mother, the Jews. In the paraphrase here Erasmus includes the ass from the Matthean narrative in order to accommodate the traditional interpretation. Cf CWE 45 291–3 with nn12, 13, 14 and CWE 48 149 n50.

Jesus' modest and gentle mien with the face of the priest, puffed up with pride; note his grim forehead, his knotted brows, his haughty eyes, his sneering mouth. Compare Jesus' bare hands with the priest's fingers covered with rings and gems. Compare Jesus' simple and common robe with his pompous and ornate dress, in which there is nothing less than purple and gold. Compare the few and humble disciples of Jesus with the more than royal procession of heralds, splendid pages, trumpets and clarions, attendants and escorts of the high priest.[91] Compare the acclamations of the children who preceded and followed Jesus and who were singing, inspired by the Holy Spirit, the verse from the prophecy of the psalm: 'Hosanna (that is, 'Bring salvation')![92] Blessed is he who comes in the name of the Lord! Blessed be the kingdom of our father David which is at hand! Hosanna in the highest!' – compare these words with the worldly acclamations of the chorus flattering the wicked Jewish high priest: 'Long live the most holy high priest! Victory to the highest priest of God! May the most blessed prince of religion rule!' That Jesus was opposed to high priests of this kind is clear from the fact that he commanded that proud and pretentious priesthood to be destroyed together with its temple.[93] They are the ones through whom even today Jesus is slain in his members, when he wishes to be the sole prince of priesthood. [138] In such a procession Jesus, the king, entered the royal city,[94] Jerusalem – a heavenly priest entering his temple – and there taught the people as becomes a king and priest.

(9) The Last Supper (paraphrases from John 13 and Matthew 26 CWE 46 159–60 and CWE 45 348–51)

[**John 13**] [159] It was the day before the Passover, and our Lord Jesus, whom nothing ever escaped, knew that the time was at hand when he,

91 Perhaps an attempt to criticize indirectly the arrogance and extravagance of the papacy. Cf the annotation on Acts 9:43 (*apud Simonem corarium* ASD VI-6 244: 559–61: 'The wealth of the church has grown immensely. One would congratulate the good fortune ... if only godliness matched it. Now the palaces of three kings scarcely suffices to receive the vicar of Peter.' The last sentence was omitted in the editions of 1527 and 1535.

92 In his annotation on Matt 21:9 (*Osanna filio David*) Erasmus explains the Hebrew word 'Hosanna' as an interjection, whose literal meaning is 'Save me,' a word used in the context of earnest entreaty or radical asseveration in dire circumstances. Modern scholars generally agree. Cf Ps 118:25–6, 116:4.

93 Cf Mark 13:2, Matt 24:2 in each case, however, a prophecy, not a command.

94 'Royal' as the city established by David to be the seat of the kings of Israel and Judea, but cf Matt 5:35. In Matt 4:5 and 27:53 it is called 'the holy city.'

too, would 'pass over' from this world and return to his Father, from whom he had come. So while he had always loved his apostles, whom he had particularly chosen as his intimates and friends, he now made his unending love for them plain. The impending storm of his death did not drive out the affection he had for them; instead, at the very point of departure [160] he displayed the signs of a rare love, for he wanted the impression that he made on their hearts in his departing to be quite firmly fixed. He had decided, therefore, that after the preparations for that last mystical meal,[95] he would ratify the bond of a friendship that would never in any way perish. And since Jesus was aware that he would soon go to the Father, he wanted to remove from his disciples' hearts all deep-seated inclination to self-seeking. So when the meal was already laid out, he rose, and removing his outer garment, put on an apron, thus appearing unmistakably as a servant. Then he himself filled a basin with water, and setting about what the world considered the most demeaning performance of service, he began to wash his disciples' feet. This sort of service was indeed ordinarily offered to guests and friends according to Hebrew custom, but what Christ did was not only a model of boundless humility but also an image of mystical meaning: that is, that those who gird themselves for the task of preaching the gospel ought to be quite pure from all earthly desires, but that such purity comes to no one except when our Lord Jesus in his goodness washes away all the filth of our weakness.

[**Matthew 26**] [348] During this, the last supper Jesus shared with his disciples before his death, he instituted that most holy symbol of his death, so that there would be continually renewed among them an everlasting memorial of his immense love by which he did not hesitate to expend his life to redeem the race of mortals. In this way the memory of his divine sacrifice could not at some time slip from our minds. [349] He consecrated this mystic symbol with the two things by which a friendship has, since long ago, customarily been bonded among persons, so that the love by which Christ laid down his life for his people might unite us also, who even ourselves frequently eat from the same loaf of bread and drink from the same cup. At the same time he recalled by a certain spiritual image the rites of the Mosaic law, according to which no expiation from sins occurs except through

95 AV seems to place the foot-washing after the supper ('supper being ended'); the Greek is ambiguous; in his translation Erasmus left the Vulgate ('supper having been made'), but in his annotation on 13:2 he clearly understands the Greek to mean 'supper having been prepared.' Cf RSV 'during supper.'

the blood of the sacrificial victim;[96] and he signified, furthermore, that he was consecrating the new covenant of the gospel profession with a mystery of that sort.[97] For when Moses had read out from the roll containing the commandments of the Law, and the people had replied: 'All that the Lord has spoken we will do, and we will be obedient' [Exod 24:7], he took from the bowl some of the blood of the victims he had slaughtered, and sprinkled the people with it, saying: 'This is the blood of the covenant which the Lord has made with you in accordance with all these words' [Exod 24:8]. All these things, in fact, pointed by means of certain figures and foreshadowings to this most holy sacrifice, by which the Lord Jesus, of his own accord handing his body over to death and pouring out his blood, was about to atone for the sins of the whole world, freely reconciling to God anyone who professed this covenant of the new testament.

[350] Now the death of Christ was not to be repeated. In order, then, that so great a blessing could not possibly slip some day from people's minds he ordained that among those who profess the gospel law memory should be renewed by frequent communion of the holy bread and the chalice. He wanted this sign to be holy and to be so venerated that, just as an abundance of divine grace would be bestowed upon those who take the body and blood of the Lord purely and worthily, so those who took it unworthily would summon weighty damnation upon themselves.[98] Accordingly, Jesus took the bread in his hands and, after he had offered the sacrifice of praise to God, broke it and distributed it to his disciples, saying: 'Take, eat, this is my body.'[99] Then he also took the cup in his hands, and when he had given thanks to the Father he drank first, and then offered it to them, saying: 'Drink from this cup, all of you. For this is my blood, the blood of the new covenant that will be poured out for many for the remission of sins. As often as you do this, do it for the remembrance of me.[100] [351] For as often as you eat of this bread and drink of this cup, you will proclaim the Lord's death until

96 Cf Lev 17:11 and Lev 16.

97 For an excellent account of Erasmus' views on the Eucharist, particularly in relation to the Reform movement, see John B. Payne's introduction to *Uncovering of Deceptions* in CWE 78 148–62. Note also the paraphrase on John 6:41–65 CWE 46 86–9 and the paraphrase on Acts 2:42 CWE 50 24 with nn115, 117, 118.

98 Cf 1 Cor 11:27–30.

99 Cf the annotation on 1 Cor 11:24: (*quod pro vobis traditur*): 'The bread distributed among many is a symbol of concord; the one body sacrificed for all a sign of friendship.'

100 For the first clause see 1 Cor 11:25, for the second Luke 17:19 and 1 Cor 11:24.

he comes,[101] not then as saviour, but as judge. In the meantime another sacrificial victim for our sins will not have to be awaited since this one alone suffices for abolishing the sins of the entire world. And I tell you, after this I will not eat from this loaf until I eat it with you, a loaf made complete in the kingdom of my Father,[102] nor will I drink further from this fruit of the vine until I drink it new with you in my Father's kingdom.' The most merciful Lord did not exclude the betrayer Judas from this sacred symbol; his purpose was that Judas should be corrected by such great gentleness. But since he received the sign of the covenant when he had treachery in his heart, he departed more polluted than when he arrived. When they had sung a hymn for the praise of God, they arose and went to the Mount of Olives.

(10) The Crucifixion (from the paraphrase on Mark 15 CWE 49 170–3)

[**Mark 15**] [170] When Pilate saw that he was running a risk, from Caesar on the one hand and from the agitated crowd on the other, he agreed to satisfy the implacable hatred of the priests, scribes, elders, and people and, although he knew that Jesus was innocent, he pronounced his death sentence. In pronouncing it, however, he acquitted the innocent man of the crime[103] and condemned the priests and the people. For he pronounced innocent the man whom he handed over to them for crucifixion. The evangelical truth will always have such Pilates. Thus condemned, Jesus was first scourged, then was handed over to the cohort to be crucified. Whereupon, Jesus, the fount of all glory, was subjected to all kinds of humiliation: Judas betrayed him; Caiaphas, the high priest, condemned him; the council mocked him; the people clamoured against him; Herod showed contempt;[104] and Caesar's governor pronounced the verdict. In all of them is Caiaphas; and in Caiaphas is Satan. It remained for the vulgar cohort of soldiers to play their part. In them, too, was Caiaphas.

[171] They brought Jesus to a place infamous as a place where criminals were executed, called Golgotha in Aramaic, which means 'skull place.' There they offered him wine mixed with myrrh to drink, but Jesus did not accept the offering. He hated the bitter wine that the vine

101 Cf 1 Cor 11:25.
102 Cf Luke 22:16, where, however, Jesus refers to the Passover, not to 'this loaf.'
103 Cf Luke 23:22.
104 Cf Luke 23:11.

of the Jewish synagogue had brought forth for him; he hated the wine of wicked men and thirsted for another kind of wine, namely the new wine of the evangelical spirit, which he himself poured into his disciples after he had ascended to heaven. When he had been raised on the cross, the men who had crucified [172] him divided his garments among themselves, casting lots to see who should get his cloak whole, for it was woven in such a manner that it could not be divided.[105] Look upon Jesus in his poverty, having nothing left now on this earth. He was suspended between heaven and earth. This is how he must be who wishes to do battle with the enemy of man's salvation: naked, unencumbered, on high.

[173] When Jesus had fulfilled everything, he uttered a loud cry and breathed his last. At that moment the curtain of the temple, which keeps that which the Jews consider most holy from the sight of the multitude,[106] was torn from top to bottom. The shadows part when the truth comes forth. Nor was there any further need for any priest to enter the shrine now that the victim had been sacrificed which alone sufficed to expiate the sins of the whole world.

(11) The Resurrection Appearances: The Companions on the Road to Emmaus (from the paraphrase on Luke 24 CWE 48 231–5)

[Luke 24] [231] While the two were reviewing many points about Jesus with each other, and conversing back and forth, there he was, the wolf, as they say, in the tale.[107] For Jesus joined them as if he too were a traveller and offered himself as a companion on the journey, though not with his familiar appearance – not that he did not have the same body he had had before his death, but because, by Jesus' deliberate choice, their vision was prevented from recognizing the person they saw. Blessed

105 Cf John 19:23.

106 Erasmus assumes a reference to the second veil that separated the Holy of Holies from the Holy Place, the former containing the ark of the covenant and the cherubim; cf Heb 9:2–3.

107 'The wolf in the tale': Erasmus' prose is frequently punctuated by vivid images taken from proverbs, or adages, of which he published (in 1500) just over eight hundred in a small first edition, but to which he added more adages in subsequent editions until the final edition of 1536 contained over four thousand. In *Adagia* IV v 50 CWE 36 175–6 he says that this proverb 'was usually said when the subject of a conversation suddenly appeared.' Jane Phillips suggests that its English equivalent is 'speak of the devil' (CWE 48 231 n19).

comradeship, when two talk of nothing else, discuss nothing else, than Jesus! Blessed are they whom Jesus deigns to join as their companion! [232] Jesus addressed them, 'What are those subjects you are discussing as you go, with a look on your faces that indicates sadness and grief in your heart?' For if someone happens along into whose bosom we can pour out our pain, doing so very often soothes our grief. Out of such a feeling one of the disciples, whose name was Cleopas, said in reply, 'It's something quite well known to all the people in Jerusalem; since you are coming from that city just as we are, how can it be that you alone like a newly-arrived visitor do not know what was done there these last few days, things that every man alive knows?' To that, as if he wanted to learn though he had in fact come to teach, Jesus answered, 'Well, what are those things?'[108]

[233] 'We were talking about Jesus of Nazareth,' they said, 'who was a remarkable man and a mighty prophet in both word and deed, not only with God but also with the entire populace, in whose eyes he had earned himself the highest authority by his miracles, his teaching, and his good deeds. The chief priests and the leaders of our people prosecuted him on a capital charge before the governor and finally condemned him to the cross. We had formed an extraordinary hope that he was going to redeem the people of Israel – we were convinced he was the Messiah long since promised by the prophets. But his undeniable death and the shameful way he died have taken this hope away from us.

When the disciples had guilelessly made clear in this account how they wavered in their heart, how small a hope they had in the Lord's promises, Jesus did not yet actually allow himself to be recognized, but like some more learned disciple of Jesus he scolded their slowness and rebuked their unbelief. 'O too little amenable to understanding the Scriptures,' he said, 'slow of heart and resistant to believing the many oracles that the prophets uttered about Jesus! Why do these things seem strange to you now, after they have happened, when the sayings of the prophets foretold that all this must happen?' Why don't you compare their predictions with what has happened? Don't the Scriptures teach that it seemed best to the divine purpose for Christ to suffer all that he has suffered and thus in a revolutionary fashion restore life by way of death, claim a kingdom by way of the cross, enter into his glory by way of shame? [234] Are you still so thick-headed that you are looking for a general as a Messiah, seizing a worldly kingdom for himself with

108 Jesus inquires as though he does not know, an example of Jesus' deliberate deceptiveness; for the 'dissimulating Christ' see *Ratio* 48.

chariots, horses, elephants, armoured troops, ballistas, catapults, tortoises, onagers, fire, sword, and bloodshed?[109] Or do you not yet understand that Scripture is spiritual, and that the might of the Messiah does not consist in the resources with which the princes of this world either claim or expand their kingdom, but in heavenly power?

When the Lord had made them more attentive with this bit of scolding, he explained to them all the scriptures that plainly foretold that what had now happened would come to pass in Christ. He showed them that there was such a quantity of harmonious prophecies, figures, and actual events that it would be a sign of outstanding stupidity not to notice them, or of remarkable distrust not to believe them. He began his discourse with Moses and the prophets; after them he selected something from every book of divine Scripture that would build up their faith in what had happened and lay a foundation of faith in what would take place thereafter. And he compared all these passages with one another in such a way that the matter was perfectly clear.

Blessed are they who have earned the privilege of hearing the heavenly teacher explicating what he had earlier made known through prophets [235] inspired by his own Spirit.[110]

(12) The Final Departure of Jesus, and His Legacy: The Church Emerging (from the paraphrases on Acts 1 and 2 CWE 50 6–10 and 13–17, 23–5)

[**Acts 1**] [6] After Jesus was alive again from the dead, he instructed both his twelve apostles and the remaining seventy disciples[111] (whom he had chosen before his death specifically for this ministry), to go into all the world and preach the gospel not only to the Jews but to all the peoples of the entire world.[112] This they were to do when they had received

109 'Ballistas, catapults, and onagers specify three kinds of Roman wheeled artillery for throwing rocks and arrows; tortoises were sheds or interlocked shields held by soldiers in formation. All were used in siege operations' (CWE 48 234 n26).

110 There follows at this point a lengthy exposition (in CWE 48 pages 235–70) showing the 'harmony' between 'prophecies, figures and actual events.' In the *Ratio* Erasmus makes this 'harmony of all things in the life of Christ and Scripture' a central point in biblical interpretation. The exposition is also appropriate to Erasmus' emphasis on the historical reliability of the gospel ('build up their faith … lay a foundation of faith').

111 Cf Luke 10:1.

112 For the mission of the twelve to the Jews only see Matt 10:5–6, for the mission to the whole world Matt 28:19.

the Holy Spirit, for Christ imparted the Spirit to them both when he breathed upon their faces and later when he sent the Spirit more abundantly from heaven.[113] Although he had already handed over to them the authority to preach the gospel he nevertheless forbade them to rush immediately into a duty so arduous. They were not to depart from Jerusalem, but they were to gather there, and spending time in fasts, in singing hymns and in prayers, to await the Holy Spirit – a second Comforter who, he promised, would be sent to them from the Father.[114]

'By my own mouth,' he said, 'I have promised; my Father will faithfully fulfil the pledge I have made in his name. The task you will be undertaking is a heavenly, not a human one. You will not teach carnal things as the Pharisees have so far taught, but spiritual, and no small persecution will rise against you because of the preaching of the gospel.[115] Accordingly, you will need to be strengthened by a power sent forth from heaven in order to be equal to the task. Thus far we have seen only the prelude to [7] certain things that are basic to carrying out the gospel. John baptized with water; he did not confer the Spirit. He preached only repentance, because the kingdom of heaven was at hand.[116] Now there is need of more able forces to draw forth the more lively strength of evangelical teaching, and to endure the storms from an opposing world. For this you need a new Spirit – an abundant Spirit, a celestial Spirit, a fiery Spirit. With this Spirit you will be baptized within a few days. For its coming prepare your hearts with sobriety, pious prayers, but above all simple trust, so that you may be fit instruments of the Spirit, which is about to display its force through you. [8] It will give strength to your souls, will call to mind everything I have taught you, and even supply any further knowledge you might need.[117] Taught by its prompting, strengthened by its support, you will be my witnesses, first in Jerusalem, shortly thereafter through all Judea, then Samaria, finally throughout all the nations of the world. I came equally for all, I died for all, the grace of the gospel is offered to all. Until now the Law has held sway among the Jews. It is the Father's will that the reign of the gospel extend as widely as the world extends.'

These were the last words Jesus spoke to his disciples, who had all gathered together in Bethany. When he had finished speaking and had

---

113 Cf John 20:22 (Jesus breathed upon the disciples), Acts 2:2–4 (Pentecost).

114 Cf John 14:26.

115 Cf Matt 10:16–23, Acts 8:1–3.

116 Cf Matt 3:1–2; for John's preaching see 83–5 above.

117 Cf John14:26, 16:13.

blessed them, he was borne upward before the eyes of all, until a white cloud withdrew the body of Jesus from their sight. The time had come for them to stop depending on the visual presence of the body, so that they might rather begin to be spiritual and might look upon Jesus with no other eyes than those of faith.

[9] The disciples left the Mount of Olives and came to Jerusalem where they proceeded to an upper room in which were staying those disciples who were especially close to Christ and several women who had followed the Lord with godly zeal when he [10] set out for Jerusalem and had ministered to him from their means.[118] Among them was Mary the mother of Jesus.

Consider now with me for a little while the first beginnings of the nascent church. The city of Jerusalem, which in Hebrew means 'vision of peace,'[119] pleases them. Those whose native land is this world do not inhabit Jerusalem, nor do they desire to find the tranquillity of the heavenly life. Those whose minds are agitated by worldly passions do not inhabit Jerusalem. The Holy Spirit does not repair to such breasts. The *cenaculum,* which is the higher part of a building, was also agreeable. For the lower parts of a house are usually occupied either by shops or workplaces. But whoever prepares himself as a dwelling for the Holy Spirit must be far removed from sordid cares. This is that holy congregation which the Lord Jesus had chosen out of all. This upper room was the first abode of the church of the gospel. See, then, what is done here. The time is not wasted in quarrels or empty tales, but all continued steadfast with a single heart in holy prayers. Where there is not oneness of heart, there is not the church of Christ. The evangelical congregation prays for the same thing. And now the rest of the disciples flocked into this upper room of the apostles. Whoever wishes to be regarded as a disciple of Jesus must be joined to the fellowship of the church.

[**Acts 2**] [13] Forty-nine days were spent in this way after the Lord's resurrection. [14] But now that the fiftieth day had arrived they had all with complete concord come together at the same time to the same upper room to receive the heavenly Spirit. Where the mind is occupied with low and sordid cares, there the Holy Spirit is not found; it has to be in an upper room. Where the breast churns with discord, hatred, and quarrels, there is no place for the Holy Spirit. Gathered together into one place, a lofty place at that, with hearts united all believe, pray, await.

118 Cf Mark 15:40–1.

119 A traditional interpretation of the name; cf the allusion in the paraphrase on Mark 11:11 CWE 49 138 with n22.

Lo! Suddenly from above there came the gift of God. For all of a sudden there came a sound from heaven as of a wind blowing with mighty force, and it filled the entire room where they were sitting, calm and quiet. This was the breath of heaven, coming from where Christ had gone, breathing eternal life into souls, giving strength and vigour to the weak and the faint. This sign was given for the ears, another sign was given for the eyes, for these are a person's two chief senses. Tongues appeared, as though in the form of fire, distributing themselves to each of the disciples, and they sat upon the head of each for some time so that we might understand this gift would be everlasting. It was the same Spirit that blew upon the minds of all, the same flame that set on fire the tongue and breast of all. Without delay, the efficacy of the heavenly gift followed the visible sign. All who were present were suddenly transformed, as it were, into heavenly persons and, filled with the Holy Spirit, began to speak in different tongues. These were not languages they had learned from human conversation, but ones the Spirit had imparted to them from heaven. To sow the seeds of the heavenly doctrine throughout peoples of every language required tongues imbued with heavenly doctrine and aflame with the fire of evangelical love. This was, therefore, the primary sign of evangelical faith, the sign the Lord had promised to them, saying, 'They shall speak in new tongues' [Mark 16:17].

[15] Sounds are not uttered without breath, without a tongue. Accordingly, the breath from heaven puts forth a heavenly sound, a tongue of fire carries off and sets aflame the hearts of the hearers. This gift comes from heaven; the disciples are only instruments through which the Holy Spirit puts forth his voice. God bestows this gift upon each person as he sees fit. The spirit is a thing of force; fire is something lively and always in motion. The apostles burst forth in public, everywhere and openly preaching to all free salvation through trust in Jesus, the one crucified just a little while before. [17] Those who were fishermen and simple folk now with eloquence from heaven expose the pride of the Pharisees, refute the propositions of the philosophers, overwhelm the eloquence of the orators.

The crowd was in an uproar. So Peter stood before the turbulent mob, intending to instruct and to stop the mouths of those who had said, 'They are full of new wine' [Acts 2:12]. Recognize Peter's rank and authority. He is the first to speak when circumstances require an evangelical orator. He had sheathed the sword unpleasing to Christ, he had unsheathed the sword of the Spirit.[120] Such should the chief bishop

120 Cf John 18:11 (sheathed the sword), Eph 6:17 (sword of the Spirit).

be. Peter rose up, but not alone, for the eleven apostles stood with him so that he should not appear to be usurping absolute power. One alone made the speech, but the one spoke with the voice of them all, just as earlier one in the name of all had professed Jesus Christ the Son of the living God.[121]

[23] Peter's speech was truly the eloquence of a fisherman, not gained from the precepts of the rhetoricians but infused from heaven and therefore powerful [24] and effective. His speech was that sword that pierces even to the dividing asunder of soul and spirit[122] by whose keen blade the hearts of the Jews were pricked. This was the seed of the evangelical word which was to be everywhere sown. The seed, according to Jesus' teaching, does not take root in the hearts of all, but here it at once found good soil that brought forth fruit.[123] For there were baptized and added to the number of disciples (who were at that time very few), about three thousand persons. These truly are the felicitous first-fruits of the evangelical crop. Through teaching and faith, water had now cleansed them from all sins; they had now drunk of that heavenly Spirit.

So those who were numbered among the disciples persevered in the teaching of the apostles (for from this, growth is most abundant) and in taking the token of an unbreakable covenant – they called this the communion.[124] The practice, handed down from the Lord, was like this: bread was broken and a small piece was given to each one; while doing this in memory of the Lord's passion, they gave thanks to the kindness of God, who had purged them from their sins by the blood of his only Son, and who had admitted them by the undeserved death of his Son into the inheritance of eternal life. They added holy prayers in which they would ask that the kingdom of the Lord Jesus be daily extended more widely, that his glory come to shine throughout the whole world, that his will be everywhere obeyed. They would ask also that those who had once professed evangelical faith might progress daily to better things through sacred teaching and heavenly grace, and that they might thus live harmoniously together, having peace with their brethren, [25] forgiving an injury if, through human frailty, some wrong had been done, and having peace with God, who is merciful to those who are

121 Allusion to the 'confession of Peter' Matt 16:13–16; cf the paraphrase on the passage 105 with n80 above.

122 Cf Heb 4:12.

123 Cf Matt 13:3–23.

124 On Erasmus' understanding of the Eucharist see 112–14 with n97 above.

merciful to their neighbours.[125] In this way, strengthened by the daily help of the divine power, they might withstand all the attacks of Satan until the eternal reward be given after long struggles. In those days, such were the sacrifices made by Christians.[126]

II. JESUS, TEACHER OF THE HEAVENLY PHILOSOPHY

[We represent Erasmus' use of paraphrase to interpret the teaching of Jesus with selections from the Sermon on the Mount and from two parables. Both the Sermon on the Mount and parables hold a special place in Erasmus' biblical reflection. His respect for the Sermon on the Mount is evident in the fact that it assumes a disproportionate place in the *Paraphrase* in comparison with the text of the Gospel – it comprises approximately 10 percent of the Gospel text, approximately 20 percent of the text of the *Paraphrase* (CWE 41 239–40 with n965). It is also crucial to his representation of Jesus in the *Paraphrase* as the Master Teacher. Indeed, in the narrative of the baptism (Matthew 3) the concluding images of 'dove' and 'voice' are interpreted in paraphrase as images of 'initiation' into the full status of 'Master' analogous to the initiation ceremonies into the authoritative position of *magister noster* in the contemporary universities. Several further features are of particular interest: the echoes of classical ethical thought in the paraphrase on the beatitudes, the radical interpretation of Christ as the completion of the Law and of his injunctions as the perfecting of the Law, the triple exposition of the Lord's Prayer, the equation of the teaching of Christ with natural law in the interpretation of the 'Golden Rule,' and the vivid representation of the 'Two Ways.'

---

125 This description of the 'holy prayers' added to the 'communion' is, in effect, an exposition of the Lord's Prayer. One will note that the doxology is omitted and that the fourth petition (bread) is interpreted as 'heavenly bread,' a view that assumes the ambiguous Greek to mean 'the bread of tomorrow'; cf CWE 45 118 with n28. Erasmus' frequent exposition of the Lord's Prayer reflects his interest in it: he offers a triple exposition of it in the paraphrase on Matt 6:9–13 (CWE 45 115–120), a lengthy exposition in *Precatio Domini* (CWE 69 59–77), and brief expositions in *Querela pacis* (CWE 27 309–10), *Explanatio symboli* (CWE 70 386–7), and *Modus orandi deum* (CWE 70 205–8); cf CWE 45 115 n19 and 136–7 with nn159 and 162 below.

126 The term 'Christians' here is, of course, anachronistic – the disciples were first called Christians in Antioch, Acts 11:26. But in his paraphrases Erasmus likes to designate disciples and believers as 'Christians,' thus inviting the reader to see in Scripture a reference to his/her own contemporary situation.

Erasmus thought parables were an especially effective method of delivering the gospel truth (cf the *Ratio* 60–2 above). They make their point by means of a story about familiar people with familiar concerns. In paraphrasing the parables Erasmus adds to the narrative quality by adding colour and drama to the setting, suggesting motives, portraying the psychology of the individuals. The parables represented below are of special interest. The parable of the Weeds among the Wheat speaks effectively of Erasmus' opposition to the death penalty for heretics. Erasmus' position was severely criticized (CWE 41 284–5, and CWE 45 215 n17). The parable of the 'Rich Man' reflects not only Erasmus' belief that avarice and the passion for wealth was a disease to be rooted out of the heart of clergy but also his view that the rich could use their wealth, so often unjustly gained, as an 'exchange' for the 'spiritual' goods that would enhance their credit with God.]

(1) The Sermon on the Mount (from the paraphrases on Matthew 5, 6 and 7 CWE 45 83–111, 111–27, and 128–39)

[**Matthew 5**] [83] When Jesus had climbed a steep hill, he began to play the role of the teacher of heavenly philosophy, indicating by the very height of the place that he was about to hand on all the things that are exalted and heavenly. Accordingly, he did not begin from the pretentious pulpit of the philosophers, or from the arrogant chair of the Pharisees, but from a grassy elevation. He turned his eyes towards the disciples, and opening his sacred mouth he began to draw out the as yet unheard-of doctrines of the gospel teaching, which are far different from the opinions of all those who seem to the world exceptionally wise.

[84] All self-professed teachers of wisdom promise happiness. Everyone, regardless of status or condition, seeks happiness. But in what things human happiness has been placed, on this question there is much controversy among philosophers, and much error in the lives of mortals. Since happiness is the goal and foundation of all wisdom, Jesus explicated this first, teaching paradoxes that are yet very true.[127] Then only a few disciples heard these things and embraced happiness. Let

127 Erasmus sets the Sermon, which is introduced as a discourse on the 'heavenly philosophy,' within the frame of traditional classical philosophy in which two much debated topics were the quest for happiness and the paradoxes, for which the Stoics were especially well known. Cf the paraphrases on Mark 1:1 (happiness) CWE 49 13 and Acts 17:18 (paradoxes) CWE 50 107 n20.

everyone hear, for he has spoken to everyone, and everyone will be made happy.

The most deadly disease of the mind is untameable arrogance that does not allow a person to be open to true teaching. Indeed, arrogance is the spring from which in general all the chief vices gush forth.[128] Accordingly, Jesus first remedied this, saying: [85] 'Blessed are the poor in spirit, for theirs is the kingdom of heaven.' Whose ears could have taken in so inconceivable a statement unless, after the many testimonies of John, of the Father, and of the dove, their authority had finally been commended and trust won by efficacious signs?[129] This humility of spirit, however, is located in one's disposition, not in external things. Where, then, does a person, who claims nothing for himself, who yields to everyone, who is dissatisfied with himself, and who neither casts aside nor hurts anyone, have a kingdom? Such a person seems closer to the servitude of an ass than to a kingdom. And yet what Truth has said is true: theirs alone is the kingdom – but it is a heavenly kingdom.

Do you think that those who are cruel and violent rule? They live as slaves, they endure many tyrannies. They are tortured by greed, anger, envy, by the desire for revenge, by fear and hope. But whoever is free from all these cares – relying on his own innocence, on God, on the rewards of the future age – such a person scorns the things that are of this world, and pursues heavenly goods. Does he not obtain a kingdom far more beautiful and magnificent than the kingdom of tyrants? Lust does not rule him, neither does greed, or envy, or anger, nor do the other diseases of the soul. Armed with faith, whenever circumstances demand he commands diseases and they flee, he commands the waves and they grow calm, he commands demons and they depart.[130] These are the things that truly make a king, and at last summon one to share in the heavenly and eternal kingdom.

[86] Jesus continued and added to this a similar paradox: 'Blessed are the meek, for they shall possess the earth as their inheritance.'[131]

---

128 An allusion, apparently, to the 'arrogance' of scholastic theologians, whom Erasmus sometimes characterized as too arrogant to be open to new ideas; cf the *Ratio* 42 n7 (above) and the *Praise of Folly* CWE 27 126–30.

129 A reference to events preceding the Sermon: the baptism of Jesus (Matt 3:13–17 – John, the Father, the dove) and the summary account of the first miracles of Jesus (Matt 4:23–4).

130 Ie such a person will be able to perform the mighty deeds of Christ; cf Matt 17:20, 'If you have faith ... nothing will be impossible,' and John 14:12, 'One who believes will do greater works than these.'

131 Erasmus follows the Vulgate in placing the beatitude of the meek before that of the mourners.

Who are the meek? They are the people who do not use force against anyone, who, after being harmed, readily pardon the injury, who would rather lose something than fight for it, who regard harmony and tranquillity of mind more valuable than a large estate, who regard quiet poverty more desirable than quarrelsome riches. People of this sort are used to being thrown off their land, and so far are they from acquiring other people's property for themselves that they are driven even from ancestral holdings. But if the property of a meek person is lost, it is a huge gain if he has avoided upheaval and has preserved his peace of mind. The world laments as unfortunate those who are forced into exile. But Christ pronounces those blessed who live in exile because of the gospel. They have been thrown out of their houses and cast out of their homelands, but the whole world is the homeland to the gospel man, and heaven is the surest home and most secure homeland to the godly.

[87] Commonly, bereavement is a thing so pitiful that some people, bereft of those they love, take their own lives. And because of this, friends are summoned who soften the bitterness of grief with consolation. But blessed are those who mourn because of their love for the gospel, who are even torn from their loved ones, who see the people they hold most dear beaten and slaughtered on account of gospel righteousness, who pass their lives in tears, vigils, and fastings. For to them will be present the heavenly Spirit, the secret comforter,[132] who will repay for a temporary grief an inestimable joy of mind to those who will soon be conveyed to eternal joys.

Everyone knows that hunger is a bitter thing, and that we should flee want. Everyone declares those people happy who have brilliantly increased their personal wealth so that they enjoy it abundantly. Yet wealth heaped up however high does not satisfy the heart, nor should a person's happiness be measured by the fullness of his stomach. Christ pronounces blessed those 'who hunger and thirst after righteousness.' Those things that feed and nourish the body [88] should be sought with equanimity. Sometimes satiety torments the full more than their hunger was tormenting them; in any case the godly do not desire anything beyond what is necessary. Happy are they who transfer their hunger and thirst from bodily and perishable things to the quest for gospel righteousness, where fullness is blessed. Indeed, this itself is part of happiness: to hunger for the bread of the soul, whoever eats whereof will live eternally; to thirst for the living water that will

132 Cf John 14:26–7.

become in the one who drinks of it a fountain of water springing up into life everlasting.[133]

The common person thinks that those who are helped by the kindness of another are happy, but I call blessed the merciful, who out of brotherly love consider another's misery their own, who are pained at the misfortunes of a neighbour, who feed the needy from their own wealth, clothe the naked, warn the erring, teach the ignorant, forgive the sinner – in short, who use whatever resources they have to lift up and restore others. Such a person will find God far more merciful towards him and God's kindness more bounteous. You have forgiven your neighbour for some small offence; God will forgive all your sins. You have used your money to relieve your brother's poverty; [89] God will give you his own heavenly wealth.

The common person calls those bereft of their eyes unfortunate, and those who lack sight say that they are not even alive. So sweet a thing it is to behold the light with one's eyes. But if seeing the sun with bodily eyes seems so desirable, how much happier a thing it is to behold God, the fount of all gladness, with the eyes of the mind![134] What the sun is to unclouded eyes, God is to unclouded minds. Therefore blessed are they whose hearts are free from every stain of sin, for to them it will be granted to see God.

Mortals generally judge those blessed who pass their lives in leisure, their affairs arranged just as they desire, with no one to trouble them. But in my judgment they are blessed who first have repressed in their own hearts the rebellion of all desires, and then are zealous to repair harmony among others also who are at odds with them, [90] even of their own accord inviting to peace those by whom they have been injured, for these will be called 'the children of God.' This is no empty title. He who is son must also be heir as well,[135] and imitation of the father gives evidence of a true and legitimate son.[136] God freely pardons all sins; God is gracious to all who come to their senses and repent and invites all to peace and friendship. However, he recognizes as his sons only those who extend the grace of forgiveness to their brothers in the same way he has offered his grace to everyone, and he will disown the haters of peace and the authors of discord.

---

133 The images of bread and water reflect John 6:58 and 4:14. Cf also Rom 15:29 ('fullness of the blessing') and Eph 3:19 ('filled with the fullness of God').

134 Cf Eph 1:18 ('eyes of the mind').

135 Cf Rom 8:16–17.

136 That true sons imitate their fathers is a recurrent theme in the *Paraphrases*; cf CWE 50 49 n6 and CWE 48 139 n24.

But some people are even irritated by kindnesses, they attack people who benefit them, and consider as enemies people who want to save them.[137] If peace cannot exist here between these, nevertheless those who desire peace will in the meantime be blessed. Someone will say: 'Who would be able to love people who repay kindnesses with hatred and evil?' It is a difficult thing, I confess, but the reward for doing so is great. What reward? Not anything of the sort the world gives the victor in human contests, [91] but the kingdom of heaven. You must prepare for this wrestling match,[138] my disciples, if the prizes of gospel happiness attract you. There is no reason why human cruelty should frighten you. No one will be able to harm you if you tenaciously hold on to justice. Persecution will not take away your innocence; it will increase your blessedness.

Even in the midst of a storm of evils you will be blessed. When they curse you with dreadful oaths, when they attack you with every kind of evil, when they hurl against you every kind of disgraceful and criminal charge – and have lied to do it – not because of any fault of yours, but from hatred for me (for it will be the height of crimes to be a Christian),[139] do not lament for yourselves. Rather, rejoice and exult on account of these very things, because the more they vent their rage in persecuting you, the more the reward grows that is stored for you in heaven by the Father.[140] God will turn their wickedness into your good; the dishonour inflicted by them he will turn into true and everlasting glory; the false assertions of wicked deeds he will turn into tokens and testaments of true piety. [92] And so I demand that you think yourselves blessed on account of these evils, that you treat with mercy your blind persecutors, and that you offer eternal salvation to those who work for your ruin.

You will not exhibit this sublime and heroic virtue unless you arrive here by the stages I have set out before you. If you utterly reject anger, if you expel the desire for revenge, if forsaking all the pleasures of this

---

137 A rather covert allusion to Erasmus himself, who suggests in the *Apologia* that he is the object of attack for the benefits he has bestowed on others; cf CWE 41 456–8. The transition between the seventh and eighth beatitudes is subtle but enlarges the scope of the personal allusion: 'persecuted' though he may be by his enemies, he still desires peace!

138 For the Christian's struggle against the forces of evil expressed as a 'wrestling match' see 86 n41 above.

139 The paraphrase anticipates the political situation in the post-canonical period when it was a criminal offence to be a Christian; cf Pliny Epistles 10.96 and 97 and Tertullian *Apology* 2 and 4.1–5.

140 Cf 1 Peter 1:4 ('stored in heaven').

world you embrace a strict manner of life, if having utterly extinguished the desire for human possessions you thirst greatly for nothing besides justice and godliness, if you are so disposed that you desire to relieve the misfortunes of all, and you desire to serve the advantage of all, if you have a mind that is sound and free from all vices and depraved desires, neither looking to nor delighting in anything other than God, if with peaceful hearts you everywhere desire to foster and repair harmony, then at last you will exhibit these qualities that other mortals are not yet able to attain even in their dreams.[141]

[93] I have chosen you not to be merely average and passable, but to be the salt of the earth. One does not need a lot of salt, but salt that is effectual, so that it affects whatever it touches and restores flavour to what is flavourless. Of course, in the great crowd of humanity one necessarily finds people who are average and scarcely even passable. In apostles, however, in bishops, in teachers, the lively and perfect vigour of gospel love should persist.[142] Otherwise, if in your case, too, your character has been made insipid by a love of praise, a desire for money, the pursuit of pleasures, lust for revenge, or fear of infamy, losses, or death, what will be left in the end to season the tasteless life of the multitude? Thus you will end up not only useless for seasoning others, but you yourselves will incur the greatest contempt from people, because you do not practise what you teach.

[94] Let your life and your teaching be such that they serve as a guide and a measuring stick of right living to all who observe you. Our world has a single sun, but it has such effective and abundant light that it shines from afar on all who dwell upon the earth. I have set you in an exalted position so that what you say and what you do will necessarily be spread through the entire world. If clouds obscure the sun, where will mortals get their light? If your teaching grows murky with errors, if your life is darkened by worldly desires, what will dispel the darkness of the multitude? You must take care, therefore, that there is no darkness in you, no folly. You are like a city on a high mountain, visible to travellers far and wide. It cannot be concealed even if it should want to; likewise the gospel teaching: it does not allow its teachers to hide.

141 This sentence with its long sequence of hypothetical clauses provides a summary interpretation of the beatitudes.

142 Matt 5:1–2 and 7:28 suggests a double audience for the Sermon: the Apostles and the 'crowd.' While the paraphrase on the Sermon allows for a certain ambiguity of audience, at this point the paraphrase has the twelve apostles clearly in view, permitting a reflection on the leadership of Erasmus' contemporary church.

[95] When you hear these new precepts – precepts that Moses did not hand down and the prophets did not teach – do not imagine that I am bringing forward something similar to what the Pharisees are accustomed to teach, for they so weigh down the Law with their own additions and human regulations that they reject and abolish what is of primary importance in it. In no way have I come either to weaken the Law or to annul it through new precepts. Rather, I have come to complete and perfect the Law.[143] The Law had its time, it had its honour, by means of types it foreshadowed what now is displayed to the world. It kept human desires in check through carnal ceremonies and precepts as if by a sort of barrier, so that people would not sink into every vice with impunity, and so they would be more ready to receive the gospel teaching now that what has been perfected is disclosed. Although carnal and crude, it profited people this much: that they recognized their own sin. Now without ceremonies the grace that washes sins away is given. The Law therefore suffers harm no more than if a feeble boy in the course of time grows [96] into a mature man, or if ripe fruit follows the leafing boughs and the foliage, or if the rising sun obscures the moon and stars.

What the Law promised is now being made manifest, what it predicted is happening, what it foreshadowed is set out before the eyes of all, what it tried to accomplish but could not is now revealed in its fullness. The light is promised to all, but in such a way, nevertheless, that the Jews have no grounds for complaining. The grace of the gospel was offered to them first; they will not possess it any less if they share what they have with many. Be assured, I do not invalidate the Law. So far am I from invalidating the Law that not an iota, not even a dot, will be lost from the entire Law: such is the extent to which everything written in the Law must be fulfilled. But it would be foolish to await a future that is already present, it would be insane so to delight in the shadows that you scorn the real things, so to cling to the imperfect that you spurn the perfect, so to embrace carnal things that you shrink from spiritual things, to become so attached to earthly things that you reject celestial things.

Among the Jews a person is regarded as contemptible and unobservant of the Law who disregards any of the things the Pharisees have added on their own, prescribing the washing of hands, pitchers, and

143 Compare the role of Christ in relation to the Law as described in the paraphrase on Galatians 3 168–9 below.

vessels. But in the kingdom of heaven, which is more perfect by far, the person who breaks even one of the least of the precepts that I now add to the prescriptions of the Mosaic law will be regarded as least worthy and most contemptible.

[97] Come now! So that it may become clearer how much I am adding to the justice of the Pharisees, and how my justice [98] does not contradict the precepts of the Law but rather supports them, let us consider the matter with a few examples.

You have heard how our ancestors were once commanded: 'You shall not kill,' [Exod 20:13] but if someone kills, after being judged and convicted, he will be punished.[144] Therefore one seems to have satisfied the Law as long as one has not killed anyone. One is apparently both just and innocent and one will be received into the synagogue. Now hear how much I shall add. For I tell you: whoever is even angry at his brother will be liable to judgment. The sublimity of our profession extends guilt so that in the new Law the unrestrained impulse of the heart for revenge is equivalent to murder in the Old. For being angry is the first step to murder. Suppose that a person does not soon regain control over his raging mind, but that unrestrained anger breaks forth into words that, while they do not strike a brother with some specific reproach, still sadden him by an obvious indication of scorn – as if he should say '*racha*,' or something similar that shows malevolent intent. In this case, inasmuch as he is closer to murder, he will not only be liable to judgment, leading to a punishment that is fairly light, but he will also be liable to the council where sentencing must be even more severe. Moreover, if the surging impulse of the heart has broken forth to such an extent that he strikes his brother with an insult that is now direct and pointed, and calls him 'fool' or some such thing, [99] he will now be liable to the most severe penalty, that is, the punishment of hell. In so many ways is a person implicated who has not yet progressed as far as murder.[145] Thus the gospel law, which punishes someone simply for being angry, does not contradict the precept of the Law, 'You shall not kill,' but removes and keeps one further away from the act the Law

144 For this process of judgment see Deut 16:18–20, 17:8–13.

145 In his annotation on Matt 5:22 (*qui dixerit fratri suo racha*) Erasmus suggests that in 5:22 'Christ distinguished three stages of emotional response in a hostile situation: the first step is to become angry, the second to indicate an emotion by some inarticulate sound, the third to break into an open reproach.' The problematic 'Racha' represented the second step. Cf the footnote in RSV and NRSV where 'Raca' is explained as an obscure term of abuse. See Erasmus' reaction to an anonymous scholar who criticized Erasmus' explanation of the word (287–8) below.

commands to be punished. Whoever, therefore, has obtained for himself gospel love, which wishes well upon even those who are wishing ill, that repays injury with kindness, this person has no need at all of the threats [100] of the Mosaic law to avoid murder.

Among the Jews he seems godly and religious who, while plotting mischief against his brother, brings some gift to the altar. But you, if by chance you are preparing to offer some gift to God near the altar and at that point it occurs to you that there is some discord between you and your brother, do not delay, do not put it off, but leaving the gift at the altar, hurry home and see to it that first of all the sweetness of friendship between you and your brother is restored. With this done you will return to the altar to complete your sacrifice. God does not suffer any loss from a gift delayed but no service is acceptable to God that love does not commend. If you say to me: 'I have done nothing wrong; let the other person who was the source of the offence first seek reconciliation,' I will not listen.[146] You will not experience God's kindness if your neighbour does not perceive your kindness towards him. Your gift will have no grace in the eyes of God if the grace of good-will does not exist between you and your brother.

[101] Thus far I have given an example concerning love and hate, in the first of which is the root of all gospel piety, in the second, the root of all ruin. But murder has for its next-door neighbour adultery, and no love is more binding than that found in marriage. Therefore on this subject, too, let us consider what the Law enjoined upon your ancestors and how much I am adding. In the book of the Law they were told only: 'You shall not commit adultery; if you do, you will be stoned by the people.'[147] And so, [102] thus far among the Jews whoever has stayed away from another man's wife, content with his own, has been regarded as holy and blameless. But according to the gospel law that I am delivering, it is not only the man who violates another man's wife by a base act, and entwines body with body, who commits adultery, but so also does the man who looks upon another man's wife with unchaste eyes. For just as a person who is angry with his brother is close to murder, so a person whose mind is already impure, whose eyes are adulterous, tends to adultery. The husband has no reason to summon you to pay the penalty for adultery, but God, in whose eyes a person has

146 Ironically, Erasmus himself seemed unable to follow this excellent advice in his relationship with Budé, who, he felt, should take the first step in restoring their broken friendship; cf 279–82 and CWE 41 323–4. Cf also 99 n67 above.

147 Cf Exod 20:14, Deut 22:20–4.

committed a shameful act once he has willed it, has reason to condemn you for adultery.

Here a man of the flesh[148] will say, 'Who can restrain himself from lusting at least in his heart for what he loves?' Rather, who will love the wife of another man – at his own peril and with injury to her husband – if he is so disposed that he not only does not want to harm any innocent person, but even strives to pay back kindness for evil to those who have injured him? 'I cannot keep my eyes closed,' he will say. Rather, it is better to pluck out your eye than through it to suffer the loss of godliness. One must so hasten to the summit of gospel perfection that whatever has kept you from attaining it must be thrown away immediately, however sweet and lovable it may be. Accordingly, if by chance your right eye becomes an impediment to you as you hasten to this goal, do not consider how dear your eye is, but consider how much more precious is the thing it keeps you from, and without delay pluck out the eye that obstructs you, throw it away, and hurry on to where you were aiming when you began. When the whole man is threatened with death, it is preferable to regain the health of the rest of the body by the loss of one limb.

[103] I have said these things to instruct by analogy, but I will now speak more clearly so that you may better understand what I intend. I do not mean that a person should himself cut off parts of his own body, since the nature of the limbs is not evil, though their misuse must be condemned. I am speaking about the limbs of the heart, for the heart also has its own harmful limbs, and it is a godly act to cut them off as quickly as possible. The limbs of the mind are the emotions. There are certain emotions that by their very nature lead to impiety, for example, anger, hate, envy, covetousness. If any one of these begins to sprout in the heart, it must be cut off immediately, for an evil is cut off both more easily and more safely at its nascent stage. Then again, there are emotions that are not exactly evil in themselves, but nevertheless sometimes given the [104] right opportunity lead one away from what is best, for example, love of one's native land, devotion to one's wife, children, and parents, or concern for one's reputation. If these limbs serve well a person who is hastening to gospel perfection, there is no reason to amputate. For my teaching is not in conflict with natural feelings, but it restores nature to its own purity. If, however, your affection for a parent or wife or children obstructs you from pursuing gospel piety, and drags you back to the world, cut away that harmful piety.

148 Cf 1 Cor 3:1–3 ('man of the flesh').

Now let us consider another example. The Mosaic law allows a husband offended by some fault in his wife to dismiss her at his own discretion. He has only to give a certificate of divorce to the wife he has repudiated, thereby enabling her to marry another man and depriving himself, as her former husband, of any right to claim back the woman he has cast off.[149] Accordingly, the husband who has divorced his wife for any reason at all has satisfied the Law, provided he has given her a certificate when she leaves. He will not be judged an adulterer, nor will anyone point to her as an adulteress. Although the Law desired that the friendship and concord between spouses would last forever, yet aware of the hardness of the Jews' hearts, it allowed divorce,[150] so that nothing more heinous might be committed – poisoning, for instance, or murder. But among those who [105] profess the New Law, I want marriage to be something holier and more inviolate. For whoever divorces his wife – unless she is an adulteress (for she has stopped being his wife if she has had sexual relations with another man)[151] – forces her into adultery, since if she marries another man she will marry not a husband, but an adulterer; and he who marries a woman who has been thus repudiated does not marry a wife, but an adulteress. The Mosaic law does not punish any of these, but the gospel law condemns them. If, then, the Law is designed to make marriage sacred and does not grant divorces indiscriminately, I have not abolished the Law but I have assisted it inasmuch as I want no divorce, except in the case of unfaithfulness, which contradicts the very nature of marriage,[152] since [106] marriage has been instituted so that a woman once bound to one husband might bear children for him alone and obey him alone.

You have heard that your forbears received from tradition the simple precept that they should not swear falsely, but if they did take an oath they should discharge it, inasmuch as they were now responsible to God, and not only to a human being.[153] Hence among the Jews only perjury is punished; one who cheats his neighbour without committing perjury

149 Cf Deut 24:1–4.

150 Cf Matt 19:8.

151 In defending his comments here about a marriage ceasing *de facto* to exist, Erasmus explained, 'God had said that in marriage "two become one flesh"; adultery results in one flesh becoming two, thus contradicting the very nature of marriage'; cf CWE 45 105 n92. Selections from Erasmus' lengthy discussion on divorce will be found in the annotation on 1 Cor 7:39 below 267–75.

152 Cf preceding note.

153 Cf Num 30:2, Lev 19:12, Deut 23:21.

is not punished by the assembly. But the gospel law does condemn and punish such a person, for in order to protect you more completely from perjury, the gospel law utterly condemns all oath swearing. As a result it is now not permitted to swear either by God or by those things that are commonly thought of as having less binding power. [107] Since all things are sacred to God the creator, to swear by anything at all ought to be a matter of scruple. Yet what need is there for any swearing among people not one of whom is distrustful thanks to his integrity, or desires to deceive thanks to his honesty. In contracts therefore there is no need to add oaths or curses or anything similar that serves through fear to bind the one who promises, and serves to give confidence to the one who demands the promise. Two words, yes and no, are quite enough to say that you will do what you have pledged to do, and that you will not do what you have promised not to do. [108] Thus, although I absolutely forbid swearing, I do not abolish the law that forbids perjury, but I render the law more complete.

You have heard what the Law has allowed our forefathers to do in avenging an injury: 'An eye for an eye, a tooth for a tooth.'[154] For it knew that their hearts were eager for revenge. Therefore it restrained the lust for revenge to the extent that from the decision of the judges a wrong would be compensated with punishment in kind, and he who had poked out someone's eye lost an eye, and he who knocked out someone's tooth was punished with the loss of a tooth. Otherwise, if the punishment for an injury had been left to the inclination of the injured person, frequently a person would take a life to pay for a knocked out tooth. Therefore the Law intended that punishment should not go further than was fair. Now I do not break this law, I strengthen it, since I teach you that [109] absolutely no vengeance should be sought for injuries however grievous, nor should any abusive word be repaid with an abusive word, or an injury with an injury. So absolute is my teaching that if someone strikes your cheek with a blow – an intolerable affront – far from slapping him back you should rather offer your other cheek to be struck, and should prefer to bear with patience a double injury than to retaliate.

[110] Take now also this precept that is regarded as the chief one in the Law: 'You shall love your neighbour [Lev 19:18] and hate your enemy.'[155] It demands kindness, but only towards those who are kind and well

154 Cf Exod 21:24, Lev 24:20, Deut 19:21.

155 On 'love to neighbour' as the chief commandment see the reference to Lev 19:18 98 above.

deserving, whereas it allows us to bear ill will towards those who injure us. You see how I do not take anything away from this precept, but how much I add to it. For, not satisfied merely with kindnesses shared among friends, I require you, the followers of my teaching, to love your enemies as well, and not only not return with hatred the hatred of those who persecute, but even to incite them to love through kindnesses.

As you practise this goodness upon everyone, both good and evil, you will show that you are genuine children of the heavenly Father, who [111] in his desire to save everyone bestows so many good things upon the worthy and unworthy. He allows his sun to be enjoyed in common both by those who worship him and those who despise him, and he allows his rain to be useful equally to the just and unjust, with his kindness calling the evil to return to their senses, inspiring the good to give thanks. The same kind of behaviour will declare that you belong to the heavenly Father, and they will believe that your teaching comes from him, if they see in you his outstanding goodness.

[Matthew 6] [111] I have made clear in what respects you must surpass the righteousness of the scribes and Pharisees if you want to be my disciples. I will now show what you must avoid when you seem to do the things they do. For there is a certain silent disease that actually spoils all the good things the Pharisees do, so that they merit no praise at all before God. To help the needy with [112] kindness is a holy thing. To converse with God through pure prayers is a godly thing. Fasting is a devout thing. By an ostentatious display of these actions the Pharisees lay claim to a reputation for a certain outstanding holiness before men, although they displease God, who looks not upon the appearance but upon the heart. They deserve this displeasure because their hearts are corrupted by vainglory. Not that good deeds must always be concealed. But one must not act out a play for human viewing, like actors performing a play on the stage, whose only desire is to please the eyes and ears of the people.

[114] Accordingly, when you pray to God, do not follow the manner of the hypocrites who, whenever they pray, delight in standing in the public meeting places and in the corners of the plazas, for no other reason than to be seen by those from whom they hope to win praise for their holiness. [115] And stay far away from the example of the pagans, who go through long and verbose prayers as if with set formulaic expressions, just as though they would obtain nothing if they did not weary God with their most verbose loquacity, constantly and emphatically repeating the same things, and outlining with a wordy enumeration what they want and when, and how they want what they want presented to them – though they often pray for harmful things. Only

the best things must be sought from God, not everything, and one must pray frequently rather than at length, with attention more than verbosity, more with the heart than with the voice. Moreover, one should not pray with a set form of words, but to whatever extent the heat of the mind and spiritual ecstasy have prompted. The Father indeed loves to be asked, not in order to be informed of your needs by a long prayer since he knows what you need even before you ask.

If you want a model of gospel prayer prescribed to you, [116] receive now [117] the form:

Our Father, you have begotten us, once unhappily begotten from Adam, now a second time from heaven.[156] You have prepared in heaven an everlasting kingdom and inheritance for us, who must be raised above earthly things.[157] You yourself are said to live in heaven because, although you fill all things,[158] you have no earthly impurity or weakness. Grant that through us, who are pure and spotless by your kindness, your name may become renowned and glorious among human beings. For whatever is rightly done by us is not our glory, since it is your gift. Let Satan's tyranny be destroyed so that your kingdom may grow ever stronger day by day, a kingdom that endures not by its resources or the protection of its guards, but by modesty, chastity, gentleness, tolerance, faith, and love, so that, once vices and wicked desires have been cast aside, your heavenly virtues may exert their own force among human beings. And just as in heaven all things have been made peaceful and there is no creature that does not obey your commands, so on earth let there at last be no one who does not obey your most holy will, while even now everyone practises (as far as the weakness of human nature allows) what will come to pass to perfection in the life to come. Nourish, Father, what you have begotten. Provide for us so that we might not lack the bread of your heavenly teaching, in order that, by its [118] daily consumption, we might be strengthened and become mature, and invigorated to fulfil your commands.[159] And when sometimes you have

---

156 Cf John 3:7. In the phrase 'a second time from heaven' Erasmus combines two meanings of the Greek *anothen* found in John 3:3 and 7: '[begotten] again' and '[begotten from] above.'

157 The language evokes images from John 14:2–4 and 1 Pet 1:4.

158 Cf Jer 23:24, Eph 4:10.

159 The Greek in the fourth petition is ambiguous, either 'daily bread' or 'coming bread' (ie 'bread of tomorrow,' the heavenly bread). Both interpretations are found in the exegetical tradition, but Erasmus emphasizes here the interpretation that understands the expression as the bread from heaven that nourishes our spiritual lives, anticipating the life in heaven; cf 122 n125 above.

been offended by our transgressions, do not turn away from us, but by virtue of your clemency forgive us the transgressions that we commit against you through our weakness, so that we might have peace with you.[160] In the same way we too nourish mutual harmony as we, among ourselves, forgive each other our mutual sins. When your favour is upon us, we fear nothing, and strengthened by concord we are more steadfast against the common enemy. If it is possible, do not, we pray, hand us over to the enemy to be tempted, for we know his malice, we know his wickedness and craftiness. But if you allow us to fall into temptation in order to test the constancy of our hearts,[161] free us, O Father, who are best of all, from that worst of all beings. May your goodness will that these prayers be fulfilled.[162]

[121] As you are hastening with all desire to the things that are best and perfect, lay up for yourselves treasures in heaven so that you might be made truly rich; the protection of these riches will not torment you with anxious concern. [123] The common run of rich people is accustomed to excuse the disease of avarice under the pretext of human necessity. 'With these things,' they say, 'one takes care of hunger and nakedness.' So say they who do not depend totally on God, but who trust in their own help. I want you to be free from this anxiety also, so that nothing as a result of this care should divert you from the desire for better things. Nature's requirements are content with very little, and there is easily at hand from any number of sources what is sufficient for the kind of people I want my disciples to be. [124] The Father will not forsake his own: to all souls longing for heavenly things, especially those without anxiety, he who bestows the greater things will add these less important things. And so, do not store up for the distant future, do not be tormented with anxiety about providing the food essential to life,

---

160 Cf Rom 5:1 'we have peace with God.'

161 Cf the story of Job handed over by God to Satan to test his faithfulness, Job 1:8–12, 2:3–6; cf CWE 45 118 n31.

162 In the *Paraphrase* on Matthew the Lord's Prayer is framed by a summary interpretation preceding the main interpretation given here and another summary interpretation immediately following it, thus in effect paraphrased three times; the paraphrase thus tripled is an indication of its importance. For this triple paraphrase see CWE 45 116–19. Following the Vulgate Erasmus omits the doxology. He included it in his New Testament text, but recognized that it was in fact a liturgical addition to the text of Scripture. Erasmus wrote a lengthy exposition of the Lord's Prayer in a separately published *Paraphrase* (CWE 69 56–77), interpreted it in *On Praying to God* (CWE 70 205–9), and in the *Exposition of the Creed* (CWE 70 386), and echoed it in *The Complaint of Peace* (CWE 27 309–10) and in the *Paraphrase on Acts* (CWE 50 24–5; cf the reference in n159 above).

about providing the clothing that covers the body and protects from the severity of the cold. Is not the body more precious than clothing? Will he who has given the things that are so much better, and who has given them to those who are free from care, be reluctant to nourish with these less valuable things and to protect what he has given?

[125] Accordingly, when you see that he values you so highly that he has imparted to your body, arranged with marvellous foresight, a soul that is rational and similar to the minds of angels;[163] that he thinks you worthy of the title of sons; that by his freely given love he has chosen you out of all – you by whose faultless lives and unadulterated teaching he might become known and glorious among the entire race of mortals, you whom he has destined to an inheritance of eternal life;[164] when you see this, cast away that worry about lowly and sordid things that makes you say, anxious and trembling: 'What shall we eat or what shall we drink or with what shall we be clothed?' Those are the words of pagans, not Christians, for pagans [126] either do not believe that God exists, or do not believe that he cares about mortals.[165]

But someone will say: 'What, then? Shall we not acquire with the work of our hands that by which we might support our wives, our children, and ourselves? By which we might alleviate the need of the poor?' By all means, but without anxiety. Work if circumstances warrant it, but work without anxiety. If money comes your way without fraud and apart from business dealings, accept it, [127] but in such a way that its care does not at all hinder you from the work of the gospel. You are doing something too important to be, with any propriety, diverted by the care for insignificant and transient things. Let your first care be for that good compared to which those things are of no importance. The kingdom of God must be established, that is, the gospel teaching by which one attains the heavenly inheritance. I have chosen you as its heralds and promoters, and I have shown you the extraordinary virtues you will need to carry out this work, that you love your enemies, and that you pray for the salvation of those who work for your destruction.

---

163 Cf 1 John 3:1, Luke 20:36. Reflection on the glorious nature of the human person was a commonplace of Renaissance thought, as in Shakespeare's *Hamlet* II ii 315–20. For a more elaborate expression of the commonplace see the *De immensa Dei misericordia* CWE 70 102–4.

164 Cf Rom 8:15–17 (sons), Eph 1:4–5, John 15:19 (chosen), Eph 1:12–14, 1 Pet 1:2–5 (inheritance of eternal life).

165 The latter was the view of the Epicureans; cf CWE 50 107 with n20.

[**Matthew 7**] [128] There is another way in which I want you to be far removed from the conduct of the scribes and Pharisees. Although they forgive themselves when they have committed the gravest sins, nevertheless towards a brother who sins they play the part of most unmerciful judges, unjustly blaming even the things that are right, interpreting perversely what is in doubt, exaggerating what is trivial, and raging with great haughtiness against the failing of others while they indulge their own far more serious sins. [129] But sometimes it befalls the haughty that the precedent of an unjust judgment falls back on its very authors, and they in turn find others to be such censors of their lives as they have been of others' lives. Consequently, do not judge others, that you might not be similarly judged by others. For just as favour provokes favour, and clemency provokes clemency, so slander provokes slander, and rage provokes rage. No one rages more fiercely against a neighbour's failings, however minor, than those who themselves are soaked in far worse vices. This one publicly ridicules his brother because he wears a garment without a cincture[166] when he himself is completely drenched with envy. There is nothing another will not say against his brother because, overcome by the weakness of the flesh, he has taken a concubine, when he himself is totally enslaved by greed and ambition. Another curses his brother because he drinks a little too much, when he himself harbours in his breast so many murders, so many poisonings, is so blind to his own swollen tumours, and is so very keen to see a little wart on another. What kind of distorted judgment is this?

[130] Although I want you to be quick to do kindnesses to everyone, tolerant towards those who inflict injuries upon you, open and candid towards those who fall through human weakness, and, finally, so disposed even towards the perverse that you prefer to correct rather than destroy them, nevertheless I do not want the mystery of gospel wisdom revealed to the worthy and unworthy without distinction. You who possess the things that are truly holy and that surpass all pearls however precious,[167] beware that you do not cast the gospel riches to the unworthy. Those are dogs who in their wholehearted devotion to profane things shrink from things that savour of sanctity; those are swine who, completely immersed in obscene pleasures, curse the pure and chaste teaching of the gospel. One must not thrust the secrets of heavenly teaching upon those who display their contempt for sounder instruction so openly that there seems to be no hope of fruit. [131] Therefore, it

166 An allusion, apparently, to monastic costume.

167 Cf Matt 13:45–6.

is to the eager, or at least the curable, that the gospel philosophy is to be communicated. And it is not to be entrusted in its entirety immediately to everyone, but as each person has offered evidence of his progress, so are the more arcane elements to be disclosed.[168]

[132] Since it would be prolix to lay down rules for every single thing pertaining to social intercourse, which is hurt or helped by insults or favours reciprocated in turn, I will give a general rule whose force has been implanted in everyone by nature. [133] Prove yourselves to be towards others the kind of person you would like others to be towards you. There is no one who, when he falls into error, does not want to be admonished lovingly and in secret rather than to be publicly exposed. There is no one in need who does not want to be relieved; no one wants his good name disparaged; no one wants to be cheated. Therefore, from this common feeling that has been placed in every mortal, let each one determine what sort of person he should be in relation to his neighbour. He should not do to another what he would not want done to himself; he should do to another what he would be glad to have done to himself. This is the sum and substance of all that the Law and the Prophets teach. If anyone is unable to read through these texts, at least everyone has within himself a rule by which to guide his actions, provided he prefers to obey reason rather than his desires.[169]

If these things seem difficult to those who love this world, if you see the great majority of people following in the opposite direction, do not let anything unsettle your mind. Access to the best things is difficult. Be more concerned about where the way leads than whether it has an easy entry. Imagine two gates, the one narrow, to which the only access is by a narrow path, a path that soon leads to eternal life; the other wide and open, to which a broad road offers access to everyone, but a road that soon leads to eternal ruin. Since the broad way restrains no one with the laws of piety, since it attracts with the things that delight the bodily senses and caress the desires of the mind, it easily entices many people to itself; however, after they have been charmed for a short time,

168 This expression of the historic 'doctrine of reserve' (ie the view that Christian knowledge should be disclosed only in the degree appropriate to the learner's worthiness and capacity to receive), appears elsewhere in Erasmus; note especially the paraphrase on 1 Cor 2:6–8 CWE 43 46 with n14 and the paraphrase on Luke 9:17 CWE 47 253.

169 In this exposition of the 'Golden Rule' Erasmus virtually equates the revelation derived from Scripture with the truth of 'natural law.' Cf the paraphrase on Matt 10:35–7, where Jesus in the paraphrase says, 'I do not abolish the law of nature, I perfect it' CWE 45 177–8 with n53.

it sends them through the wide gate into unspeakable calamities, and those who have been deceived by false goods it hands over to true evils.

[134] By contrast, how narrow is the gate that leads to life, how constrained the way! For it offers nothing to soothe the flesh; it is harsh to many. It immediately casts in one's way the things that are burdensome even to nature: poverty, fasting, vigils, endurance of wrongs suffered, chastity, sobriety. This gate does not receive people who are puffed up with pride, or who are bulging with extravagance, or who are laden with the baggage of riches. It receives only the naked, and those who have been freed from all the desires of this world, and those who have, as it were, stripped off their bodies and been rarefied into spirit. You, however, are in no danger from those who make their way towards death, sporting with lust, excess, pride, greed, and the other desires, and laughing their insane laugh. Rather, it is against those who become your companions, having the appearance of godliness, though they are its enemies, that you must be on your guard. They talk of God the Father, the gospel teaching, the kingdom of heaven. Their clothing is plain, their faces are pale with fasting, their bodies are emaciated, they pray at length, they give to the poor, they instruct the people and interpret the holy books, and they come to you under the guise of these things, as if clothed in the skin of a sheep, though beneath they are ravenous wolves and manglers of the gospel flock. The wolf changes his voice, even professes the name [135] of Christ, professes the gospel doctrine. He feigns the works of godliness so he can more effectively use the simplicity of others for his own desires. Therefore you must take care to beware of these.[170]

[138] Whoever hears my words, and does not merely hear them but lets them sink into his innermost affections,[171] so that he expresses what he has learned through his actions, such a one, I say, is like a thoughtful and prudent man who, in order to construct a solid and strong building, first of all looks to find a solid and unmovable foundation on which to build a base that will withstand all the assaults of storms. To be sure, when the sky is serene any building whatever stands easily, but winter proves a structure's strength. At one time the force of the rain falls and strikes upon it, at another time the rivers swollen by rain shake it with their mighty onrush, then again the fury of winds pounds against it,

170 A barely disguised attack on monks and monasticism. For similar attacks see the *Enchiridion* and the *De contemptu mundi* CWE 66 20–3 and 173–4.

171 The notion that Scripture is to be 'transferred' into the affections is emphatically expressed in the *Ratio*; cf 41–2 above.

and yet, though buffeted in so many ways, it stands unmoved because it rests upon a solid foundation. On the other hand, whoever hears my words, but only hears them, and neither transfuses them into his affections, nor expresses them in actions, is like an imprudent builder who does not foresee the coming storms and places his building upon sand, obviously a shifting and utterly untrustworthy foundation. Later there rushes upon the house the force of the rain, the violence of the floods, the blast of the wind, and the house is wrenched away and removed from its foundations and falls with a great crash because the structure was resting on a useless foundation. Let your first care therefore be for the foundation. Fasting, almsgiving, prayers are like a splendid building. If, however, one who does these things looks for the empty praise of people, or for gain, or pleasure, everything will come crashing down if ever the raging storm of temptations rushes against it. On the other hand a person, whose affection has been fixed on the teaching and promises of the gospel, and who awaits from God alone the reward for deeds rightly done, will stand firm and unbroken [139] against all the machinations of Satan, even against death itself.

(2) Parables of Jesus

Parable of the Wheat and the Weeds
(from Matthew 13 CWE 45 212–16)

[**Matthew 13**] [212] Now to return to the sequence of the foregoing discourse, the Lord Jesus related also another parable to show that one must beware of another bane if one wants to store pure and unspoiled wheat in one's barn. This bane is when Satan attempts by means of false apostles and impious bishops and heretics to corrupt heavenly teaching to accommodate their own evil desires, as they twist it with deceitful interpretation, and mix true things with false, the sound with defective.

The parable goes like this: [213] 'The kingdom of heaven is like the householder who, since he was a good man, had sown good seed in his field. While the family servants were sleeping, there came secretly a certain enemy, who wanted to harm the householder. Since that enemy was not able to take away the seed by night, because it was already planted safely in the ground, he set about doing harm by craft: he scattered useless cockle seed and mixed it with the sown wheat. With this done he went away. At first no one noticed the treachery. But when the seed had now emerged as blades, and the stalks were weighed down with ears, then at last the cockles that were sown with the wheat began to appear, their difference now obvious. Then the slaves, at a loss to imagine how this had happened, came to the householder and said: "Master, did you not sow good seed in your field? How then did the cockle get mixed in?" The master, surmising an author of the injurious act, said: "An enemy has done this, a man who so wishes me ill that he takes pleasure in doing me harm, even if he gains no advantage for himself." Then the slaves said, "Do you want us, then, to go and gather the cockles, and clean the crop?" The master said: "By no means, lest by chance while you pluck out the cockles you unwittingly uproot the neighbouring wheat. Allow the wheat to grow along with the cockles until harvest time. Then I will make it the responsibility of the harvesters that before they harvest, they first gather the cockles that are mixed in, and put them separately into little bundles as fuel for the fire, and then store the pure wheat in my barn."'

[214] Then Jesus sent the crowd away and went home. When he was alone at home, his closest disciples came to him asking him to explain to them the parable about the cockles mixed with the wheat. Jesus, not at all annoyed, told them in a clear manner. He said, 'The good householder who sowed the good seed is the heavenly Father; the field in which [215] he sowed is the entire world, not just Judea. The wheat that sprang up, a good crop from good seed, are those people who, as a result of gospel teaching, become worthy of the heavenly kingdom, making their lives and their deeds correspond to what they profess. The bad cockles, which are mixed in with them from the bad seed, are wicked people who profess the gospel teaching insincerely. The enemy who secretly mixed in his own seed by night – from which arises perverse teaching – is the devil. The slaves who want to collect the cockles before the time is right are those who think that false apostles and heretics should be removed from our midst by the sword and by death, though the householder does not want them to be destroyed, but to be tolerated, if by chance they might come to their senses and repent, and be turned from cockles into wheat. If they do not repent, let them be saved for their judge, to whom they will pay the penalty some day.

The time for harvest is the consummation of the age. The reapers are the angels. Therefore, in the meantime, evil persons mixed with the good must be endured, since they are tolerated with less harm than they could be removed. But when that final time comes, when the good will be separated from the bad, then the Son of Man, judge of all, will send his angels, who will purge his kingdom. Those who troubled the good [216] he will gather together apart from the others and deliver them to the fire of hell. There they will be afflicted with never-ending torments.

But those who have sprung from good seed and have persevered to the end will gleam like the sun in the kingdom of their Father.'

Parable of the Rich Fool
(from the paraphrase on Luke 12 CWE 48 30–4)

[**Luke 12**] [31] An opportunity presented itself that enabled the Lord to remove from deep within the hearts of his disciples [30] the desire for money. [31] For someone said, 'My brother is holding our joint inheritance; he refuses to be pinned down and is putting off the division of the property. Tell him to divide the inheritance with me.' But Jesus, as if displeased at being interrupted in his heavenly task for sordid cares replied, 'Fellow, with what brazenness do you interrupt me over a trivial thing! Doesn't this world have judges to settle such petty lawsuits? I was appointed not so that one might be made richer, but so that everyone might come to eternal life.'

Then turning to the disciples and the others who were there he began to dissuade them from the pursuit of wealth – not that wealth is a bad thing in itself, but because it is folly to set wealth as the primary safeguard of one's life and to be called away from the things that concern eternal bliss by the pursuit of it. 'Be continually on guard,' he said, 'against everything that borders on greed, for often under pretext of need and prudence the gloomy vice creeps up, which once let in leads a person astray into every sort of disgrace. [32] Plenty does not make for happiness but for worry, and nature's needs are in fact satisfied with little.'

To implant this more deeply in the people the Lord added a comparison by which everyone might examine and test his own disposition. [33] 'There was a rich man,' he said, 'whose fields had produced very abundant crops. Yet he, never thinking about relieving his neighbours' poverty but just as if the produce was for only one person, was worried about storing it, not about disbursing it. For he said to himself, "What shall I do? The yield of grain is too great for my barns to be able to store the crop." If he had let himself be guided by love when he was in such mental turmoil, love would have said to him "Look around at how many are in need of what you have in excess. Acknowledge to whom you owe even your year's productivity. God has favoured you with capital from which you may garner the interest of heavenly deeds. Exchange transitory goods for permanent ones, earthly for heavenly, human for divine. Thus your generosity will have been your gain." But since he preferred to be guided by folly and thoughtlessness, at their urging he said to himself, "I will tear down my old barns and build bigger ones, and put all this year's yield, and the rest of my goods, in them, so nothing is lost. And then free of all care I will say to my soul, 'Soul, you have a large supply of things put by that will be enough for many years; relax, eat, drink, and enjoy yourself.'"

[34] 'While the rich man was turning over in his mind this daydream of long-term happiness, suddenly the voice of God came to him, saying, "You fool, since life itself is not guaranteed you, why are you storing up for years to come? For only in this life can you enjoy the things you are putting away, and no one is guaranteed life for even a single day. Why are you promising yourself many years? This very night they will require your soul of you. And the things you have acquired – whose will they be? They certainly won't be yours. You will have to leave them to your heir, or to anyone else who seizes them. But spiritual riches, which you could have acquired by disbursing your wealth, would have accompanied you even in death." Here you have the example of a man who stores up for himself the riches of this world and who is only rich for himself but not rich before God, for God desires that relief be provided among his members through those who are well-to-do. And those who become poor in this way are more blessedly rich.'

CHAPTER FIVE

Paraphrases on the Pauline Epistles

[In 1499 Erasmus visited England at the invitation of William Blount, Baron Mountjoy, whom he had been tutoring in Paris. During the visit he met John Colet, who was then at Oxford, but later became Dean of St Paul's Cathedral and refounded and endowed St Paul's School. Colet was an avid interpreter of St Paul and a theologian with whom Erasmus had vigorous discussions at Oxford, some of which are recorded in his early letters (cf Epp 108–11). After Erasmus returned to Paris he undertook to write a commentary on the Pauline Epistles but eventually gave up the attempt because, he said, he had discovered that he needed Greek at every point (cf 4 above). In 1511 he took up a lectureship at Cambridge and very soon wrote to Colet that he might even start lecturing 'on your (ie Colet's) St Paul' (Ep 225:22). He left Cambridge in 1514, and as he was on his way to Ghent his horse suddenly took fright with a resulting injury to Erasmus' back so severe that he could not dismount without help. Then and there he vowed to God and to St Paul that if the sainted 'apostle to the gentiles' would heal him he would write a commentary on his Epistles, a promise he was never to fulfil. Nevertheless, Erasmus' continuing interest in the apostle was manifested in numerous ways. His first *Paraphrase* was on the Epistle to the Romans, for which he wrote an 'Argument' (ie an introduction) of unusual length. As a preface to Acts he transformed a brief Greek 'Travelogue' into a major document detailing the sequence of events in the life of Paul, and relating the events to a chronology that correlated the details of the apostle's life with the chronology of Roman imperial history. In his later years he was approached by Jacopo Sadoleto, papal secretary and cardinal, who sought his advice while attempting to write a commentary on Paul, and by the Lutheran Philippus Melanchthon who sought his approval for a commentary on Paul he had already written. Thus Paul, both the man and the preacher-theologian, loomed large in the life and thought of Erasmus. The selections that follow attempt to catch Erasmus' vision, as suggested in his paraphrases, of this extraordinary apostle. We begin by attempting to trace Erasmus' efforts to imagine a biography of Paul, which included the Apostle's understanding of who he was as an apostle; for this I draw upon Erasmus' paraphrastic elaboration of Paul's own statements in the Pauline Epistles (section I). Thereafter we shall see how in the *Paraphrases* Erasmus suggests the theological and moral vision that he believed characterized and motivated St Paul (section II).]

I. IMAGES OF PAUL

(1) A Character Sketch (from the Dedicatory Letter to the *Paraphrase* on 1 and 2 Corinthians, Ep 916:408–50 CWE 43 16–18)

[Erasmus' *Paraphrases* on the Epistles, whether published individually or in a set, were always preceded by both a dedicatory letter to a distinguished individual and an 'Argument' – an account of the contents and circumstances of the writing. Erasmus often used the Argument to speak of the author's style; in the *Paraphrase on the Two Epistles to the Corinthians*, dedicated to Erard de la Marck, prince-bishop of Liège, the dedicatory letter offers, after a long account of the early church and the contents of the first Epistle, a remarkable portrait of the apostle Paul, excerpted here.]

This Paul of ours is always skilful and slippery, but in these two Epistles he is such a squid, such a chameleon – he plays the part of Proteus or Vertumnus[1] turning himself into every shape that he may shape [the Corinthians] anew for Christ; with such freedom does he himself twist and turn like a man who threads the windings of a maze, and appearing to us in a fresh guise every time. How humble and ingratiating he sometimes is, as he beseeches them by the mercy of Christ and begs them to

1 In classical mythology Proteus was the old man of the sea who transformed himself into different shapes to escape those who tried to lay hold of him to compel him to tell them the unknown; cf Homer *Odyssey* 4.384–570. Erasmus frequently alludes to Proteus as an image representing changeability and accommodation to circumstances; cf eg the annotation on Rom 1:4 ('who was predestined') CWE 56 10 with n9. Vertumnus was the old Roman god of the seasons, constantly changing his shape. Cf *De copia*: 'more inconstant than Vertumnus, more unstable than Proteus' CWE 24 388.

bear with his foolishness for a space! Then again he cries in harsh and threatening accents 'Do you seek a proof of Christ speaking in me?'[2] Elsewhere he abases himself and calls himself an off-scouring, misbegotten, and unworthy of the name of Apostle; and then becomes grand and exalted and sets himself even above the greatest of the apostles, crawling upon the ground at one moment, and the next appearing to us out of the third heaven.[3] Now he praises the piety of the Corinthians, now thunders against their faults.[4] Some things he demands openly; others he suggests by a kind of underground approach. Sometimes he is an unready speaker who knows nothing save Jesus, and him crucified; sometimes he speaks wisdom among them that are perfect. In one place he acts the part of an intelligent and sober man; in another he dons the mask of one who is foolish and beside himself.[5] Now he boldly claims his own rights, now courteously resigns them. In one place he speaks from the heart, sometimes resorts to irony, with 'Forgive me this wrong.'[6] You may find that he gives an appearance of inconsistency; but he is most like himself when he seems unlike, and most consistent when he seems the reverse. Always Christ's business is his main concern; always he thinks of the well-being of his flock, like a true physician leaving no remedy untried that may restore his patients to perfect health.

The greatest scholars labour to explain the intentions of poets and orators; but in this orator far more toil is required if you are to understand what he has in mind, what he aims at, and what he is avoiding; so full of tricks is he everywhere, if I may so express it. Such is his versatility, you would hardly think it is the same man speaking. At one time he bubbles up gently like a crystal spring, at another pours roaring down like a great torrent, carrying many things before him; now flows peacefully and gently, now spreads himself as though into a spacious lake. Again, he sometimes plunges underground and reappears suddenly in another place; then, when it suits him, meanders unexpectedly, caressing now this bank and now that; sometimes fetches a long digression and turns back again upon himself. I am the more amazed at

2 Cf 2 Cor 10:1–2 (ingratiating), 11:1 (foolish), 13:3 (threatening).

3 Cf 1 Cor 4:13 (off-scouring), 15:8–9 (misbegotten, unworthy), 2 Cor 11:5, 12:11 (exalts himself), 1 Cor 2:3–4 (crawling on the ground), 2 Cor 12:1–4 (third heaven).

4 Cf eg 1 Cor 11:2, 17 (praise, blame).

5 Cf 1 Cor 2:2–3 and 6 (knows Jesus crucified, speaks wisdom), 2 Cor 11:21–3 (speaks as a fool).

6 Cf 1 Cor 9:3–7, 12 (claims and resigns rights), 2 Cor 12:13 (irony).

some people who, although they have hardly a smattering of grammar and no idea what it is to write, yet suppose an understanding of Paul's language to be an easy and almost childish thing.[7]

(2) Conversion, Call, and Commission (from the paraphrases on Romans 1 and Galatians 1 CWE 42 15 and 99–103)

[However difficult it may be to construct a biography from the letters of Paul, he is nevertheless highly self-revealing in them. It is surprising that he says relatively little about his conversion and call, perhaps the fullest account of which is given in the Epistle to the Galatians. But Erasmus' technique of paraphrasing encouraged him to explicate what seemed to him implied in the first few verses of Romans, offering a sharp contrast between past and present. It is with that passage that we begin.]

[**Romans 1**] [15] I am Paul, though formerly Saul, that is, I have become peaceful, though formerly restless,[8] until recently subject to the law of Moses, now freed from Moses, I have been made a servant of Jesus Christ. Not that I am a deserter or forsaker of my former tradition, but I have been summoned to the duty of this mission, and I am now more happily separated than I was before, when as a champion of the pharisaical sect, I wandered about in error, impiously pious, ignorantly learned. But now at last I am truly worthy of the name Pharisee,[9] inasmuch as I have been set apart and chosen by Christ himself to undertake a task far more glorious, namely, the preaching of the gospel of God. This gospel is by no means new but one long ago promised by him, the gospel concerning his Son who was born in time of the lineage of David according to the infirmity of the flesh, but was also revealed to be the eternal Son of the eternal God according to the Spirit which sanctifies all things. Through him I have obtained not only this grace,[10] which observance of the Law could not have conferred, but also the duties of an apostle, in order that, just as the other apostles have spread

7 For an Erasmian account of the difficulties of Pauline prose see the Argument to the Epistle to the Romans CWE 42 12–14.

8 Erasmus reflects speculation on the names 'Saul' and 'Paul,' which, according to some, meant, respectively, 'restless,' and 'peaceful.' See the annotation on Rom 1:1 ('Paul') CWE 56 4.

9 The word 'Pharisee' means 'set apart.'

10 Ie the grace resulting in his conversion; Paul is thus the recipient of a double grace: conversion and commission.

the gospel among the Jews, so I might preach it among gentiles of every race to prevent them from being overwhelmed by the burdens of the Law but to submit to the faith preached to them concerning Christ and to rely upon this, not upon the empty wisdom of the philosophers.

[**Galatians 1**] [99] At one time I was devoted to Judaism and pleased my people, persecuting in every possible way those who professed the name of Christ. But so long as I please men I displease God, who wished Moses to be set aside and Christ his Son to be brought to light. As long as I was a servant to the Law, I was concerned about protecting the prescriptions of Moses, and I sought praise from man. Now God has called me to something different, and by God alone I desire to be commended. Accordingly, after I once dedicated myself to Christ, I never was slave to the ceremonies of Moses which I knew had been rejected on account of the light of Christ. [100] For although several times, while living among the Jews, I have observed some of the rites of my fathers in order to allay a disturbance, nevertheless I have never regarded those rites as an aid to salvation. I accommodated myself for a time to the feelings of my own people in order to win more to Christ.[11] But now I must publicly and freely cry out against the Mosaic rites and solemnly renounce that which turns into an injury to Christ.

I want you to know, brethren, that the gospel that we have delivered to you is not subject to human authority, so that it should be changed at the whim of any person. For I did not procure my gospel from any human being nor was I taught it by man, that I should be compelled either to depend on the authority of anyone or to follow his interpretation. Christ himself saw fit to reveal to me the mystery of the abolition of the old Law, and of the introduction of the new law. I do not think that what I tell you is obscure. For I believe you know already, through my reputation, how eagerly I formerly displayed my Judaism through my love of the Law, and how I abhorred the gospel of Christ, the secret of which I had not yet received.[12] I went so far as to attack, in every possible manner, the new congregation which at that time had begun to gather by the Spirit of God around the teaching of the gospel. In fact, in Judaism, which alone at that time I judged to be holy and pious, I gained so much praise

---

11 Cf eg Timothy circumcised (Acts 16:3); also Paul's vow taken to accommodate Jews in Jerusalem (Acts 21:23–6), although in relation to the (generally accepted) early date of Galatians a reference to the vow taken at a later date in Paul's ministry is anachronistic here.

12 'Secret,' ie the 'mystery' (mentioned just above). In the text here the secret revealed to Paul was that the gospel was open to the gentiles without subjection to the Mosaic law.

among my own people that I distinguished myself above most men of my age. [101] The more doggedly I clung to the traditions handed down by my forefathers, the more religious I was considered. For I erred in judgment, not in heart,[13] and I opposed the author of the Law out of zeal for the Law. God allowed this for a time by some secret plan of his. Accordingly, when it pleased God – who had designated and selected me already long ago for this undertaking when I was still in my mother's womb – to reveal his will toward me, and when he called me to this service by his own gracious goodness, in order to use me as an instrument to make known his Son Jesus, what do you think I did? Did I hesitate to undertake the duty assigned to me?[14] Did I distrust the oracular command of Christ?[15] Did I discuss my gospel with any apostles of my own race? Did I go to Jerusalem, so that my gospel might be supported by the authority of those who, because they were called to the apostolic rank before me, are highly esteemed? None of these!

As a matter of fact, immediately after I discovered the error of my ways, after I accepted my command from heaven, I went without delay to Arabia and did not shrink from presenting the name of Christ to wild and barbarian races. And I preached the grace of the gospel with no less zeal than I formerly had preached the Mosaic law. After I left Arabia, I returned to Damascus where I had first begun to preach the name of Christ after I was baptized. Then after three years I came to Jerusalem in order to visit Peter rather than to confer with him.[16] However, I stayed with him no more than fifteen days, because he seemed to hold first place among the apostles. I was not eager to see any of the other apostles except James. I do not lie. God himself is my witness.[17] After

---

13 A common rationalization of God's choice of the persecuting Paul for the high calling of an apostle; cf 1 Tim 1:13 and the paraphrase on Acts 9:15 CWE 50 65.

14 For Paul as instrument see Acts 9:15. To act without hesitation is, in Erasmus' view, a sign of true faith. See the paraphrase on Rom 4:20 CWE 42 31.

15 For the oracular command see Acts 9:15 and 26:16–18.

16 Both Erasmus' translation and his annotation on 1:18 ('to see Peter') suggest that in Erasmus' mind the 'visit' was more than a courtesy call (cf just below, 'an appropriate courtesy'); cf the annotation on Gal 1:18 CWE 58 17.

17 Neither in his *Paraphrase* on Acts 9 nor in that on Galatians 1 does Erasmus attempt to reconcile the two accounts of Paul's activities immediately after his conversion. His paraphrase here on Gal 1:15–20 stresses the immediacy with which Paul began to carry out his designated mission; in this Erasmus may reflect Jerome's reading of the text reported in his annotation on Gal 1:16 ('I did not acquiesce in'): 'When he had set me apart … to preach him among the Gentiles immediately, I did not confer … '; cf CWE 58 14–15. But Erasmus was puzzled by the apparent discrepancies between the two narratives; cf 'Travels of the Apostles' CWE 41 957–8 with n35.

these things I went into the regions of Syria and Cilicia, proclaiming everywhere the name of Christ. For in these regions also some congregations of Jews had begun to unite in the teaching of Christ. But I was little known by sight to them, even though I myself was a Jew by birth. This only had they learned from rumour, that I was the one who had suddenly been changed by [102] the divine will from a persecutor of the Christian faith, and that I had now become a preacher of that faith; that the faith which I at one time opposed with all my might I now defended at peril to my life.

[**Galatians 2**] [102] When I had already preached the doctrine of the gospel for fourteen years, chiefly to the gentiles, I went again to Jerusalem with my associates Barnabas and Titus, whom I wanted to be witnesses to this fact. I did this, however, not as an appropriate courtesy as was the case earlier, but commanded by a divine oracle in order that it would be all the more clear to the Jews that salvation is no longer to be sought through circumcision, but through faith in the gospel. I discussed with them my gospel which up to now I preach among the heathen by Christ's command. I spoke primarily to those who were most influential among the Jews, to the end that none of them who still believed in combining the Mosaic law with the gospel of Christ would publicly assert that in the race course[18] of the gospel I had been running, or was still running, in vain.

[103] After I had shared my gospel with them, they perceived that the duty of preaching the gospel among the gentiles had been entrusted to me by Christ, just as the duty of preaching it among the Jews had been delegated to Peter. As a result, Peter, James, and John (for they seemed to be the pillars among them) extended their right hands in agreement and fellowship with Barnabas and me. They requested only that while preaching the gospel among the gentiles we remember the poor who were living in Jerusalem, in case anyone wished to collect some relief for them.[19]

(3) Paul's Apostolic Mission

[The highly dramatic conversion of Paul and his apparently simultaneous call ensured that his life would be dominated by his sense of mission.

18 'Race-course': cf 1 Cor 9:24. A marginal note in the 1522 edition of the *Paraphrase on Galatians* identifies this meeting with that of the Council of Jerusalem described in Acts 15.

19 Cf 1 Cor 16:1–3, also 2 Cor 8–9 noting especially 8:8 and 9:5 where Paul stresses that the Corinthians were free to 'give as they wished.'

While his mission was in the first instance defined by his call, time and the vicissitudes of his ministry would enable him to understand more broadly its significance and dimensions. In his *Paraphrases* on the Epistles Erasmus is able to highlight some essential aspects of the Pauline self-understanding. The *Paraphrases* emphasize Paul's commission to evangelize the gentiles as the stewardship of a divine mystery, a secret revealed to Paul at the divinely appointed time in history, thus giving to Paul a role in salvation history not entirely dissimilar to that of Christ. But Erasmus also saw in the Epistles another aspect of the Pauline role in human salvation, the role of both priest and victim, priest in 'offering' to God the gentiles who have believed the gospel he preached to them, victim in that his sufferings were a sacrifice effective on behalf of the salvation of human beings in some manner similar to, if not quite equivalent to, the sufferings of Christ. In the *Paraphrases* on the Pastoral Epistles Erasmus creates a tone both authoritative and paternalistic appropriate to the apostle who has the 'care of all the churches' (2 Cor 11:28), thus suggesting a man whose mission placed upon him the burdens of a bishop of bishops, giving advice in a firm but kindly manner to those who will themselves serve as overseers.]

(a) Steward of the Mystery (from the paraphrase on Ephesians 3 CWE 43 320–2)

[**Ephesians 3**] [320] I, Paul, am eager to win you gentiles for him (although the Jews resent it), if, as I hope, you have heard that the sphere of responsibility assigned to me by Christ himself is this: to dispense especially among the gentiles, to whom you belong, the good news of salvation which, until now, some people used to think belonged to the Jews alone.[20] This secret,[21] formerly hidden from the other apostles, Christ has revealed especially to me. He not only foretold to Ananias that I would publish his name abroad among the gentiles, but he himself also bade me play the part of his ambassador by going to the gentiles far off.[22] Formerly it seemed abhorrent that ungodly people and devotees of idol worship should be called to the fellowship of the gospel, although that is what had been decided by God long before the world was created, and through divine inspiration it was in some

20 Paul witnesses to the responsibility assigned and to the resentment of the Jews in his speech to the Jews in Jerusalem as recorded in Acts 22:3–22; cf 22:10, 14–15, 21–2.

21 For the secret as 'mystery' (paraphrasing 3:3) see 176 n61.

22 Cf Acts 9:10–16; for 'ambassador to the gentiles' see 2 Cor 5:20, Acts 13:47.

manner [321] revealed to the prophets.[23] However, that gentiles attain the good news of salvation by faith alone and without the help of the Mosaic law – this had not been revealed to the race of mortals in the way it is now being revealed through me.

The authority to preach this gospel has been assigned to me; nor am I neglecting the responsibility entrusted to me – even to the point of undergoing chains and imprisonment – thus far labouring constantly in the work of the gospel. Not that I myself by my own strength am equal to so lofty a responsibility; but the very one who assigned this office to me is also of his own accord adding his assistance. I am not boasting of my lofty status. I acknowledge that I am the least of the saints. But nevertheless to me, who am the least, it has pleased the divine goodness to entrust a task by far the greatest, namely, that among gentiles (who have been until the present completely ignorant of God), I should promulgate and proclaim [322] the unsearchable riches of Christ that he is offering abundantly to all; and that what up to now lay hidden, I should bring to light, I mean the fact that the benefit of the gospel is to be dispensed now to all nations. Previously it was thought to have been conferred on the Jews alone, although from eternity it had been determined otherwise by God, both the creator and the director of the universe. This plan of his own divine mind he willed to be secret until now, because it was precisely in these times that he willed it to be published, and published through his church. This wisdom is now becoming known, not only to the whole earth, but also to the first and foremost of angelic minds and also to the foremost of the demons that dwell in the heavens and the highest part of the atmosphere.[24]

(b) Priest and Victim, Sacrificer and Sacrifice (from the paraphrases on Romans 15, 2 Corinthians 4, Colossians 1, and Philippians 2 CWE 42 85, CWE 43 223–4, 405–6, 375)

[**Romans 15**] [85] I perform the duty, of which I was indeed unworthy, but which was entrusted to me, by the grace of God. I submit to the will of Christ whose work I zealously perform with all my strength, so that by bringing the gospel of God to light among you gentiles, I might offer a pure sacrifice to him. However, I believe that by far the most pleasing

23 Cf Isa 45:22–3, 49:6.

24 For the demons (paraphrasing 'principalities and powers,' 3:10) and their dwelling place see CWE 43 322 n14.

sacrifice to him would be for me to present you to God himself as those worthy of him, like a sacrifice made pure and holy, not by carnal ceremonies, but by the Holy Spirit who is the one and only author of true holiness.

[**2 Corinthians 4**] [223] We ourselves, daily, through our weakness, are afflicted with evils, yet with God's help we persevere unconquered in the evils that have to be endured. While we in all [224] ways are indeed oppressed by adversity, yet we are not distressed; we are reduced to penury, but are not in penury destitute; we suffer persecution, but are not in persecution deserted; we are cast down and trampled upon, but not, however, so as to perish; and in this respect we are imitating, to the best of our ability, the Lord Jesus whom we preach. He died once on behalf of all. We, exposed every day to the dangers of death, carry about, as it were, his death in our body, as we spend this life for you. We do this so that, just as we imitate the death of Jesus by dying on your behalf, so too the life of Jesus, the life through which he lived again after death, might be shown in our body; and indeed that life of his will be shown in our body either when we are snatched by him from death, or when, by showing contempt for the life of the body, we openly bear witness to and affirm the resurrection of bodies. So it happens in a new way that the immortal life of Christ becomes more manifest to you through the affliction of our body, which is subject to death. It is indeed death that makes its assault against our person, but the fruit of life, which is born of our death, redounds to you, for whose sake we expose ourselves to these evils.

[**Colossians 1**] [405] As matters now stand, I am so persuaded that the gospel is true that not only do I feel no regret or shame, but I even suffer joyfully and count as my glory the scourges, the prisons, the fetters that I endure not for my crimes but for your salvation. For although the Jews protest, I teach that you belong to the gospel grace no less than the Jews themselves. Why should I not say that I am suffering for your salvation, for which Christ suffered? Why should an apostle be reluctant to do what our leader was not loath to do? He not only suffered in his own body on our behalf, but he also suffers in ours, somehow, as if filling up through his deputies[25] what could appear to have been inadequate in his afflictions; not that his death of itself does not suffice, but that in some way the affliction of head and members, of prince and

25 'Deputies': Latin *vicarios*, ie 'vicars.' Cf CWE 43 405 n40, citing Theophylact: '... when the general is away his deputy ... stands in for him and personally receives the wounds intended for him.'

deputies, is one; the more abundant it is, the more it overflows to add to the full measure of your salvation, indeed, not only of yours but of Christ's whole body, which is the church. [406] I am carrying out the task assigned; the care of the church has been entrusted to me. Christ has assigned his own responsibilities to me; he has handed over the care of his body, especially that portion of the care that is directed towards welcoming the gentiles to the gospel, so that I may fulfil by my work what he seemed to lack, and might divulge what has been concealed from many past generations and from the gentiles, namely, that not only for Jews but also for gentiles an approach lies open, through faith, to gospel salvation.

[**Philippians 2**] [375] I am confident, while you persevere, that I, too, will boast at the coming of Christ that I have not laboured in vain, nor run to no purpose in the stadium of the gospel,[26] since I have gained such disciples for Christ. So far am I from regretting the efforts through which I have presented you to God as a most pleasing victim, that if, in addition to the offering and the sacrifice of your faith, I, too, should be made a sacrificial offering, I would rejoice as much on my account as on yours: on your account since I have offered you to Christ, a most pleasing victim, as converts to the gospel; on mine, seeing that when such a sacrifice has been completed, I myself, too, must be entirely immolated. For just as I see that my afflictions have resulted in your advancement, so I know that my death will be advantageous for the gospel, and for this reason death, too, when it comes, will be pleasing to me.[27]

(c) Bishop of Bishops (from the paraphrases on 1 Timothy 3 and 4 CWE 44 18–21 and 26)

[**1 Timothy 3**] [18] There are important qualifications that you must look for in those who in your judgment ought to be put in charge of the people. It is only right for the one who excels in rank to excel also in virtues. Many seek the prestige perhaps but fail to consider how much responsibility this prestige brings with it. Anyone who desires to become a bishop solely because of ambition, or for the sake of financial gain, or to have dictatorial powers desires his own destruction. He is not paying sufficient attention to the meaning of the word bishop. It is not the name of a rank, but of a function, an office, a responsibility.

26 Cf n18 above.

27 In the annotation on Phil 2:17 (*supra sacrificium*) Erasmus explains how Paul is both victim and priest; cf CWE 43 375 n38.

It means 'overseer' and one who looks out for the advantages and needs of others. You will not entrust this honour to anyone unless you discover that a person has the proper qualifications to be a bishop. To give you a firmer basis for making this judgment I shall sketch in a few words a picture of the true bishop.

First, the integrity of his life must be such that no charge of any kind can be brought against him. It is simply incongruous for someone to present himself to the others as their teacher and as one who has the authority to demand innocence from them while failing to practise what he teaches in his own life and behaviour. [19] Secondly, chastity is an important qualification in the selection of a bishop. Therefore, if a candidate who spurns sexual pleasures completely is not available, you must certainly make sure that the candidate is or has been married only once. A first marriage may appear to have been undertaken in order to have children, but even among pagans repeated wedlock creates the suspicion that the emotions are out of control. I do not preclude other men from entering a second marriage if abstinence is beyond them, for to lay this restriction on the entire congregation is too harsh. But it befits a bishop to be so totally free from fault that he cannot even be suspected of having a fault.

Now there is a special quality which must be looked for in a bishop. He has to have an aptitude and inclination for teaching – not for teaching Jewish myths or the supercilious, inflated philosophies of this world,[28] but the things which make us truly godly and truly Christian. The first duty in a teacher is to know what is best. The next is that he teach willingly, calmly, diligently, lovingly, without arrogance, in a timely way. For evangelical teaching is such that it wins over by gentleness, not by shouting. [20] Look also for a man who takes care of his private property and consider his ability in the management of his household affairs, for a home is nothing but a miniature state, the head of a household nothing but the ruler of a tiny community.

In the selection of a bishop one must also look at how long a man has been a Christian. Baptism to be sure grafts a person into the body of Christ, but this person does not instantly acquire perfect godliness. Baptism opens the entrance into the church, but it is left to each person at this point to strive vigorously towards the goal of holiness. We are reborn through baptism, but it is still left to us to gain stature and strength over an extended period of time by growing to maturity through daily

28 Cf Titus 1:14.

increases in godliness. Therefore, care has to be taken that a neophyte – I mean, one who has recently enlisted in the fellowship of faith – not be put in charge of so important an office, for he may be puffed up with pride and acquire a dangerous self-confidence. It is not unlikely that, ensnared in the net of ambition, he will behave too proudly in the office entrusted to him and will not escape the slanders of the evil-minded. Pagans will misconstrue his behaviour and say that he [21] sought out the Christians with the aim of becoming pre-eminent among them since he was a lowly figure among his own kind. 'It's a good thing he left us,' they will say. 'He has the reward for his change of religion. He preferred to be a Christian bishop than to live among us as a private person.' He who has given proof of his true godliness and of his own modesty by the passage of time will be safe from such suspicions.

[**1 Timothy 4**] [26] Command and teach these things bravely and steadfastly so that you clearly display the authority of a bishop, since you are convinced that our teaching has issued from Christ himself. There is no reason for you, young as you are and placed in such an important position, to be timorous or to give way before the wickedness of those teaching a different doctrine. You must not look to the number of years you have lived but to the position you hold. If people see the reflection of a holy mind in all your speech, if they observe modesty and purity in the conduct of your life, if they perceive a love worthy of a bishop in the performance of your duties, if they behold a heart trusting in God in its endurance of evils, if they see you untouched in any respect by human passions, they will readily respect you as though you were their senior.

(4) Defence of Apostolic Identity (from the paraphrases on 1 and 2 Corinthians and Galatians CWE 43 119–20 and 269–72, 273–5, and CWE 42 130)

[It is clear from the Epistles to the Galatians and the Corinthians that Paul struggled for years to assert his legitimacy as a true apostle. The paraphrases selected below represent Erasmus' elucidation of some of the more pointed discussions in the apostolic defence. They conclude with an interpretation of the famous 'stigmata' Paul claims to have received.]

[**I Corinthians 9**] [119] Am I not an apostle, just as the others are who boast of this title? Have I not at Christ's bidding been sent to the gentiles? But if I am an apostle just as much as the others, why do I have less apostolic power and authority? Has it not also been granted to me to see our Lord Jesus Christ? – if it seems important to anyone (as it is), that he was witnessed by others after the resurrection.[29] But if apostles are measured by the services they offer and by their noble deeds, what is there in which even here I am found wanting? Is it not an apostolic deed to gain Corinth for Christ, a city once so bound over to worldly desires? And yet with the Lord's help it was through me that this deed was accomplished. Whether I am an apostle to the Jews,[30] let those decide who are eager to mix Christ with Moses. Surely I am an apostle to you, who believe in Christ through my urging, who have perceived that divine power assists my speech.[31] You, therefore, are my work if deeds are required (although any praise here is owed to Christ, not to me). Are you not my certificate, [120] by which I could show that the apostolic ministry has been assigned to me for the glory of Christ? This is the way I customarily answer those who keep asking by what proof I show myself to be an apostle. Now if I have accomplished in you whatever the highest apostles[32] have anywhere accomplished in others, how am I less an apostle than they?

[**2 Corinthians 11**] [269] I have to ask your indulgence to allow me to say something about myself, something true, so that no one will attribute to my folly the fact that I myself am trumpeting my own praises. What I am doing has the appearance of foolishness, I know. But I am driven to this pass by the ostentation of those whom you tolerate, even while they foolishly boast. [270] They want it to seem important that they are Hebrews, just as if it makes any difference to God from what stock you are sprung; and yet, if it is something to be born a Hebrew, I too am a Hebrew. They are Israelites; I am too. They are descendants of Abraham; I am too. For they vaunt themselves on empty titles of this sort; and yet in such things we are their equals, if we should like to boast.

Even in regard to those things that truly do contribute to apostolic glory, we outshine them. They are ministers of Christ – let us grant it – but I am more so (to speak foolishly, but to speak the truth nonetheless).[33] I have shown that this is so, not through arrogance, nor by taking gifts, nor by boasting of family origin, but by the very proofs

---

29 Acts 1:22 implies that the essential qualification for 'apostleship' is to have seen the resurrected Christ. Paul affirms in 1 Cor 15:8 that he has seen the risen Christ.

30 Cf Gal 2:7–8.

31 Cf 1 Cor 2:4.

32 'Highest apostles': cf Gal 2:9, and the paraphrase on 1 Cor 3:4–5 CWE 43 54.

33 In the *Praise of Folly* CWE 27 144–5 Erasmus ridicules with splendid sarcasm the misinterpretation of this passage (2 Cor 11:23) by a 'certain renowned theologian'!

that truly attest an apostolic heart. I have endured more labours than they; far more grievously have I felt the lash; more often have I been cast into prison; more frequently have I run the risk of death. But if you wish some instances to be recounted in detail: five times I received forty lashes less one, when I was beaten by the Jews; three times I was beaten with lictors' rods;[34] once I was stoned; [271] three times I was shipwrecked; I spent an entire night and day on the high sea in the greatest despair of life. But why should I go on enumerating individual instances, since frequently, for the sake of the gospel, I was in danger, not only in sailing, but also in journeys by land? Repeatedly I encountered dangers from rivers, dangers from brigands, dangers from the persecution of the Jews, dangers from the violence of the gentiles, dangers springing up in the city, dangers in the desert, dangers in the sea when I came close to being slaughtered by the sailors,[35] dangers from these falsely called 'Christians' who were resisting our gospel.[36] Not to recall, for the moment, the constant labours and hardships undertaken for the sake of the gospel: the frequent nights without sleep, the hunger and thirst endured times without number, the frequent times without food,[37] the hardships of [272] cold and nakedness endured. But what I have recounted thus far pertains only to the affliction of my body.

In the meantime, I was experiencing no less severe affliction of spirit. Daily I was pressed and weighed down on every side by the concerns I have on behalf of so many churches. So close are they to my heart that whatever happens to them I count as happening to me. For whose ills do I not grieve as my own? Who is weak, through whose suffering I do not myself become sick? Who is hurt, through whose injury I do not myself suffer the deepest distress? If there must be boasting, I shall boast of what proves my frailty rather than my greatness. Let others boast that through their commendation of the gospel they are considered important, that they are growing rich, that they reign under the pretext of Christ. I personally think it a finer thing to boast that for the sake of Christ I have been cast down and afflicted. The God and Father of our Lord Jesus Christ knows that I am telling no lie.

---

34 'Lictors rods,' ie punishment by Romans as distinct from punishment by Jews (eg by stoning). The lictors were attendants of Roman magistrates; they carried bundles of rods as symbols of the magistrate's authority and as instruments of punishment.

35 An allusion evidently to Acts 27:42–3; if so, to include it here is anachronistic.

36 Cf Phil 1:17. 'Falsely called "Christians"': in NRSV 'false brethren'; on the anachronistic use of 'Christian' in the *Paraphrases* see CWE 41 172–3 with n680.

37 Cf Acts 27:33–6.

[2 Corinthians 12] [273] Thus far I have recounted evidence demonstrating that I have been beset with calamities and woes, evidence which, according to human judgment, makes a person despicable rather than glorious. Is one to boast or not? Yet it is sometimes expedient to boast, especially when the tenor of our talk has led us to visions and revelations of the Lord Jesus. Although those 'apostles' of yours fabricate many such revelations and vaunt them insolently, I shall recount only one so that I may not seem even here to be their inferior. I shall do so under compulsion and against my will, and not for my glory, but for God's. [274] I know someone who, fourteen years ago, was caught up, whether in the body or out of the body, I do not know – God knows – but nevertheless he was caught up all the way to the third heaven; from here, again, he was caught up into paradise. In both places he heard certain ineffable words that it is not right for a mortal to utter. On behalf of a person of this sort, I shall boast, since such great felicity has come to him by God's kindness. About myself, meanwhile, I shall make no boast, except to recall the events that show me afflicted and abased.[38]

Perhaps it would not be quite safe for me to boast about these things that make us important and border on the danger of arrogance. Accordingly, so that I might not be too exalted by the loftiness of the revelations, or more highly regarded among people than is good, the gracious will of God permitted a goad and affliction of the body to be given me. Its purpose is both to remind me forcibly of myself and to prove to all that I am mortal, subject to ills we all share. Hence, to afflict me as I do Christ's work, a messenger and servant of Satan was given, in order to hinder my gospel and to harass me with the most savage persecutions, just as if, hurling me down and pressing upon me, he were to beat me on the head, so that I should not be unduly elated.[39] Since the situation was fiercely annoying for me, three times I asked the Lord to free me from this affliction. [275] But he, having my interest at heart more than I myself, responded after this fashion: 'Paul, be content with my kindness towards you; you are not to press your demands any further. The fact that you are being pummelled by afflictions pertains, at the

38 In his annotation on 2 Cor 12:5 (*pro huiusmodi gloriabar*) Erasmus notes that Paul writes in a way that deliberately conceals the fact that the person who received the vision is he, himself.

39 The paraphrase points to two interpretations of the 'thorn in the flesh' (2 Cor 12:7): a physical ailment, such as frequent headaches, a view common in the tradition (to which there may be a concealed allusion in the expression 'as if [Satan] were to beat me on the head'), and the view Erasmus prefers, ie harassment of Paul's evangelical mission. Several views are described in the annotation on the verse (*et ne magnitudo*).

same time, both to making my glory illustrious – for while you are safe under my protection you cannot be conquered, no matter how great the storms – and to your salvation, inasmuch as the more you are afflicted by the evils of the body, the richer you grow in the goods of the spirit.' Thus it happens that God's strength finds its true end in human frailty, and weakness completes power.

[Galatians 6] [130] Let no one hereafter give me trouble. There is no way in which I can be torn away from evangelical truth, either by any disgrace or by afflictions. For everywhere I carry about on my body as the signs and brand-marks of my Lord Jesus Christ, all the dishonour which has been branded on me because of him, such as prisons, floggings, chains and stonings, and all other evils that I have endured for the name of Christ. I display these as trophies and count it to my glory that insofar as is permitted, I am deemed worthy to represent the cross of Christ which I preach.[40]

(5) The Final Years

[While precise knowledge of the final years of the Apostle is no doubt unattainable, we learn from the book of Acts that after his third missionary journey to western countries he returned to Jerusalem to deliver alms collected from the 'gentile' churches he had visited. His presence in Jerusalem created a riot as a result of which he was imprisoned in Caesarea. From there he was taken to Rome for trial after he had appealed to Caesar, where he was put under 'house arrest.' Inferences from the Epistles encouraged a tradition to develop that assigned a double imprisonment to Paul, the first following his arrest recorded in Acts, resulting in a trial and his consequent release, upon which he engaged for ten more years in further missionary work. He was then imprisoned again and after a trial (now his second) was beheaded. Erasmus accepts this tradition in his *Paraphrases*. But before these later events, while Paul was still free, we have from his own pen a remarkable expression of the understanding he had of his apostolate: a mission to gentiles that extended across Asia and Europe, and in particular to gentiles hitherto untouched by the gospel. This conception

40 'Represent' here translates the Latin *imitari* 'imitate,' which perhaps reflects more decisively Erasmus' understanding of his apostolate as an identification with the apostolate of Christ. Cf CWE 42 130 n7: 'In his annotation on Gal 6:17 (*stigmata*) Erasmus explains "stigmata" from the image of slaves who were branded to mark them as the possession of their master. So Paul, as a slave of Christ, has been branded by the wounds he had received, bearing in his body the marks of the cross of Christ.'

he describes in a few sentences in what is commonly thought to be the last Epistle we have from him, the Epistle to the Romans. We begin here with Erasmus' paraphrastic interpretation of Paul's understanding of his apostolate, and conclude with Paul's response in Erasmus' words to his situation as a prisoner.]

(a) From Syria to Spain (from the paraphrase on Romans 15 CWE 42 85–6)

[**Romans 15**] [85] To some extent I can be proud, and rightly so, not boasting about myself before men, but rejoicing before God for the happy outcome of my preaching.[41] However, I do not attribute this to myself or my own industry but to Jesus Christ whose work I am doing and with whose help I perform the duty of preaching. For my heart does not endure to recount the exploits of others. Lest I should seem to claim for myself praise for the deeds of others, I shall mention only those things that Christ has brought about through my ministry, namely, that the gentiles previously devoted to the impious worship even of idols, now submit to and obey the gospel, stimulated in part by my words and deeds, in part by the magnitude and power of signs and portents which have been produced through me to confirm the reliability of my teachings. But these things were not produced through my power or strength, but through their author, the Spirit of God, of whom I am nothing other than an instrument [86] and a minister. Therefore, while I boast about the success of my preaching, I preach the glory of Christ, not my own. For I have not preached the gospel in the usual manner, but up to this point I have preached in those provinces where the name of Christ had not yet been heard in order that the foundations of the Christian religion might be more broadly laid, and the boundaries of the sovereignty of Christ might be further extended. Nor did it seem right to build on top of foundations laid by other apostles. But considering that it was more difficult to establish the beginnings of religion than to protect and increase gains once they had been made, I judged that the former pertains more to the work of the gospel.

Now that I have travelled through Achaia and Macedonia, I see that there remains no place in these regions in which I have not laid the foundations of the Christian religion, and for many years now I have

41 Cf 1 Cor 1:23. Erasmus emphasizes here as elsewhere the role of preaching in Paul's mission; cf CWE 43 36 with n36.

been moved by the desire to see you [Romans]. Adequate opportunity (I hope) will be given for fulfilling my desire when I set out for Spain. At the present time, however, I have resolved to make a journey to Jerusalem in order that I might present to the Jewish Christians living there the gifts of the Macedonians and the Achaians that have been entrusted to me.

(b) A Double Imprisonment (from the Argument to 2 Timothy and the paraphrase on 2 Timothy 4 CWE 44 40 and 53)

[**Argument**][42] [40] Since in the previous Epistle Paul had led Timothy, his agent in Ephesus, to expect his return and there was now no way that he could do this because he was being held in chains in Rome, he sends a letter encouraging him not to be dejected by the storm of persecutions but following Paul's own example to prepare his soul for martyrdom. Dangerous times were threatening because of certain persons who, under the pretext of godliness, were trying to overturn true godliness and in this way to boost themselves. They thought that Christian godliness consisted in words, not, as is the case, in the purity of the soul. Then, after attesting that the day of his own death was near and that he had now been abandoned by most people, he tells Timothy to come quickly to him in Rome and to bring Mark. He wrote at Rome when he was appearing for the second time before Nero's court.[43]

[**2 Timothy 4**] [53] Do your best to come to me as soon as possible. Imprisonment prevents me from walking here or there at will to carry out the work of the gospel, and I have been abandoned by almost everyone. There are some things which I am eager to commit to you orally before my departure. Demas has left me; he prefers to enjoy the delights of this world than to share my sufferings in the expectation of an immortal reward. In this spirit he has taken himself off to Thessalonica. Crescens has been called away to Galatia on business. Titus has gone off to Dalmatia. Luke alone stands by me, the inseparable companion of all my fortunes. Alexander the coppersmith has not only abandoned me in these storms, but has also done me many wrongs. It is not my place to

42 For 'Argument' see 39 and 147 above.

43 'Nero's court' represents the Greek *praetorion* 'praetorium,' which Erasmus assumes is the emperor's court in Rome, but the word was also used to designate the headquarters of provincial governors, as in John 20:28. For the two imprisonments, the first referenced in Acts 28:16 and 30, followed by a period of ten years of missionary work, the second resulting in Paul's death see Eusebius *Church History* 2.22.2–3, and CWE 44 40 n2.

punish him, but the Lord will requite him as he has deserved. You too beware of him for your own good. For he was so far from standing by me that he even strongly opposed our case.

When I had to plead my case the first time before Caesar's courts,[44] no one stood by me. They were all terrified with fear and forsook me. That is only human and understandable; I would not want it to be charged against them. The Lord, however, did not abandon me, bereft as I was of human help, but stood by me and gave me strength so that the heralding of evangelical faith would be completely persuasive and its fame would reach the ears of all nations. He wanted the teachings of the gospel to be spread far and wide, and it was, I think, with this plan that he drove me hither and yon through different lands and had me carried finally even to Rome. With his help I was delivered from the jaws of the most savage lion. I am confident, moreover, that the same Lord will deliver me also in the future from all the evil actions of the ungodly. And in fact, if death is inflicted in this life, he will nevertheless preserve his servant and soldier for his heavenly kingdom. To him be glory for ever and ever, amen.

Do your best to convey yourself here before winter cuts off travel.

II. ERASMIAN PERSPECTIVES ON THE PAULINE THEOLOGICAL VISION

[The selections below reflect Erasmus' paraphrastic response to three major aspects of Pauline theology as they emerge from the Epistles. First, Erasmus sees in both Romans and Galatians an attempt by Paul to explain the significance of Christ in terms of salvation-history: the great time-periods, first, before Moses and the Law, second, Israel under the Law, and third, the time of grace inaugurated by Christ. In the paraphrases Erasmus confronts the reader with the question emphatically raised: 'What is the function of the Law in the slow movement of history?' The paraphrases on both Romans and Galatians lead the reader to see the period of Law in relation to sin, particularly the sin of the individual. In both the purpose of the Law is to restrain a people from sin and so to prepare it for the high ethical demands of the age of grace. In the *Paraphrase* on Romans, however, the paraphrase shows that far from achieving its purpose the Law actually became a 'stimulator' of sin. In addition the *Paraphrases* point to another

44 Cf the preceding note.

overarching purpose of the Law: to prefigure and prepare a people for the coming of Christ and the period of grace, a period in which love replaces Law, as the selection from 1 Timothy so effectively demonstrates. Erasmus' representation of the Law was seen as essentially negative by Béda and the Paris theologians, and in his revisions of the 1530s Erasmus took some small steps to brighten the impression, though the selections given here belong entirely to the original *Paraphrases*. The question of the function of Law ultimately leads to the place of Israel in salvation-history, and Erasmus' paraphrase on Paul's great answer to that question in Romans 11 echoes brilliantly the resounding confidence of the apostle. While the grand scheme of history portrayed here will undoubtedly fire the imagination of every reader, modern readers will find perhaps even more fascinating the representation of the psychology of the sinner in the paraphrase on Romans 7.

Three passages have been selected to represent Erasmus' reflection on the death of Christ, as it appears in the *Paraphrases* on the Pauline Epistles. Taken together, the passages in paraphrase point to what is often understood as the three classic interpretations of Christ's death: his death as an atonement, his death as a victory over the powers of evil, and his death as a model for imitation. The final selection in this section reveals Erasmus' understanding of 'mystery' as found in the Pauline corpus: a secret to be revealed. The revelation turns out in paraphrase to be virtually a statement of the 'rule of faith' embodied in the classic creeds.]

(1) Moses and Christ in the Destiny of the Human Race (from the paraphrases on Romans 7, Galatians 3, 1 Timothy 1, and Romans 11 CWE 42 41–3, 112–14, CWE 44 8–9 and CWE 42 63–4, 67–9)

[**Romans** 7] [41] Now the Law of Moses, inasmuch as it foreshadowed Christ by means of figures and ceremonies, was given only for a certain time. When the light came forth the shadows yielded; when the truth appeared the likeness of truth departed. Because the Mosaic law was mortal (so to speak) it is not surprising if it is now dead. Consequently, as long as the time of the Law lasted the Law was in force, and it had authority over those who had submitted to it. Now, however, you have been joined to Christ as the bride to the bridegroom, and, liberated from your old bonds, you have submitted to the authority of a new bridegroom. [42] As long as we were subject to the gross and carnal Law as to a husband, the Law seemed to rule over us as though with the authority of a husband, while desires, more fierce thanks to the opportunity provided by the Law, were so strong in our bodies that we were dragged into sin in the manner of slaves. Thus we begot unhappy offspring from our unhappy union, bringing forth whatever was born only for its death and destruction.[45] But now that we have been liberated from the lordship of the Law it is not right still to hold to this carnal husband, that is, to the letter of the Law. Rather, we should serve a new bridegroom, one who is heavenly and spiritual.

Perhaps some slanderer will suppose that I condemn the Law itself as the author of sin, since I said that as the servants of the Law we have fallen headlong into sin and death. For he will say that just as it is characteristic of righteousness to produce life, so it is characteristic of sin to produce death; if the Law brings forth death, the Law itself could appear either to be sin or at least in league with sin.[46] God forbid that anyone draw this conclusion. The Law is not the author of sin; it is the revealer of sin. Sin lay hidden and deceived us, in a way, before the Law existed, while everyone acquiesced in his own desires and thought that whatever especially pleased him was permitted and that it was right to desire anything he found delightful. Therefore, I indulged myself as though I did not know that the desire for another man's property was a sin, had not the Law forbidden me to desire it. And indeed the Law was brought in with the intention of restraining sins. But due to our sin, the results were quite the opposite of the intention. Inasmuch as the Law revealed sin and did not add strength to enable us to fight back against our vices, it happened that the lust for sin took advantage of this opportunity and was all the more aroused, for human nature is more inclined to those things that are prohibited. Thus, since before the Law was revealed I had no knowledge of certain sins while of others I did have knowledge (but understood that I could do them, as they had not been prohibited), my mind felt relatively slight and sluggish temptations to commit sin. For we love those things more indifferently that we are permitted to have whenever we please. But so many forms of sin were revealed by the disclosure of the Law that a whole troop of

45 In the paraphrase on Rom 7:1–3 (omitted here) Erasmus worked out elaborately the Pauline comparison between the Israelites and the Law and a wife obligated to be subject to her husband only as long as he was alive. The paraphrase continues the comparison here; hence the reference to the 'offspring of our unhappy union,' the union implied in the contract between God's people and the Law.

46 Béda and the Paris theologians severely criticized Erasmus for presenting the Law in his *Paraphrases* in a way that seemed to denigrate it; cf CWE 82 90–113.

passions was aroused by the prohibition and redoubled its efforts to incite us to sin. Thus, by this means sin received strength and vigour. Before there was a Law sin [43] was sluggish and virtually dead. But I in the meantime lived as if outside the Law, or rather I thought I lived – as if it were permitted to sin with impunity. But, when the precept forbidding me to sin intervened, sin not only was not restrained but actually seemed to gain new life and to receive new vigour. But while sin was gaining new life, I who seemed before to be alive, now died, recognizing through the Law that I was guilty, and sinning nevertheless. And the result was that what had been established for the support of life became death for me, not however by the fault of the Law, but by my own fault. For since the inclination to sin was innate in me, my sick mind, eager to sin, seized the opportunity provided by the Law. And so the devil, using a good instrument in a wicked way, seduced me into sin, taking the opportunity provided by the Law, and through sin he struck me down so that I found myself a prisoner and in the power of another. Consequently, there is no reason here for us to accuse falsely the Law which has been given by a good God, and thus sets forth holy, just, and good precepts. For whatever prohibits evil must be good.

[**Galatians 3**] [112] But someone might say: 'If we were intended to hope for salvation from this source,[47] for what reason did God afterwards add the useless Law?' It was not completely useless. For even if it does not confer innocence, it restrains the licence to sin, holding back evil desires by means of ceremonies which serve as a kind of barricade. The Law would not have been given if our unbridled malice had not required it. And yet it was not given to bind everyone forever, but for a time fixed beforehand by God, during which [time] it prefigured Christ by images, deterred people from sin by punishment, and invited them by promises to strive for innocence. For this purpose the Law was established with God as its author, and conveyed through angels, but conveyed by angels in such a way that power over all of it remained with Christ, and he, standing midway,[48] intervened between the Mosaic law and the grace of the gospel, in such a manner that he was the end of the former and the beginning of the latter. He interposed himself between

47 'This source,' ie 'faith.' Preceding this passage Erasmus has paraphrased Gal 3:1–14, drawing out the Pauline doctrine implied in the text that, as the promise to Abraham shows, the 'blessing,' ie salvation, was 'established on the sole condition of faith,' hence here the 'source' of salvation.

48 Erasmus follows the view predominant in Christian antiquity that the 'mediator' ['intermediary' RSV] of Gal 3:19 and 20 is Christ; modern exegetes generally agree that Moses is intended here.

God and men in such a way that he included in himself the nature of both, for he intended to reconcile the one to the other. But a conciliator who intercedes has to intercede among several parties. God, however, is one, and there was discord between him and the human race. Consequently, a third party was necessary who would share both natures and reconcile them to each other. He would placate God by his death and lure men by his teaching to the true worship of God.

[113] For a time, then, the Mosaic law served the purpose of restraining the Jews, as if hemming them in with a wall, in part by threats of punishment, in part by the expectation of the promise, in part by foreshadowing the coming of Christ. Thus when Christ came, he would not find them fallen headlong into every kind of impiety and hence unworthy and unreceptive to the grace of the gospel. Through the promises of the Law, therefore, they dreamed in one way or another about the mystery of the gospel. They were therefore dependent on the tutelage of the Law only until that could be disclosed which the Law had outlined in shadows, and until they could awaken and see exhibited in a bright light what previously they had awaited as through a dream.

Therefore, the Law did not offer perfect righteousness, but it had been given, as though it were a pedagogue,[49] to an untutored people so that if a regard for virtue could not yet hold them to their duty, the fear of punishment might restrain [114] them from great outrages. Thus gradually making progress, they might be led to Christ, through whom alone, after they had abandoned faith in their earlier ceremonies, they could expect true righteousness. However, a pedagogue is not given to boys to be with them always, but only until they have grown up and by their own will are attracted to honourable things. Then they have no need to be restrained from crime by fear of punishment, but through the encouragement of their father they are voluntarily and willingly drawn toward honourable things. Thus a father, although he maintains a unique affection for his children, nevertheless forces them to serve for a time a pedagogue whose master they are soon to become. In the same manner, God restrained his own people by the severity of the Law when they were still young and uncultivated, until, by laying hold of evangelical faith, they should be restored to him, and cease to be under the jurisdiction of a pedagogue, but instead live freely as free-born sons under the mercy of a most kind parent.

49 In the Greco-Roman world the 'pedagogue' was a slave who acted as preceptor or governor of a child.

[1 Timothy 1] [8] It is love that directly comprehends and fulfils the entire meaning of the Law of Moses,[50] but this love must issue from a pure heart and from a mind whose conscience is clear and from a faith incapable of pretence. Sincere love dictates far more rightly what is to be done than any number of regulations. If it is present, what need is there for the Law's commands? If it is not present, what does observance of the Law contribute? Since ordinary human love is frequently flawed by personal feelings, it is often found together with an insincere way of life and is sometimes incapable of complete trust. But evangelical love nowhere deceives, does not hesitate, cannot falter in the obligations of godliness. For it has no other object than the glory of Christ and the salvation of a neighbour; it depends on nothing else than Christ. We do not say this because we condemn the Law of Moses. [9] We both know and state that the Law is good unless someone employs it in an unlawful way. The ultimate purpose of the Law was to lead us to Christ. The person who sees clearly and discerns in what respects the Law, which was given for a limited time, must yield to the gospel and in what it must retain permanent force; who understands how one must adapt its gross letter to the spiritual teaching of the gospel; who understands that those whom the blood of Christ has redeemed from the tyranny of sin and who under the impulse of love willingly do more than the Law of Moses prescribes have no need of either the fear or the admonition of the Law either to be restrained from wicked deeds or to be aroused to do their duty; to this person certainly the Law is good. People who are driven and swept along by the Spirit of Christ take the lead on their own and outstrip all the regulations of the Law. Once they have obtained the gift of righteousness, they shrink from all unrighteousness. Therefore, the Law, which deters from wrongdoing through fear of punishment, was not created for them at any rate. They willingly and gladly do what the Law demands even if they do not keep to the literal words of the Law.

[Romans 11] [63] But does my teaching imply that the gentiles have been adopted by God because of their faith, although previously they were strangers to God, while on the contrary the people previously chosen by God have now been rejected outright because of their unbelief? By no means. For it is not at all reasonable that God has now rejected a people whom he has freely acknowledged up to the present time as chosen and as peculiarly his own. Clearly, if God had rejected the

50 Cf Matt 22:34–40.

whole nation, I myself would not be preaching Christ. Thus God has not allowed the whole nation of the Jews to be separated from him. And he has not allowed the whole remaining race of mortals to die in their own sins, even though from both groups there are few who believe. So what happened? Surely the Israelites, due to their unbelief, failed to obtain what they had sought by trusting in the Law. The only ones to obtain it have been those who qualify through election, not circumcision. Neither circumcision nor observance of the Law was at all useful for the rest. But they were so blinded by malice that no matter how many portents they saw, [64] they did not believe them. Even though they had been waiting so long for Christ, when he came they looked at him with the eyes of the body and failed to see him with the eyes of the mind. For they do not wish to enjoy the things that have been set before them, and they have turned against things that have been exhibited before their eyes and ears. They have not taken the trouble to lift their eyes to heaven and to acknowledge the kindness of the creator toward them. No, they are attached to the lowly letter of the Law, and despise sublime things; they are devoted to temporal things and reject eternal things. They carry around the books of Moses, though they do not understand them.[51] They read the prophets and deny the promise given by them.

But someone will ask, 'What is the purpose of all this? The Jews have been blinded, taken captive, bowed down, become deaf. Have they so fallen that they have completely perished? Is there no hope that they will rise again?' Perish the thought! On the contrary, their fall was temporary and it worked to your advantage, since it was the opportunity for you gentiles to be accepted into salvation. Then in turn even the Jews, through the example of the gentiles, will be forced at the very end of the world to a zeal for true piety. [67] When the number of gentiles has been filled, and when the Jews see that the whole earth abounds in the profession of the Christian faith, that their city, temple, sacred things, and people have been dispersed and scattered,[52] they will finally begin to regain their vision and understand that Christ is the true Messiah.

[68] But perhaps we are going deeper into the sanctuary of this secret than is right for a man to speak about among men.[53] As I gaze upon the

51 Cf Acts 15:21 and 2 Cor 3:15.

52 A reference to the view prevalent among early Christian authors that the destruction of Jerusalem and the dispersal of the Jews was a sign of the inauguration of the Messianic age; cf Tertullian *Adversus Judaeos* 3.

53 Cf 2 Cor 12:1–4.

ineffable purpose behind the divine plan I am dumbfounded, and since I am not able to explain, I choose to cry out: O the depth of the divine wisdom most abounding! How little can the judgments of God be understood or perceived by any human mind! How little can the purpose of his plans be detected by any created intellect! Who has ever known the mind of the Lord, or who was present in his deliberation? Indeed, God takes thought for the salvation of mankind by a plan we cannot understand but which could not possibly be better. For he wishes his own kindness to be felt by us in such a way that we are not able to claim anything for ourselves. Whatever is good proceeds from God as from its source and is conferred through him as through its author. [69] Therefore, to him alone are owed honour, praise, and glory for all eternity.

(2) The Death of Christ Interpreted (from the paraphrases on Romans 3, Colossians 2, and Romans 6 CWE 42 24–5, CWE 43 413–16 and CWE 42 37–8)

(a) Christ's Death the Means of Propitiation

[**Romans 3**] [24] Moreover, just as parts of the Law were [given] previously to reveal human sin, which had previously been less evident, so now through the gospel, righteousness has [25] been revealed which does not need the support of the Mosaic law, although the Law and the prophets have given witness to it. Righteousness, I say, not of the Law but of God, and this not through circumcision or through the ceremonies of the Jews but through faith and trust in Jesus Christ, through whom alone true righteousness is conferred, not only upon the Jews, or upon this or that nation, but without distinction upon each and every one who has faith in him.

For just as this disease is common to all, and all alike have regressed to a point where they are not able to boast before God about their own righteousness, so justification must be sought by all from the same source. It is certainly not paid back as a reward earned through the observance of the Mosaic law or even through the observance of the law of nature.[54] Rather it is given freely by the divine goodness, not

54 By pointing to both the Mosaic law and the law of nature Erasmus invites a reference to the divine scheme of saving-history divided into discernible chronological periods: the period inaugurated by the Mosaic law and the period before the Mosaic Law when humanity lived by the law of nature, a law whose force continued, however, among gentiles who did not have the law of Moses.

through Moses but through Jesus Christ by whose blood we have been redeemed from the tyranny of sin.[55] To be sure, the Jews formerly had their own means of propitiation[56] clearly a shadow and type of the future; but God has now revealed that Christ is the true propitiation for all, in order that we, formerly hostile on account of our sins, now might be reconciled to God, not (as with the Jews) through the blood of beasts, but through the most holy blood of Christ himself, which washes away all the sins of all people. In this way he reveals his righteousness to all men, while through the Son he pardons the errors of their former life with the intent that they afterwards do not fall back again into sin. He does not forgive because they have merited it, but because he himself has promised [forgiveness]. Nor did he endure sinners until then because he was ignorant of their sins or approved them, but to make known his righteousness at this appointed time, so that it might be clear that he is by nature and of himself truly righteous, and that he is the one and only author of human righteousness.

(b) Christ's Death Annuls the Contract

[**Colossians 2**] [413] Just as he, in dying, laid aside the body subject to death and, in rising, received an immortal body, so you, through a baptism according to the Spirit, have died along with him, after all the sins of your former life have been set aside; and not only have you died with him but you have been buried together with him at the same time.[57] Accordingly, after thus laying aside the body that was subject to sin (and indeed sin is the soul's death), through Christ you have risen along with him, free from sins not through your own merits, but only because you simply believe that God, who by his power raised Christ from the dead, is by his might doing the same in you so that since all sins have been freely remitted through the Son's death, you may henceforth live with him, not guilty of any sins, but hastening towards true immortality in unflagging zeal for innocence. Therefore, to God

55 The ceremonies for the sacrifice of an animal as a means of atonement with blood for the sins of the people are described in Lev 16:1–34.

56 'Means of propitiation': Latin, *propitiatorium*, the word used in the Vulgate of Exod 25:17–22 and Heb 9:5 for the 'mercy seat.' For his New Testament translation of the Greek *hilasterion* Erasmus adopted the Vulgate's *propitiatorium* in Heb 9:5, but in Rom 3:25 he translated with the Latin *reconciliatorem* 'reconciler': ' … the redemption in Christ, whom God set forth a reconciler through faith with the intervention of his blood [or, 'interposing his blood'] … ' Cf Rom 3:25 in RSV.

57 Cf Rom 6:1–4.

the Father are owed all the things that are generously bestowed on you through the Son.

[414] I repeat, all our sins are forgiven us, once and for all, and forgiven in such a way that there is no danger that they might be imputed to us in the future because we had sworn in formal terms to obedience of the Mosaic law, no danger that on this account the adversary might be able to bring us to trial for non-observance of the Law, as if bound by a written document. On the contrary, that long-standing, binding contract on account of which the devil was pressing us hard, Christ has annulled by the profession of gospel faith, on account of which the offences of our former life [415] are not being imputed to anyone. Whatever could be exacted from us on the terms of this binding contract, Christ has paid on the cross on which the contract was torn to pieces and completely destroyed.[58] Nor is there any reason for us to fear the tyranny of Satan after Christ on the cross conquered, through his own death, death's source, by recovering us like glorious spoils snatched away from demonic principalities and powers over which he triumphed when he had conquered them. For then did he frankly and openly display them not only to men but also to angels when he had vanquished and indeed despoiled them, carrying them in a triumph, as it were; and displaying his adversaries ruined and shattered, not through the help of angels or men, but by his own power, he hung upon [416] the cross such a magnificent trophy that, high above, it was visible to all.[59]

58 In his annotation on Col 2:14 (*chirographum decreti*) Erasmus explains that the *chirographum* was a 'personally signed contract,' while the 'decrees' were either human or divine laws, hence the expression, 'the contract' or 'bond which stood against us with its legal demands' (RSV). The affirmation or 'profession' of the Law and our consequent sense of guilt convicted us of our transgression of it, as we had not fulfilled the contract; for this we owed the penalty. But on the cross the contract was so completely destroyed that not a trace of it remained, and thus the penalty of death was transformed into the gift of eternal life.

59 The imagery derives from Roman military practice. 'Spoils' were a technical term for the armour captured by a victorious Roman leader from the enemy supreme commander whom he had slain. When a general had achieved outstanding success on the battlefield he might be given a 'triumph,' a public ritual procession in which distinguished persons captured from the enemy were conveyed, visible to all who observed the procession. A 'trophy' was a 'commemorative display of captured armour set up on the battlefield at the point where the enemy turned back. For Erasmus the trophy seems to be the contract itself nailed to the cross' CWE 43 416 n50; cf also 415 n47. For further discussion on the triumph see CWE 44 14 n11 and CWE 48 147 n45; the term appears also in the description of the burial of Stephen in the *Paraphrase on Acts* CWE 50 57 cf n11.

(c) Christ's Death the Model for Imitation

[Romans 6] [37] Since we have obtained the baptism of Christ, it is not fitting for you to avoid what that baptism either effects or denotes. For when we are baptized in the name of Christ, together with him we die to our former sins that have been abolished by his death, and not only do we die together with him, but we are also buried with him, and this through the same baptism. Hence, just as Christ was called back to eternal life, so we have been awakened through Christ from the death brought by sins. Now we imitate Christ's death if we so completely lose feeling for all our former desires that we seem dead to them. Whoever truly imitates the death of Christ is received into the number of the righteous; he has ceased to be subject to sin, from whose tyranny he is now free. Therefore, if we have died together with Christ in his death and have been freed from our former sins, we believe that by the kindness of this same Christ we shall henceforth live together with the living Christ if our conduct is innocent and blameless, and we shall so live that we shall never again fall back into death. And in so doing, we shall reproduce the image of Christ as far as possible.

[38] Therefore, following the example of Christ, consider that you, too, have died once for all to sin. Your former sins and desires have been snuffed out, and you have become new. So reflect that, as those brought back to life, you are living a life immortal to God by whose kindness you have obtained innocence. No one lives to God except one who is alive to piety, righteousness, and all the other virtues. For since we are incorporated into the body of Christ and have been made one with him, it is necessary that the members correspond to the head. But Christ is the head. Since he ever lives to God, it is fitting that we likewise should live to God through the same Jesus Christ our Lord. Just as Christ has once for all been raised from the dead and does not suffer again any tyranny of death, likewise you must struggle so that sin, once destroyed, does not recover its lost tyranny over you and renew the authority of death. Rather, you should take care from now on so to conduct yourselves in every aspect of your existence that it will be clear from your whole life how, together with Christ, you have left behind things which belong to death and have been transformed into newness of life.

(3) The Mystery of Christian Truth Revealed (from the paraphrase on 1 Timothy 3 CWE 44 22–3)

[1 Timothy 3] [22] The Christian church is the pillar and foundation of truth. Our temple is much holier than the temple in Jerusalem; it does not hide its mysteries in shadows and figures, in cherubim, pomegranates, bells, the ark and similar enigmas,[60] but displays to us solid and genuinely evangelical truth. [23] Certainly it is beyond controversy that the mystery of evangelical godliness,[61] that mystery which frees us once for all from every superstition, is far and away the greatest thing in this temple that stands open throughout the whole world. It is not a table or an ark[62] or a sacrificed animal that is displayed, but it is Christ himself who is displayed and preached. Formerly unknown and unremarked, he has now become so visible that in his human life he was even seen and handled in the flesh by men,[63] while he received so much power in the Spirit that he abolished the sins of all and conferred, and continues to confer, through faith alone the righteousness that the Law was unable to effect. So far was this mystery of ours from being hidden away that it was the object of admiration even to the eyes of angels as they sang 'Glory to God in the highest, and on earth peace, good will to men.'[64] Other mysteries cease to be objects of respect if they are spread abroad. Our mystery has been proclaimed to both Jews and Gentiles alike. Nor was this proclamation ineffective. The simple speech of the gospel, supported by the evidence of miracles, has persuaded the whole world, as no philosophy or human eloquence could have done, of something which would otherwise seem completely contrary to the order of nature. Lastly, after the punishment of crucifixion Christ came back to life by his own power and with angels visibly waiting upon him he ascended into heaven,[65] thus showing us where all our hope must be directed. What is more holy than this mystery? What more sublime? What more certain? or more clear? If we truly believe it, if we live lives worthy of it, what reason is there to pay any attention hereafter to the petty regulations of Judaism? It is we who possess the mystery of true godliness.

---

60 For the construction and furnishings of the Jewish temple see 1 Kings 6–7.

61 On the meaning of 'mystery' see CWE 43 93 n30: 'Erasmus defines *mysterium* ... as "something hidden, and known to the few, and which is to be shared only with the initiates."' Here, Erasmus transforms the traditional meaning: the mystery of godliness is the gospel reflected in the narrative of Christ's life made public by proclamation. See 153 and n21 above.

62 Ie the table of 'showbread' and the 'ark of the covenant' in the temple.

63 Cf 1 John 1:1.

64 Luke 2:14 (AV and similarly in Erasmus' Latin translation).

65 For the angels see Acts 1:10–11.

III. ERASMIAN INTERPRETATIONS OF PAULINE ETHICS

[This section highlights four major aspects of Erasmus' ethical thought as reflected in his interpretation of the Pauline Epistles. In the first selection we see a rather typical tropological interpretation of 'sacrifice,' focusing attention on the integrity of the interior and emotional life. In the second, Erasmus reflects his strong conviction that one must take every precaution to avoid disturbing the public order established and maintained by governments, both good and bad, for public order is an innate prerequisite of the God-ordained structures of society. The third makes a strong characteristically negative evaluation of wealth as inherently 'non-Christian,' while the fourth shows Erasmus tackling the difficult question of free-will, and modifying his view over the course of years, possibly under the influence of Luther, but also, as he himself suggested, reflecting his continued reading of Augustine.]

(1) Sacrifices Worthy of a Christian (from the paraphrase on Romans 12 CWE 42 69)

[**Romans 12**] [69] Therefore, now that by the gift of God you have been brought over from your former superstition to the true religion and are free from the burden of the Mosaic law, I beg and implore you, brethren, through these mercies of God, that henceforth you sacrifice victims to him worthy of this profession – not goats or sheep or oxen that are chosen as pure animals and suitable for sacrifices, for this custom belongs to the heathens and Jews. It is enough to have indulged until the present in base sacrifices of such a kind, but in the future God requires from you far different kinds of rites, another kind of worship, other victims, namely, that you offer your own bodies to him.

This should not be done by mutilating your members,[66] but by subduing your evil desires. You should not offer dead beasts but a living, truly pure, and holy sacrifice, pleasing and acceptable to God – a rational sacrifice, in which the mind rather than a brute beast is the victim. As long as the Law remained carnal, God allowed the bodies of beasts

66 Erasmus seems to have in mind the 'common run of preachers' who understand 'rational worship' as a 'moderate maceration of the body'; cf the annotation on Rom 12:1 ('reasonable service') CWE 56 321–2 with n5; here, however, 'mutilating your members' may also suggest circumcision.

to be sacrificed to him. But since the Law has begun to be spiritual, sacrifices must be made to God with spiritual victims.[67] Sacrifice your disposition to pride rather than a young calf, slay your boiling anger instead of a ram, immolate your lust instead of a goat, sacrifice to God the lascivious and seductive thoughts of your mind instead of pigeons and doves. These are the sacrifices truly worthy of a Christian, these are the victims pleasing to Christ.[68] God is spirit, and he is won over by gifts of the spirit. He demands to be worshipped not by ceremonies but by pure affections. Cut away from your heart superfluous and unbecoming desires instead of cutting away the foreskin from your body. Let the Sabbath be for you a mind free from the tumult of disturbing passions. Christ has offered himself for us; it is right that we in turn should sacrifice ourselves for him. And so it will come about that just as by your profession you have been separated from this world and incorporated into heaven, so in your life and your feelings you will be at variance with your former life, and you will be transformed into new persons, as it were, that is, into heavenly creatures as far as possible – if not yet by the immortality of the body, then certainly by a new state of mind.

(2) Obligations of a Christian in Public Life (from the paraphrase on Romans 13 CWE 42 73–5)

[**Romans 13**] [73] Should persecution by rulers and magistrates break out against you because of your profession of Christianity, you must endure it even though it did not arise from any fault of yours. Persecutions must not, however, be provoked or invited by refusing to do what these leaders in their own right demand and what can be done without offence to God. The state stands firm through order, it ought not to be disturbed under the pretext of religion. There are disgraceful desires, there are vices, in which it is not right to go along with others. [74] On the other hand, there are things in which, because of the nature of the times, one ought to go along even with the heathen for the sake of public peace and order, lest those who somehow ought to be restrained

67 Cf the paraphrase on Rom 8:3: ' … in the one Mosaic law there are, as it were, two laws, the one base and carnal … conveyed by Moses, having little power … ; the other spiritual and effective, which Christ delivered to us' CWE 42 45. To critics who thought he denigrated the Law Erasmus frequently responded with this distinction: his negative comments were directed to the carnal part of the Law, not to the spiritual part, ie the part that implicitly conveyed the truth revealed by Christ.

68 Erasmus clearly liked this tropological (metaphorical) interpretation of 'sacrifice,' cf eg the *Enchiridion* CWE 66 71.

by fear should become worse by your example. For we may divide all things into three classes.[69] The first are those which are truly heavenly, and which, inasmuch as they are peculiar to Christ, are in every case to be preferred to all other things. The second class are things which belong wholly to this world, for example, desire and sin. These you must flee in every possible way. Between these there is a third class, which is neither good nor bad in itself, but which is nevertheless necessary for protecting the order and concord of the whole state. However, I should not want you to throw into confusion what may indeed be but the shadow and outward form of justice that this world has, provided it does not plainly conflict with the righteousness of Christ. Persecution must be borne, and likewise worldly authority, even if it should be somewhat unfair, so that when they persecute you they may not seem to do so on a well-founded pretext, as indeed they might well seem to do if you alone reject the public laws that have been received by all. Christ has not sanctioned such laws, but he has not condemned them either; he gave no thought to them, as it were, because he had more important things to do.

Therefore, whoever belongs to the human race should obey public laws. He should submit to magistrates, who bear a sort of image of God[70] and who, through punishing evil, do the work of God in one way or another. And to that extent, certainly, the power of those men comes from God. Consequently, whoever resists a magistrate who is performing his duty – even an ungodly and heathen one – resists not the one who is performing his duty, but God, from whom all authority derives, from whom also the justice of the law arises. For just as God wished that there should be order among the members of his own body, so in the whole commonwealth in which there are both good and evil, he wished that there should be a certain order. And order is good in itself, even if someone abuses a magistracy. Consequently, those who disturb this order fight against God, its author. And those who fight against God will justly pay the penalty.

[75] And because they carry on affairs that are public, and what is public pertains to all, for this reason you pay a tax to them as a reward for their service. Even if they are impious, nevertheless, because they administer public justice and because God is justice, they are the

69 For this division in the ethical thought of Erasmus (the good, the bad, the indifferent) see *Ratio* 48 with nn31 and 34, also the *Enchiridion* CWE 66 61.

70 Erasmus explains in the *Education of a Christian Prince* CWE 27 220 what it means to say a prince bears the 'likeness of God.'

ministers of God and in a way rule for him as long as they apply their efforts to the mandate given them by public authority. So they should be obeyed in what is right; but if they order impious things, God must be obeyed rather than men.

(3) Christians and the Pursuit of Wealth (from the paraphrase on 1 Timothy 6 CWE 44 36–8)

[**1 Timothy 6**] [36] The pursuit of wealth and the pursuit of godliness cannot coexist in the same person.[71] Men whose souls have once been taken over by the desire to become rich are provoked into many shameful acts and fall into a snare and into many desires that are as foolish as they are ruinous. For this particular desire does not come unaccompanied, but brings with it a long train of evils – arrogance, pride, ambition, violence, fraud, injury, debauchery, carnal pleasures, and other plagues of this kind. Their burden gradually sinks a person into death and destruction, and he becomes pestilent and deadly not only to himself but also to the others in his charge. Anyone who is motivated by greed can do nothing with integrity, nothing without corruption. Greed is so far from honest goodness that it is the seed and root of all evils even if wealth seems to display a sort of admirable happiness. Enticed by this bait, some in their pursuit of wealth were depraved by desires and strayed from the sincerity of evangelical faith when they placed before their eyes another guide than Christ. While they were foolishly chasing after the sweet life, they entangled themselves in many sorrows, acquiring with a great deal of trouble something which they can safeguard only with anxiety and worry and which, if it should chance to be snatched away, would wound their heart and do a grave injury to their greed. Such are the possessions of those who have dedicated themselves to the god Mammon.[72]

[37] I have shown how dangerous the pursuit of wealth is to Christians. If there are among our people, however, any who happen to have received that wealth which leads this world to call them rich and

71 But cf the paraphrase on Matt 6:25–34 where Erasmus permits the follower of Christ to have 'money that comes one's way,' 138 above.

72 This could also be translated, 'to Mammon as their god.' In his annotation on Matt 6:24 (*et mammonae*) Erasmus notes that the Greeks sometimes speak of wealth as a god; in fact, however, there was no actual god in classical antiquity named 'Mammon.' Erasmus, in the annotation just cited, claims the word is Aramaic; cf CWE 44 36 n9.

blessed, and to look up to and to revere them like demigods, instruct them that they are not to adopt a haughty attitude because of their confidence in this wealth and that they are not to think that their felicity can be safeguarded by material goods. These goods are, first of all, hollow and meaningless, and, secondly, they are uncertain because if chance does not snatch them away, death certainly does. Let them put their trust instead in the living God who never fails either the living or the dead because he himself is immutable. From his beneficence comes whatever this world supplies in sufficient quantity from the year's produce, which is for our immediate use, not for the accumulation of riches. Let them direct their energy instead to exercising themselves in good works so that they may become truly wealthy and grow rich in good deeds rather than in estates. Let them consider whatever possessions [38] they happen to acquire belong to all and not just to themselves. For this reason they should be ready to share with the needy and should not treat with disdain the rest of the people who are poor, but should adopt instead a pleasing and mild manner for the meetings and intercourse of social life.

(4) Free Will (from the paraphrase on Romans 9 CWE 42 55–7)

[Erasmus and Luther exchanged letters first in 1519, when the correspondence between the two was cordial, and Erasmus gave a qualified approval to Luther's central concerns. But Erasmus found Luther's approach to reform too violent; after Luther's excommunication (January 1521) several persons in high position, including Henry VIII and Popes Adrian VI and Clement VII requested Erasmus to write against Luther. Erasmus finally did so in 1524 choosing for his subject 'free will.' As soon as his book, *De libero arbitrio*, had been published Philippus Melanchthon told him that 'all Luther's contentions, taken by and large, either revolve around the question of free will or involve the use of ceremonies.' He continued, 'On the first of these I see that you disagree.'[73] This challenge to Luther would lead to three further publications, one by Luther, *De servo arbitrio* (1525), and two by Erasmus, the *Hyperaspistes* I (1526) and II (1527). Erasmus himself was in fact somewhat ambiguous on the subject: though he championed free will in his debate with Luther, in 1527 he wrote to Thomas More, 'If I follow Paul and Augustine very little is left to free will.'[74] Erasmus'

73 Ep 1500:12–13.
74 Ep 1804:88–9, cf 82–109.

ambiguity is reflected in the changes made in 1532 in the paraphrase on Romans 9:14–22. I give here the text of *1532*, but have marked with asterisks the passages concerned, adding in a footnote the passages as they appeared in the first edition of 1517.]

[**Romans 9**] [55] And let no impious person distort the things we have said and contend that blame should not be ascribed to men but to God, who arbitrarily rejects or chooses those who have merited or were guilty of nothing. Far be it from anyone to harbour such a thought and to interpret in this way what God says to Moses in Exodus [33:19]: 'I will have mercy on whom I have mercy, and I will have compassion on whom I have compassion.' *So then,[75] it is not by willing or by exertion that salvation is attained, but by the mercy of God, for in vain do we desire, in vain do we strive, unless a willing God draws us to him. Moreover, he draws to himself whomever he chooses, even those who have merited nothing, and rejects those who are guilty of nothing. *However,[76] it does not follow that God is unjust to anyone, but that he is merciful toward many. No one is condemned except by his own guilt. No one is saved except by the kindness of God. *Thus,[77] he thinks those worthy whom he wishes, but in such a way that if you have been drawn to him by his mercy you have reason to give thanks; but if you have been abandoned to your own obduracy you have no reason to complain. For God does not harden human minds to hinder them from believing in the gospel of Christ; but to illuminate the magnitude of his kindness and to reveal the glory of his power, God uses the stubbornness of those who, through their *own* obduracy, refuse to believe. For that is how we should interpret what is said to Pharaoh in Exodus [9:16]: 'But for this purpose I have raised you up that in you I might show my power and that my name might be proclaimed throughout the earth.'[78]

From words of this kind the ungodly seizes the opportunity and says: 'If he has mercy on whomever he wishes, and hardens whomever he wishes, how can he afterwards blame us? Since it is impossible to resist the will of God, let him charge it to his own account rather than to ours

75 In *1517* 'as if': ' … on whom I have compassion, as if it is not by willing … '

76 This sentence replaced a sentence of the *1517* text reading 'Or rather, some part of it depends on our own will and striving, although this part is so minor that it seems like nothing at all in comparison with the free kindness of God.'

77 In the *1517* text the sentence was shorter, as follows: 'Thus he thinks those worthy whom he wishes, but in such a way that you have reason to give thanks, you have no reason to complain.'

78 Vulgate, cf AV.

if we sin.' Listen now to my reply. No one resists the will of God, but the will of God is not the cause of your destruction. He did not harden the heart of Pharaoh in such a way that he himself caused Pharaoh's stubbornness, but although he knew the tyrant's arrogance was worthy of sudden destruction, nevertheless little by little he used heavier punishments against him by which [56] Pharaoh might have been corrected if his own evil will had not stood in the way. But the divine leniency provoked his impious mind even more. God, therefore, turned Pharaoh's evil into his own glory.

I could say more things on God's behalf, but God hates all arrogance. However, what is more arrogant than a man (than which nothing is lowlier) disputing with God as if he were contending with an equal? For who would tolerate it if a clay vessel expostulated with its maker and said: 'Why have you formed me in this way?' What clay is in the hand of the potter, we all are in the hand of God. *So[79] says the Lord himself through the prophet Isaiah. He forms whatever pleases him, making one vessel for a base and lowly function, another for an honourable function. No matter what the reasons for his actions may have been, the potter is answerable to no one, and it is not proper for the clay to demand from him the reason for his decision. *The clay[80] in itself is nothing other than clay. If the potter forms an elegant drinking-cup from clay, whatever honour attaches to this belongs to his own artistry. If the potter forms a chamber-pot, no injustice is done to filthy and worthless clay. Therefore if God abandons someone in his sins, thus he was born, there is no injustice. But if he calls someone to righteousness, his mercy is a free gift. In the case of the former, God reveals his own righteousness so that he may be feared. To the latter he discloses his own goodness so that he may be loved. It is not the part of a man to require a reason from God for his decision – why he calls this one later and that one earlier, why he accepts one who has done nothing to deserve it and abandons a man who has incurred no guilt. A man is far more lowly in comparison with God than is clay in comparison with its human craftsman. If it is monstrous arrogance for the clay to argue

79 The sentence was added in *1532*, hence absent from the 1517 text; for the reference see Isa 29:16, 45:9.

80 [The clay … guilt]: These sentences were added in *1532*, hence were absent from the text of 1517, when the passage read, ' … the potter is answerable to no one, and it is not proper for the clay to demand from him the reason for his decision. A man is far lowlier in comparison with God than is clay in comparison with its human craftsman … '

with its creator, is it not greater arrogance for a man to dispute about the purposes of God which are so far above us that we are scarcely able to grasp a shadow or a dream of them? Begin to believe and cease to debate, and then you will understand more quickly.

And the potter can make a mistake, God cannot. It is enough for you to believe that God, since he is omnipotent, can do whatever he wishes. But at the same time, since he is best,[81] he does not desire anything but the best. He ought not to be blamed if he uses our evils for a good purpose. On the contrary, this itself is a proof of his supreme goodness, that he turns the evil of others into good. God has not made you into a filthy vessel. You have defiled yourself, and you have devoted yourself to dishonourable purposes. After this, if God[82] through his own wisdom makes use of your evil for saving the pious and for glorifying his own name, you have no cause to complain about it. You are paying a just punishment for your evil will. The pious are rendered more cautious by your example, and they give thanks more eagerly as they become more aware, because of your blindness and destruction, of [57] how much they owe to the divine kindness. Pharaoh had no cause to accuse God; he was overthrown by his own evil will, and yet his evil will made clear the glory of God among the Hebrews.

81 A standard epithet applied to God, even to the pagan Jupiter, 'greatest and best.' Cf 263 n196.

82 In *1517* God speaks here in his own person: ' … if I through my wisdom make use of your evil … and glorifying my own name … ' This may have been inadvertent, and it was corrected to third person in 1521.

CHAPTER SIX

Paraphrases on Hebrews and the Catholic Epistles

[The selections from Hebrews and the Catholic Epistles are taken in the order of the publication of the *Paraphrases* on these Epistles, the order in which they appear in CWE 44. The selections have been chosen either on the basis of their inherent interest or because they touch on focal points in Erasmian thought. The paraphrase on 1 Peter 1:3–21, 4:1–2 attempts to clarify the relationship of Christ's suffering and death to baptism and Christian morality, and to explain the meaning of the affirmation in the Creed that 'Christ descended to the dead.' In the paraphrase on the passage in 2 Peter Erasmus delivers a sly thrust against contemporary theological education, and, perhaps more substantively, grounds Christian truth in the evidence of eye-witnesses and in the authority of inspired Scripture properly interpreted. Erasmus creates a lively interest for the reader of the paraphrase on James by his vitriolic, and at points autobiographical, excursus on 'the tongue,' and in paraphrases in both James and 1 John he addresses theological topics of universal interest: the relation of faith and charity, and the meaning for the Christian of the biblical concept of 'the world.' Finally, we offer here a long selection from Hebrews 11, that remarkable chapter on faith providing a field so suited to the exercise of Erasmus' rhetorical skills.]

1 PETER

Christ, Saviour and Exemplar (from the paraphrases on 1 Peter 3 and 4 CWE 44 98–100)

[1 Peter 3 and 4] [98] It is glorious for you to imitate your prince. This was the way he made the glory of God the Father clear. Completely innocent, he was arrested, put in chains, scourged, spat upon, crucified, and died for our sins though he himself had no sin. Righteous, he paid the penalty for the unrighteous; guiltless, he paid the penalty for the guilty, gladly obeying the will of the Father in order to present us, who were sinners, pure and unstained to the Father. We too, then, following his example, are to live among the harmful without ourselves doing any harm and, while being good, are to suffer for the salvation of those who are evil. He died only once and was given eternal life in return for temporary suffering so that we who have had our sins removed once for all might not relapse into the same sins. Christ atoned for us. Because of the weakness of the human body that he had assumed he was delivered to death, but he was recalled to life by the power of the Spirit, which could not be overcome by any sufferings. For during the time when his lifeless body was enclosed in the tomb, alive in the spirit he penetrated to the region of the dead, and went to those spirits who had themselves likewise been stripped of their bodies and were residing with the dead, proclaiming to them that the time was now at [99] hand for them to receive the reward for their godliness. For they had in the past feared the justice of God and had not sought vengeance for wrongs done to them, but, doing no harm themselves, had lived among people who did harm. But to those who, in the days of Noah, did not believe, he announced that they would suffer what they deserved. Therefore, when the deluge came rushing down, it destroyed everyone except the eight who alone followed Noah's counsel, and entrusted themselves to the ark.

What Noah's ark signified for those eight who were saved, baptism now signifies for you. Baptism if properly received saves from destruction and washes away filth not from the body but from the soul. Refused, it destroys forever and sinks one in still heavier waves of wickedness. Therefore, that which, when faith is added, is a source of salvation to others, brings destruction to the disbelieving and rebellious. However, it is not enough for you that your sins have perished and the warped desires of your old life have perished in the flood of baptism. There must also be present in you a conscience which throughout the whole of your life after baptism continues to respond to God's gift. Christ died, but only once; he rose again never to die thereafter. Through baptism the sins of our past life are destroyed for us once for all through Christ's death, but on the condition that, having been brought back to life again in him for innocence, we never afterwards relapse into sins in so far as it is in our power not to do so. [100] This will happen if we put our mortality aside, as it were, and aspire with our whole heart and soul to that heavenly life whose inheritance awaits those who obey the gospel.

[1 Peter 4] [100] Therefore, since Christ, your prince and head, did not indulge in the pleasures of this life but reached heavenly glory through the temporary sufferings of the body and, armed with patience, overcame his adversaries, it is right that you who profess yourselves his disciples should arm yourselves with a similar firm purpose in your heart. An innocent way of life is the securest armament. Whoever has died with Christ in the flesh has so ceased from the sins of his past life that it is clear to all that he has died to human desires. He no longer itches with the craving for fame, is no longer aroused by the lust for revenge; whatever is left of the span of life given in this poor body he lives out entirely for the will of God.

The Nature of Evangelical Truth (from the paraphrase on 2 Peter 1 CWE 44 114–15)

[**2 Peter 1**] [114] Since what you have received from us is absolutely certain, you must not deviate from it. For our teaching is not like that of the philosophers, who, with cleverly devised fables and man-made subtleties, try to persuade people of what they themselves obviously do not understand since they disagree with one another about it.[1] We have certainly not followed their course but have revealed to you the power and coming of our Lord Jesus Christ and we preach to you his majesty, which we have beheld with our own eyes. After God the Father had clothed him with a beauty and a glory that made his face as bright as the sun and made his clothes surpass the whiteness of snow, the greatest honour of all was added, the witness of his Father's own voice: 'This is my beloved Son who has delighted my heart. Hear him.'[2] No more complete or more magnificent testimony could be produced. If the oracles of the prophets who shrouded their prophecies about Christ in riddles have very great weight with you, so manifest a proclamation from the Father himself about the Son ought to have even greater weight. The prophets concur with the Father's voice provided that one interprets them correctly. They in a sense prepare the mind for evangelical truth through their promises when they sketch and, as it were, outline what evangelical preaching portrays completely. [115] The predictions of the prophets will be useful only if those who read them remember that the prophetic part of Scripture is obscure because

1 In his annotation on 2 Peter 1:16 (*non enim indoctas fabulas*) Erasmus suggests that these words from Scripture characterize fairly some of the debates of the contemporary theologians!

2 For the details of the Transfiguration see Matt 17:1–8, where the Vulgate text compares the garments of Christ to snow.

of its cloak of figurative speech and cannot be understood without interpretation. This interpretation does not belong to everyone alike and is not subject to the arbitrary views of any one person. For the prophets who made these predictions did not make them from their own understanding and will. Since they were holy men and free from all human desires, the Holy Spirit inspired their minds, and using them, so to speak, as his organs of speech made his own mind somehow known to us through them. What men produce from their own human understanding can be grasped by the human intellect. But what has been produced by the inspiration of the divine Spirit requires an interpreter who is inspired by the same Spirit.

JAMES

Faith and Charity (from the paraphrase on James 2 CWE 44 150–1)

[James 2] [150] What is faith without love?[3] Love moreover is a living thing; it does not go on holiday; it is not idle; it expresses itself in kind acts wherever it is present. If these acts are lacking, my brothers, I ask you, will the empty word 'faith' save a person? Faith which does not work through love is unproductive; no, it is faith in name only. An example here will make clear what I mean. If someone says blandly to a brother or a sister who lacks clothing or daily food, 'Depart in peace, keep warm, and remember to eat well,' and after saying this, gives him or her none of the things the body needs, will his fine talk be of any use to the ones in need? Such people will be no less cold and hungry for all his fine talk, which is of no [151] help to their need. He gives them only verbal support, but does nothing in actual fact. A profession of faith will certainly be equally useless if it consists only of words and does nothing except remain inactive as though dead. It should no more be called faith than a human corpse merits the name of human being. Love is to faith what the soul is to the body. Take away love and the word faith is like something dead and inert. It will do you no more good before God to confess in words an idle faith than fine speech benefits a neighbour in need when he must be helped with action. The person who offers no

3 One should note the manner in which the relation of faith and charity is presented in the annotations on 1 Cor 13:2 and 13, 242–7 below.

tangible proofs of his faith but repeats every day, 'I believe in God, I believe in God,' seems to be mocking God. His belief is only a matter of words, for he possesses a faith that serves no purpose.

Someone will now appear perhaps who, eager to separate things that are by nature most closely joined together and cannot be split apart from each other, might say, 'You have faith, I have deeds. Let each one of us be satisfied with his part. Let your faith be enough for you. I am content to have for my part good deeds.' On the contrary, neither part is sufficient by itself. As for you who boast of faith – if you really have it, you ought to show it by your actions. If the faith you have is dead, the mere fact that you have it is futile. As for you who on the other hand vaunt your deeds – they are not enough by themselves to obtain the crown of immortality unless they issue from love, which is the inseparable companion of saving faith. Loving acts of charity are for us what flowers and leaves are for a tree. If they bloom at the proper time, they show that the roots of the tree are alive and are providing the sap by which the leaves and flowers are nourished. Good deeds are correspondingly beneficial if they are not done for vainglory or for popularity, because of fear or shame, or from hope of gain, but from a living faith which has persuaded us that whatever is done to a neighbour for God's sake is done to God, and that its reward is not to be expected from anyone except God.

The Tongue (from the paraphrase on James 3 CWE 44 154–7)

[**James 3**] [154] To have complete authority over the belly is an achievement, to control the eyes and ears is likewise an accomplishment, and it is something again to keep the hands in check. But to keep the tongue under complete control is the most difficult of all. The tongue is a tiny part of the body, but all the rest is virtually dependent upon it. Human speech is an effective and powerful force for either the benefit or the ruin of the multitude. It penetrates the minds of its hearers; it implants or weeds out pestilent beliefs; it arouses or calms passionate hatreds; it moves people to war or disposes them to peace. In sum, the tongue can propel a hearer in any direction at all.

[155] Look at how tiny a fire can kindle a huge mass of timber. Where did that raging and rapidly spreading fire come from? From a single spark. In the same way there can come from the human tongue both the greatest benefit and on the other hand the ultimate ruin to human life. The tongue is a world and collection of all the vices. A small spark is, as it were, the seed from which the whole fire grows. Similarly every evil

in life is taken from the tongue as though it were their storehouse. Just as a bit of fire combines with a mound of tinder so that gradually fire mingles with the entire pile, so the tongue mingles with the members of the body in such a way that, if it is not checked, it stains and infects the whole body with its plague and keeps a person's entire life from the cradle to extreme old age ablaze with the fire of every vice. But nature did not place the violent power of this evil in the tongue. This evil was inspired from the fire of Gehenna, which first infects the mind with evil spirits. The pestilence in the mind then breaks out on a larger scale through the organ of the tongue, and finally catches others too with its contagion so that the evil cannot be checked by any force.[4]

[156] Although every kind of animal that earth and sea and air contain has been tamed in the past and is being tamed every day, no method, no art has yet been found to tame the intemperate tongue. Yes, this one evil is still wild and violent, and is not only incapable of being controlled but even drips with a deadly poison. Indeed, the tongue is doubly baneful with its insuperable ferocity and its deadly poison, which it breathes on anyone it wishes even from a distance. The disease would be less frightening if it were simple and harmful in one way only. As it is, the evil takes many different and various shapes in order to injure more grievously and readily, and is often more deadly when it disguises itself under the appearance of good. There is nothing better or more attractive to everyone's eyes than godliness. The tongue does the most harm under the pretext of godliness when it mixes things that cannot cohere. For the person who is cruel and slanderous towards a neighbour cannot be pious towards God. And yet with this organ we praise God, calling him Father, and with the same organ we revile and slander a neighbour created in the likeness of God. [157] When someone tries to make slander acceptable under the guise of godliness, what else is it than dosing wine with hemlock to make the poison more deadly by mixing it with the most wholesome substance? They have in their mouth 'Lord, be merciful' even as they cruelly rage against a brother with their tongue. They have on their lips, 'Our Father,' even as they pierce again and again with the lance of their tongue the neighbour for whose salvation Christ was pierced.[5] They pour out praise for the gentleness of Christ,

4 The paragraph paraphrases James 3:6, a somewhat problematic verse: 'And the tongue is a fire. The tongue is an unrighteous world among our members, staining the whole body, setting on fire the cycle of nature, and set on fire by hell' [RSV].

5 Cf John 19:34.

who answered his slanderers calmly,[6] while they themselves assail with lies even the one who benefits them.[7] They proclaim themselves angels[8] and heralds of Christ while they are the organ of the devil. They not only do such opposite things with the same tongue but often even from the same pulpit they begin with the praises of God and then launch into the denigration of a neighbour.[9] The ruin with which they infect the minds of the audience is all the greater because under the fictitious appearance of religion they cover and disguise the deadly poison which they draw forth from their infected heart through the organ of the tongue. I ask you, brothers, does this not remind you of some kind of monster?

1 JOHN

The World, the Flesh, and the Devil (from the Paraphrase on 1 John 2 CWE 44 182–3)

[**1 John 2**] [182] By 'world' I do not mean this world whose creator is God and in which we live whether we wish to or not. I call 'world' those futile desires for the meaningless things in which the common herd of men, oblivious to true goods, place their happiness.[10] No place, however isolated, no special garb or diet or title removes you from this present world. Only a mind free from those desires that I mentioned can do that. What does this world contain that does not lead to destruction? There are three things that most of all deceive the foolish and unwary: the pleasure of the flesh, the incitements of the eyes, the pride and noise of life. The world is a magician, and its tricks are the hollow pleasures

6 Cf eg Luke 22:66–71, John 18:19–24.

7 Erasmus undoubtedly has in mind his own situation, as his complaints in the *Apologia* prefacing his editions of the New Testament indicate; cf CWE 41 456–8. Cf. 127 n137.

8 Probably an allusion to monks, who were sometimes said to 'live the angelic life'; cf CWE 45 58 n5.

9 A reference evidently to Erasmus' own experience, related in the annotation on 1 Peter 4:7 (*et vigilate*): a preacher during a sermon delivered in Erasmus' presence accused Erasmus of a double sin against the Holy Spirit: presumption and an assault on truth.

10 Compare the paraphrase on James 4:7: 'When I say "world" I mean precisely those misplaced passions for visible things through which the world promises a kind of happiness.' For a review of the word 'world' in Erasmus' writings see CWE 43 370 n7. See also the paraphrase on John 15:18 CWE 46 180, and the annotation on Gal 4:3 ('we were serving as slaves under the elements of the universe') CWE 58 65–6.

through which it caresses the body's senses for a moment so that the soul may be temporarily diverted from its pursuit of heavenly goods. For that heavenly Spirit which God the Father imparts to his children who have been truly reborn through Christ inspires the passion for those heavenly goods.

Satan too has his spirit through which he inspires a baneful love for material things which are neither real nor lasting for those who have devoted themselves to this world. He inspires the evil joys of sexual love [183] that tickle the body's members with a foul and foolish itch. He inspires the fondness for fine food and drink that entice throat and palate. He inspires the comfortable sweetness of relaxation and sleep to make the mind grow more listless from lack of use. He inspires lewd songs and obscene stories with which to cajole the ears. He inspires the allure of beautiful shapes and spectacles of every kind with which to delight the eyes. He inspires the pomp of prestige and the noisy stir of wealth, incitements to ambition. In short, from every side he diverts people's minds from true and everlasting goods to the hollow idols of false goods. Anyone who is captured by a desire for these things should realize that he is not being moved by the Spirit of the Father in heaven but by the spirit of the world.

HEBREWS

Encomium on Faith (from the paraphrase on Hebrews 11 CWE 44 243–52)

[The author of Hebrews offered in chapter 11 an outstanding example of his rhetorical skills; the chapter accordingly provided an excellent ground for Erasmus to display his own undeniably sophisticated rhetorical abilities, as the passages excerpted here attest. But the paraphrase on the chapter is perhaps more significant as an opportunity well utilized by Erasmus to characterize the nature of faith. Erasmus had claimed that Heb 11:1 did not offer a definition of faith, a claim that was challenged. In *1527*, in an annotation on Rom 1:17 in the fourth edition of his New Testament, Erasmus attempted to define faith, not in terms of formal definition but by a consideration of expressions of faith in use in Scripture and in everyday life. This (*1521*) paraphrase on Hebrews 11 anticipates the later definition in the annotation of *1527* (excerpted below) by elucidating the implications of the narrative of the great exemplars of faith in Hebrew literature. Here in the paraphrase on Hebrews 11, the range of vocabulary Erasmus used to designate faith is relatively small, especially in comparison with his study of faith in the annotation on Rom 1:17, but I have included in brackets the Latin for the relevant words with the hope that readers will find this a convenience in comparing this passage with that annotation.]

[Hebrews 11] [243] Nothing makes the godly more attractive to God[11] than to have a sure confidence [*fiducia*] about him. For to have no doubts about God's words is evidence of a mind that holds only the best thoughts about him, since the things of which God speaks are nowhere apparent to the human senses and cannot be proved by human arguments. There are things that the mind conceives of only through hope, since they do not exist anywhere in any physical way. Most people believe [*credo*] that such conceptions are insubstantial and no different from dreams. They think it foolish to believe [*credo*] something to be true [244] which cannot be shown to the eyes. And yet this faith [*fides*] through which the righteous man will save his life when others perish[12] is not some vulgar credulity [*credulitas*]; it is the solid and firm foundation of those things that can be apprehended neither by the senses nor by man-made arguments. Firm hope makes them so present to the mind that they appear to be held in the hands right before the eyes. Hope does not persuade through man-made proofs but through a sure confidence [*fiducia*] in God their source that those things which cannot be seen in themselves are absolutely sure. The Jews have faith [*fido*] in their own works, but our confidence in God[13] is the one thing that makes us pleasing and dear to him – and not only us; anyone who reviews the history of the world, starting with the creation, will find that it was above all on the grounds of their faith [*fides*] that all those ancestors of ours who are renowned and remembered for their godliness deserved what they attained.

First, do we not owe to faith [*fides*] our understanding that this whole world and everything it contains were created by the word of God and the mere command alone of its creator? For otherwise who could persuade us that things that are seen come into existence from things that are not seen or that what exists is made from what does not exist? Philosophers following human reasoning think that the universe is uncreated and no more had a beginning than did its fabricator.[14] As for us, however, we believe just as if we had actually seen what could never in

11 The paraphrase on 11:1 anticipates 11:6; 'Without faith it is impossible to please [God].'

12 Perhaps an allusion to 'righteous Lot' (2 Pet 2:7) is intended.

13 'Our confidence in God': in Latin 'this.'

14 Cf Aristotle *Physica* 8.1.

fact have been seen and cannot be inferred by the reasoning power of the human mind, and we base our belief on [*fretus*, ie 'relying on'] the divine books that tell how the world was created by the command of God who we know is all-powerful and cannot lie.

[246] Now how many times did Abraham give proof of his extraordinary confidence [*fiducia*] in God? First, though a man has nothing sweeter than his native soil, nevertheless when he was told by God to leave his native land and dear ones behind and to emigrate to an unknown land, he obeyed the divine voice without hesitation,[15] without the stimulus of anybody's example, without having any plausible proofs to make him hope that he would be coming into the hereditary possession of some land, of which up to that time he knew neither the name nor the location. So sure was his confidence [*fiducia*] that God would fulfil whatever he promised. It was from the same confidence [*fiducia*] that, no matter what happened, Abraham was never led to lose faith in [*diffido*, ie 'distrust'] God, who had promised the land.

[247] Was it not also an outstanding proof of Abraham's faith [*fides*] that when, to test the sincerity of his faith [*fido*] in him,[16] God told him to sacrifice his son Isaac, without a moment's delay he started to do what he had been told, although Isaac was his only son and it was in his name that the descendants had been promised? For the words of God's promise were, 'In Isaac your seed shall be called' [Gen 21:12]. Abraham did not start arguing with himself: 'Where will my descendants come from if I kill him in whom my hope of descendants exists?' Instead he carefully weighed in his mind the fact that God, who had made the promise, could not lie and, if it should so please him, was able to raise up, even from the dead, his lifeless son to be the propagator of the race.[17] Abraham believed in the resurrection of the dead, and for this reason it was granted to him to bring back home his lifeless son restored to life – restored, that is, because it had been in Abraham's power to kill him. For this reason Isaac was even then an image foreshadowing the future resurrection of Jesus Christ.

[248] It was, moreover, the faith [*fides*] of the parents that saved Moses right after he was born. [249] But while his parents duly deserve their praise, it was to Moses' own credit that, after he had grown up and had been adopted by Pharoah's daughter, he rejected the honour of being a

15 To obey without hesitation is for Erasmus a chief mark of faith; cf 151 with n14 above.

16 Ie 'to test how sincerely he trusted God.'

17 Compare the characterization of Abraham's faith in the paraphrase on Rom 4 CWE 42 26–32.

member of the king's family. Having proclaimed publicly that he was a Hebrew, he chose to suffer affliction in common with the people of God rather than to maintain an impious pretence and secure the advantages of a life at court. He disdained what was in his possession and turned the eyes of faith [*fides*] to those things that were far distant from the senses, relying on [*fretus*] God who does not allow the godliness of men to be cheated of the rewards it has earned.

Because he relied on [*fretus*] God's support, he dared even greater things than these. He was not afraid of the wrath of a savage tyrant and did not hesitate[18] to labour to bring about the flight from Egypt. He disdained the king, whom he beheld with his eyes. With an unbroken spirit, he had faith in [*fido* ie 'he trusted'] the invisible aid of the invisible God just as though he saw him face to face with his own eyes. It was due to the same confidence [*fiducia*] that while he understood that the avenging angel would kill every one of the first-born of the Egyptians, he had no fear at all for his fellow Hebrews. Instead he instituted the yearly ritual of eating the paschal lamb with whose blood they sprinkled the threshold, lintel and doorposts of their houses.[19] Relying on [*fretus*] this sign, they were not afraid for themselves in the midst of the slaughter of the Egyptians.

What caused the walls of Jericho to collapse suddenly on the seventh day after the Hebrews marched around them seven times? For they were not being battered in by any machines, but at the [250] sound of the priests' trumpets and the shout of the people an entrance was given at the point where each of the Hebrews had taken his position in their ring around the city.[20] Was it not the faith [*fides*] of the people and of Joshua the leader? Joshua was convinced[21] that God could do everything and that what he had promised to do would undoubtedly be done.

Since among so many extraordinary deeds of our ancestors not a single outstanding exploit was performed without the aid of faith [*fides*], what point is there in continuing to review them one by one? Time will fail us if I go on to speak about the commander Gideon who, relying

18 'Did not hesitate': *dubitavit*, which has also the sense of 'waver in opinion,' 'doubt,' 'question.'

19 According to Exod 12:7 blood was sprinkled only on the lintel and the two doorposts.

20 Cf Josh 6:1–21. The narrative does not explicitly speak of specific entrance points, cf 6:20.

21 'Was convinced … undoubtedly': *persuaserit sibi … haud dubie* – each expression in its own way emphasizes the certainty with which Joshua held his conviction.

on [*fretus*] God's aid, dared with three hundred men to attack the forces of the Midianites, or about Samson, or David, or Samuel. [251] Time would fail me if I continue to review all the examples of this kind. I may pass over in silence for the moment the many outstanding prophets[22] who, relying on God [*fretus*], counted the threats of tyrants as nothing, or about the many men renowned for their religious devotion who, without human resources, but with the support of God in whom they had placed total confidence [*fiducia*], performed wonders and left to posterity a memory of themselves from their outstanding deeds. Of all these their faith [*fides*] must be given the credit for what they did. They obtained from God through prayers of faith [*fido*][23] what was impossible in the normal course of nature. Why, the confidence [*fiducia*] of women even brought it about that mothers saw their dead children called back to life! Men, stretched on the rack and half dead from different kinds of torture, preferred to expire in pain than to obey the ungodly commands of princes. With great confidence [*fiducia*] they gave up for God the life which they knew they would receive back with interest in the resurrection of the dead. Still others because of their tenacious zeal for truth and righteousness were objects of ridicule to people who derided and slandered them as madmen and criminals. Not only were they visited with reproaches [252] because of the confidence [*fiducia*] they had in God, but their sincerity was also tested by scourgings as well as by chains and imprisonment. They were stoned to death. They fell, slain by swords, convinced that not even death could tear the godly away from God. Some were cast out of their own homes and exiled from their towns. They wandered over the desert like wild animals, covering themselves as best they could with goatskins and sheepskins, suffering from the lack of necessities, hard pressed on all sides by the savage threats of their persecutors, and afflicted by the varied ills of this life.

Although all these have not yet obtained the reward promised for godliness, which will occur in the resurrection of the body, nevertheless they have earned everlasting praise for their steadfast confidence [*fiducia*]. Someone may say, 'Why is each one not given his or her reward immediately after death?' Evidently God has decided that the entire body of Christ will receive the glory of immortality at the same time. For we are all members of the same body and those who have gone

22 For the identification, somewhat problematic, of the prophets and the great heroes of faith in the narrative that follows see CWE 44 251 n42.

23 'Prayers of faith': *votis fidentibus* 'trusting prayers.'

before us are willingly waiting so that together with their physical bodies and the whole company of their brothers all will come equally into the inheritance of eternal glory and will be joined at the same moment to their Head.[24]

24 Cf 1 Thess 4:15–17. Exegetes have interpreted 11:40 in various ways. Erasmus here follows the interpretation of Thomas Aquinas; cf CWE 44 252 nn51, 52.

CHAPTER SEVEN

The *Annotations* on the New Testament

[I noted in the introductory chapter the stimulating variety of subjects Erasmus addressed in his *Annotations* (cf especially 8–9 and 16–17 in reference to the second and fourth editions of the New Testament). The annotations were intended in the first instance to defend his translation and clarify the sense of the Greek text. But the genre permitted the discussion of a wide-ranging field of topics (cf 21). As an avenue facilitating defence and clarification, the annotations invited discussion, necessarily pervasive, of the text and language of Scripture, but this discussion itself presupposed debatable views about the authority and canon of Scripture. In addition, few passages of Scripture fail to invite reflection on theological issues, issues indeed that were often heatedly contested in the sixteenth century, some of which are subjects of debate still in the twenty-first century. Moreover, when Erasmus dedicated his New Testament to Pope Leo, his affirmation that his work was undertaken with the hope that it would contribute to the restoration of a religion fallen into decay rationalized his frequent attempts in the annotations to contrast the word of Scripture with the state of the current church, bringing into view with a sharp critique ethical and, indeed, even liturgical problems. Beyond that the humanist instinct to describe places and assess human character led to some of the most interesting passages in the annotations. The selections below roam through this work of Erasmus and attempt to order his thoughts, sometimes apparently quite spontaneous, within the categories just described. Selections from Romans and Ephesians are referenced according to CWE page number; selections from the other New Testament books are referenced according to ASD series, volume and page number, and, in the case of long annotations, line number as well.]

I. SCRIPTURE

(1) The Canon of Scripture – Annotations on Acts 1:1 and Hebrews 13:24

From the annotation on Acts 1:1 (*primum quidem sermonem* 'in the first book') [ASD VI-6 177–80:23–38, 52–73]

[The selections from this annotation appeared in *1516* (first paragraph, but cf n3) and *1527* (second paragraph). The annotation reflects Erasmus' sensitivity to some of the historical problems arising from the investigation of Scripture, in particular the problems of canon and historical reliability. The argument here implies that historical reliability is a necessary prerequisite for admission into the canon of Scripture, but Erasmus also expects canonical writings to have a certain 'gravity.' He begins the annotation by extolling Acts as a biblical book: the narrative of the book is, he thinks, really a continuation of the gospel story, of which the birth and growth of the church is an intrinsic part, and wishes that Luke had carried further the narrative of the remarkable deeds of the apostles. The annotation continues:]

[**ASD VI-6 177–80**] [23] For this reason I am the more surprised that the Greeks treated this book so indifferently, and that among the ancient Latin writers no one arose to illuminate with commentary a work so remarkable, so utterly replete with gospel grandeur and gospel faith. As far as I know nothing else of this sort exists apart from some place-names Jerome has identified, and those only few and briefly noted (though perhaps this little work should not be attributed to Jerome).[1] It was late in time when the Epistle to the Hebrews was received into the canon. There is some doubt about the Epistle of James. For many years Italy did not recognize the book of Revelation as Scripture; Greece even now does not fully approve it as a canonical book.[2] About Acts,

1 A reference to the *Expositio de nominibus locorum vel civitatum ... in libro Actuum apostolorum 'An exposition of the place-names ... in the book of the Acts of the Apostles.'* This dictionary of place-names was the work of the Venerable Bede (c673–735), though in Erasmus' day it was generally ascribed to Jerome.

2 On the adoption of these books into the canon see Ferguson *Early Christianity* 206–10, especially 208, 'The most disputed books of the New Testament in the fourth to the sixth century were Hebrews, 2 Peter, Jude and Revelation.' Erasmus discusses further the question of authorship and canonicity in the first and last annotations on James, 2 and 3 John (last annotation), and Revelation (last annotation). For Hebrews, see the next selection.

however, there never has been any hesitation. The[3] fact that the Manicheans did not accept the book, as Augustine points out in his book *Against Adamantius the Manichean*,[4] quite properly gave the Book of Acts more weight among the orthodox precisely because heretics, who were alike both ridiculous and ungodly, did not like it. It is appropriate, therefore, that Christians should strive with even greater zeal[5] to become acquainted with the origins of their own society so that once they have learned how the church grew from infancy to maturity they will recognize the means by which a religion fallen into ruins must be restored.

[52] For my part, I have no doubt that the Holy Spirit wanted this book to survive to give certitude to our faith; at the same time the Spirit did not want the narrative of events to be continued further, in part so that we should not find the infancy of the church a matter of doubt, in part so that through a diversity of narratives we should not gradually fall away from Christ to human concerns. The inviolable authority of the Holy Scriptures had once and for all to be confined within boundaries so that their authority would not be diminished by a multitude of books. For if you read the writings of the others who are said to have lived near the time of the apostles, writings published as a record of events that either the authors themselves saw and heard or learned from others who had witnessed them,[6] you will think you are reading fables (if I may use the expression) if you compare them with the gravity and intrinsic reliability of the narrative of Acts. Among these writers there are some who created fictional narratives from what they found in Scripture, while there are others who through intellectual incapacity or faulty memory passed on what they either had not heard or had not understood. I think the writings of Clement and Papias, perhaps also Dionysius, are of this sort. Certainly Papias is criticized by Eusebius in his *Church History* on the ground that he failed to grasp what he had

3 This sentence was added in 1519.

4 The reference to *Contra Adamantium Manichaeum* seems to be incorrect, but cf Augustine *De utilitate credendi* 7. The Manicheans originated in the third century AD. They were dualistic, claiming that in the created world light was trapped in darkness, but redemption released the light. The church regarded them as a Christian heretical sect; see Ferguson *Early Christianity* 707–8, and 259 n183 below.

5 'Greater' because Acts, unlike some other books, is universally accepted among orthodox Christians as canonically authoritative.

6 An allusion to 1 John 1:1 and Luke 1:1–3: John professes to be a witness himself to the saving events recorded; Luke, on the other hand, professes to construct a narrative not as an eye witness, but as a careful investigator relying on the witness of others.

learned from John, and consequently his writings provided for many an opportunity for error.[7] But if there is reason to suspect error or failure in those who had lived with the apostles at the very beginning, what do you think would have happened if the authority of such narratives or writers had passed down to posterity in sequence over a long period of time? Eusebius of Caesarea composed his *Church History* with the greatest care and fidelity, but many things are reported there that do not have the high seriousness appropriate to history.[8]

From the annotation on Hebrews 13:24 (*de Italia fratres*) [ASD VI-10 378–84:809–39, 866–901]

[In this annotation the question of canonicity arises in relation to authorship: on the one hand the late acceptance of Hebrews into the canon argues against Pauline authorship, on the other hand authorship in itself need not be the sole criterion of canonicity; whoever was the author of the Epistle, the church was right to include it in the canonical Scriptures. It is particularly interesting to follow Erasmus' argument against Pauline authorship, an argument both conjectural and subjective. The annotation was introduced in *1516*, and insertions were made in each subsequent edition without respect to chronological order; in the excerpts below all editions except that of 1522 are represented.]

[ASD VI-10 378–84] [809] Good reader, I would not want your esteem for this Epistle diminished because many people question whether its

---

7 Clement of Rome, by tradition third pope in succession after Peter, wrote a letter to the Corinthian church, but the reference here is to the pseudepigraphical writings that circulated under the name of Clement, writings commonly known as the Pseudo-Clementine literature; cf the annotation on Rom 16:14 ('*Hermas, Petroba, Hermes*') CWE 56 429 and CWE 56 96 n16, where Erasmus speaks disparagingly of the writings as a forgery; also Ferguson *Early Christianity* II 964, where the fictional correspondence of Peter and James is noted. Pseudo-Dionysius, long assumed to be the Areopagite converted by Paul (Acts 17:34), was a Neo-Platonizing Christian of the fifth–early sixth centuries. Four extant works are attributed to him: *The Divine Names*, *Mystical Theology*, *The Celestial Hierarchy*, *The Ecclesiastical Hierarchy*. Papias, early second century bishop of Hierapolis (in Asia Minor) who wrote a book on the *Oracles of the Lord*, claimed to have been a follower of the disciples of the apostles, and related 'strange parables and teachings of Christ' that had come to him from 'unwritten tradition'; cf Eusebius *Church History* 3.39, where Papias is said to have been a 'man of exceedingly small intelligence.'

8 Eusebius of Caesarea in Palestine (c260–c339) composed several apologetic works, but is most famous for his *Church History*, an historical account of Christianity from the time of Augustus, Roman emperor (24 BC–14 AD) to that of Constantine (emperor 312–337 AD), whom he greatly admired.

author is Paul or someone else. Regardless of authorship, the Epistle is on many counts one eminently worthy to be read by Christians. In expression it is vastly different from the style of Paul, but in heart and mind it reflects the Apostle exactly. Several features suggest (but do not prove) that it was written by someone other than Paul. First, this is the only Epistle of all those written by Paul in which his name is not mentioned. [822] Second, for many years, in fact right to the time of Jerome, the western church did not accept this Epistle in its canon of Scripture, as Jerome himself observes.[9] Third, although Ambrosiaster comments on all the Pauline Epistles, he writes nothing on this one.[10] [828] Fourth, although no one cites Scripture more skilfully and appropriately than Paul, yet [in Hebrews 2:5–9] the author cites Ps 8:4–6 in a sense precisely opposite to its intended sense, for he applies the passage to the humiliation of Christ, while the entire psalm extols the grandeur of the human condition. [836] Further, St Jerome, citing this Epistle in some of his writings, seems to have doubts about the authorship, for example in his commentary on Jeremiah 31 he says, 'The apostle Paul, or whoever it was that wrote the Epistle, cites Hebrews' [31:4] [866] And Origen, as we read in Eusebius, said that there were many who, on the basis of style, questioned whether this Epistle was a genuine Epistle of Paul, though he himself with complete confidence ascribed it to Paul.[11] [870] Indeed, the most convincing argument against the Pauline authorship is the style and character of the expression, which is utterly different from that of St Paul. [875] For example, Paul's Greek often retains Hebrew idioms, but of this there is not a trace in this Epistle. [879] I shall at this point withhold my own opinion, but it is probable, as Jerome indicates in his *Catalogue* of illustrious writers that the author of the Epistle is Clement of Rome, third pope after Peter.[12] [890]

---

9 Jerome Epistle 129.3. In this letter Jerome declares himself willing to accept Hebrews as canonical, but admits that the western church does not customarily do so. This portion of Jerome's letter is cited in CWE 83 82.

10 Ambrosiaster is the name given to a fourth century commentator on the Epistles of Paul, Romans to Philemon – thirteen Epistles in all. The commentary does not include Hebrews. Erasmus identified him with Ambrose, bishop (from 374–97) of Milan and hence bilingual (cf n 117 below). In later years Erasmus questioned the identification; nevertheless Ambrosiaster continued to appear in Erasmus' texts as 'Ambrose.'

11 Eusebius *Church History* 6.17.

12 See *Jerome On Illustrious Men* 5.10 (FOTC 100) translated by Thomas Halton (Washington 1999) 13. The traditional list of popes that followed Peter places Clement after Linus and Anacletus (Cletus).

Moreover, in the 'Letter to Dardanus' Jerome states clearly that though the Epistle was not accepted as canonical by the Latin Church, many Greek writers did accept it, not as an Epistle of Paul, but as the writing of a churchman – Barnabas rather than Clement, or according to some, Luke.[13] [897] And yet today, some people think that anyone who questions the Pauline authorship is worse than a heretic. If the church declares definitively that this Epistle was authored by Paul, I gladly submit my understanding to the obedience of faith, but as far as I can see, it does not seem to be an Epistle of Paul.

(2) The Authority of Scripture

From the annotation on Matt 2:6 (*et tu Bethlehem* 'and you Bethlehem') [ASD VI-5 98–100:753–90, 805–46]

[In this annotation, introduced in *1516* and greatly extended in *1519*, Erasmus raises a question of perennial importance: how can the Scriptures be authoritative if there is manifest error found in them? Although in later discussions Erasmus would extend the line of argument taken here, he never deviated far from it: the Scriptures are the result of the combined effort of the Holy Spirit and fallible men, the Holy Spirit guiding according to his wisdom but not dictating verbally, while human beings employed their natural abilities to create the biblical narrative; hence memory lapses were possible and presented no challenge to our faith in Scripture as long as the errors do not affect the 'substance' of our faith. The annotation very soon came under attack (cf Ep 769:43–68). Indeed, Erasmus' whole enterprise in translating and paraphrasing the New Testament raised questions about the sacrosanct character of Scripture, forcing Erasmus to articulate carefully his fundamental view of the nature of Scripture. We should note, however, the final sentence in this selection, where Erasmus concedes that we may not always be able to account for Scripture as we have it. Likewise, in the *Ratio* he had acknowledged the fact that there were indeed difficulties and contradictions in Scripture (57 above). The difficulty, even apparent contradiction, noted in the present annotation arises from a comparison of the text of Micah 5:2, and its citation in Matt 2:6. For the convenience of the reader I set out the text of Micah and that of Matthew:

Micah 5:2 NRSV: 'But you O Bethlehem of Ephrathah, who are one of the little clans ['thousands' (AV)] of Judah, from you shall come forth for me one who is to rule in Israel.'

13 Cf Epistle 129.3 (cf n9). Jerome writes similarly in *On Illustrious Men* 5.10 (cf n12).

Matt 2:6 NRSV: 'And you, Bethlehem in the land of Judah, are by no means least among the rulers ['princes' (AV)] of Judah, for from you shall come a ruler who is to shepherd ['rule' (AV)] my people Israel.'

In the selection given here the first paragraph was introduced in *1516*, the remainder was added in *1519*.]

[ASD VI-5 98–100] [753] This testimony[14] is taken from Micah 5. St Jerome frankly admits that Matthew's citation does not agree in every respect with the text found in the Septuagint[15] or in the original Hebrew. He explains that this was due either to the Gospel writer who made a special effort to report the response of the scribes and Pharisees as they gave it [to Herod] in order to show their negligence in sacred Scripture, or, as some think, to the evangelists themselves who quoted testimonies of this kind not directly from the written page but from memory, and so, as happens, made mistakes. Indeed, sometimes one finds some difference even in sense,[16] as though the writers discreetly disregarded the words.

In case a weaker brother or a crabby critic should take offence, I shall not hesitate to quote the actual words of Jerome.[17] [770] It is clear that in this passage Jerome, fine scholar though he was, found himself in very difficult straits from which he was scarcely able to extricate himself. His first explanation, which he attributes to himself, seems too forced, too contrived. In the first place, the citation is introduced by the words, 'as it is written by the prophet,' but these words can be attributed as

14 'Testimony': Latin *testimonium*, a term commonly used to refer to biblical texts cited to validate or illuminate statements or events described in the New Testament or other early Christian literature.

15 A translation of the Hebrew Bible into Greek, according to legend by seventy-two (or seventy) translators (Latin *septuaginta* 'seventy'). Begun in the third century BC the translation was not completed until the first century BC. The translation is often cited by the Roman numeral LXX '70.' One of the major tasks Erasmus set himself in publishing his New Testament with annotations was to determine the source of the citations from the Old Testament that are found in the New. Jerome had made a similar effort, but in order to show that the citations were taken from the Hebrew, though this required that discrepancies be 'explained.' Erasmus generally found that such citations were not taken directly from the Hebrew.

16 Cf Jerome *Commentary on Micah* (on 5:2).

17 The passage as quoted from Jerome was added in *1519* – in order (as Erasmus says here and often elsewhere in introducing quotations) to divert malicious doubt; it is omitted in the selection here, since Erasmus has in the previous paragraph summarized it well: the discrepancy is due to either 1/ Matthew's intention to report the words of the scribes and Pharisees 'to show their negligence in Scripture,' or 2/ memory lapses on the part of the evangelist.

convincingly to the Gospel writer as to the Pharisees. Second, one will nowhere find the scribes and Pharisees censured because they did not know the Law; they were criticized because though they had eyes they did not see, corrupted as they were by ambition and avarice. [779] It was rather to the Sadducees that the words, 'not knowing the Scriptures' were applied.[18] [786] Jerome's second explanation, which he attributes to others, is rather more troublesome, that is, that as a result of memory lapses the Gospel writers in citing Scripture frequently differ from the words of the Hebrew, sometimes even from the sense. Although he reports this as the opinion of others, he does not speak against it as though it were irreverent. In fact, he admits that in Matthew the sense is directly opposite to that of the prophet.

[805] Certainly, an accusation of falsehood in the Gospel writers is abhorrent, but not likewise a memory slip. The authority of the whole of the sacred Scriptures is surely not immediately shaken if somewhere they vary in words or sense, provided the substance of the matters at hand and on which our salvation depends remains firm. That divine Spirit, who controlled the minds of the apostles, permitted them to be ignorant of certain things, at points to make mistakes and to err either in judgment or in sentiment. This, however, offered no disadvantage to the gospel but actually turned the very error into a support for our faith. Similarly the Spirit might also have regulated the instrument of apostolic memory in such a way that if in characteristically human fashion the memory failed in some respect, the failure does not lessen faith in the Holy Scriptures but actually stimulates faith among those who might otherwise have been able to complain that the narrative was deliberately designed to insure agreement [between the texts]. [819] That heavenly Spirit has directed this entire mystery of our salvation with hidden counsels and in ways concealed from human intelligence.[19] We do not have the ability, nor is it appropriate to Christian modesty, to prescribe how the Spirit should manage its business. Christ alone was called the truth,[20] he alone was free from every error. [826] To be sure, the highest authority is owed to the apostles and Gospel writers, but perhaps Christ, with some plan hidden from us, wanted something human to remain in them too, clearly perceiving that this itself was conducive to the restoration of the human race. He could have once for all freed his followers from all ignorance, all error, but Peter transgressed

18 Cf Matt 23:23–6 and Luke 11:42–4 (Pharisees), Matt 22:23–9 (Sadducees).

19 Cf Rom 11:33–4.

20 Cf John 14:6.

after he had received the Holy Spirit, in fact transgressed so gravely that he had to be rebuked by Paul. Paul disagreed with Barnabas, which was possible only if one of the two was wrong.[21] But if we are completely convinced that the authority of all Scripture totters if the slightest error should be found therein, it is at least more than likely that of all the copies the Catholic church now uses none is so perfect that either chance or someone's zeal has not sprinkled in some fault. [838] Some people think that problems of this sort cannot be explained, fearing that through one or two little words the authority of Scripture would be undermined. [843] I prefer to believe that either the text has been corrupted, or, if something has been changed, it has, in the divine plan, been changed for the better, or, finally, that the text is in fact sound but in our weakness we cannot penetrate the mystery.[22]

(3) The Text and Language of Scripture

(a) Establishing the Text

From the annotation on 1 John 5:7–8 (*tres sunt qui testimonia dant in caelo* 'there are three who bear witness in heaven') [ASD VI-10 540–8:255–8, 271–84, 318–25, 337–57]

[Erasmus frequently claimed that his translation followed his Greek text. While he did collate a relatively small number of Greek manuscripts, he made no attempt to establish a critical edition of the Greek text. The Greek text printed parallel to the Latin translation did not include an apparatus for variants, but Erasmus was able to discuss the text and variants in his annotations, where he provided the evidence of manuscripts and the witness of the Fathers to the text, and applied on occasion some of the principles of textual criticism still accepted, such as the principle of the 'more difficult reading,' ie that in a choice of variants the one more difficult to construe is likely to be the correct one; in addition he often attempted

21 Cf Gal 2:11–14 (Peter), Acts 15:36–41 (Paul and Barnabas).

22 Erasmus' 'critical approach' to Scripture as it appears in this annotation was not without qualification. See, for example, the annotation on Rom 1:4 ('from the resurrection of the dead of Jesus Christ'), where in the course of an attempt to give the biblical words a better construction, Erasmus writes, 'I would not be understood to imply that the reliability of Matthew, who tells the story [of the saints arising from their tombs at Jesus' death, Matt 27:50–3], is less certain than if all the [Gospel writers] had reported the same thing – for we do not put the reliability of the Gospel writers to the same test as that of other historians … ' CWE 56 20.

to determine the correct text on the basis of reasonable conjecture. The text of 1 John 5:7–8 proved to be particularly problematic, and Erasmus addressed the problem at length in his annotation in editions from 1522 to 1535. The Latin Vulgate text of this passage traditionally offered parallel 'witnesses' to Jesus as both divine and human, the witness in heaven and the witness on earth, as in AV:

'There are three that bear witness in heaven, the Father, the Word, and the Holy Ghost, and these three are one; and there are three that bear witness on earth, the Spirit and the water and the blood, and these three agree in one.'

Modern scholarship approves rather the reading with only one set of witnesses:

> 'There are three that bear witness, the Spirit, the water, and the blood, and these three agree.'

The additional words in the Vulgate (comprising what is often called the Johannine comma) seemed to many of Erasmus' contemporaries an essential weapon to use against the Arians, for the words seemed to point definitively to the essential unity of the Trinity. Following his Greek manuscripts, Erasmus omitted the comma in the first two editions, but in 1521 a Greek manuscript found in England that included the comma (codex Montfortianus) was brought to his attention, and against his best judgment he included the words in the editions from 1522 to 1535. The manuscript now in the library of Trinity College, Dublin, has long been thought to have been forged specifically to force Erasmus to include the words in his New Testament, a point that is, however, open to question (cf Andrew Brown in ASD VI-4, introduction 27–111). The following excerpts from the annotation convey the tenor of Erasmus' response to his critics, and reflect the emphasis he placed on the evidence of manuscripts and patristic authors in determining the text of the New Testament, in the case of patristic authors considering both their direct quotations of a text and their commentary on it. The excerpts conclude with an allusion to Codex Vaticanus, still regarded as one of the most reliable witnesses to the text of the New Testament. The greater part of this annotation appeared first in *1522*, in response to the criticism of Edward Lee and Diego López Zúñiga. The evidence of manuscripts from Constance and of codex Vaticanus was added in *1527*, while the argument based on the evidence of Augustine's *Contra Maximinum* was added in *1535*.]

[ASD VI-10 540–8] [255] Saint Jerome in his preface to the Catholic Epistles suspects that this passage has been corrupted by Latin translators, and that some have omitted the witness of Father, Son, and Holy Spirit.[23] Further, Cyril cites this passage in agreement with my edition.[24] [271] Bede, carefully commenting on this passage, explaining meticulously and at length the threefold witness on earth, makes no mention of the witness in heaven of Father, Son, and Holy Spirit – and he was a man with great facility in the language and diligent in inspecting the ancient manuscripts.[25] [276] In the manuscript supplied to me from the library of the Minorites in Antwerp, I found in the margin a comment about the witness of Father, Word, and Spirit, but it had been added by a fairly recent hand who did not want the words omitted. In the Paris edition of Bede there is no mention of Father, Son, and Holy Spirit. Bede followed Augustine in his book *Against Maximin the Arian*. Although Augustine leaves no stone unturned to prove from canonical Scripture that the Holy Spirit is God and all the Persons are of 'one being,' he nevertheless does not adduce the added words, though he is otherwise persistent in showing that Spirit, blood, and water signify Father, Son, and Holy Spirit.[26]

[318] But someone will say, 'The [heavenly witness] was an effective weapon against the Arians.'[27] First, since it is agreed that long ago in

23 This preface to a commentary on the Catholic Epistles was authored not by Jerome but by Pseudo-Jerome. Cf CWE 72 404–5 with n283. The preface appeared in early printed Bibles placed before the Epistle of James.

24 Cyril (c375–444), bishop of Alexandria (412–44), was a bold defender of Trinitarianism as defined in the councils of Nicaea (325) and Constantinople (381). Erasmus refers to Cyril's *Thesaurus on the Trinity*, where Cyril cites only the witness of 'spirit, water, and blood.'

25 The Venerable Bede (c673–735), English monk and priest at Wearmouth and Jarrow is best known for his *Ecclesiastical History of the English Nation*, but he also wrote a *Commentary on the Seven Catholic Epistles*. For his 'Dictionary of place-names' cf 199 n1. Erasmus seems to have come upon the manuscript in the Minorite Library in 1520, and was thus able to refer to it in preparing the 1522 edition of his New Testament; cf 12 above. See CWE 44 xv n28.

26 Cf Augustine *Contra Maximinum Arianum* 2.22.3.

27 'Arians': the name is derived from Arius (c280–336), a priest, and a popular and distinguished preacher in Alexandria. Although Arianism was subject to some modifications in the course of time, it always insisted on a subordinationist view of Christ. Arians held that the 'Son' is not eternal, but was created before the creation of the world. Because Christ was a creature whose being was derived from God he could never be called God in the full sense of the word and was therefore not equal to the 'Father.' Arius was condemned by the Council of Nicaea (325) at which the term 'homoousios,' meaning 'of one substance,' was incorporated into the Nicene Creed to exclude the Arian heresy. Arianism flourished, however, under some of the emperors in the fourth century, but Nicene orthodoxy is usually thought to have won a decisive victory at the Council of Constantinople in 381. See the annotation on Rom 9:5 234–6 below.

both the Greek and Latin manuscripts the text varied, this text will not be a weapon against those who will undoubtedly and with equal right adopt the text that promotes their side. But suppose there were no question about the text, since what is said about the witness of water, blood, and Spirit, that these are one, refers not to the divine oneness of nature but to the agreement of their witness, do we think Arians so stupid that they would not interpret the words in this passage about the Father, Word, and Spirit in precisely the same way?

[337] Still, I will not hide the fact that a Greek manuscript has been discovered in England in which are found the words lacking in most Greek manuscripts. [343] On the basis of this codex, therefore, I have restored what is said to be lacking in the manuscripts I have seen. I suspect, however, that this codex has been corrected to agree with our Vulgate text.[28] I have consulted the two extremely ancient manuscripts in the Library of St Donatian in Bruges. Neither had the witness of Father, Word, and Spirit. Both copies from Constance did add the witness of Father, Word, and Spirit after the witness of spirit, water, and blood, but without the words 'these give witness.'[29] [353] Moreover, Paolo Bombace, a scholar of integrity, at my request wrote down this passage word for word from a very old manuscript in the Vatican Library, and it does not have the witness of Father, Word, and Spirit. If you are impressed by sheer age, the book was of great antiquity, if you are impressed by papal authority, the witness was sought from the papal library.[30]

---

28 For codex Montfortianus see the introduction to this annotation. See also CWE 72 403–11 and especially 404 and 408 where Erasmus indicates that he would have added the 'heavenly witness' if he had found it in a single Greek manuscript.

29 Erasmus had discovered these Latin manuscripts in the Donatian library in Bruges in the summer of 1521, when, as councillor to Charles V, he followed the court to that city. His friend, Marcus Laurinus, Dean of the College of St Donatian, gave him access to the library. Another friend, Johann von Botzheim, canon of the cathedral in Constance, Switzerland, had sent him Latin manuscripts of the Epistles when he was preparing the fourth edition (*1527*) of the New Testament. For Laurinus and Botzheim see respectively 286 and 297 n18.

30 Paolo Bombace, an excellent Greek scholar, served as secretary to various members of the papal court and thus had access to the papal library. He was appointed papal secretary in 1524, but was unfortunately killed in the sack of Rome in 1527. Although Bombace had sent the text of 1 John 5:7–8 early in the summer of 1521, Erasmus did not receive it until September, too late, apparently for its evidence to be incorporated into the 1522 edition, hence the discussion of it appeared first in *1527*.

(b) Characterizing the Language

From the annotation on Acts 10:38 (*quomodo unxit eum* 'how he anointed him') ASD VI-6 250–4:665–742

[This annotation was introduced in *1516* with the claim briefly stated that the apostles wrote vernacular, hence sometimes faulty, Greek rather than the standard and correct Greek represented in the literary treasures of the classical period. This view implicitly challenged an exalted view of biblical inspiration and was open to the charge that it denigrated the Holy Spirit who authored the words of Scripture. In response to the charge Erasmus vastly enlarged the annotation in *1519* (with a few additions later), expressing a view that he would articulate more fully in his controversies with Béda, Cousturier and Pio, that the Scriptures are the joint endeavour of the human and divine. The annotation was motivated in *1516* by the observation that 'some manuscripts read, "whom he anointed him."' Erasmus explained that the double object ('whom … him'), was not normal Greek but a characteristic of Hebrew idiom, here carried over incorrectly into the Greek. The *1516* portion of the annotation concludes with the word 'Demosthenes' in the fourth sentence below. The remainder of this selection was added in *1519*, an addition that seems to have been motivated by the criticism of Johann Maier of Eck (cf n39, below).]

[**ASD VI-6 250–4**] [665] It is uncertain whether Peter spoke these words in Hebrew or Greek.[31] And yet even when the apostles write Greek they often reflect the idiom of their native language. Today, too, those who speak Latin but are otherwise uneducated ignorantly import into their speech some vernacular expressions, for example French people mix in French, the British English, the Germans German. After all, the apostles learned their Greek from the speech of the common people, not from the orations of Demosthenes.[32] Thus it seemed good to the divine wisdom to draw the world to its own philosophy without any help from human eloquence. That gift of tongues did not have to last

31 A reference to Peter's speech in the house of the centurion, Cornelius, Acts 10:34–43. Erasmus' uncertainty may suggest a question whether a gentile centurion would know Hebrew, but perhaps also whether at this stage Peter knew Greek well; Erasmus proposes in the *1519* addition to this annotation that the apostles learned Greek as a result of living among Greeks in Greek-speaking countries.

32 Demosthenes (c384–22 BC) is perhaps the most famous of the ancient Greek orators. At least sixty of his orations are still extant.

forever. It was sufficient that it was available when the need required. Likewise those early disciples did not always raise the dead, did not always heal the sick, but only when it was useful for religion and the gospel. Once only do we read that the apostles spoke miraculously in other languages.[33] (Also in chapter 19 of the same book those who had been baptized and received the Spirit are said to have spoken in tongues and prophesied.)[34] However, it is more likely that on the occasion of Pentecost the apostles had spoken in a single language, and through divine power were understood by all alike.

As a matter of fact, I do not think it is necessary to attribute without hesitation to the miraculous just anything the apostles happened to do. They were men, they did not know everything, they were sometimes wrong. Even after Peter had received the Holy Spirit Paul reproached and instructed him. Paul disagreed with Barnabas so vehemently that they separated.[35] Perhaps it was more suited to the gospel of Christ that it should be proclaimed to the common people in simple and unpolished speech, and that the speech of the apostles should correspond to their manner of dress, their manner of dining, to the whole manner of life that they shared with common people (apart, of course, from the things that pertain to the spirit and religion), so that pride in human eloquence should not be able to claim anything for itself in this business. Christ often left his disciples to their own resources: they hungered, they thirsted, they were wearied with the labours of the body, the cares of the soul, they felt advancing age and other weaknesses of the human condition. But he was also at hand whenever he wanted to make known to the world his majesty, and in using his disciples to spread the gospel, he controlled their bodily organs precisely as he knew it would especially contribute to his own divine plan and to human salvation. In fact, it is no wonder if, when Greek was spoken in Egypt and Syria, Cilicia and almost the whole of Asia Minor, the apostles knew Greek apart from any miracle, especially when they later lived for so many years among Greek-speakers. And certainly they did not write a Gospel immediately after the Ascension. Someone who speaks French will speak French well within a year even if the person previously has no knowledge of the language. Do we wonder that the apostles after so many years acquired a modest facility in Greek?

33 Ie at Pentecost, Acts 2:1–13.

34 Acts 19:1–6.

35 Cf Gal 2:11–14 (Paul rebuked Peter) and Acts 15:36–40 (Paul disagreed with Barnabas).

I am perfectly aware that Paul places the kinds of tongues and their interpretation among the gifts of the Spirit. He even boasted that he speaks in tongues more than all the rest.[36] This is probably not the place to consider further to what exactly he was referring, but even if he was referring to something like the event of Pentecost when the Holy Spirit was poured out upon the apostles, we should add that this gift did not bestow upon them a precise and finished skill in languages; rather it provided a skill just sufficient to facilitate most effectively the work of the gospel. In the same way, if someone happened to be granted the gift of prophecy in order to explain some particular passage of Scripture, the ability to explain any passage at all was not forthwith granted for all time, because as Paul testifies God gave his gifts to individuals according to the measure of their faith.[37] Likewise, if, in particular circumstances, a knowledge of languages was given to someone, it is not obvious that he at once possessed the same ability among any group of people with respect to any subject at all.

We commonly suppose that Augustine also had the gift of prophecy in explaining the sacred Scriptures,[38] and yet there are places where he did not arrive at the true and genuine sense of Scripture. Jerome did not, I am sure, lack the gift of languages, and yet in some passages experts in Hebrew disagree with him. But if anyone contends absolutely that the knowledge of languages was divinely infused into the apostles and that this gift continued with them without interruption throughout their lives (on the ground that whatever is done by divine power is more perfect than what is done simply in the natural order of things or through human industry as Chrysostom says)[39] how is it that the speech of the apostles is not only unpolished and unrefined but unfinished, disordered, and sometimes with obvious solecisms?[40] No one can deny what the facts themselves so plainly reveal. The Holy Spirit was

---

36 Cf 1 Cor 12:7–12 (kinds of tongues, interpretation), 1 Cor 14:18 (Paul speaks in tongues).

37 Rom 12:3.

38 Erasmus understood the chief function of prophecy to be the interpretation of Scripture. See the paraphrase on 1 Cor 13:2 CWE 43 158 with n4.

39 This passage has a close parallel in Erasmus' response (15 May 1518) to the criticism of Johann Maier of Eck, Ep 844:63–108. A precise parallel to the thought expressed in the brackets has not been found in Chrysostom, but may represent an idea more generally stated in several homilies; cf ASD VI-6 252 715:16n.

40 'Solecism,' ie the incorrect use of language. Erasmus charged the Translator of the Vulgate with all kinds of solecisms, adding to his New Testament of *1519* a list of forty-five solecisms he had noted in his annotations of *1516*. The list appears in CWE 41 under 'Errors in the Vulgate.'

pleased with speech that was simple, yet at the same time was pure and sound and free from the linguistic improprieties that usually impede understanding. The Greek expositors, to whom Demosthenes and Plato were intellectually accessible and crystal clear, everywhere struggle with difficulties of this kind when they interpret Scripture. How often does Origen note the absence of proper language in Paul! How often does he stumble over confused order, unfinished sentences,[41] ambiguities. Chrysostom does not deny that this is the case in Paul, and in many passages Jerome admits that it is so, openly attributing to Paul an imperfect knowledge of Greek.[42] The same Jerome attributes to Luke a better knowledge of Greek than of Hebrew, simply because as a native of Antioch he was better trained in Greek, and he also acknowledged that Paul was more fluent in Hebrew than in Greek because he was a native Hebrew speaker, whereas he learned Greek by instruction. [733] Why did the ancient commentators dare to say that Paul desired Titus because Titus was more proficient in Greek than he was?[43] Such comments would be close to blasphemy if you insist on the view that the gift of tongues was miraculous. And yet some of the most highly approved doctors of the church are not afraid to publish this view in their books!

I have discussed this question at greater length perhaps than the design of these annotations demanded, but I do not want anyone to think that I spoke irreverently or rashly in asserting that the apostles learned Greek from popular speech, not from the orations of Demosthenes. Apostolic authority must be measured not from the character of their speech but from their habit of mind. Inelegant speech in the apostles ought not to offend a devout reader any more than an unkempt appearance or vulgar clothes.

(c) Defining the Words

[In his translation of the New Testament Erasmus sought not only to restore the original text according to the Greek, but also to make the Latin approximate more closely the real Latin spoken by Latin speakers in antiquity and

---

41 'Unfinished sentences': Latin *anantapodotis*, a word defined in ASD VI-6 20 as 'a hypothetical proposition wanting the consequent clause.'

42 See, for example, Jerome's *Commentary on Galatians* 3.1a trans Andrew Cain FOTC 121 (Washington 2010) 118: '[Paul] although inelegant in speech, is nevertheless not so in knowledge.' Chrysostom in his *Homilies* does not generally comment on Paul's style, ASD VI-6 253:74n.

43 Cf the annotation on 2 Cor 2:13 (*non habeo requiem in spiritui meo*).

to clarify the language of Scripture. While this meant in the first instance choosing the proper Latin word to represent the Greek as precisely as possible, Erasmus used the annotations not only to justify his choice of Latin words but also to reflect on the connotation and nuances of words. The sample that follows will indicate Erasmus' method and suggest the perennial value of some of his comments. The words selected below follow their order in the *Annotations*, ie the order of the biblical text; they are identified in English by their rendering in RSV, except for those in Romans, already translated in CWE.]

HYPOCRITE
Matt 6:2 (*sicut* ***hypocritae*** 'as the hypocrites')

[The annotation was introduced in *1516*; the rhetorical questions at the end were added in 1519.]

[**ASD VI-5 150–1:965–74**] The Greek word *hypocrites* signifies a stage-player, that is, one who, feigning to be someone, acts out a story in front of the people. We call such persons 'actors.' Hence our [Latin] words for public proclamation or acting correspond to the Greek word *hypocrisis*. In fact, the Greek word can be used of anyone who puts on a pretence or feigns. Thus in Paul: *agape anhypokritos*, that is, 'love not feigned, 'without pretence.'[44] With respect to mimic gestures the Apostle's words fit well, for he has just said *pros to theatenai*, that is, 'that they might be seen,' which is the whole point of acting, and hence the word 'theatre.'[45] What pantomimist, what stage-player is any more a 'spectacle to be seen' than those who with meaningless lip-motion and strident voice want to appear to be praying to God and conversing with him?[46] Or those who with Jewish ceremonies counterfeit holiness?

WORD
John 1:1 (*erat* ***verbum*** ['In the beginning] was the word')

[Erasmus introduced a short note in *1516* (a) to explain the meaning of the Greek *logos*, translated in the edition of 1516 as *verbum* (so the Vulgate) but

44 Cf Rom 12:9, 2 Cor 6:6 (RSV 'genuine love' in both passages). The prefix 'an' gives the word a negative value, the equivalent of 'not.'

45 Erasmus refers to the expression in Matt 6:1: 'Beware of practising your piety before men in order to be seen by them.' The Greek *theaomai* 'I view,' 'gaze at' is used specifically of spectators in the theatre, hence the Greek *theatron* 'theatre.'

46 'Conversing with [God]': Erasmus liked the expression for designating 'prayer.' Cf Hilmar Pabel *Conversing with God: Prayer in Erasmus' Pastoral Writings* (Toronto 1997).

in *1519* and thereafter as *sermo* and (b) to explain also the significance of the definite article in the full expression 'the logos.' Both his explanation of the definite article in *1516* and his change in *1519* from *verbum* to *sermo* were challenged, the former notably by Edward Lee, the latter by several critics one of whom was a bishop who spoke his disapproval publicly; in defence Erasmus greatly enlarged the annotation, drawing material from his published defence of 1520, the *Apologia de 'In principio erat verbum'* (see CWE 73 xii–xix). I omit here the discussion of the definite article, which presupposes a knowledge of Greek (but cf CWE 72 172–5). The discussion of *logos/verbum* illustrates well the wide reach of Erasmus' exploration of language. In the selection below, the first three sentences belong to the 1516 edition, the fourth to *1519*, the remainder to *1522*, reflecting Erasmus' response to his critics.]

[ASD VI-6 30–4:7–39, 89–95] [7] The Greek *logos* denotes several things: word, discourse, speech, reason, manner, calculation, sometimes it designates a book. The noun is derived from the Greek verb *lego* 'I say' or 'I gather.' Jerome thinks that several of these fit well the Son of God.'[47] I am puzzled to know why Latin speakers preferred *verbum* [word] to *sermo* [discourse]. Although I knew that *sermo* expressed more accurately the Greek *logos* used here in the Gospel, nevertheless, due to a sort of superstitious fear I did not, in my first edition, replace the Translator's *verbum*, for I did not wish to give any occasion to slander. I merely observed somewhere that in the Holy Scriptures the word *sermo* frequently designates the Son of God.[48] Then, when I discovered that this occurred in so many places, and that in this very passage the church once read, 'In the beginning was the *sermo*'; moreover, that Cyprian and Augustine both read the passage in this way,[49] I supposed that no one would be offended, especially since I publish my New Testament with

---

47 Jerome Epistle 53.4.

48 The change from *verbum* to *sermo* in the March 1519 edition of the New Testament had given rise to criticism shortly after the edition appeared. Erasmus published a response in two versions both under the title *Apologia de 'In principio erat verbum,'* the first in February 1520 short, the second in August of the same year much longer. See the introduction to the translations of the two versions, 1520a and 1520b, *'Defence of "Word,"'* in CWE 73 xii–xix. In the *Defence* Erasmus shows at length from the writings of the Fathers that *logos* is frequently translated in the Scriptures by *sermo*.

49 Cyprian cites the passage with *sermo* in *Ad Quirinum, Adversus Judaeos* 2.6; Augustine in various places, cf eg *Tractates on John* 108.3 (on John 17:17) FOTC 90 trans John W. Rettig (Washington 1994) 281.

its annotations for private, not for public reading. What harm if in a book read in private I should write 'speech' or 'utterance' or 'discourse' or 'expression' or anything else that meant the same thing? Since, therefore, there would have been no reason to reproach me even if in Holy Writ the word *sermo* had never been used to designate the Son of God, why should I now be blamed, since in so many ways *sermo* expresses the Greek *logos* more accurately and more suitably than *verbum*; since, moreover, *sermo* is found so many times in use by orthodox writers, both ancient and modern, and since it is in public use in churches today and long ago the church read as I have translated?

[35] *Sermo* explicates more completely what the evangelist meant by *logos*, because to Latin speakers *verbum* does not mean speech as a whole, but a single word, though sometimes – but not often – it is used of a brief expression like a maxim or a proverb as [when we say] 'It is an "old saying" [*verbum*].' But Christ is said to be the *logos* for the reason that whatever the Father says is spoken through the Son[50] [many corroborative citations from the Fathers and medieval writers follow here].

[89] 'But its novelty offends us' they say. Offends whom? Those who slander? To those who like to be regarded as profoundly learned theologians, what is found in sacred writers [as I have demonstrated] ought not to be new, while the unlearned would have paid no attention to a novelty if some preachers had not cried out provocatively before the people (adding pointless verbal abuse) that Christianity is finished and done for now that we have a new Gospel. How stupid! Has the Gospel been remade because *sermo* is substituted for *verbum*?

BORN ANEW

John 3:7 (*et* ***nasci denuo*** 'and be born anew')

[Erasmus recognizes the ambiguity of the Greek; it is an ambiguity still widely recognized; see eg the marginal notes in AV and RSV. The annotation was brief – in *1516* a single sentence, concerned solely with the meaning of the Greek word. The excerpt that follows here was added in *1519*.]

[ASD VI-6 72:960–5] [960] Chrysostom observes that the Greek adverb *anothen* is ambiguous: it can mean 'again' or it can mean 'above' or 'from heaven,' as in John 19 'You would have no power over me if it were not given you from above' [19:11].[51] Cyril adopts this sense in John

50 Cf John 17:8.

51 Cf Chrysostom *Homilies on John* 24:2 (on John 3:7).

3: one who is born again through the Holy Spirit is born, as it were, from heaven.[52]

BABBLER

Acts 17:18 (***seminiverbius*** 'babbler')

[Acts 17:18 records that some Epicurean and Stoic philosophers met Paul in Athens, and some wondered what this 'babbler,' ie Paul, would say. The Vulgate had translated the Greek *spermologos* by *seminiverbius* 'word-scatterer.' AV, RSV, NRSV all translate 'babbler,' DV 'word-sower,' NEB 'charlatan,' TOB jacasse, ie 'magpie,' 'jabberer' (AV offers a marginal alternative, 'base fellow'). The detailed examination of the word in the annotation on the verse reflects well the efforts Erasmus made to locate the precise meaning of a word semantically problematic and to set out to view its implicit imagery. The passage illustrates also one of Erasmus' methods of semantic exploration, the analysis of the component parts of a word along with its usage in classical and biblical expression. The annotation was introduced in *1516* and enlarged primarily in *1519* (when Hesychius and Demosthenes were cited) with a small addition in each of the subsequent editions.]

[ASD VI-6 284:413–39] [413] The Translator has formed the Latin word on the model of the Greek compound. But what does *seminiverbius* mean to Latin-speakers? A more felicitous coinage would have been *verbisator* 'word-sower,' that is, 'one who spreads strange rumours among the crowd.'[53] Hesychius understands the [Greek] word to mean 'trifler' or 'one who gathers seeds.'[54] Hence a bird from the crow family was called a *spermologos*. [425] Demosthenes used the word in his speech 'On the Crown.' [A commentator] says that this reproach is directed toward a good-for-nothing, a worthless man, one thought to be of no account. [433] But Demosthenes calls Aeschines a *spermologos*, a contemptuous appellation because Aeschines would say anything at all for the sake of

52 Cyril *Commentarius in Johannis evangelium* 2.1 (on 3:7).

53 The Translator evidently understood the word to be formed from the Greek *sperma* 'seed' and *logos* 'word,' and so coined the Latin expression *seminiverbius*. This Vulgate coinage Lewis and Short explain as *semino* 'I sow' and *verbum* 'word.' Erasmus objects that even if we accept this derivation, a better coinage would have been *verbisator*, ie two Latin nouns in combination giving the expression 'sower of the word.'

54 Hesychius was a lexicographer, probably of the fifth century AD. See CWE 56 91 n10.

financial gain, the kind of man we call a 'wrangling advocate.'[55] [435] Paul here, still unknown, seemed to some of the Athenians to be someone of this sort. Hence the verb *spermologein* is used in the sense of 'to trifle.' Leonardo Bruni of Arrezo [1369–1444] translated the word by *rabula*, that is, a man of intemperate and annoying loquacity.[56] But it cannot be understood as 'word-sower' as Augustine thinks,[57] since the Greek is a compound of two words, 'seed' and 'gather' – 'gathering seeds.'[58]

GRACE

Rom 1:5 (**grace** and apostleship)

[In the Argument to the *Paraphrase on Romans* Erasmus listed 'grace' as one of the words that have a special meaning and use in the Pauline writings. The annotations comment on the word fairly frequently, though seldom at any length. Following the comments on the word in Romans 1:5 further annotations on 2 Corinthians 8:6 and Colossians 4:6 are added here to show the wide range of meanings Erasmus understood the word to have. All three annotations were introduced in *1516*, with small additions later.]

[CWE 56 18–19] 'Grace,' too, is a Pauline word, a word Paul repeatedly emphasizes, desiring to exclude carnal reliance on the Mosaic law. In Greek, however, *charis* sometimes means 'a kindness' that is conferred without recompense – whence also the verb *charizesthai* 'bestow' or

---

55 In 336 BC Ctesiphon, who had proposed to crown Demosthenes in a public assembly in recognition of his services to Athens, was indicted by Aeschines, who like Demosthenes was a distinguished orator. Demosthenes defended Ctesiphon in the speech commonly known as 'On the Crown.' In the passage Erasmus cites here (*De corona* 133) modern texts read *semnologos* 'bombastic phrase-monger.' Cf *Demosthenes De corona and De falsa legatione* trans C.A. Vince and J.A. Vince rev Loeb Classical Library (Cambridge MA 1939) 107.

56 Leonardo Bruni (c1370–c1444), a distinguished humanist in Florence translated many Greek works into Latin. He was famous for his polished Latin prose; cf CWE 28 415 with n595. The reference here is to Bruni's translation of the speech by Demosthenes cited. *Rabula*, however, may be a conjecture by Erasmus; cf ASD VI-6 284:436n.

57 Cf Augustine *Contra Cresconium* 1.12–15.

58 On this interesting word Ernst Haenchen writes, '[The word] is originally used of birds that pick up grain, then of scrap collectors searching the marketplace for junk, and further of anyone who snapped up the ideas of others and spread them about as his own without understanding what they meant, and, finally, of any ne'er-do-well.' *Acts of the Apostles. A Commentary* 14th ed trans Bernard Noble and Gerald Shinn, trans rev and updated by R.McL. Wilson (Philadelphia 1971) 517 n12.

'give freely'; sometimes 'favour,' for example, 'You have found *gratiam* [favour] with God';[59] sometimes an 'obligation for an act of kindness,' for example *echo charin* [I owe thanks, am grateful].

By 'grace' [Paul] here[60] means that he was called back from error and not only called back, but also chosen to call, with authority, others to the grace of the gospel.

2 Cor 8:6. (*et consummaret in vobis etiam* ***gratiam*** *istam* 'so he should also complete this generous undertaking among you')[61]

[ASD VI-8 408:385–7] Here again the Translator has rendered *charis* by *gratia,* though it would have been better rendered by 'good deed,' or 'liberality,' or as I have translated, *beneficentia* 'kindness' [literally, 'well-doing'], a word Cicero frequently used.

Col 4:6 (*sale sit conditus* '[Let your speech always be gracious,] seasoned with salt')

[ASD VI-9 384:718–23] [The sense is] let your speech always have grace, seasoned with salt, meaning 'In the conversations of you Christians with pagans, your speech should be pleasant and unassuming, but with wisdom added thereto.' We can apply this to ourselves whenever we must deal with people in power: we should not provoke them with abusive or bitter speech, only to make them worse than they are, but by prudently controlling our speech we should gradually induce improvement if they go wrong.

FAITH

Rom 1:17 ('from **faith** unto **faith**')

[In the edition of 1527 Erasmus added an entirely new annotation on Romans 1:17, defining at unusual length the word 'faith,' *pistis* in Greek, *fides* in Latin, and related words such as *fiducia,* 'trust.' It seems likely that the motivation for this extensive annotation derived from Béda, who had not only challenged Erasmus' paraphrase on James 2:17 where the paraphrastic writer claims that a dead faith did not deserve the name of faith,

---

59 Luke 1:30. This sense of the word, used in Gabriel's greeting to Mary, is explicated more fully in the annotation on Luke 1:28, where Erasmus describes the criticisms with which his paraphrase on the verse was greeted. For the annotations on Luke 1:28–30 see 225 with n76, for the paraphrase see 76 with n5.

60 Ie in Rom 1:5, 'I have received grace and apostleship … ' This brief paragraph was added in *1527*.

61 Cf DV translating the Vulgate: 'We desired that Titus would finish among you this same grace.' In context, Paul sends Titus to the Corinthians to oversee the collection of a gift for the 'saints in Jerusalem.'

but saw Erasmus more broadly as Lutheranizing in his view of faith. The Paris theologians were to follow Béda's lead, in responding to whom Erasmus began by defining faith in a manner that paralleled this *1527* annotation. But the question of the definition of faith came into purview as early as 1520 when he had been criticized for refusing to accept Hebrews 11:1 as a 'definition' of faith. The definition here thus both filled a long-recognized lacuna, and offered an immediate response to a theological challenge. Notably, in defining the word here Erasmus consistently appeals to usage, examining the ways in which the word is normally used in particular contexts, but he does not conclude without a clear statement of the word's significance for Christian thought and experience. For Béda, see ASD IX-5 120, for the Paris theologians CWE 82 70–1, for the earlier critics CWE 72 321–2 (Lee) and ASD IX-2 242–3 (Zúñiga); and for an important discussion on faith and charity see the annotations on 1 Corinthians 13:2 and 13:13 242–7) below.]

[**CWE 56 42–4**] The Latin language has no word exactly corresponding to [the Greek] *pistis*. In Latin, one who believes the words of another is said to have *confidence* [*fides*] in him; one who makes a solemn promise is said to give a *pledge* [*fides*]. One who performs what he has promised is said to fulfil his *trust* [*fides*]. One who is not believed lacks our *trust* [*fides*] – [we have] no *faith* [*fides*] in the appearances [he puts on]. One who does not adhere to an agreement breaks *faith* [*fides*]. We read much about the *faithfulness* [*fides*] of servants towards their masters. In Latin, therefore, *fides* belongs sometimes to one who promises, sometimes to one who fulfils a promise, sometimes to one who believes, sometimes to one who is believed; sometimes it is a general term, as when we say 'there is no *faith* [*fides*] left in the world,' meaning that no one fulfils what he promises, and that no one *trusts* [*fidere*] another.

In Greek, too, *pistis* [faith] sometimes means the *reliability* [*fides*] of one promising or fulfilling, sometimes the evidence by which we persuade. One is called *pistos* [trustworthy] who does not deceive. He trusts [*pisteuei*] who gives credence or *relies upon* [*confidit*] or entrusts.

In Latin, we speak in a positive way of *trusting* [*fidens*] and of *trust* [*fiducia*], which resides only in the believer [*in credente*]; in a positive way likewise [we use the infinitives] *to entrust* [*confidere*] and *to trust* [*fidere*]; but *self-confident* [*confidens*] and *boldness* [*confidentia*] have a negative connotation. Sacred literature, however, frequently uses these words loosely, for it often uses *fides* [faith] for *fiducia* [trust] in God almost in the sense of hope; sometimes for the belief or conviction by which we assent to the things handed down to us about God – by which even the demons believe.[62] Sometimes the word *faith* [*fides*] embraces all these meanings: that assent to the truth both of the historical record and of the promises, and the *trust* [*fiducia*] that arises from his omnipotent goodness, not without the hope, that is, the expectation, of the promises. So far, indeed, does one speak of the *faith* [*fides*] of human beings.

However, one also speaks of the *faith* [*fides*] of God, a faith he manifests in his promises; hence God is said to be *trustworthy* [*fidus*] *or faithful* [*fidelis*], that is, *pistos*, because he does not deceive.[63] Sometimes [the Scriptures] speak of the *faith* of God [*fides dei*][64] by which we *trust* [*fidimus*] in him rather than in man; it is said to be 'of God' not only because it is directed towards him, but also because it is given by him; sometimes [the Scriptures speak of the faith] of both [God and man] as in 'The righteous shall live *by faith* [*fides*] – of God who does not deceive in what he has promised, and also of man who *trusts* [*fidit*] in God.'[65] To both belongs the phrase used here, 'from *faith* [*fides*] to *faith* [*fides*].' For just as God at appointed times began to reveal his nature and to fulfil his promises, so man's knowledge of and *trust* [*fiducia*] in God grew by stages. Few believed the prophets until the Lord displayed before their eyes what they had promised. Again, from what we have seen, and now see, our *faith* [*fides*] is strengthened concerning the things that were predicted about his final coming.

EXPECTATION
Rom 8:19 ('for the **expectation** of the creation')

[Erasmus clearly took delight in revealing for his readers the vivid images, particularly images of action, inherent in some Greek words. This and the three annotations that follow (on Philippians 1:20 ['eager expectation'], Romans 8:26 ['helps'] and Romans 8:26 ['makes request']) are illustrative. The annotation on Philippians 1:20 follows in thematic rather than canonical order.]

[CWE 56 216–17] [The Greek noun] *apokaradokia* does not mean simply 'expectation' but 'eager and anxious expectation.' The Greek word is composed of three parts: *apo* [from], *kara* [head] and *dokein* [to seem], because those who earnestly desire to see something raise their heads and keep a constant watch. Hilary speaks of an expectation 'far off,'

62 Cf James 2:19.
63 Cf eg 1 Cor 1:9, Heb 10:23.
64 Cf Mark 11:22: thus the Greek; translated 'have faith in God' (NRSV).
65 Cf Heb 2:4.

because with head stretched forward we look into the distance.[66] [First sentence *1516*, remainder *1535*]

Phil 1:20 (*secundum* ***expectationem*** '[it is my] eager expectation')

[**ASD VI-9 280:107–11**] The Greek word connotes more than 'expectation'; it implies a compelling desire, hence the compound. He did not say merely *prosdokia* ['an awaiting'] but *apokaradokia*, evoking an image of one straining with head bent forward in order to see. [First sentence *1516*, second *1527*]

HELPS

Rom 8:26 ('likewise also the Spirit **helps** [our] infirmity')

[**CWE 56 221–2**] [The Greek verb] *synantilambanesthai* ['helps'] means 'to be present with aid for one who is struggling in something he has undertaken.' Just as we strive, looking forward with endurance, so also the Spirit gives its aid to the weary, as though stretching out a hand to those who struggle.[67] [*1516*]

MAKES REQUEST

Rom 8:26 ('the Spirit **makes request**')

[**CWE 56 222**] *hyperentyngchanei*. [The Translator] sometimes translates the Greek verb as 'makes request,' sometimes as 'appeals' or 'intercedes.' This occurs whenever one goes to a person on behalf of another's affairs, as one might approach a prince to commend the cause of a friend.

It must be observed that he has said *hyperentyngchanei*, for the prepositional prefix [*hyper* 'above,' 'over'] usually indicates superiority. The sense is this: even though one's spirit sometimes seeks things that would be harmful, nevertheless, the Spirit breathes upon the souls of some and corrects their misguided commands as one in charge of all appeals. [First paragraph *1516*, last paragraph *1527*]

EVIL

1 Cor 5:8 (et **nequitiae** 'and evil')[68]

[Words signifying good and bad often require defining. In the following example Erasmus employs the context to give specificity. The excerpt is from *1516*.]

---

66 Hilary *Tractatus super psalmos* 148.2.

67 Cf the similar explanation of the similar Greek verb *antilambanesthai* in Acts 20:35, 'The verb evokes in particular the image of one who extends the hand to prevent someone from falling or to restrain one who is about to depart' [ASD VI-6 306].

68 1 Cor 5:8 RSV: 'Let us therefore celebrate the festival not with the old leaven, the leaven of malice [Greek *kakia*] and evil [Greek *poneria*], but with the unleavened

[ASD VI-8 98:972–5] The Greek noun [*poneria*] signifies *malitia* [malice] and *versutia* [cunning]. [Paul] sets out two [Greek] words, *kakia* and *poneria*, the opposites of which soon follow, 'sincerity' and 'truth,' for 'malice' is the opposite of 'integrity of motive' and 'cunning' is the opposite of 'truth', that is, of 'ingenuousness,' 'candour.'

II. THE BIBLICAL TEXT IN THE CONSIDERATION OF THEOLOGICAL ISSUES

[Throughout the more than two decades of his work as a biblical scholar, Erasmus always insisted that his work on Scripture was that of a philologian, preparatory work for the more dignified and important work of theologians. But he emphasized that theology must always proceed on the basis of a sound philological understanding of Scripture. The following selections reveal the intersection in Erasmus' work of philology and theology.]

(1) The Holy Family

[Erasmus' comments below reflect the devotion and respect paid to the Holy Family in the early sixteenth century. Matthew has given prominence to the role of Joseph in the birth stories, while Luke provides the fuller source for reflecting upon the role of Mary and the boyhood of Jesus. In the *Paraphrase on Matthew* Erasmus' Joseph may be simply foster-father, but he is, nevertheless, endowed with a righteousness commensurate with his responsibilities. His goodness does not, however, obliterate his common humanity, for in his ignorance he is capable of 'suspicion or at least astonishment.' The conviction that Mary as God-bearer must be pure and unstained demanded a careful interpretation of the Lukan birth stories, while the evangelist's account of Jesus' childhood raised questions, addressed in the *Paraphrase*, about the nature of his divinity.]

(a) Joseph

From the annotations on Matt 1:19 (*cum esset vir iustus* 'since he was a just man' and *nollet eam traducere* 'he was unwilling to put her to shame') [ASD VI-5 78:308–22 and 84:451–61]

[The first paragraph was introduced in *1516*, the second was added in *1519*.]

---

bread of sincerity and truth'; instead of 'malice and evil' NEB translates 'corruption and wickedness.'

[ASD VI-5 78 and 84] [308] The Greek participle leaves us free to understand the clause [as either causal or concessive]. Here the participle expresses the reason why Joseph was unwilling to expose Mary, that is, 'because' he was a just man.[69] It is remarkable that the evangelist calls Joseph a just man because he was unwilling to take Mary to court or to punish her, when the law declared that he should punish her.[70] But the evangelist calls Joseph 'just' not on account of a single virtue, the first of the four moral virtues, but because of his absolute goodness in all respects.[71] His action sprang from some extraordinary and unaccountable goodness when, upon seeing the swelling belly of his spouse and the indubitable signs of conception, he neither reprimanded his wife, nor complained to her family, nor was tortured with jealousy, nor took her to court demanding punishment, but he repressed his anxiety and considered silently a secret divorce. He saw her pregnant and did not yet know the mystery about which he soon learns from the angel. [451] When the angel admonished Joseph not to fear,[72] he added the reason: 'Because that which is conceived in her is of the Holy Spirit' [1:20]. This explanation clearly shows that the fear had arisen not from reverential awe, but from suspicion or at least from astonishment.

If anyone thinks it is a little harsh to say that Joseph had some doubts about Mary's chastity, he should listen to Augustine, who in Epistle 54 speaks even more harshly: 'Hence Joseph, to whom the mother of the Lord was engaged, when he discovered that she was pregnant, and he knew that he had not had sexual relations with her, for this very reason would necessarily have believed that she had committed adultery. Still he did not want her to be punished, although he did not approve of her shameful act.'[73]

---

69 The Greek construction is, '[Joseph] … being a just man … resolved'; the participle thus permits the translator to understand either 'since Joseph was a just man' (causal), or 'although Joseph was a just man' (concessive). The Latin 'cum' has the same ambiguity. Erasmus explains that the intent is causal; read as concessive the intent would be, 'Joseph, although he was a just man, did not carry out the law, as a just man should do.' But Joseph's justice went beyond the justice of the Law; *because* he was an absolutely just man he did not carry out the Law!

70 Cf Lev 20:10.

71 The four moral virtues: justice, wisdom, temperance, and courage, often called the four cardinal virtues. Cicero offers an extensive discussion of the four virtues and concludes that justice is the chief virtue; cf the *De finibus* 5.23.65. Erasmus thus defines the Greek word *dikaios* 'just,' often translated 'righteous'; cf 1:19 NRSV.

72 'Be not afraid to take Mary your wife for that which is conceived in her is of the Holy Spirit' (Matt 1:20).

73 Augustine Epistle 153.4.9.

(b) Mary

[Three annotations on Luke 1:28–9 reveal the intensity of theological concern in the sixteenth century over the church's teaching about Mary. The concern is evident in the reaction to Erasmus' translation of these verses and his comment in the *1516* annotation about the annunciation of the angel. Three problematic expressions found in the Vulgate are in question: (*ave gratia plena* 'Hail [Mary] full of grace'), (*benedicta tu* 'blessed art thou [among women]'), and (*quae cum audisset* 'which when she had heard'). Erasmus understood the first as 'Greetings, favoured one' (so NRSV, also AV); modern critical texts generally omit the second expression as insufficiently attested, while Erasmus replaced the third with 'which when she had seen' (so AV). The excerpts below from these three annotations follow the text of ASD without distinguishing the cue-phrase of each: VI-5 458–60: 377–86 (*ave gratia*), 398–401 (*benedicta*) and 405–46 (*quae cum*). Since the annotations reflect a complex discussion of assertion, criticism and response extending over several editions the dates of the editions in which the texts appeared are given in square brackets.]

[ASD VI-5 458–60] [*1516*] [377] The address of the angel has the character of words expressing love towards a maiden. The expression suggests something amorous.[74] That is why the maiden was greatly troubled and thought, 'What sort of greeting is this?' [Luke 1:29]. [*1519*] Origen has noted that this kind of greeting is found nowhere else in Scripture; accordingly, the very novelty increased the maiden's astonishment.[75] In fact, the Greek word *potapos* ['what sort of'] is itself emphatic, indicating a strange and extraordinary greeting, for the customary Hebrew greeting expresses peace. But it was most appropriate that she who would conceive the author of true pleasure should be greeted with an expression of joy, and that she who would give birth to Jesus, the end of feeble ceremonies and the prince and author of saving grace, would be addressed with the word 'grace.'[76]

---

74 'Amorous' from *1516* to *1522*, but in *1527* Erasmus replaced the word here in the annotation with the words 'sweet and endearing' as a result of the severe criticism he had received, reflected in the response to the 'storm' mentioned below.

75 Origen *Homilies on Luke* 6.7 (on 1:28) FOTC 94 trans Joseph T. Lienhardt S.J. (Washington 1996) 27.

76 The Vulgate's *gratia plena* translates the Greek *kecharitomene* (1:28) a perfect passive here in the sense of 'favoured one,' a sense implied in the word *charis* (ie 'grace,' as it is often translated), but in 1:30 *charis* clearly has the sense of 'favour': You have found *charis* 'favour' with God.

[*1516*] [398] The Greek word for 'blessed' carries the sense of 'praised,' 'lauded,' or 'of a distinguished reputation,' which[77] in the first instance refers to something amatorial, suggestive of marriage, at which the maiden was troubled, for she had not yet been informed of the celestial mysteries.

[*1516*] [405] [We must read] 'when she had seen him,' the reading of Ambrose, whose text continues, 'she was disturbed at his entrance,' and who explains in his comments that virgins are usually disturbed and frightened at any approach of a man and they fear any address by a man.[78] [*1527*] [415] The *Catena aurea* reports the words of some Greek, from which it is clear that he read 'had seen' not 'had heard: 'Since Mary was accustomed to receive visions, the Gospel writer attributes her confusion not to the vision but to the words of the angel.'[79]

[422] When I had briefly observed that the angel's greeting was in some way amatory, that he had appeared as a suitor and that for this reason Mary was at first disturbed, good heavens! what a storm a critic raised! – a storm that blew up again from another critic[80] – though St Thomas reported these words in his *Catena*, as he would never have done if they were ungodly and blasphemous. [435] I only mentioned 'suitor,' a word that is just as honorable as 'betrothed,' while 'amorous' is not an obscene word, for engaged couples write 'amorous' letters. Still they cry out that my words are blasphemous, and speak of 'lust' and 'fornication.' I shall not consider the implication of the citation above of that Greek, that it was precisely because Mary was accustomed to visions that she was troubled not at his appearance but by his words. [443] I am satisfied that he read 'had seen.' Otherwise, if his appearance had not been mentioned, it would have been pointless for

77 'which … mysteries'; so Erasmus wrote in *1516*. But in 1520 Edward Lee strongly objected (CWE 72 [note 32] 131–7). Erasmus made virtually no change in the edition of 1522, but later Pierre Cousturier (cf 15–16, above) also challenged Erasmus' comments, and in the edition of 1527 Erasmus omitted the offensive words but not without severely criticizing his critics, as the 'storm' mentioned below shows (cf n80). Cf ASD VI-5 399–401 critical apparatus.

78 *Expositio Evangelii secundum Lucam* 2.7.

79 The *Catena aurea* (*'Golden Chain'*) is a commentary by Thomas Aquinas on the four Gospels comprised of citations from various commentators to effect a continuous exposition. Thomas' 'continuous exposition' was given the name *Catena aurea* in its first edition.

80 Erasmus refers to Edward Lee whose comments were published in 1520 (CWE 72 131–7), and to Pierre Cousturier who had become a Carthusian monk in 1511 and in 1525 had attacked the concept of new Bible translations (*De translatione Bibliae*) while he was Prior of the Carthusian house in Preize, near Troyes.

him to observe that she was disturbed by his words, not his sudden appearance. Accordingly, I think it is respectful to believe that a modest maiden was troubled at the first sight of a young man and at a form of greeting that was both novel and alluring.

From the annotation on Luke 1:48 (*humilitatem ancillae* 'the lowliness[81] of his handmaiden') [ASD VI-5 464–6:516–44]

[The first two sentences are from *1516*; the remainder was added in *1527*. One will note that in *1527* the answer to the theologian here is primarily philological in character.]

[**ASD VI-5 464–6**] [516] The Greek *tapeinosis* here means 'insignificance,' not the moral virtue the Greeks call 'humility.' The sense is, 'Even though I am the least of servants, still you have not shunned me.'

[519] Anyone who wishes may laugh at these grammatical notes of mine provided he admits that theologians – indeed theologians three and four times over – have tripped up on them. When I was preparing the fourth edition of these annotations, a certain theologian of Paris, who regards himself as the chief pillar of a tottering church, demonstrated from this passage that it was from the virtue of humility that Mary deserved to become the mother of God, accusing me of 'Lutheranism' because in explaining the words of the angel 'you have found grace,' I wrote [in my paraphrase], 'This is not a matter of your merit but of divine favour.'[82] Certainly, to whatever extent it was a matter of grace it was not of merit, and I do not deny that there was some degree of merit, but as a paraphrast what I found written in the Gospel I interpreted, what I did not find I had no obligation to touch upon.

Let us grant that the Greek word *tapeinosis* here has the sense of the 'virtue' expressed in Greek by the word *tapeinophrosyne*, in Latin by *modestia* 'an unassuming estimate of oneself' [ie humility]. Let us grant as true that Mary's humility merited such great felicity. On this

81 RSV 'low estate.'

82 The accusation was made by Noël Béda, an influential member of the Paris faculty of theology, and was answered by Erasmus in the *Supputatio*, which, like the fourth edition of the New Testament, was published in March 1527. Béda's criticism had been directed specifically to the paraphrase on Luke 1:28–30, but as Erasmus had reiterated the point in the paraphrase on Luke 1:48 the response to Béda was appropriate here. The Paris theologians included the criticism in their *Censures* (1531) to which *Erasmus* replied in *Clarifications* CWE 82 233–4.

view, how are her statements consistent? She calls herself a servant and begins to magnify the Lord, then extolls herself, saying that by her virtue she merited an honour so great that she, a maiden, should give birth to God. If she deserved this, what room is there for the grace of which the angel spoke? If she deserved this because of her humility, is it not inconsistent for her to say, 'For behold, from henceforth all generations shall call me blessed?[83] – for no one is said to be fortunate because of anything achieved by one's own virtue.[84] Moreover, how do her words, 'For he has done great things for me' fit this view? She did not say, 'He has rewarded me magnificently!' Nor did she add, 'because he is just,' but 'because he is powerful and merciful,' as she soon says, 'His mercy is from generation to generation.' My intent here is not to detract from the merit of the Most Holy Virgin, but to show that what that great theologian has brought forward against my interpretation actually opposes the view he tries to defend.

From the annotation on Luke 2:35 (*et tuam ipsius animam* 'and a [sword will pass through] your soul') [ASD VI-5 485–7:79–124]

[The first sentence appeared in *1516*, the remainder was added in *1519*.]

[**ASD VI-5 486–7**] [79] 'Pierce' would have been more appropriate than 'pass through.'[85] Augustine wrote that when Mary, the mother of Jesus saw that her son had died, she too wavered somewhat in her faith, but only for a short time, that is, until he rose again from the dead; [Scripture says] 'the sword passed through': her doubt did not remain fixed deep in her soul, but merely 'passed through.'[86] [97] Theophylact points

83 Here and in the remainder of the paragraph Erasmus cites passages from the *Magnificat*, showing that Mary's words in Luke 1:46–57 point not to any claim of virtue but to God's grace.

84 In this sentence Erasmus equates *beata* (Greek *makaria*) 'blessed' with the Latin *felix* 'fortunate' as he frequently does in his paraphrase on the 'beatitudes' in Matthew 5. He understood the Greek word to connote the happiness derived from unmerited advantages that befall one, a characteristic sense also of the Latin *felix*.

85 'More appropriate' (Latin *venustior*, literally 'more graceful') because while the translation 'pass through' represented accurately the Greek, it is more pleasing to use the idiom more appropriate to the action of a sword. Erasmus desired a translation that not only represented the Greek accurately, but was also pleasantly readable.

86 The reference is actually to Ambrosiaster *Questions on the Old and New Testaments* 77.2. The work was long identified as belonging to Augustine. For Theophylact, mentioned next, see his *Commentary on Luke* 22:36.

out that we could understand the sword here as the pain of suffering or some doubtful thought when she saw her son dying on the cross, the one who had been born in a special manner and was famous because of his many miracles. Chrysostom, I think, did not shrink from holding this view of Mary for he attributes to Mary the sort of affection most mothers have towards their sons from whose achievements they hope to derive some glory for themselves.[87] [112] Origen, too, even more obviously shows that the sword of scandal struck Mary's heart. 'Why do we suppose,' he says, 'that when the apostles were scandalized,[88] the mother of our Lord was free from offence? If in the passion of the Lord she felt no offence, Jesus did not die for her sins. But if all who have sinned and come short of the glory of God[89] are justified and redeemed by his grace, certainly Mary also was offended at that time.' Soon Origen adds, 'The sword of unbelief will pass through you, and you will be struck with the dagger of wavering doubt, and your thoughts will tear you in pieces.'[90] [119] In the twentieth homily, he attributes to Joseph and Mary a faith not yet perfect when they reprimand their son and take him out of the temple.[91]

I make no judgment about the opinion of others. I have no wish to be contentious on this matter, but neither do I approve either the temerity or the obstinacy of those who attribute to Mary anything they dream up, then uphold their opinion as though it were a Gospel oracle, crying 'heretic' if anyone expresses doubt!

From the annotation on Luke 2:50 (*et ipsi non intellexerunt verbum* 'and they did not understand the saying') [ASD VI-5 490:192–7, 222–9]

[The first paragraph was added in *1519*, the second in *1527*.]

[ASD VI-5 490] [192] How will this passage be treated by those who (with more pious zeal than circumspection) attribute to the Blessed Virgin as much beatitude at that time as she possesses now? When Christ responded [to his parents] he certainly spoke clearly enough, yet the

87 Chrysostom *Homilies on Matthew* 44.1 (on Matt 12:46). See the annotation on Matt 12:46 (*quaerentes te*) below.

88 Cf Matt 26:31–2, in AV 'offended,' in RSV 'fell away,' in NRSV 'became deserters.'

89 Cf Rom 3:23–4.

90 Origen *Homilies on Luke* 17.6–7 (on Luke 2:35) FOTC 94 trans Joseph Lienhardt S.J. (Washington 1996) 73.

91 Origen *Homilies on Luke* 20.4 (on Luke 2:51) FOTC 94 85.

Gospel writer adds the observation that his parents did not understand what Jesus said. One should also note how sharply the boy answered his parents when he had been rebuked – virtually 'rebuking' his parents who were rebuking him.

[222] Some people attribute to Joseph alone the fear of the parents,[92] likewise the rebuke given to their son. Finally, [some interpret] 'they did not understand the saying'[93] as though the clause did not apply to the Virgin, who was less concerned for the safety of her son than for the possibility that the parents had in some respect failed in their duty. I acknowledge that the desire to attribute to the Most Holy Virgin the most perfect endowments is indeed godly, but I also think it is not far from a dangerous brashness to define beyond the warrant of Scripture the steps by which Christ led his mother to a perfect understanding of himself.

From the annotation on Luke 2:51 (*et erat subditus illis* 'and he was subject to them') [ASD VI-5 490–2:232–52]

[The annotation was added in *1527*.]

[**ASD VI-5 490–2:232–52**] Some hold the (not very sensible) view that Christ even in his gospel ministry owed obedience to his mother. But a public administrator is not subject to the authority of his father, nor does a father have the right to prescribe to his son as bishop how he should administer gospel teaching. Even worse is the view of others that the Blessed Virgin can, even now, command Christ as though he is a man, and that this is the meaning of the liturgical chant, 'Show yourself as mother, let him receive our prayer through you etc'; that is, 'instruct your son to hear us.'[94] If so, then we are to entreat the mother rather than the son, and all power was not handed over to Christ even according to his human nature if he is obligated to her command, nor has she even yet surrendered to her son her maternal authority although the Father handed over to the Son all power in heaven and on earth.[95] [248] [As a

92 Ie the fear reflected in their anxious concern when the parents discovered that their son was not with them as they journeyed home from Jerusalem; cf Luke 2:48.

93 Ie they did not understand what Jesus said to them, 'Why were you searching for me? Did you not know that I must be in my Father's house?' [Luke 2:49].

94 The quotation is from the vesper hymn *Ave maris stella* ('Hail, Star of the Sea') used at feasts in honour of Mary.

95 Cf Matt 28:18.

boy] the Lord did not need his mother's admonitions, but to provide an example he gave unswerving obedience not only to his mother, but to Joseph also, who was not his father. I find the expression 'owed obedience' difficult when applied to Christ: one who owes, sins unless he pays what is owed.

There is a customary complaint that comments like these offend the ears of the godly; well, then, the opinions I have noted certainly offend my ears!

From the annotation on Matt 12:47 (*quaerentes te* 'seeking you')[96] [ASD VI-5 218–20:621–44, 656–8]

[The excerpt was almost entirely added in *1519*, but cf n102.]

[**ASD VI-5 218–20**] [621] If only the whole Christian people would be so dedicated to the veneration of the Most Blessed Mary that they would emulate her virtues in all their pursuits! But the common folk today – with a sort of pious partiality – attribute too much to her or Chrysostom attributed too little when he expounded this passage in his twelfth homily. This is what he says: 'And yet, some incivility is evident in the mother's behaviour. Consider therefore the importunity of both the mother and the brothers of Jesus. When they should have entered and listened with the rest of the crowd, or at least waited outside until Jesus had finished his address and then made their approach, they called him outside in the presence of all, since they were motivated by a certain desire for display and ostentation.'[97] [631] Expounding the narrative of the wedding at Cana in the Gospel of John, Chrysostom even more obviously attributes to Mary some desire for honour and renown: 'For she wished now to win popular favour and become herself more distinguished thanks to her son … Like any mother Mary thought she had the right to instruct her son in everything, though in fact she had an obligation to revere and worship him as Lord.'[98]

96 The reading of the Vulgate; texts that include 12:47 read, 'seeking to speak to you'; cf AV, NRSV.

97 Chrysostom *Homilies on Matthew* 44.1 (on Matt 12:46); Erasmus indicates that he is citing the passage from a Latin translation.

98 Chrysostom *Homilies on John* 21.2 (on John 2:4).

Augustine seems to attribute to her a certain lack of faith.[99] We make her totally immune from original sin, [639] but [Chrysostom][100] seems to attribute to her 'actual' sin – unless perhaps the emotion he attributes to her is free from all fault.[101] So, indeed, I prefer to think, for just as ignorance can be without fault, so can doubt and the feelings of a mother.[102] [656] But in these matters I am not interposing my opinion. I only wish that the zealous commitment of some to the heaping up beyond all measure of all things concerned with the saints would be directed rather to a commitment to emulate the kind of life that made them truly blessed.[103]

(c) Jesus

From the annotation on Luke 2:52 (*et Iesus proficiebat etc* 'and Jesus increased etc') [ASD VI-5 492:253–75]

[The church's teaching about the divinity of Christ had obvious implications for understanding the boy miraculously born as God incarnate, and might well seem to imply a fullness of deity in the child from its birth. Erasmus attempts to explain the divinity in a way that does not exclude the obvious humanity: a full divinity whose 'gifts' were gradually imparted in the normal stages of human growth. The annotation was added in *1519*.]

[ASD VI-5 492] [253] I am aware of the various interpretations of this passage.[104] Some say that Christ 'increased' not because of anything added to him after he was conceived in his mother's womb, but because

99 Augustine Epistle 75.3, 6.

100 Latin *hic* 'this one.' The previous sentence was inserted in *1522*; as *hic* was present in the 1519 text it would clearly have referred to Chrysostom, whose name preceded.

101 On the distinction between original and actual (or personal) sin see CWE 56 139–61 with nn11 and 12 (annotation on Rom 5:12 ['in whom (or, in which) all have sinned], excerpted below).

102 This sentence was added in *1522*.

103 For further discussions by Erasmus on Mary (including the doctrine of the Immaculate Conception) see CWE 82 233–36 and CWE 40 1020–22, Ep 1126:327–37 with n40, Ep 1196:60–71 and CWE 56 159 n70 (on the Immaculate Conception), and 'Mary' in the General Index of CWE 84. See also the colloquy 'A pilgrimage for Religion's Sake,' in which Erasmus presents a satiric account of the veneration of Mary in the sixteenth century, CWE 40 621–50.

104 The annotation has in view the entire verse: 'And Jesus increased in wisdom and stature and in favour with God and man' [RSV].

he increasingly expressed and revealed more and more the gifts with which he was [at conception] completely endowed, and did so not only before men and women whose salvation he had at heart but also before God whose glory he was making luminous. Others say that Christ always possessed the same gifts, but they were his first by the divine beneficence, later through human effort and practice. I am not refuting these views, but I should like the reader to consider whether one can without damage to a sincere faith agree to this: that while it is beyond question that Jesus received from the divine beneficence all the gifts with which he, as a human person, was endowed, yet God imparted those gifts in certain stages to the human nature he had assumed. Note that we read about the development of Jesus' twice in the same chapter: in chapter 2 Luke says, 'The child grew and became strong filled with wisdom [2:40]'; that he became strong seems to imply some increase in strength. Again in the present passage [2:52] we read more specifically that 'Jesus increased in wisdom and age[105] and favour with God and men.' Since Luke speaks of the three – wisdom, age, and favour – in a single expression, it seems that just as Jesus advanced by stages in age so he had increased in gifts by actual increments. I do not care if this view conflicts with some formulations of the Scholastics or with the opinion of anyone. My concern is whether what Luke clearly wrote contradicts sincere faith, which, after all, must be the standard by which we measure everything. And I make my proposal, such as it is, with no other intent than that the reader should give it some consideration.

(2) The Divinity of Christ

[From primitive times Christians have struggled to articulate the relationship of Christ to God, to understand and to honour the divinity of Christ. As we have seen above (208 n27) a crisis arose with the preaching of Arius in the early years of the fourth century. Some critics thought Erasmus' writings on the New Testament reflected his own diminution of the divine status of Christ. In the selections that follow here Erasmus insists on approaching the subject philologically: he does not define the nature of God, but insists on reading the text of Scripture in a straightforward and honest way.]

105 Erasmus recognized the ambiguity of the Greek word *helikia,* which both the Vulgate and he translated as 'age,' but which may also be translated 'stature.' It is clear from subsequent comments in this annotation that he accepts here the meaning 'age'; in his paraphrase on the verse, however, he represents both meanings, observing that increase in stature results naturally from increase in age; cf CWE 47 100 n98.

From the annotation on Rom 1:7 (***a deo patre et domino nostro Iesu Christo*'** 'from God the Father and our Lord Jesus Christ') [CWE 56 31–2]

[This annotation was introduced in *1516*, with additions in *1519* and *1527*.]

[CWE 56 31–2] [31] The Greek expression is ambiguous. It can, indeed, be read: 'from our Father and the Father of the Lord Jesus Christ' in which case you would understand that we have the same Father as he; or: 'from our Father and from the Lord Jesus Christ' and in this case you would understand that the grace he invokes for these people comes simultaneously from the Father,[106] whom Paul customarily calls 'God' – a word peculiar, as it were [to the Father] – and from the Son, whom he most often likes to call 'Lord' but 'God' very rarely. In fact in the fifth chapter of this very Epistle he openly calls him a man: 'Much more has the grace of God and of the Lord abounded for many in the grace of one man, Jesus Christ' [5:15]. And in the Acts of the Apostles Peter calls him a man – 'a man approved by God' [2:22]; likewise Paul before the Athenians: 'the man he has appointed' [17:31]. I incline to the second reading especially because this form of expression detracts from neither the lordship of the Father, nor the deity of the Son. My aim in this annotation is nothing else than [32] to point out the character of apostolic speech.[107] Tertullian makes the same observation in the book he wrote against Praxeas: 'And so I shall not speak of gods or lords at all, but I follow the Apostle, so that if the Father and Son both must be named, I shall call God "Father," and Jesus Christ I shall name "Lord." Christ, [when mentioned] alone, however, I shall be able to call "God."'[108]

Annotation on Rom 9:5 (***qui est super omnia deus*** 'who is above all things God.') [CWE 56 242–4]

[This annotation was developed over the five editions, but radically revised in the final edition of 1535, which is the version excerpted here.

106 The ambiguity arises from the Greek, which has the pronoun 'us' rather than the possessive adjective 'our,' reading literally, 'from the Father of us and the Lord Jesus Christ,' thus permitting two possible constructions: either 'from the Father of us and [from] the Lord Jesus Christ' or 'from the Father of us and [the Father of] the Lord Jesus Christ.'

107 In so boldly declaring his aim Erasmus disavows any intention of supporting Arianism, and affirms his responsibility as a biblical scholar.

108 Tertullian *Adversus Praxean* 13. 9–10.

In the excerpt immediately above, the ambiguity arose from the grammar; in this passage the ambiguity arises from the syntax which obscures the punctuation (punctuation is lacking in ancient manuscripts).]

[CWE 56 242–6] [242] This passage can be construed in three ways.

[Erasmus' somewhat complex description of the three ways follows here; they may be formulated thus:

1 'from whom is Christ according to the flesh – Christ who is above all. God be blessed forever.' Erasmus believes that this interpretation attributes divinity to Christ but does not specifically equate Christ with God.
2 'from whom is Christ according to the flesh, which Christ, since he is God above all, is blessed.' This reading specifically equates Christ with God.
3 'from whom is Christ according to the flesh. God who is above all be blessed forever.' Erasmus argues that this reading, while not denying the divinity of Christ or excluding divinity from him, cannot be used as a defence against Arianism.[109] Erasmus notes 'linguistic difficulties' with both the first and second reading. He continues:]

[243] The third reading has no difficulties, at least on linguistic grounds – 'from whom is Christ according to the flesh'; here a period ends the sentence. Then from a consideration of such great goodness of God, an expression of thanks is added: 'God who is above all be blessed forever.' Thus we would understand that the Law that was given and the covenant and the prophets and finally Christ sent in a human body – all of these things God, through an ineffable plan, provided to redeem the human race. Here if you take God to be the whole sacred Trinity (a meaning that frequently occurs in sacred literature, as when we are commanded to worship God alone and serve him alone)[110] Christ is not excluded. But if ['God' here] means the person of the Father (as is frequently true in Paul, especially when Christ or the Spirit is mentioned in the same passage) – [then] although from other passages in Scripture it is clearer than day that

109 Cf English translations: 'of whom came Christ, who is over all, God blessed forever' DV, AV, NRSV; 'of their race is the Christ. God who is over all be blessed forever' RSV, NEB.

110 Cf Luke 4:8.

Christ, no less truly than the Father or the Holy Spirit, is called God, nevertheless this particular passage does not effectively refute the Arians, since nothing prevents it from being referred to the person of the Father. And so those who claim that from this passage it is clearly demonstrated that Christ is openly called God, seem either to place little confidence in the witness of other scriptural texts; or to attribute no intelligence to the Arians; or they have not considered carefully enough the Apostle's language. [Erasmus now notes (244–5) a fourth reading, which, however, he regards as 'contrived, mere trifling'; he concludes:] [246] Now if the church teaches that this passage must be interpreted only in relation to the divinity of the Son, then the church must be obeyed, though this [will do] nothing to refute the heretics or those who listen only to Scripture; but if [the church] says that this passage cannot, according to the Greek, be explained in any other way, it affirms what the facts immediately disprove.

(3) Original Sin

From the annotation on Rom 5:12 (***in quo omnes peccaverunt*** 'in whom [or, in which] all have sinned') [CWE 56 139–48]

[Erasmus' method in this annotation is noteworthy. While, as we have seen, his interpretation often proceeds from an analysis of the Greek and an appeal to the evidence of the Fathers (as indeed it does here), in this annotation his appeal to context is particularly striking. As elsewhere, he insists here that the issue is essentially a textual one; sound theology can emerge only from an honest appraisal of the text. The annotation was introduced in *1516*; short additions were made in *1519* and *1527*, but the annotation was revised and greatly lengthened in *1535* to become the longest annotation of all those in Romans. The excerpts are taken from the 1535 edition.]

[CWE 56 139–48] [139] Some refer 'in whom' to Adam, in whom a latent posterity was concealed, and so in him all have sinned. Others interpret the Greek phrase to mean 'in this, that' or 'inasmuch as.' Those who insist upon the first sense [ie 'in whom'] furnish, from this passage above all, support for [the doctrine of] original sin. Those who like the second sense refer the Greek phrase [*eph ho* 'in which'] neither to

Eve nor to Adam, but to the thing itself without qualification, that is, 'in this, that all have sinned.'[111]

[There follows here a discussion to show 1/ that according to the common definition of sin, new-born infants cannot be said to be guilty of sin; and 2/ that the Greek phrase in question (*eph ho*) is not normally used to mean 'in whom.' Erasmus has thus removed fundamental objections to his interpretation that here in Romans 5:12 Paul is speaking not of original sin but of the actual sin of each individual, an imitation of the sin of Adam. He continues:]

[141] There is, then, nothing in the words here that cannot be accommodated to the sin of imitation. Two syllables alone – [*eph ho*] – appeared to stand in the way, and I have shown that they scarcely convey that sense which is the only one some would have. I am not the first to advance this interpretation, for this whole [142] passage is explicated in the same way by whoever he was whose scholia on all the Epistles of Paul bear the name of Jerome.[112] For to these words, 'Sin entered, and death through sin' [5:12a] he appends this comment, 'by example or pattern.' Then after these words, 'and thus it passed through to all' [5:12b] he follows with, 'while they thus sin, they also likewise die.'[113] Then to the words that follow 'in which all have sinned' [5:12c] he adds a comment like this: 'That is, in this, that all have sinned, they sin through the example of Adam.'[114] I acknowledge that this work is not by Jerome, but its content bespeaks the work of a learned man.

111 So Erasmus translated.

112 This set of commentaries (called scholia here) on the thirteen Epistles of Paul appears to be the work probably of Pelagius with interpolations by an unknown scholar identified as 'pseudo-Jerome.' Pelagius (c350–c425), probably British by birth, but in Rome by 390, was the most prominent figure among a reform-minded group who insisted on the freedom of the human person in moral action for which each person was consequently responsible; Pelagius was therefore a proponent not of the doctrine of original sin but of 'imitative' sin, ie the actual sin of each individual in imitation of Adam. He is famous for the controversy between him and Augustine. See Ferguson *Early Christianity* 887–9. The text of the commentaries has been edited by Alexander Souter in *Pelagius' Expositions of Thirteen Epistles of Paul* Texts and Studies 9 (Cambridge 1922–31).

113 Cf Souter *Pelagius' Expositions* II 45:11–22.

114 Souter *Pelagius' Expositions* III 8:14.

From Origen, however, it is not so easy to gather what his view was, for he is, of himself, often slippery in argument, [and is so] especially since we have him translated freely with many things added, removed, or changed.[115] [143] But you can be sure that [Origen] is talking [144] about the sins of individuals, because he says: '"All have sinned and fall short of the glory of God" [Rom 3:23]. And therefore if you were to mention even that righteous man Abel, he cannot be excused, for "all have sinned."' [Origen] passes on from Abel to Enosh, from Enosh to Enoch, from Enoch to Methuselah, from Methuselah to Noah, from Noah to Abraham, demonstrating with proofs that individuals have sinned by their own sins.[116] I think it is clear enough from these words that Origen interpreted this passage in terms of the sin of imitation.

I do not say this to call into question whether there was some original sin, but to point out that those lie who say that I alone record this interpretation, and that it is a fabrication peculiar to Pelagius and me. I condemn the opinion of Pelagius, and I am aware of the consensus of the ancients on this matter; [but] the dispute is concerned only with the sense of this passage, whether properly it refers to original sin. In the first place, it is generally acknowledged that the beginning of this whole disputation [in Romans] arose from a point other than the question of original sin; and that the thrust of the disputation moves towards a different end. For in the first chapter [Paul] reproaches the gentiles because, contrary to the law of nature and to their knowledge of philosophy, they had degenerated to every kind of wickedness; in the second chapter he reproves the Jews because they did not observe the Law, in which they boasted; in the third chapter he concludes that both the Jews and gentiles are equally guilty and in need of the grace of God; in the fourth, he teaches that Jews and gentiles are saved not as a result of their own works, but through faith, and that the promise made to Abraham belongs to all who resemble him in their faith; in the fifth he teaches that forgiveness of sins and the gift of righteousness, that is, of innocence, comes to all through the freely given love of God, who

115 Origen's *Commentary on Romans* was translated by Rufinus of Aquileia (c345–411). Erasmus justly criticizes Rufinus as a translator 'who not only permits himself to work in some opinions of his own, but even omits whole books … ' (annotation on Rom 3:5 ['is God unfair who inflicts wrath'] CWE 56 94). See the introduction to *Origen. Commentary on the Epistle to the Romans Books 1–5*, trans Thomas P. Scheck, FOTC 103 (Washington 2001) 10–14.

116 Origen *Commentary on Rom* 5:1 (on 5:12); for the citations here see Scheck ibidem 313–15. For the sequence Enosh–Enoch see Gen 4:17–26 (AV, NRSV), where the sequence is reversed.

has washed away the sins of all through the blood of his Only-Begotten. Up to this point [ie Rom 5:11] there is nothing that is not applicable to personal sins (to use a scholastic term). [145] It is clear that the words [in 5:13] that follow [on 5:12] – 'For until the Law sin was in the world, but sin was not imputed' [5:13] etc – most of the Doctors explain as referring to the 'sin of imitation.' In fact even the passage [in 5:15] – 'For if many died through the trespass of one' etc – which again it seemed possible to refer to original sin – [Ambrosiaster] interprets thus: 'That is, if by the trespass of one, many died imitating his transgression, much more the grace of God' etc. Again, the words [in 5:18], 'As through the trespass of one, [the judgment was] for condemnation upon all' etc, the same Ambrosiaster explains thus: 'That is, just as through the trespass of one all who likewise sinned deserved condemnation, so also by the righteousness of one all who believe will be justified.'[117] From here on, [Paul] orders the discussion in such a way that you understand he is talking about the sins specifically of individuals. [146] How then will [Paul's] discussion remain firmly on course if the words that both precede and follow are understood to refer to the sins of individuals, while suddenly in the middle a sin of a different kind is thrown in?

[148] The reckless claim made by someone, that all the ancients, both Greek and Latin, with striking agreement interpret this passage to refer to original sin, is, then, false, since the Greek Origen and the Latin scholiast interpret it otherwise.[118] Consequently, it is not true that this opinion is peculiar to Pelagius and me, since Ambrosiaster, too, interprets what both precedes and follows to refer to the sins of individuals and seems to touch upon the sin of Adam only in the middle.[119] But it is even more false [to say] that this interpretation is in conflict with the special character of Pauline speech and the proper sense of the Greek words, since I have made it clear that both the character of the language, and the sequence and course of the discussion, fit more smoothly the view that I am showing to be possible.

117 For Ambrosiaster as Ambrose see 202 n10. Erasmus' identification of him as the bishop of Milan, and a speaker of both Greek and Latin, would give his interpretation special weight here, where the significance of a Greek preposition was in question. For the citations here see Ambrosiaster *Commentary on Romans* 5:13, 15, and 18.

118 Erasmus has also examined the comments (omitted here) of Chrysostom and Theophylact on the passage, and shown that they too believe that Paul is speaking of the actual sins of each individual.

119 Ie the contextual references must on principle determine our interpretation of the critical passage.

(4) Marriage as a Sacrament

From the annotation on Eph 5:32 (***sacramentum hoc*** 'this [is a great] mystery')[120] [CWE 58 209–10]

[The Greek *mysterion* 'mystery' was frequently translated in the Vulgate as *mysterium*, but sometimes in the later canonical Epistles and Revelation as *sacramentum*, and this was particularly significant in Ephesians, where in 5:32 the translation could seem to support the inclusion of marriage as one of the seven sacraments. In his annotations Erasmus frequently commented on the Greek word (cf eg n121 below). The annotation on Ephesians 5:32 was brief in *1516*; thereafter additions in *1519* and *1522* were interwoven in the text, the larger additions in *1519* motivated primarily it seems by the criticism of Edward Lee and reflecting allusions and ideas in the large *1519* annotation on 1 Cor 7:39, excerpted below. Once again, we see Erasmus' philological approach to theological problems.]

[CWE 58 209–10] [209] *mysterion*, that is, '*sacramentum*.'[121] I wanted those people to know this who use this passage to make matrimony one of the seven sacraments according to the special and exact meaning of this word. That matrimony is a sacrament is not, of course, in doubt, because it is likely that this tradition originated with the apostles or at least with the holy Fathers, and thence came all the way to us. And yet long ago orthodox scholastics did have doubts; indeed, a different opinion met approval. For some have observed that when Dionysius expressly considers the sacraments of the church and carefully explains the ritual and ceremonies of each, he makes no mention of matrimony.[122] Jerome, even in the several books in which he disputes about matrimony, nowhere calls it a sacrament.[123] Neither indeed does

---

120 Cf Eph 5:32 in DV: 'This is a great sacrament, but I speak in Christ and the church.' Erasmus translated, 'This is a great mystery, but I speak concerning Christ and the church.' For further discussions on marriage as a sacrament see the *Response to the Annotations of Edward Lee* (Note 188) CWE 72 296–303, the annotation on 1 Corinthians 7:39 abbreviated below 267–75, and *Institution of Christian Matrimony* CWE 69 226–35.

121 Cf the annotation on Mark 4:11: '*mysterion*,' that is, concealed or secret, not to be shared with the profane, a word the Vulgate sometimes renders as *sacramentum*.

122 Erasmus refers to Pseudo-Dionysius and his book *De ecclesiastica hierarchia* in which the sacraments are discussed. For Pseudo-Dionysius and *The Ecclesiastical Hierarchy* see 201 n7 above.

123 In the late fourth century, when Jerome was asserting the values of the celibate life, several opponents attacked his position, Helvidius, Jovinian and Vigilantius. In this passage Erasmus mentions Jovinian in particular, a monk from Milan who wrote

Augustine speak of matrimony in these terms, though he looked upon matrimony more favourably than Jerome, even writing a book *On the Good of Matrimony*.[124] It might seem more surprising that not even Jovinian, the champion of marriage, ever mentions the word 'sacrament.' If he had done so Jerome would have had to engage him on the point when he was refuting his books, especially since he responded so meticulously. This sort of reasoning, I know, is easily answered by scholars.

My comments are not intended to call into question whether marriage is a sacrament, for I am entirely in favour of the high status it enjoys; rather, I have spoken thus because it does not seem that we can effectively infer from the Apostle's words that it is a sacrament. In fact, the adversative, 'But I [speak],' clearly shows that this great mystery pertains to Christ and the church, not to husband and wife. For the sacrament is not 'great' in this, that a man is joined to his wife – this is normal practice even among pagans. [210] St Augustine, in his book to Valerius on marriage says, 'This sacrament the Apostle has called "great" in Christ and in the church. What therefore is great "in Christ and the church" is in every individual husband and wife very small, but nevertheless a sacrament of an inseparable union.'[125] Further, as I had begun to say, in this passage the Greek word [*mysterion*] does not mean sacrament of the kind meant when the church speaks of 'the seven,' but 'a thing hidden and secret,' a word Paul frequently used of other things that are far different from the nature of the sacraments. Writing to the Thessalonians he speaks of the 'mystery of iniquity,' and again in 1 Corinthians 13, 'If I know all mysteries.'[126] The ancients

a book (now lost) supporting marriage and opposing the concept of the perpetual virginity of Mary. But Erasmus may have in mind here some of Jerome's letters also, such as Epistle 22, the letter to Eustochium, on virginity.

124 In 401 Augustine wrote his book *On the Good of Matrimony* as a corrective to Jerome's harsh denunciation of marriage in his book *Against Jovinian*. While Augustine upheld the superiority of celibacy, he also affirmed the goodness of marriage. However, Augustine does speak of marriage as a sacrament, if not specifically one of the seven (cf *De bono coniugali* 15.17, 18–21), and includes marriage as a sacrament of the church, though perhaps not with what became the traditional understanding of sacrament; cf just below the citation from *On Marriage and Concupiscence*. For an excellent, if brief, study of Augustine on the sacraments see Fitzgerald *Augustine through the Ages* 741–7.

125 Augustine *De nuptiis et concupiscentia 'On Marriage and Concupiscence'* 1.21.23. This treatise in two books was addressed to Valerius, an official at the Emperor's court in Ravenna.

126 Cf 2 Thess 2:7 and 1 Cor 13:2.

called an oath or a binding obligation a sacrament – I suppose because they were transacted with certain secret ceremonies. I do not deny that matrimony is a sacrament, but I want us to consider whether from this particular passage it can be demonstrated that we can properly speak of a 'sacrament' in the sense in which baptism is said to be a sacrament.

(5) Faith and Charity

(a) From the annotation on 1 Corinthians 13:2 (***charitatem non habeam*** '[if] I have not charity') [ASD VI-8 252–6:700–47, 767–94]

[This is an extensive annotation introduced in its full length in the final edition of the New Testament, 1535. It seems to have been motivated largely by the objections of Béda and the Paris theologians, who saw in Erasmus' *Paraphrases* several statements in which Erasmus drew an inseparable connection between faith and charity. They argued from Paul's statement in 1 Corinthians 13:2 that faith and charity are separate gifts of the spirit, and can exist separately. Hence Erasmus devotes the annotation to a demonstration that the two are inseparable. The discussion presupposes the Pauline account of 'gifts' in the preceding chapter (12:8–11), where 'tongues,' 'faith,' 'knowledge' all are mentioned and to these allusion is made in 13:1–2. In the first half of the annotation Erasmus undertakes to show that in patristic literature faith and charity are regarded as inseparable, to show also that conditional (ie hypothetical) statements ('if … then') are fictional (as in 13:1–3), used for the purpose of argumentation in debate, but are not intended to represent actual reality. He then continues:]

[**ASD VI-8 252–6**] [700] I think the Apostle is speaking here [in 13:2] not about just any 'faith' or 'prophecy,' but about the gifts of the Spirit after the ascension of the Lord. [710] Since true faith embraces many things – an assured assent to all that has been handed down to us as necessary to eternal salvation, and a confident trust in the mercy of God and his promises realized both in this life and in the age to come – how would such a gift come to us apart from charity? Now I agree with those who understand the expression 'all faith' [13:2] to mean perfect faith, and no one, I assume, will deny that Paul here is speaking not of just any charity, but of true and evangelical charity, for if he were comparing this with the other gifts as dead, the lofty status of charity would be meaningless. After all, what would be the point if he were saying that true charity is more excellent than the kind of prophecy Balaam spoke, or the kind of faith the demons possess?[127]

It is probable, then, that Paul in [1 Corinthians 13:2] in order to emphasize its superiority compares true and evangelical charity with the true and perfect gifts of the Spirit, separating in a purely hypothetical way things that belong intrinsically together. One thing is certain: whenever the Lord or the apostles speak of faith they mean a 'living faith.' For example, 'Your faith has made you well' [Matt 9:22 RSV], and 'If you have faith as a grain of mustard seed' [Matt 17:20 RSV]. The blessed Paul throughout all his Epistles emphasizes nothing more insistently than grace and faith. He teaches that we are justified through faith, that by faith we stand, that people of faith will gain the blessing, and that Christ dwells in us through faith.[128] Finally, in Hebrews [chapter 11] he sings the praises of faith. Similarly Peter in Acts, 'Purifying your hearts by faith' [Acts 15:9], and John writes that we overcome the world through faith.[129] How then is one at fault who joins charity as an inseparable companion to this faith so often asserted in the books of the New Testament? Now since faith begets the works of charity – as the Apostle writes to the Romans, 'Whatever is not of faith is sin' [Rom14:13], while to the Galatians he speaks specifically of the faith that works through charity[130] – the works of charity must therefore be attributed to faith. How then is it appropriate to separate charity from faith, that is, the root from the branches?[131]

But some people find it problematic if someone says that a person obtains righteousness, that is, forgiveness of sins, through faith alone [*sole fide*]. To me, at least, it seems that these people either do not know or have forgotten that words like 'alone,' 'singular,' 'only,' are frequently used both by non-Christians and by the orthodox to designate not what is solitary or unaccompanied, but what is outstanding or preeminent, as when the satirist says, 'Virtue is the one and only nobility,' he means that the highest and most outstanding kind of nobility is the luminous distinction of one's name, a distinction arising

127 Cf Num 24:3–9, 15-24 (Balaam), James 2:19 (demons).

128 Cf Rom 5:1 (justified through), 2 Cor 1:24 (stand by), Gal 3:7–9 (blessing gained by), Eph 3:17 (Christ dwells in us through).

129 Cf 1 John 5:4.

130 Cf Gal 5:6.

131 For the image see Rom 11:17–19, John 15:1–5.

from one's own virtue.[132] When we say that someone is endowed with singular prudence we are not stripping the person of the other virtues but are attributing outstanding wisdom. Again when someone says in the Comedy, 'He alone is a friend to a friend,' he does not mean that apart from him no one is a friend to others, but that this particular person is in a surpassing way a friend to his friend.[133]

[767] Using the same figure of speech, Paul calls God alone wise and immortal, not thereby excluding angels and prophets, for in the Gospel the five virgins are said to be wise, and in addition to Solomon wisdom is predicated of several in canonical literature.[134] Similarly in Luke, the ninth chapter, when we read that 'Jesus was found alone' [9:36], the three disciples are not excluded, but Moses and Elijah with whom he had just been speaking. Finally, when the blessed Thomas Aquinas in the liturgical sequence says, 'Faith alone suffices to strengthen the sincere heart,' the word 'alone' does not exclude charity and the other virtues, but only human reason and sense experience.[135] [785] Accordingly when someone says that persons are justified by faith alone, charity or the works of charity are not forthwith excluded, but human philosophy or ceremonies or the works of the Law, or the life lived before baptism, or something similar, which is understood from the drift of the speech. In fact, in Paul the word 'alone' is not added.[136] What difference does it make since in so many places Paul presses upon us that Abraham was pronounced just apart from works, that we are all justified by faith and not from works, for if from works then grace no longer has a place.[137] All of Paul's Epistles abound with this kind of talk, and yet nowhere does he separate charity from purifying faith, and so many times exhorts to works of charity.

---

132 Cf Juvenal *Satires* 8.20.

133 Terence *Phormio* 562; cf the interesting note in the early twentieth century (2nd) edition by Sidney G. Ashmore (Oxford 1910) 184, '"*solus*" is of course an exaggeration. He befriends his friends as no one else can do.'

134 Cf Rom 16:27 and 1 Tim 1:17 (in AV and Erasmus' text, but not in NRSV]), Matt 25:1–12 (virgins); for the proverbial wisdom of Solomon see 2 Chron 1:7–12 and 9:1–2, and for other 'wise' persons see Gen 41:39, Deut 1:15 and Matt 23:34.

135 A reference to the hymn attributed to Thomas Aquinas; cf the translation by Edward Caswell, 'Now my tongue the mystery telling' (*pange lingua*) ' … if senses fail to see, faith alone the true heart waketh, to behold the mystery.'

136 The expression is found in James 2:24.

137 Cf Rom 4:1–5:1, 11:6, Eph 2:8–9.

(b) From the annotation on 1 Corinthians 13:13 (***maior autem horum*** 'the greater of these [is charity]') [ASD VI-8 264–6:904–76]

[Before *1535* this was a very short annotation, addressing a strictly philological problem: the Greek literally reads, 'faith, hope, charity, these three, but the greater of these is charity.' The Vulgate adopted the Greek idiom, rather than translating into good Latin the intended sense. Erasmus explained that the expression reflected Greek idiom, where the comparative is used for the superlative, hence here the intended sense is, 'the greatest of these.' The long *1535* addition is directed to two other problems. 1/ What does Paul mean by saying '"*now*" abide faith, hope and charity' [13:13]? Recognizing that these are divine gifts, Erasmus suggests that Paul is speaking of them with the grand view of saving-history in mind, thinking specifically of their utility in the present moment for the welfare of the human race, hence the 'now.' He then proceeds to the second problem, 2/ How can charity be said to be the greatest of these gifts, greater even than faith?

1/ In answer to the first question Erasmus admits that he finds the passage puzzling, but suggests that Paul's thought in 13:8–13 advances in a somewhat digressive way: the gifts necessary to the witness of the primitive church will cease as the church grows to full stature, which it has now done; the gifts of faith, hope, and charity, however, remain, since without these there cannot be a church. Then the Apostle thinks of the greater perfection of the future heavenly world, when we will see not as in a mirror but face to face and will be known as we are known. There even faith, hope, and charity will 'vanish away.' 'Now,' however, in our present life they still remain. But surely charity cannot cease in heaven, where there is perfect charity! What then is the nature of the charity that 'now' remains with us but is not needed in the celestial world? Erasmus writes:]

[**ASD VI-8 264**] [904] Certain gifts, like the gift of tongues, essential in the first stages of the church's life, are now no longer operative, for these were signs given for unbelievers, not for believers. Paul seems to have pointed in this direction when he says, 'When I was a child etc' [13:11], as though some gifts were given to the church in the process of maturing, gifts that would cease when the church had arrived at the 'measure of the fullness of Christ' [Eph 4:13]. From the expression of this perfection, the biblical text seems to move to the greater perfection of the future life, for the words 'then shall we see face to face' [13:12] are not applicable to the church militant. If we grant that in this remark the Apostle has digressed slightly, as he sometimes does elsewhere, we would understand his main intent in this way: even if the other gifts cease in the church, faith, hope, and charity will never cease, for without these we would not have the church of Christ but a synagogue of Satan.[138]

In the celestial life, of course, neither faith nor hope nor charity will remain since 'faith is the substance of things hoped for, the evidence of things not seen' [Heb 11:1], and 'why does one hope for what one sees?' [Rom 8:24]. But it seems incongruous that in the heavenly world charity is not operative, where charity will be complete and perfect. With all due respect to the opinion of others, my own opinion is that the Apostle here [in saying 'now'] is speaking not of that whole and complete charity by which we love God above all things and our neighbour on account of God, but only of that one function of charity through which we are able to help our neighbours. [930] This particular function of charity will cease in the heavenly world, where no one will need to be assisted by the kindness of another, though in this life there is no one who does not need his neighbour's help.

[2/ Erasmus proceeds to the second problem:]

[**ASD VI-8 264–6**] [932] Perhaps someone will want to ask, 'How is it that Paul here says "charity is the greater" when the Lord in the Gospel and Paul in his letters so notably preach faith?' For just as no gift is pleasing to God without charity, so no gift is received without faith, indeed no gift is even given without faith. Faith is, as it were, the hands of the soul with which we receive and embrace the bounty of the Spirit, without which not even the works of charity are pleasing to God. Moreover, faith is by nature prior to charity, since it is through faith that we come to know God, while nothing is loved unless it is known. Now that which brings to birth or produces seems more excellent than that which is born or produced. Finally, Paul everywhere credits human salvation to faith rather than to charity.[139]

[943] Besides, if charity is the greatest of gifts, then in chapter 12, which immediately precedes and in which the gifts of the Spirit are recounted, the chief place ought to be given to charity. In fact, however, faith finds some place there, but charity is not even mentioned.[140] To this one can only reply that although the term itself is not found expressed

138 For the expression see Rev 2:9.

139 Cf eg Rom 1:16, Gal 3:1–6, 23–4.

140 Cf 1 Cor 12:8–10; 'faith' is mentioned in 12:9.

there, the many functions of charity are mentioned, as 'word of wisdom,' 'word of knowledge,' 'the grace of healing,' 'the working of miracles,' 'prophecy,' 'the discerning of spirits,' 'administrations,' 'interpretation of speeches'[141] [DV]. Through these works charity expresses itself. One who displays the branches and fruit sufficiently commends the root. And since this whole passage urges the advantage of a neighbour, on this principle the gifts that are more profitable to the many are called the better gifts, and charity the greatest because it accommodates all things to the advantage of the church. There is no reason, however, why the same thing should not be regarded as both superior and inferior to another according to the perspective from which it is viewed.

Perhaps someone will further ask how, since no gift of the Spirit – not even charity –is given or is pleasing without faith, Paul, in his catalogue of gifts lists faith as though, among the members of the mystical body, it is present in some but not in others.[142] [964] But, as Theophylact notes, in that catalogue the term 'faith' does not point to that belief and trust in God through which all graces are given, but only to that faith through which miracles are performed, a faith that is neither given to all nor is necessary for salvation.[143] It seems clear enough that the Apostle refers to this kind of faith when [in 13:2] he says, 'If I have all faith so as to remove mountains' [RSV]. This faith, too, can be said to be perfect in its own class though it is not absolutely perfect in relation to the full force of the word 'perfect.' For perfect faith is the root and source of all spiritual gifts, even of charity itself. To charity, however, belongs whatever good comes to one to contribute to the advantage of his neighbour, whether that good is spiritual or moral or natural or fortuitous.

III. ERASMIAN PERSPECTIVES ON CHURCH AND SOCIETY

[The selections from the annotations above have illustrated Erasmus' work as a philologist engaged with the text and meaning of Scripture. But Erasmus' annotations seem to have been modelled to some extent on a long tradition of desultory commentary to which spontaneous remarks

141 Erasmus quotes the Vulgate of 12:8–10 for all these 'functions of charity' (including 'interpretation of speeches') except 'helps' and 'administrations' found in 12:28.

142 A reference to the list in 1 Cor 12:4–10, quoted in full in the annotation, omitted here.

143 Theophylact *Commentary on 1 Corinthians* 12:9.

on tangential subjects were appropriate, such as the annotations of Aulus Gelius in late antiquity (cf CWE 41 50–1, and 21 above). In any case Erasmus repeatedly insists, as in the letter to Pope Leo X dedicatory to his New Testament in 1516, that he saw in Scripture the means to the 'restoration of religion' ie Christianity. Indeed, the prefatory essays to his New Testament suggest that he wanted it to be seen as a symbol of and call for reform. His annotations were thus an avenue for him to express his perspectives on the condition of the church and of society, and to call for reform. It is probable, in fact, that some readers will find that it is in comments of this kind that his annotations hold their greatest interest: they offer engaging insights into ecclesiastical conditions in the sixteenth century, conveyed to us in passionate and mordant prose. In the selections that follow Erasmus focuses our attention on the burden of ecclesiastical regulations, on the excesses of monasticism, on the prevalence of war in Christian Europe, on the disturbing condition of the Liturgy, on divorce, and on a theological education for clergy entirely inappropriate to their calling.]

(1) On Ecclesiastical Regulations

From the annotation on Matt 11:30 (***iugum meum suave*** 'my yoke is easy') [ASD VI-5 206–10:305–6, 322–441]

[In *1516* the annotation consisted of a single sentence explaining why Erasmus had replaced the Vulgate's *suave* 'sweet,' 'pleasant' with *commodum* 'agreeable,' 'gentle.' In *1519* Erasmus enlarged the annotation to offer a major critique of the sixteenth century church; apart from the third paragraph (*1522*; but cf n149) the selection below follows the text of the 1519 edition.]

[**ASD VI-5 206–10**] [305] By 'yoke' [the Gospel writer] means 'rule,' 'the power to command.' Christ wants us to understand that this commanding authority is kind and gentle, in no way harsh, not at all severe. [322] Truly the yoke of Christ is gentle and his burden is light if, beyond what he has imposed on us, nothing further is imposed by the petty regulations of human beings. He asks for nothing more than love for one another;[144] nothing is so bitter that charity cannot season and sweeten it. Whatever is in accordance with nature is easily borne; nothing, however, agrees more with nature than the philosophy of Christ,[145] which is

144 Cf John 13:34.
145 Cf the introduction to *Paraclesis*, 23–5 above.

almost entirely directed towards the restoration of our fallen nature to its original innocence and integrity. But just as among the Jews human regulations added an oppressive weight to the Law, which was in itself burdensome, so we must always take special care that by the addition of human regulations and decrees we do not turn the law of Christ, in itself gentle and light, into a burden that is heavy and harsh. Such things creep in at first in such a way that either they are disregarded as trivial and of no consequence, or, commended by their façade of piety, men and women even of integrity (though hardly of foresight) willingly embrace them. Once accepted they spread bit by bit and grow to huge proportions, and oppress and overwhelm those who no longer welcome them. This happens either through force of custom – a merciless and tyrannical power – or by the authority of princes, who for their own gain use and tenaciously maintain what was rashly accepted.

How pure, how uncomplicated is the faith handed down to us from Christ! How similar to it the Creed put forth by the apostles themselves, or at least by apostolic men! To this simple faith the church, shaken and torn by the discord of heretics, then added much. Soon there were as many creeds as Christians.[146] [345] Development continued little by little until finally some of the definitions (called 'articles') of the scholastics or certain novelties of some midget men whom arrogance inspired to think up opinions or invent dreams, have almost become equated with the articles of the apostolic faith – opinions or dreams though they be.

About these opinions neither the different schools agree nor do even the professionals of the same school agree among themselves, and not even in their own circles do the definitions remain fixed but are changed with the times. When first they crept in, they were regarded by the schools as only probable opinions; soon they passed beyond the confines of the school into books, and burst forth even into public sermons. But what originates in rash and seemingly inconsequential efforts to define is frequently strengthened and augmented by a stubborn determination to maintain. Examples of this are our complex conclusions

146 In the *Explanation of the Creeds*, a late work dedicated to Thomas Boleyn, father of Anne, Erasmus speaks at length of the Creeds, mentioning the Nicene Creed (325 AD), the Constantinopolitan Creed (381 AD) and the Athanasian Creed (ninth century); cf CWE 70 241–59 especially 253. But there were other formulas and definitions, in effect creeds, drawn up by Synods, eg the Chalcedonian Definition (451 AD), and some churches used variations of the great standard creeds. For Erasmus' understanding of the origin of the Apostles' Creed see CWE 39 432 n16.

about the nature of the divine persons; [360] also our pronouncements (as though divinely authorized) on the nature of the mysteries.[147] It would contribute more to godliness if we would take from such things whatever is conducive to holy living. But the practice of making pronouncements, a habit originating in antiquity, has now gone so far that it cannot be tolerated. There are people who start by formulating an insipid syllogism, and from a passage [of Scripture] little understood or from some petty human regulation produce an article of faith.

Whether or not we are Christians is determined from these things, though such definitions do not in the slightest contribute to Christian godliness. [374] Long ago St Augustine lamented that the church of Christ was so oppressed that the condition of Jews was almost more tolerable than that of Christians.[148] What if he saw that free people of Christ entangled [as it is today] in so many laws, so many ceremonies, so many snares! A people oppressed not by the undisguised tyranny of men but of secular princes, bishops, cardinals, popes, and above all, their assistants who,[149] under the mask of religion, serve their stomachs. The very sacraments, instituted for the salvation of mankind, some of us use for our own gain, our pride, our tyranny, for the oppression of the poor Christian populace. No kind of clothes was forbidden to the Jews except that woven from linen and wool.[150] Now how many regulations there are about clothes! What monstrous superstition about garments and colours![151] And from trifles of this sort we are counted as Christians, although these things in themselves are neither honourable nor base but subject to change depending on circumstances and the shifting taste of mortals; in fact, Christ never said a single word about them. The Jews had few fasts, and yet no one called it a mortal sin if someone had not fasted on the explicitly established days. We, on the

---

147 Ie the sacraments.

148 Cf Augustine Epistle 55.19–35. The same allusion is found in the dedicatory letter to the *Paraphrase on the Two Epistles to the Corinthians*; cf Ep 916:266–77 or CWE 43 11 with n45, and in *On Eating Meat* CWE 73 70 n25.

149 'Who … stomachs': this biting remark was added in *1522*.

150 Cf Deut 22:11.

151 Erasmus frequently complains about the fastidious concern over monastic garb. In his annotation on Matt 23:5 (*ut videantur ab hominibus* 'that they might be seen by men') he speaks of the diverse and novel forms and colours of dress and adds that in comparison with Christians who place a superstitious emphasis on such things the scribes and Pharisees seem positively honourable. Cf also CWE 84 207. Though a monk Erasmus himself had laid aside his monastic habit, and received a papal dispensation exonerating him from the consequent penalties; cf Ep 517:14–25 and the introduction to it in CWE.

other hand – how often are we oppressed with abstinence from food! To these fasts we are not invited but compelled under penalty, as they say, of eternal damnation. The Jews were forbidden certain kinds of fish and animals, creatures in any case not particularly wanted for consumption. We waste away for a good part of the year by eating fish, we become bloated through starvation. Neither old age nor disease provides an excuse; only money buys relief from the law.[152] For the Hebrews the number of fast days was modest. The age of Jerome knew very few beyond the Lord's Day. Now there is neither limit nor measure to festive days. At first only a few were established in order to provide some leisure for the practice of godliness; now they should be suppressed to exclude opportunities for crime – except that avarice persuades the priests to consider their advantage rather than true religion.[153]

What shall I say of the intricate and inextricable chains that bind vows? From some of these relief can be purchased but only with immense sums of money, from others there is absolutely no escape. How much more agreeable were the terms of marriage for a Jew than they are for us![154] With how many snares do we entangle marriage, with what vexatious trumpery – simply to maintain scholastic dogma! In how many ways do we constrain the sacrament of penance and confession, with how many decrees do we encumber it![155] This is to say nothing about the burden of prayers weighed down with even daily accretions. [409] The thunderbolt of excommunication is everywhere ready and waiting, on all sides anathematizations hasten to the attack. The sacrosanct authority of the Roman bishop, which ought to be efficacious only in support of the affairs of the church, some use in absolutions, dispensations, pardons, indictments. Affairs relating to the sacerdotal office are so involved that you could learn thoroughly all the philosophy of Aristotle sooner than the practice of a priest. In church there is scarcely time

152 Perhaps even more than monastic dress fasting was the object of bitter attacks by Erasmus. See *On Eating Meat* CWE 73 75–85, and for the events that occasioned this little work CWE 73 xxiv, and ibidem 105 for the horrific death of the central figure in the events. Erasmus had an intense dislike of fish, claiming that eating fish made him sick; he was granted a papal dispensation that allowed him to avoid eating fish. For a vivid account of the consequences of fasting in his own life see the colloquy 'A Fish Diet' CWE 40 713–14 and 751–4 nn263–78.

153 For crime on festive days see Ep 1039:190–209.

154 See the annotation on 1 Cor 7:39 excerpted below 267–75. Erasmus describes the complex ecclesiastical laws and regulations associated with marriage vows in the *Institute of Christian Marriage* CWE 69 258–65, 389–90.

155 For regulations associated with confession see *Manner of Confessing* CWE 67 47–50.

to explain the Gospel. A good part of the sermon has to be given over to the pleasure of the commissioners.[156] Sometimes the most holy teaching of Christ must either be suppressed or twisted to their interests. At such things the godly silently groan.

[430] To heal these ills there generally has remained one great anchor – a General Council.[157] Now, however, these very evils apply to the head of the Commonwealth, and no hope of healing remains unless Christ himself turns (or at least arouses) the hearts of popes and princes to attend to true piety, or unless theologians and preachers with full consensus teach and inculcate what is worthy of Christ. Of this one thing we must all be constantly admonished: to embrace the liberty in the manner St Paul has taught us, that is, not to make our liberty an occasion for the flesh, so that on the pretext of liberty we serve sin more shamefully.[158] Let us shake off the heavy yoke imposed by men, but only as we take up the truly gentle yoke of Christ.

(2) On the Mendicant Orders

From the annotation on Mark 6:9 (*calceatos sandaliis* '[he instructed them to take nothing, but to] wear sandals') [ASD VI-5 385–8:881–931, 946–9]

[This annotation, added entirely in *1535*, the last edition of the New Testament published by Erasmus in his lifetime, is directed toward a critique of the practices of the mendicant friars. It begins with a discussion of the mendicants' footwear. From a comparison of Mark 6:9, Matthew 10:10 and Luke 10:4, the friars justified the use of sandals but not shoes. Erasmus argues here that the distinction, based on a literal reading of these passages, is not justified: shoes as such were not forbidden by the evangelists. Erasmus soon turns to what becomes the central focus of concern: the legitimacy of begging practised by the mendicant friars, and the more general issue of poverty and riches in Christian ethics.]

---

156 Ie the commissioners of indulgences who took time from the sermon to encourage people to buy indulgences. Jacques Chomarat, however, identifies them as: 'autorités laïques dont le prédicateur communique aux fidèles les décisions,' *Grammaire et rhetorique chez Érasme* (Paris 1981) 469 n3.

157 In this passage Erasmus appears as a supporter of the Conciliar theory, ie that the highest authority in the church is located in a council of bishops. Erasmus offers an interesting discussion on the relative authority of councils and pope in the colloquy 'A Fish Diet' CWE 40 689:27–691:4; see Craig Thompson's notes on the issue CWE 40 732 nn96, 97, 98.

158 Cf Gal 5:13.

[ASD VI-5 385–8] [881] It would be simpler to say that Christ wanted to persuade his disciples that they should approach the task of preaching without baggage or encumbrances, that their only care should be to proclaim the kingdom of heaven; and since they were still in the early stages of their training he spoke in plain but vivid terms. I do not think that Christ would have been displeased if one of the apostles wore shoes because of the roughness of the road or a sore foot. It was with the same intent that he forbade them to greet anyone on the way, speaking in hyperbole to urge the utmost zeal in hastening the work. [892] It does not belong to evangelical perfection scrupulously to represent Christ in externals. He did not come into the world to teach us what shoes or what clothes we should wear.

Just as the mendicants are eager to make Christ go barefoot, so they are eager to make him a beggar. Poverty is appropriate to Christ, mendicity diminishes his dignity. Inescapable need is the only valid reason for begging. Papal constitutions have had this in view when they warn that no one should be received into the rank of presbyter unless he has the means for his livelihood.[159] Why? So that presbyters would not be forced to beg, which diminishes the dignity of a priest. That regulation is nonsense if mendicity is part of evangelical perfection. When he was staying in Corinth Paul did not go around begging in the lodging houses or on ships – certainly not door to door – but to avoid asking anyone for support he stitched skins together at night for making tents.[160] Christ was generous to those in need, so far was he himself from begging, and sometimes he sent the apostles to buy food.[161] It is not improbable that the Lord had his own means, either from the resources of his father and mother or even from his own labour. Otherwise, if he had no house or furnishings, how do we read that he moved from Nazareth to Capernaum where he had a residence?[162] It is also likely that he was dressed in clean and honourable clothes, otherwise the soldiers would not have divided among themselves the seamless garment they had torn.[163] Moreover, the gifts freely given of rich friends and godly women have nothing

159 Cf ASD VI-5 387:896–8n: 'Perhaps a reference to the Decretals of Sixtus ... [citing the Latin, which I translate] "The religious should not be installed as rectors in churches unless provisions are sufficient to relieve the burden of their expenses and maintain them appropriately."'

160 Cf Acts 18:3, 1 Thess 2:9.

161 Cf John 4:8, 13:29.

162 Cf Matt 4:13 and Mark 2:1; also the paraphrase on Matt 9:1 CWE 45 151 with n3.

163 Cf Matt 27:35, John 19:23–4.

to do with begging.[164] Nor does the fact that he himself said the Son of man has nowhere to lay his head have any weight. This statement does not properly refer to lack of resources but to all those things in which the soul of humans dedicated to the world take repose.[165] This is situated in the emotions, not in external things. A longing for glory is more dangerous than a longing for wealth. What are those striving for who want to be seen as apostolic men, men of evangelical perfection, by begging both in private and in public? It is for them to say, not for me. Certainly we never read that the Lord begged, nor do we read anywhere that the apostles begged or that the Lord ever ordered them to do so.

Poverty itself is not, in fact, a virtue, nor is wealth a vice. There are two kinds of poverty. On the one hand there is a kind of poverty that provides only a frugal living with nothing superfluous, the kind beautifully adapted to gospel philosophy; on the other hand there is a kind that weighs down and presses hard upon one and frequently entices to more serious crimes than does wealth. Accordingly Solomon prays to avoid both riches and poverty alike, wealth because it sometimes causes one to forget God, poverty because it entices one to steal and to lie under oath, a form of blasphemy to be sure.[166] Poverty drags people into many other evils, sacrilege, sorcery, prostitution, robbery, parricide. Those therefore are to be commended who use well wealth that has been acquired without fraud, and those are to be commended who bear patiently and cheerfully a forced poverty. At the same time, I think those are not to be disparaged who of their own free will embrace poverty, provided it leads to the provisioning and the propagation of the kingdom of God, but it is to be rejected if it obstructs. [946] And yet, how great is the number of those who profess poverty to escape poverty! Or, by accepting an abbacy, even to come into the possession of enormous riches! Gospel perfection derives not from the profession of the three vows – poverty, chastity, and obedience – but from the imitation of Christ.

(3) On War

From the annotation on Luke 22:36 (***sed nunc qui habet sacculum*** 'but now the one who has a purse')[167] [ASD VI-5 584–94:703–10, 732–816, 839–62]

---

164 Cf Luke 8:3.

165 Cf Matt 8:20; in the paraphrase on this verse, however, Erasmus does indeed emphasize Jesus' poverty and lack of all possessions CWE 45 146.

166 Cf Prov 30:8–9, where the words are attributed to 'Agur, son of Jakeh' [RSV].

167 The annotation discusses the entire verse: 'But now the one who has a purse must take it, and likewise a bag. And the one who has no sword must sell his cloak and buy one' [NRSV].

[Erasmus frequently lamented the evils of war. One finds his opposition to war expressed in both incidental comments and in major publications – in the famous adage 'War is sweet to those who have not tried it' (*1515*, *Adagia* IV i 1 CWE 35), in *The Education of a Christian Prince* (*1516*, CWE 27 282–8), in *Complaint of Peace* (*1517*, CWE 27 300–22), in the colloquy 'Military Affairs' (*1522*, CWE 39 53–60), in the letters prefacing his *Paraphrases* on Matthew (*1522*), Luke (*1523*) and Mark (*1523–4*), *Paraphrases* dedicated respectively to Charles V (Ep 1255), Henry VIII (Ep 1381) and Francis I (Ep 1400). But Erasmus was not an absolute pacifist. In 1530 he somewhat grudgingly conceded (with conditions) that 'it is lawful to fight off the Turks unless God sends a clear sign to prohibit it' (CWE 64 237). In the same 'Discussion' (*On the Turkish War*) he calls attention to some of the principles that underlie the theory of the 'just war,' a theory reaching back into pagan antiquity and adapted to Christian theology by the early Fathers. Preceding the 1527 edition of the *Annotations* some people were pressing Erasmus 'to state whether [he] believes all war is forbidden to a Christian.' In this annotation on Luke 22:36, after decrying once again the evils of war, Erasmus answers the query by articulating in principle the theory of the 'just war.' The annotation was already long in *1516* (extending here to n181); in *1519* he acknowledged the right of princes to 'use the sword' in the interest of justice and public discipline and anticipated briefly the *1527* addition (cf n188) wherein he clarified his position with a discussion of the just war.]

[ASD VI-5 584–94] [703] My dear Christian reader, I ask you: is there anyone so glum that he can restrain his laughter when he considers how ridiculous are the comments written on this passage by some modern exegetes?[168] Or is there anyone so given to laughter that he would not frown in indignation at interpretations that so vitiate this heavenly teaching? Nicholas of Lyra, for example, in the estimation of many a distinguished doctor, distorts the words of Christ in this way: Christ, he says, is warning the apostles that when the storms of persecution are brewing they should fortify themselves with two things – provisions

168 By 'modern exegetes' (Latin *recentiores*) Erasmus refers to the scholars of the high Middle Ages. He names here Nicholas of Lyra (d1349) whom Erasmus often associated with the earlier Hugh of St Cher (d1263). See CWE 44 134 n12. The comments of these two often appeared with the *Gloss*, a compilation (twelfth and thirteenth centuries) of comments printed in the margins of the Vulgate Bible.

and the protection of arms – so that they would not lack food or be overwhelmed by their persecutors!' Hugh of St Cher insists even more shamefully on the same interpretation.

[732] Now if the Lord was telling his disciples to prepare the means for livelihood and defence, are not clothes necessary for living? Yet he orders his disciples to sell their cloaks! Accordingly, [we should understand that] just as with these words [ie sword-cloak] Christ was preparing the apostles to suffer bravely the savagery of persecutors, so with reference to 'taking the bag' he was preparing them to endure hunger and all the customary unpleasant concomitants of warfare. The prediction of evils[169] is not an exhortation to prepare provisions and defensive weapons, but an exhortation to the endurance of evils that more readily overthrow us if they come upon us unforeseen. As long as the Lord was here as a mortal he had abundantly supplied the needs of the disciples without any concern on their part, and had kept them safe from the onslaught of evils. They were consequently weak and ill-prepared for the storms of evil that were threatening. After all, it was just before his death that they were even contending over the primacy.[170] In anticipation of these evils he was warning them that they should not trust in their own strength, but should be on their guard against the advancing storm of persecutions. How should they be on their guard? Exactly as he himself showed them by both example and admonition: 'Watch and pray that you do not enter into temptation' [Matt 26:41]. We read that after they had received the Holy Spirit, they did precisely what the Lord had taught them.[171] He wanted them to depend on him not in the manner of children, but as men who join to their own effort the support available from heaven. This is the interpretation of Chrysostom. [756] Consider his words: 'Bringing the chicks out of their nest, he tells them to use their own wings.'[172] Does Chrysostom mean that they are to get ready spears, helmets, shields, and cannon balls? If so, then what is the difference between a war-mongering mercenary and an apostle?

But the objection is made that when circumstances change, it is permitted to change the pattern of life: in time of peace such things are forbidden, in time of war they are permitted – as though there has been any time at all when good people have been free from persecution! As though Christ, now that he is about to die, recants all those teachings of

169 Erasmus may have in mind the prediction of persecutions in Luke 21:7–19.

170 Cf Luke 22:24–7.

171 Cf eg Acts 4:23–31.

172 Chrysostom *Homilies on Matthew* 84.1 (on Matt 26:51–4).

his: about not resisting evil, about loving and helping enemies, about blessing those who curse us, about the blessed state of the meek and of those who suffer persecution for the sake of righteousness, about turning the other cheek if someone strikes you, and many other things of the same sort.[173] Recanting all such teaching he now urges his disciples to prepare provisions and equip themselves with all the paraphernalia of a soldier. Really?

[774] Further, why should we regard of any importance Christ's instruction to his disciples if he was teaching them to do what pirates and brigands do of their own accord? Is this that heavenly doctrine he so wished to share with us that he left heaven and came down to earth? [781] Let us suppose it was the intention of Christ that his apostles should equip themselves with an iron sword, loitering about like brigands, equip themselves also with the provisions military leaders require, how (to press the details) does one explain that he tells them to sell the cloak and buy a sword? Surely he is not sending them to war with a sword in hand but wearing no clothes! [795] Consider the subsequent events as reported in the other Gospels. He later severely reproaches Peter because he uses a sword, and he orders him to put it back in its sheath, adding that those who fight with a sword perish with the sword, that any number of legions were available to him from his Father if he had wished to defend himself by force.[174] Moreover, when, in the biblical narratives, did the apostles ever do what Christ emphatically ordered his disciples to do?[175] [800] We read that they fled, we read that they returned an answer, we nowhere read that they wore breastplates and carried swords.[176] Why in all those [apostolic] letters do they dare to disagree with all their preceptor's teaching [as my opponents understand it]? They all with one voice teach endurance, they ask that our enemies be overwhelmed with kindness, that coals of fire be heaped on their heads. Paul asks that we overcome evil with good,[177] he boasts of the hardships he has endured, he never boasts of enemies overthrown and destroyed. So often does he arm the Christian recruit

173 Dominical sayings from the Sermon on the Mount (Matthew 5) and the Sermon on the Plain (Luke 6:27–36).

174 Cf Matt 26:51–3, John 18:10–11.

175 'Ordered them to do,' that is, to take up the sword in self-defence, as the 'modern exegetes' have interpreted the verse?

176 Cf Matt 26: 56, 70–4 (flee), but Erasmus may be alluding to later events as recorded in Acts and the Epistles; cf eg Acts 8:4, 9:23–5; Acts 26:1–4 (return an answer).

177 Cf Rom 5:3–4, 12:12, 20–1.

with the gospel armour, the helmet of salvation, the shield of faith, the sword of the Spirit![178] Where among these is there any reference to that sword we devise?

In my view there is no heresy more destructive, no blasphemy more wicked than that of a person who (to recall the example of the Philistines) blocks up with earth the wells in the gospel field, those wells that derive from Christ their vein of living water flowing forth into eternal life,[179] and turns the spiritual sense of Scripture into the carnal sense, perverts the heavenly doctrine into earthly doctrine, twists or rather corrupts the most holy teachings of Christ, and does so when the interpretation is contradicted by all the teachings of Christ, contradicted by the life of Christ, contradicted by apostolic teaching, denied by so many thousands of martyrs and opposed by the interpreters of old. [839] And yet there is hardly a single precept of Christ that some people do not pervert by their comments and petty distinctions. These are read and affirmed by theologians thought to be of the highest calibre, quoted as though they enjoyed the authority of an oracle. They[180] are publicly taught; princes hear these things, which incite them to war – as though they were not sufficiently frantic for war without incitement! So it is that Christians stir up trouble, go to court, fight for possessions, power, revenge, almost more insanely than pagans have ever done.

[847] Those[181] who think that the right to go to war must not be taken away from princes are of no concern to me. I will not even talk about how at the present time princes fight, and there is no need to teach them what they do all too keenly of their own accord – if indeed what they do is to fight and not rather to collude to destroy the people, and on the pretext of war to establish their own tyranny. There is one view I will not tolerate, and that is that we make Christ the author of such doctrines. [858] I am aware that Augustine cites this passage [Luke 22:36] in his work *Against Faustus the Manichaean*. It is clear, however, from his citation that he does not want the apostles, in fact not even emperors to go to war unless fully confident of their own righteous intention, unless the cause is just, unless it is a war against the sacrilegious and the worshippers of demons, and unless it is undertaken for the sake of the

178 Cf 2 Cor 11:18–29 (hardships), Eph 6:14–17 (armour).

179 Cf Gen 26:15–25 (wells), John 4:14 (living water). Cf the *Ratio* 61 above.

180 This sentence is a *1519* addition.

181 This long addition of *1519* including the discussion on the 'right of Princes' concludes just before the addition of *1527* for which see n188.

public peace.[182] [877] There is, to be sure, a question whether Augustine is consistent in his comments on war, for though in many, many places, speaking as a Christian he abominates war, he does seem to defend it when he writes against the Manichaeans and the Donatists.[183] [890] But [the inconsistency can be explained] by the general truth that in conflict with opponents everyone twists Scripture to support his own view.

[901] Accordingly, I think a more straightforward interpretation is this: Christ was trying to remove little by little common dispositions from the hearts of the disciples. He had first freed them from a concern for provisions,[184] he wanted now to liberate them also from the fear of punishment and death. He knew what in that troubled time would come into the minds of men who were still not fully trained, and so he allowed them for the moment to misunderstand the comment about the swords in order to remove more effectively from their hearts the desire for revenge.[185] If he had said nothing about the sword, apostolic men might have thought it a legitimate means of defence whenever their lives were endangered. But now he developed the subject and chose his words in such a way that no one could possibly doubt that the use of the sword was forbidden to apostolic men.[186] Previously, he had sent them to prove themselves and to get some taste of gospel ministry, but only

---

182 Cf Augustine *Contra Faustum Manichaeum* 22.74–7. Erasmus appears to extrapolate from these chapters the conditions Augustine sets for permitting Christian rulers to go to war. 'Righteous intention': Latin *pietas*; Augustine wrote *pietas in Christo* 'Christian devotion.' Cf the article on Augustine's views on war in Fitzgerald *Augustine through the Ages* 875–6.

183 Manicheism originated in the third century AD, under its founder, Mani. It was proscribed by the Emperor, Diocletian, and as it came to be regarded as a Christian heresy it was persecuted by Christians. It taught a radical dualism of light and darkness; by a process of redemption light entrapped in matter was liberated. Donatism was a Christian schismatic movement originating in North Africa after the persecution of 303–5 initiated by Diocletian. It objected to the leniency of the church in its treatment of those who had handed over the Scriptures during the persecution, and insisted that sacraments administered by anyone in a state of sin were invalid. Hence those baptized by such were required to be re-baptized. It received its name from its first great bishop, Donatus. Augustine was a bitter opponent of the Donatists.

184 Ie when Christ had set the apostles out on their mission to Judea, Mark 6:7–9, to which Erasmus refers again just below.

185 Cf Luke 22:38.

186 'Apostolic men': ie Jesus' disciples, but Erasmus seems to imply also a reference to all bishops, who were considered successors of the apostles, and some of whom in Erasmus' day personally engaged in warfare, perhaps most notably Julius II, 'the warrior pope.'

within the borders of Judea. Although here natural human concerns looked for provisions and the accessories appropriate to a comfortable journey, he ordered them to set out without purse, without staff, and yet they lacked nothing, since good men of their own accord supplied their necessities. But since the climax and ultimate end of gospel preaching would be martyrdom, and nothing is more to be feared than death, he wanted his disciples to be prepared for this struggle also, not only by the example of his death but also by his admonition. Accordingly, in order that from that previous experience he might inspire confidence in the face of what was to follow, he reminds them of their former mission: 'When I sent you without bag and purse and shoes did you lack anything?' When they replied, 'No! Nothing at all,' he calls them to a higher, more demanding standard: 'Do you see that you have lacked nothing though to this day you are destitute? This then should not be a concern that weighs upon you; but just as there is no reason to be concerned over provisions and the resources needed for living, so there is no reason why you should be solicitous about defending yourself if at some point a persecutor threatens torture or death. You will overcome tyrants with the same resources as I. In fact the more you are deprived of human resources the better equipped you will be for this warfare. Thus if anyone has cloak or purse, let him divest himself even of these so that he will be less encumbered. He needs only my sword, which so thoroughly prunes and cuts away all affections that anyone furnished with it will fear neither torments nor death, to say nothing of hunger or lack of clothes.'

In speaking thus I am not taking away from princes the right to wage wars providing Christian principles are taken into account. Ambrose praises emperors who, to protect a Christian peace, set themselves up as a wall, so to speak, against the barbarians. Nevertheless even he admits that to do so falls short of the pure gospel that Christ in this passage teaches his disciples.[187] But what does this have to do with priests who go to war all the time, and do so for power, for plunder, for worldly glory? What[188] does this have to do with Christian princes who embroil the globe in ceaseless wars because of their ambition, their anger, their

187 Cf eg Ambrose's letter to 'The Emperors and Princes, Gratian, Valentinian, and Theodosius' asking the imperial power to restore the peace (Ep 12 in PL 12, but Letter 40 in *Saint Ambrose Letters* FOTC 26 trans Sister Mary Melchior Beyenka (Washington 1967 [1954]) 213–15); cf also *De obitu Valentiniani 'Consolation on the Death of Valentinian'* 4.

188 The remainder of this annotation was added in *1527*; see the introductory note.

avarice or other passions that gratify their own personal interests? What has this do to with those wars that are waged with such adverse (not to say 'monstrous') results that frequently the invader does less damage than the defender?

[944] However, if someone presses me to state clearly whether I believe all war is forbidden to a Christian, I shall first ask that person to tell me what St Martin meant when he said, 'Let the one who is going to serve as a soldier take your bonus.[189] I am a Christian; I am forbidden to fight'; also what St Jerome and other orthodox writers meant by so often condemning war between Christians.[190] But if to this question I receive no response I shall say that war is not suitable to an apostolic man, nor is the Christian religion to be spread by arms only; that a prince should undertake no war that can be avoided by negotiation; and that when a war has been started it must be fought with as little loss of blood as possible and ended as quickly as possible.[191] I should say, in addition, that to fight even such a war falls short of the gospel standard and should not be justified by precepts found in the Gospels. Many things not taught by the Gospels are conceded, like swearing an oath or litigating at court. Pagans accept the 'right of the sword'[192] if the laws are observed. Evangelical piety, however, would rather heal than kill. [959] Still, Christ did not take away from magistrates their power in public office, which serves divine justice even though the magistrates are idolaters. Finally, there are in human affairs many necessary evils that are tolerated because they exclude worse evils; this does not mean that they are approved as representing gospel doctrine.

---

189 'Bonus': soldiers were sometimes rewarded with what was called a 'donative,' in effect, extra pay.

190 Cf Sulpicius Severus *Life of St Martin* 4.3. P.F. Hovingh (ASD VI-5 595 n948) suggests that in the allusion to Jerome, Erasmus refers to the latter's comment in his commentary on the parable of the weeds and the wheat in Matt 13:29–43, a parable in which Erasmus in his paraphrase on it argued against the death penalty for heretics, carefully noting that his interpretation did not take away the 'right of the sword' from the prince (cf 123 and 142–4 above). In the fourth century hostilities between the 'orthodox' and heretics were very severe. Cf Jerome *Commentary on Matthew* 2 (on 13:37) FOTC 117 trans Thomas P Scheck (Washington 2008) 163.

191 Erasmus articulates here a Christian version of the 'just war theory,' a theory well defined in pagan antiquity; cf Cicero *De officiis* 1.11.34–7. For the Christian tradition of the just war theory see eg for Augustine Fitzgerald *Augustine through the Ages* 875–6, for Thomas Aquinas the *Oxford Dictionary of the Christian Church* ed F.L. Cross, 3rd ed rev ed E.A. Livingstone (Oxford 2005) 1731.

192 Ie the right to carry out a death sentence for criminal action. For the right of magistrates to use force to maintain justice see the paraphrase on Rom 13:1–5 CWE 42 73–5.

(4) On the Liturgy

[The three annotations that follow next reflect Erasmus' critique of various aspects of liturgical practice. In the first Erasmus asks for the proper pronunciation of Greek loan words commonly used in the Liturgy, in the second he points to the absurdity resulting from the misreading of Scripture during the liturgy, and in the third he exposes his relatively well-known hostility to contemporary church music.]

(a) Proper Pronunciation

From the annotation on John14:26 (***Paracletus autem Spiritus Sanctus*** 'But the Comforter,[193] the Holy Spirit') [ASD VI-6 140–2:506–26, 532–53]

[Erasmus begins the annotation by suggesting that those who are superstitiously scrupulous in their prayers should at least pronounce the words of Scripture correctly. He notes that the ecclesiastical pronunciation of the word Paracletus (properly, with the penultimate syllable long), incorrectly shortens that syllable, thus cheating God of one beat of time. He then broadens the discussion to the *Kyrie eleison*, still familiar in many contemporary church circles of the twenty-first century; it is with this that our selection below begins. The first paragraph was introduced in the edition of 1516; the remainder was added in *1519*. Erasmus begins our selection with a certain genial humour.]

[**ASD VI 6 140–2**] [506] It is even more harsh when in the *Kyrie eleeson* ['Lord have mercy'], words repeated innumerable times every day, speakers cheat the divine ears of two syllables, pronouncing the first word in two syllables, the second in three. Since this disgraceful act is committed on occasion perhaps a hundred times every day, if you calculate the total over forty or fifty years I doubt that you would restore what you owe if you did nothing for a solid year but repeat *kyrie eleeson* doing so with its seven distinct syllables.[194] In my estimation, it is right to pay back to God what we have cheated him of. After all, we have countless laws to ensure that we pay someone back if we have wrongly taken even a penny. If it is sacrilege to take a little gold from anything sacred, how much more serious is the sacrilege when

193 'Comforter' (AV), 'Counselor' (RSV), 'Advocate' (NRSV).

194 Cf ASD VI-6 141 506–9n, where Hovingh notes that elision and iotacism 'lead to four syllables instead of six'; cf just below *kyrghelayson*.

the very one who is the author of everything sacred we defraud of the most sacred thing of all!

Now it is not only sacrilege but it seems to me to be insult and blasphemy as well when they persistently take the 'h' from 'Christ,' and address their king with exactly the same appellation as they would address the 'crest'[195] of a hen or a cock. Would Christ, who is 'greatest and best,'[196] bear this insult if he were as crabby as some people are difficult in their dealings with others, or if God were as unjust toward human beings as human beings are towards one another? If you, an insignificant man, were in the presence of a king you would not dare to say 'Perdinand' for 'Ferdinand,' or 'Pilip' for 'Philip'[197] and do you not fear to say 'Crist' for 'Christ' in the midst of those most sacred mysteries where it is forbidden to distort even a single jot?[198]

[532] But, not to seem too harsh, I would gladly excuse such a fault as long as people err through ignorance, but after they have been lovingly admonished by those who have knowledge of such things, then, since it requires no more effort to pronounce correctly than incorrectly, if they persist in their mistaken habits and knowingly continue to err, spurning and rejecting the admonition of the learned, I see no way at all that they can be absolved from a very grave sin. Nor will the fact that a vast number similarly err help their case. God is a judge neither corrupted nor overwhelmed.

What then do we think we should say about those who for more than fifty years have so grossly erred (and erred not only in these matters), and when they have been corrected not only do not repent of their ways and thank the one who has corrected them, but with sardonic laughter hoot and hiss him off the stage, regard their benefactor as an enemy, attack him at their banquets, cry 'heretic.' They call me arrogant if, when occasion invites, I point out some such thing even in a friendly way; they regard themselves as holy and humble and prefer to persist in a confessed error so as not to seem ignorant, and rather than acknowledge their own mistake they cast aspersions – even the accusation of heresy – upon a brother who has been helpful. In the canon of the mass[199] would they put up with someone who says 'phater' for 'pater'

195 'Crest': in Latin '*crista*,' ie the 'cock's comb,' while 'Christ' in Latin is *Christus*.

196 'Greatest and best,' an expression applied in antiquity to Jupiter to reflect his power, majesty and goodness; cf 184 n81 and CWE 27 169 n13 and 28 384.

197 References are to Ferdinand, brother of the emperor Charles V and ruler of the Austrian duchies, and Philip (1478–1506), the father of Charles and Ferdinand; Charles had a son also named Philip.

198 'Jot': Latin iota, echoing Matt 5:18.

199 The canon of the mass is the prayer of consecration that begins immediately after the *Sanctus*; cf 'canon of the mass' in ODCC 280–1.

['father'] or *'pilius'* for *'filius'* [son']; it is worse to say 'Crist' for 'Christ' or *kyrghelayson* for *Kyrie eleeson* – in such a few expressions to go wrong in so many ways that there are more errors than syllables!

(b) The Public Reading of Scripture

From the annotation on Rom 8:33 ('who will make accusation against the elect of God?') [CWE 56 230–1]

> [The lack of punctuation in the Greek manuscripts often creates difficulties for the translator (cf 235 above). While the difficulty in this passage may arise from punctuation, the solution to the interpretation of the passage lies in grasping the sense in the sequence of the language. As Erasmus points out, with a little reflection the intended meaning is unmistakeable. Here Erasmus objects in particular to the meaning implied by the public misreading of this passage in the liturgy, which seems to suggest that Christ condemns his elect! The first paragraph introduced the annotation in *1516*; the remainder of this selection was added in *1519*.]

[CWE 56 230–1] [230] In this passage Paul's meaning is very clear if we understand that the question implies denial so that the sense is: No one will dare to charge those whom God has not only called but also chosen. Accordingly, the words that follow ['who is to condemn? Is it Christ Jesus etc'] should be read as emerging from one and the same question, implying the answer 'Impossible.' And yet even in churches we hear these words read as statements, not questions,[200] and falsely, indeed with insolence towards Christ, unless ignorance excuses so great a fault – which is not really a legitimate defence.

[231] Origen seems to bring the two clauses together in the way I do: It is God who justifies; who is to condemn? Then 'Christ Jesus who died' seems to read as though spoken by one who is making not an inquiry, but a statement. Assuming that the answer to the previous question ['who is to condemn'] is now complete (for we have answered 'No one'), we begin a new and cumulative series of proofs, so that the

200 Cf NRSV, reading the text of 8:33 as a statement: 'Who will bring any charge against God's elect? It is God who justifies. Who is to condemn? It is Christ Jesus who died, yes who was raised, who is at the right hand of God, who indeed intercedes for us. Who will separate us from the love of Christ? Will hardship, or distress … ? But NRSV margin punctuates with a question mark: ' ... Who is to condemn? Is it Christ Jesus who … intercedes for us'? The biting comment at the end of this sentence ('and falsely … defence') was removed in *1535*.

sense is, 'Christ is the one who died for us, yes, who rose again, who is seated at the right hand of God and pleads for us; who will accuse those who have been chosen, or who will condemn them?' Thus from so many proofs heaped up together, the single consequence follows that there will be no one to bring charges against us or condemn us. To me at least this reading seems the truer.[201]

(c) Church Music

From the annotation on 1 Cor 14:19 (***quam decem milia*** 'than ten thousand [words]')[202] [ASD VI-8 274–8:157–97, 205–16]

> [This annotation, reflecting so vividly Erasmus' dissatisfaction with the current state of church music, was introduced in *1516*, with a major addition in *1519* and a few shorter additions in *1522* and *1527*. It caught the eye of the Paris theologians, who strongly objected to his criticism. In his response to the theologians Erasmus quoted from the annotation, a passage translated in CWE 82 204 (ASD VI-8 274–6:157–166) from which I take the translation (with slight modifications) in the first paragraph below. This paragraph was introduced with the annotation in *1516*; the remainder of the selection given here was, with two exceptions (cf nn205, 210), added in the 1519 edition. Craig Thompson places Erasmus' comments on music in the context of his life and of the Renaissance in the colloquy 'A Pilgrimage for Religion's Sake' CWE 40 669–70 n161, which offers a good bibliography for further reading.]

[ASD VI-8 274–8] [157] In this matter the custom of the church has changed remarkably. Paul would rather speak five words with understanding than ten thousand in the Spirit. But nowadays in some regions they sing in the Spirit all day long;[203] there is no restraint or end to the singing, whereas they hear hardly once every six months a wholesome sermon exhorting them to true godliness. For that is what Paul calls speaking with understanding. I will say nothing about the sort of music introduced into divine worship that does not allow even a single word to be clearly

---

201 Thus Erasmus reads the words as a statement, but insists on reading the statement with the right emphasis, not 'who will condemn? Christ Jesus,' but 'who will condemn? Certainly not Christ, as his victory proves.'

202 Cf the entire verse: 'Nevertheless in church I would rather speak five words with my mind, in order to instruct others also, than ten thousand in a tongue' [NRSV].

203 In his late work *Ecclesiastes* (*1535*) Erasmus comments on the music of his day in virtually the same way as in this annotation; cf CWE 68 700–1 with n1212.

perceived, and leaves those who sing no freedom to pay attention to what they are singing. Only a jingle of words strikes the ear and caresses with its momentary petty delights. Even this should be tolerated if it were not that your average priest and monk believes that such practices constitute the utmost godliness, in this differing widely from St Paul.

Why does the church hesitate to follow such a great authority? Or rather, why does it dare to differ from him? What else is heard in monasteries, in colleges, in almost all churches except a din of voices? In Paul's day there was no melodious singing, only the spoken word. A later age grudgingly admitted singing, but only as the clear and rhythmic articulation of words, still evident in the mass when we chant the Lord's Prayer, though in that earlier age the common people understood the language used, and would respond 'Amen.'[204] But now the common people hear only words that signify nothing, and the articulation is generally such that they do not hear even the words, only the sound strikes their ears. At first singing was adopted under the guise of piety, but then little by little it has developed to the point where there is no measure or end of psalms, songs, canticles, and hymns for the dead. What is worse is the fact that to provide such things priests are bound with obligations almost more stringent than their obligation to offer what Christ taught. Moreover,[205] the laity are compelled to hear such stuff at the cost of providing for wife and children – surely the most sacred duty of all.[206] By all means let churches have singing during the Liturgy, but keep it within bounds. We are compelled [to hold in mind] these things in our private lives, and we take the public chorus with us in ship, cars, hotels. We are judged pious or ungodly by whether we attend to or neglect these things. Someone is more avaricious than Crassus, more scurrilous than Zoilus,[207] yet he is regarded as pious because he sings these petty

---

204 Eph 5:19 and Col 3:16 seem to provide evidence of singing in the services of the Christian communities from virtually the earliest times. However, in his paraphrases on these verses Erasmus does not specifically locate the context of singing in the church services; cf CWE 43 344–5 with n30 and ibidem 423. For a useful account of the development of music in the corporate services of early Christianity see Ferguson *Early Christianity* 787–90.

205 This sentence was added in *1522*.

206 In his *Apologia Against the Patchwork of Alberto Pio* Erasmus offers an interesting justification of this statement, referring to his experience among the English; cf CWE 84 218–19.

207 Marcus Licinius Crassus, first century BC, formed with Caesar and Pompey the 'First Triumvirate' in 60 BC. He was famous for his wealth and was dubbed 'Crassus the Rich.' Zoilus, grammarian of fourth century BC, became known especially for his harsh criticism of Homer.

prayers with a clear voice even if he doesn't understand a word. I ask you, what understanding of Christ do people have who believe that he takes delight in a vocal din of this kind?

As though this were not enough, we bring into our sacred edifice a sort of affected theatrical music, a confused chattering of diverse voices such as, I think, would never have been heard in the theatres of Greece and Rome.[208] Everything is filled with the noise of trumpets, cornets, pipes, and sambuccas,[209] while human voices compete with these. We hear love songs and unseemly little ditties to which harlots and mimic actors dance. People rush into a sacred edifice to charm their ears as if it were a theatre. Meanwhile we pay huge sums to organists, to crowds of boys whose entire youth is wasted in learning this sort of yelping while they learn nothing good. A vile medley of squalid, unreliable debauchees (as most are) is maintained, and the church is loaded down with enormous expenses on account of something that is even destructive. [205] Now[210] those who are too dull to be able to learn music do not feel satisfied on a festival day unless they contribute to some sort of depraved singing they call the 'faux-bourdon.' This neither follows the notes nor observes the harmony.[211] [211] Our music merely indulges the affections of fools and looks to the cravings of the stomach. [214] Let us sing in the Spirit, let us sing Christian hymns, let us make music sparingly, but let us make music more especially in our minds.

(5) On Divorce

From the annotation on 1 Corinthians 7:39 (***liberata est a lege, cui autem vult, nubat*** 'she is free to marry anyone she wishes') [ASD VI-8 146–8:786–821; ASD VI-8 158–84:10–46, 195–306, 337–69, 459–502]

[In the edition of 1516 this annotation was completed in a mere two lines – Erasmus did not address the issue of divorce in it. He had, however, briefly done so in his annotation on Matthew 19:8, where he had noted that while the church had generally relaxed the absolute demands found in Matthew

208 Cf Erasmus' description of the music with 'variegated harmony of voices' in CWE 82 206 with n745.

209 'Sambucca,' a triangular stringed instrument with a shrill tone (mentioned in the Vulgate of Dan 3:5).

210 This and the next sentence were added in *1527*.

211 English spelling, 'faburden.' 'Perhaps from the French *faux-bourdon*, literally, "false hum," a type of improvised polyphony popular in England from the 15th century to the Reformation' *Shorter Oxford English Dictionary* 6th ed Lesley Brown et al (Oxford 2007).

5:21–48 divorce remained an exception, though 'hearts were hard now' as in Moses' day. Moreover, the prescription in Matthew, definitive as it was, left one free to enter a second marriage after divorce, which, again, was not allowed by the church of the sixteenth century.

In the edition of 1519 Erasmus tackled decisively the issue of divorce, shaping afresh his annotations on Matthew 19 and 1 Corinthians 7; the *1516* comments on divorce in the annotation on Matthew 19:8 were omitted and a new annotation on Matthew 19:3 introduced ('from whatever cause'), which in the course of nearly a page summarily anticipated the extended argument of the annotation on 1 Corinthians 7:39 (ten pages in *1519*). Subsequent additions enlarged the annotation on 1 Corinthians 7:39 to fourteen pages in the final edition of 1535.

For a careful summary of Erasmus' position on divorce, including the divorce of Henry VIII, see CWE 39 321–3 n16.

The excerpts given here, with connecting summaries in English, are intended to reflect the most essential points in Erasmus' long argument. With two exceptions (identified in the notes) the excerpts are taken from the 1519 edition.]

[**ASD VI-8 146–8**] [786] I know that it is a firmly established tradition among Christians that once a marriage has been consummated it cannot be dissolved except by the death of one of the partners. [791] But if good people have always been willing to change their views for the better, and if it is appropriate to adjust laws, like medicine, to suit the condition of the disease, we might consider whether we might profitably do the same thing here, and if so, whether it is permitted to dissolve certain marriages – not rashly, but for very weighty reasons, and not by just anyone but by ecclesiastical authorities or by duly established judges – and whether, once the marriage is dissolved, both partners are free to marry whomever they wish, or whether at least the one who was not the cause of the divorce is free to do so.

[811] First of all, then, it belongs to apostolic godliness to be concerned for the welfare of all (so far as permitted), and certainly for the church to come with solicitude to the help of its weak members. We see people in the thousands locked together in an unhappy marriage to the destruction of both partners, who perhaps could be saved if they were separated. I think godly people would desire this if it could be done without violating the divine precept. If this is not possible, I believe it is in any case a godly wish, especially since charity sometimes desires the impossible. Moses desires that he be eliminated from the book of life; Paul desires to become anathema from Christ on

behalf of his brothers.[212] There have, at least, been those who thought that once a marriage had been dissolved it was possible to marry again – so that no one should without further consideration suppose that what I am proposing is unheard-of and on every count absurd, something to be hissed off the stage, unworthy of being called into question.

[Erasmus now reviews at length (more than three pages in the 1535 edition) the patristic and medieval literature that favours the case for permitting divorce and remarriage. He then proceeds to an argument from 'natural justice.']

[ASD VI-8 158–84] [10] Now no one can deny that the laws of Christ are much the most equitable and by far the most excellent, whether they are compared with natural law or with human laws.[213] [15] Does it seem fair that a husband should be compelled to live with a wife notorious for her profligate behaviour for which he was in no way responsible and which he cannot remedy (in fact, to live with such a woman is simply not to live); or if he separates he is compelled to spend the rest of his life bereft, deprived and, as it were, emasculated? Suppose it is right for the one who was the cause of the divorce to be deprived of the right of a second marriage, why should the one who is not at fault (except that he made an unfortunate marriage) be punished? Whoever heard of punishing fortune, especially by divine law, provided fault is absent? What else is this but to add affliction to the afflicted, who deserved help instead?

[40] 'But'[214] someone will say, 'the law has been prescribed for marriage that, once contracted, it may not be dissolved, and those who know this law offer of their own accord their neck to the noose.' This, however, is precisely the point at issue: can the rigor of this law be relaxed in some way, since often there are cases of such a kind that it seems cruel not to help one in danger. If our law seems to be opposed to the fairness of natural justice we must see whether what we read on this matter in the Gospels and apostolic Epistles should be interpreted

212 Cf Exod 32:32 (Moses), Rom 9:3 (Paul).

213 In this paragraph Erasmus appeals to the common sense native to all of us. In Latin the adjective *aequus*, becomes the thematic word, meaning 'fair,' 'just,' 'reasonable,' here translated 'equitable,' 'fair,' 'right.' For natural law in Erasmus see CWE 45 232 n8.

214 ['But' … danger] Added in *1522*.

in a different way. Let us be permitted to do here what we do not fear to do in other passages of Scripture.[215]

[Erasmus launches into a long review that reveals how opinions on church doctrine and practice have differed and changed in the course of time, with the implication that the marriage canons might also be modified. He then turns to a consideration of the texts of Scripture that have been used in the support of the church's rigorous position on divorce. He begins with Matthew 5:21–2 and reiterates at length the argument briefly articulated in the *1519* annotation on Matthew 19:3.]

[195] In this one case [ie divorce] we hold tenaciously to a law pushed to its extreme, although elsewhere we accept almost any alleviating interpretation. [Christ] forbids us to swear at all,[216] in fact he forbids swearing, and does so with much greater severity than he forbids divorce, insisting on it at length, yet on account of a few pennies we swear indiscriminately, giving this excuse, 'one must not swear *rashly*.'[217] Why not likewise, 'One must not divorce his wife rashly?' He forbids us to be angry, but then we add 'rashly.' He forbids us to speak abusively to anyone; we even strike people on the face, and finally kill with the excuse, 'Not with the intent to harm, but to correct.' [211] And – not to continue with details – we are asked to love our enemies, to do good to those who treat us badly, to bless those who curse.[218] We respond with a consideration: 'I shall wish for a better mind in my enemies; I am not required to exhibit the tokens of friendship.' There is, finally, the excuse put forward in every case: 'These are precepts for the perfect.' [218] Christ spoke these words not to the crowd but to his disciples, and did so on the mountain where he was portraying that purest part of his body that he calls 'the kingdom of heaven,' where laws are not needed.[219] What need is there

215 A reference to other scriptural injunctions given as absolutes but qualified by the church, above all, the ethical injunctions of Matthew 5, as Erasmus proceeds to discuss.

216 For the radical injunctions to which Erasmus now refers see Matt 5:21–48.

217 In fact the Vulgate text of Matt 5:22 read 'Whoever is angry with his brother'; Erasmus' Greek text read 'Whoever is angry with his brother rashly'; cf AV 'Whoever is angry with his brother without a cause.'

218 Cf Matt 5:44, as in Erasmus' text and AV; the Vulgate read, 'Love your enemies, do good to them that hate you' [so DV], RSV has only 'Love your enemies.' But cf also Luke 16:28 and Rom 12:14.

219 Cf Matt 5:21–5. In his paraphrase on the Sermon on the Mount Erasmus is ambiguous about Jesus' audience, but cf CWE 45 93.

for the precept, 'You shall not kill' when no one even when harmed becomes angry or curses, when everyone prefers to concede his just right rather than go to court? What need of a law forbidding adultery when no one desires what belongs to another? Why an oath where no one tries to cheat and everyone trusts. [228] Grant the kind of people Christ desires and there would be no need of either a bill of divorce or an oath. But if on account of the very many weak who are now in the church in such large numbers, no one is forbidden to go to court, no one is forbidden to swear provided he does not perjure himself, no one is compelled to return good for evil, why do we demand from all without distinction this one injunction about divorce? Today we see among Christians not only the constant quarrelling of the partners but even worse behaviour – murder, sorcery, and witchcraft. Why, then, when the Jews, because of the hardness of their hearts were permitted for any cause whatever to cast away their wives so that they would not commit some worse act against them, do we not apply the same remedy since the disease is the same? Paul does not approve second marriages, and yet for the sake of chastity he permits what he dare not demand, judging it better 'to marry than to burn.'[220] And do we not moderate the severity of our laws on divorce? The Jews interpreted the Mosaic text about a bill of divorce to mean that the husband had the right to cast his wife aside for any trivial reason, suppose, for example, she had some physical blemish.[221]

[The allusion to 'any cause whatever' brings Matthew 19:3–9 into view. Erasmus briefly explains why Christ excepted 'fornication' [19:9].

[242] Christ limited the reasons for divorce to a single cause, adultery, not because adultery is more wicked than other shameful deeds but because it contradicts the grounding principle of marriage. Matrimony makes one individual out of two; adultery severs that bonded union.[222] Christ therefore granted divorce to his disciples on this one ground; he did not take away what Moses had granted, but denied that it had been so from the beginning.[223] If the human race had persevered as it had been created there would be no divorce at all. Christ calling his disciples back to humanity's original innocence does not want divorce since he does not want his people to be hard of heart. And yet Paul makes a

220 Cf 1 Cor 7:8–9, also 1 Tim 3:2, Titus 1:6.

221 Cf Deut 24:1–4.

222 Cf Matt 19:9. Erasmus justifies the exception on the same grounds in the paraphrase on Matt 19:9; cf CWE 45 271–2.

223 Cf Matt 19:8.

concession to human frailty, frequently relaxing the precept of the Lord. Why could the Roman pope not do the same?

[But Matthew 19:6 provides a further argument against divorce: 'What God has joined together let no one separate.' Erasmus points to some of the major causes of unhappy marriages, noting the problems raised by the theory of 'consent.']

[251] There is a fairly straightforward refutation of the objection that 'what God has joined together let no one separate.' God has joined together what is properly joined together; God separates what is rightly separated. Among the pagans, in fact even among the Jews, matrimony was not valid without the consent of the parents or guardians, and yet among both a marriage could in some way be dissolved. Christians enter marriage with excessive ease, and once consummated, it cannot be broken apart. Boys and girls are secretly joined in marriage by panderers and bawds; fools and drunkards tie the knot – and a beginning so disgraceful is indissoluble, and, what is more, a marriage thus begun becomes a sacrament! [261] I admit that there is no marriage without mutual consent, but it must be sober consent, not consent extorted by craft or in the midst of intoxication, but consent given with the counsel of friends, as is appropriate in something that can never be undone and that deserves to be numbered among the sacraments of the church. But when, after investigating the case carefully, a bishop or other legitimate judges dissolve the kind of marriage I have described, this is not a case of 'man separating what God has joined together.' In fact, what youth, wine, rashness, ignorance has wrongly glued together, what the devil has wickedly bound together through his ministers, the panderers and bawds, this God rightly separates through his servants.

[Erasmus turns to the second major question (outlined in the first paragraph of this selection): whether once a marriage has been properly dissolved the partners are free to marry again. He begins by setting Christ's words in their social context showing by inference that in forbidding divorce Christ assumed only the particular constraints familiar to his audience.]

[269] They say, 'But the church does approve divorce, on the condition, however, that both partners remain unmarried.' I ask you, did Christ have in mind this kind of divorce? [In Matthew 19] he is questioned by Jews, he answers Jews. The Jews did not know of any divorce except a divorce that removed the right of a man to remarry the woman he

had divorced and that gave him the right to marry another. [279] Now if Christ was speaking about 'true divorce' where do we get this new kind of divorce that is divorce more truly in name than in reality? [285] Why do our laws add so many cases in which divorce is accepted? [288] If we can make changes to the precepts of Christ, why do we not take thought for the welfare of those who are not well joined together? If no change is permitted, why have they dared to make so many exceptions? The papal laws allow a partner who has converted to marry again if the other partner will not convert from an irreligious and blasphemous life; Christ did not make this exception, yet we dare to do so.[224] A woman may marry again if she separates from a man who cannot perform his expected manly function; she cannot marry again if the man divorced was a patricide. It is an 'error of condition' if a woman marries a slave who she thought was free-born, and this invalidates a marriage even after it has been consummated. Someone[225] will say, 'in this case a marriage was not dissolved but simply declared not to have been the true marriage it seemed to be.' [301] Why not with the same reasoning come to the rescue of a couple in an ill-advised marriage; let that also be declared 'not a true marriage' which was contracted between boys and girls without parental authority though they are still under parental care, contracted, moreover in circumstances of drunkenness and the trickery of bawds.[226]

[305] Let us now examine the reasons the ancients gave for not granting a second marriage, even in a case of adultery.

[Erasmus passes in review the arguments from Jerome and Augustine against a second marriage, then comes to the argument based on the concept of marriage as a sacrament.][227]

[337] [Theologians] bring forth the argument from the 'sacrament' to defend the position that every marriage once contracted is indissoluble. Let us pursue this further. Augustine, who finds in marriage three goods, calls the third good the 'sacrament,' but he does not mean one of the seven sacraments. Dionysius, though he enumerates specifically

224 For this 'exception,' known as the 'Pauline Privilege,' see the paraphrase on 1 Cor 7:15–16 CWE 43 96 with n39.

225 [Someone … bawds]. This passage was added in *1522*.

226 Erasmus discusses at considerable length the issues of parental authority, consent, and validity of marriage in the *Institutio christiani matrimonii* CWE 69 239–75.

227 On marriage as a sacrament, ie a mystery, see CWE 69 225–31 and 240–2 above.

each sacrament, and explains the virtues, the rites, and ceremonies of each, makes no mention of marriage.[228] [349] Further, although Greek and Latin writers have in many, many books discussed marriage, there is not a single place they clearly and distinctly mention marriage as among the seven sacraments – not even Augustine when he promotes marriage, insisting upon the goods of matrimony.

[360] When the Fathers, following Paul, sometimes call marriage a sacrament, I think they mean that in joining husband and wife, since this is the closest possible form of friendship,[229] there is represented a certain type and image of Christ joining the church, his bride, to himself. Indeed, a marriage duly maintained most certainly is a holy and sacred thing, and yet it is possible that a type of a holy thing may not in itself be holy as in the case of Bathsheba torn from Uriah and joined to David.[230] Further, it is not necessary that a type of a holy thing correspond in every way; otherwise it will not be a sacrament when a man has a sterile wife or when a woman endures a husband who is a drunkard or disreputable or a gambler.

[Erasmus turns to the consideration of passages from the Pauline Epistles. He offers expositions of each of them to show that these Epistles do not provide a valid defence of the church's position on the indissolubility of marriage. The last of the passages, 1 Corinthians 7:10–11, he regards as 'the most difficult of all,' for it seems to offer very solid support for the Church's traditional practice. He quotes:]

[461] 'To the married I give charge, not I but the Lord, that the wife should not separate from her husband (but if she does, let her remain single or else be reconciled to her husband), and that the husband should not divorce his wife' [RSV]. Paul seems to be speaking here about Christian marriages, that is, a marriage in which both partners are Christian.[231] [468] It seems also that he is speaking not about serious wrong-doing, like adultery or even worse, but about minor offences on account of which divorces were

228 Cf Augustine *De bono conjugali* 24.32; Pseudo-Dionysius does not mention marriage in *De ecclesiastica hierarchia*; for Dionysius and his works see 240 n122 above.

229 'Friendship': Latin *amicitia*. While the word is standard for 'friendship,' Erasmus in speaking of marriage clearly intends the word to connote an 'alliance,' 'bond,' 'union,' effected and maintained by love. See his description of this bond in *Institutio christiani matrimonii* CWE 69 219–29, in the course of which he observes that 'the bond of marriage surpasses any friendship however close' (CWE 69 222).

230 Cf 2 Sam 11.

231 Ie not the marriage of a Christian and a pagan – an allusion to 2 Cor 6:14, 'Do not be mismatched with unbelievers.'

frequent in Greek society. [473] And it is the woman who [is cast aside because she] offends who is to be reconciled, not the woman who has been offended. If the offences are mutual, but not major, the Apostle forbids the woman to marry another man, thus precluding a return to her husband; she is to remain unmarried in the hope that the two can be reconciled. [477] The man is told only that he is not to cast off his wife for offences of this sort. He does not add that if he divorces her he should remain unmarried. The Apostle speaks here only of woman because Jewish custom did not allow the woman the right of divorce. [487] In any case, Paul seems to have forbidden the woman to leave her husband on account of minor offences to enable reconciliation and return to her husband, but if the two do separate she should refuse a second marriage. He is not giving his approval to the view that a woman separated from her husband should remain unmarried if the husband is unwilling to restore the relationship, but he is saying rather that this is preferable to breaking up the old marriage and beginning a new one.

But suppose a case of the following kind had been put before Paul: a fool contracts marriage with a fool, a boy with a girl, wine, rashness, bawds have played a part, the couple have been craftily led into a trap – and there are plenty of marriages of this kind, untold thousands are kept cruelly ensnared. The marriage begins with an unreflected assent; it is a marriage provided only that intercourse has followed, indeed even if it hasn't. The couple are entirely incompatible, so different is their manner of life and character; there are constant quarrels, irremediable hatred, they fear poisoning, murder, they look for every kind of evil. Neither partner can live a celibate life; if they stay together both twice perish, but with another marriage there is hope that both will be saved. If the Apostle were dealing with cases like this, perhaps he would respond differently, according to circumstances, would relax the rigor of his former counsel, and would, I think, interpret these passages with greater civility than we interpret them.

[Erasmus concludes this, his longest annotation, with further criticism of the doctrine of consent and a plea for parental guidance in the engagement of young couples, and finally by a detailed account of the considerations that led him to his present position.]

(6) On the State of Contemporary Theology in the Universities

Annotation on 1 Timothy 1:6 (***in vaniloquium*** '[have turned] to meaningless talk' [NRSV]) [ASD VI-10 10–30:88–116, 168–72, 206–31]

[The long annotation on 1 Timothy 1:6 invites reflection on Erasmus' longstanding hostility to the scholastic education that characterized theological education in the Universities. He had expressed his contempt for it in his satirical letter to Thomas Grey in 1497, mocking its focus on syllogisms, on 'instances, quiddities and formal qualities' and the 'very super-subtle subtleties that are today the boast of the sons of Scotus' (Ep 64: 50–1, 78–9). In a more serious vein he resumed the attack in the relatively brief *Methodus* that prefaced his New Testament (*1516*), where he proposed an alternative method of education based on a literary reading of Scripture rather than on the logical, propositional method of the scholastics. In the *Methodus* he had complained of 'all the petty questions of the theologians' of which 'there is neither number, nor measure nor end.' When the *Methodus* was vastly enlarged to become the *Ratio verae theologiae* (*1518/1519*) Erasmus illustrated 'scholasticism' by citing some of these petty questions, and in subsequent editions added yet further examples (cf 70 n101 above). The annotation on 1 Timothy 1:6 spoke to the same issue and with a similar development: a relatively short annotation in *1516* became lengthy in *1519*, with further additions in *1522* and *1527*. The initial and final lines of the annotation translated here catch well the tone and substance of Erasmus' discussions on this subject. In the selection below the first paragraph belongs to the 1516 edition, the next two to *1519*, the fourth paragraph was added in *1527* (one exception noted [n246]), while the final paragraph was inserted in *1522*.]

[**ASD VI-10 10–30**] [88] *In vaniloquium* '[have wandered] into vain discussions' [RSV].[232] [*eis mataiologian*]. If you consider the sound of the words, *mataiologia* is not so different from *theologia*, though there is in fact the greatest difference between the two. Accordingly, we too [like the persons to whom Paul here refers] must be careful not to pursue theology in such a way that we fall into mateology, endlessly crossing swords over insignificant trifles. Let us discuss rather those things that transform us into Christ and make us worthy of heaven. What is the point of contending over the number of ways sin can be understood, whether it is a privation only [ie a lack of good] or a stain inherent in the soul. The concern of the theologian should rather be that everyone abhors and hates sin.[233]

For so many centuries we have disputed whether the grace by which God loves and draws us is the same as the grace by which we love one

232 Cf NRSV above, 'have turned to meaningless talk.' Compare the discussion here with a similar one in *A Discussion of Free Will* CWE 76 9–12.

233 On sin as a privation or stain, ie either a lack of original righteousness or an inveterate vice see CWE 56 153 n11.

another, and[234] whether it is something created or uncreated. This rather should be our concern, that through pure prayers, an innocent life, and righteous deeds, God deems us worthy of this gift. We dispute without end what distinguishes Father from Son and both from the Holy Spirit – whether the distinction is in the substance or the relation, and how they can be said to be three, none of whom constitutes 'another' since they are one essence.[235] How much more to the point to act in all ways so that we might with holy piety worship and adore that Three-in-one[236] whose majesty we dare not scrutinize, and so that we might express as far as we can that ineffable concord by our own concord in order to obtain at some time admission into that fellowship. We debate how it is possible for the fire that tortures the ungodly to have any effect upon the incorporeal when the fire itself is material. How much more important to strive with all our might that the fire find nothing in us to burn.

If these questions were being discussed for the sake of relaxation or without contention it would be tolerable. But now some people spend their whole life in questions of this sort, and discussions progress to shouting, genuine dissension, insults, sometimes even to blows. What a swarm of questions we stir up about baptism, about the Eucharist,[237] about the sacrament of penance! To be ignorant of some of these issues is of little consequence; in fact, some of them are the kind about which you can make assertions but the assertions can neither be proven nor refuted. It is more to the point that we bend our efforts, and exhort one another to this end, that we respond to the sacrament of baptism with a life worthy of Christ, that we attend with frequency and purity those sacred repasts, so that there should be little in our lives that needs to be burned away by the branding-iron of penitence. [168] Let us give our attention not to vanities but above all to that which Christ wanted us to know, to what the apostles taught, what genuinely effects charity 'from a pure heart and a good conscience and faith unfeigned,' which alone Paul calls the end and perfection of the entire law.[238]

---

234 [and … uncreated] added in *1527*. See Erasmus' definitions of the 'kinds of grace' in *A Discussion of Free Will* CWE 76 31–2.

235 For the clarification of this aspect of Trinitiarian doctrine see *A Discussion of Free Will* CWE 76 10 n26.

236 Erasmus has not used here the historic Latin term *Trinitas* but *Ternion* signifying a unit of three; cf 296 n17.

237 'Eucharist': Latin *synaxin*, here clearly referring to the Eucharist, but for its wider meaning see CWE 84 51 nn245, 246.

238 Cf 1 Tim 1:5, Col 3:14, Rom 10:4.

[206] How is such an extensive and assiduous pursuit of heathen philosophy appropriate to the profession of the apostolic life? The mouth dedicated to the gospel prates about nothing but Averroës and Aristotle.[239] These people[240] are loathe to touch money, yet spend their whole life in the books of blasphemous philosophy! The early Christians who had learned such things in paganism gathered from their books certain things for the purpose of Christian instruction. Now those who profess the simplicity of Christ and are nourished by evangelical preaching are compelled to learn such things almost by heart. I know a certain theologian who said that nine years was not enough to understand what Scotus wrote on only the Preface of Peter Lombard. I heard another declare that it was not possible to understand a single proposition in the whole of Scotus unless one had memorized all Scotus' metaphysics![241] [220] I do not make these comments to advocate the condemnation of dialectic and philosophy taught in the universities; I simply disapprove an immoderate devotion to trifles. [224] 'The time is short,' the Apostle says [1 Cor 7:29], and a vast enterprise is in hand; why do we attend to these lengthy and wasteful discussions? Let the best things be taught, and as far as possible in abbreviated form, cutting away the unnecessary.[242] [227] Our[243] concern is rather with those things by which we are transformed into Christ.

And so we will be [transformed] if we practise innocence with all our strength, abstaining from every disgraceful deed, if we strive to our utmost to show Christ's love by doing good to all, if we imitate his tolerance so that instead of retaliation for harm done to us we actually repay the injuries with kind deeds.[244]

---

239 For Erasmus' critique of Scholastic education based on, hence presupposing, a knowledge of Averroës and Aristotle see the *Paraclesis*, especially 31 with n16.

240 Erasmus refers to monk-theologians who as monks have taken the vow of poverty.

241 For Duns Scotus and Peter Lombard see the *Paraclesus* 31 with n15 and 35 with n28 (Scotus) and 35 n27 (Lombard).

242 Thus the *Ratio* attempted to show a 'short-cut to true theology.' For a similar contrast between two methods of education, one long and tedious, the other short and effective see CWE 41 275–6, where Erasmus replies to a challenge by Pierre Cousturier who thought Erasmus' method was the long and laborious way!

243 This sentence is part of the *1519* addition.

244 An abbreviated statement of the philosophy of Christ; cf the *Paraclesis* 30 and the *Ratio* 46–7 above.

IV. PEOPLE AND PLACES

[Erasmus was gifted with a talent for vivid and dramatic description, as may be seen in his letters, for example, in the portrait of John Colet in Ep 1211, or in the account of his meeting with Cardinal Grimani whose astonishing library he was privileged to see (Ep 2465:5–60). In his annotations Erasmus frequently diverges from the philological discussion to comment on incidents, people, and places. These comments are sometimes critical, sometimes laudatory, but invariably add colour and zest to his annotations, inviting from the reader the kind of curiosity that is stimulated by fascinating tales or good gossip. The comments are often brief, but at two points Erasmus offers an extended description of two people he wishes to extol. In both cases the encomium becomes not only a laudation of persons but also of humanism. We begin with these.]

(1) Two Distinguished Humanists

(a) Guillaume Budé

From the annotation on Luke 1:4 (***eruditus es veritatem*** 'the truth ... [about which] you have been instructed) [ASD VI-5 450–2: apparatus criticus 2, 6–66, 83–108, 114–24]

[The story of this annotation is, in effect, a story about a friendship won and lost. Guillaume Budé (1468–1540) came from a family that had attained noble rank in the fifteenth century. He had served as secretary to Charles VIII, king of France 1484–98, and soon after Francis I ascended the French throne (1515) he again became closely associated with the court. However, his primary interest throughout his life was the cause of learning. A self-taught Grecist, he devoted himself to humanism: by 1508 he had published 'Annotations' on the *Pandects*, a collection of writings of the ancient Roman jurists, and by 1515 a study of ancient coinage, *De asse* (*On the As* [a Roman coin]). Upon the publication of the New Testament in 1516 Erasmus wrote to Budé, informing him of the publication and recommending Froben as a printer. Budé at once acquired a copy, and had read only the prefaces when a friend informed him of the magnificent compliment Erasmus had paid him in his annotation on Luke 1:4. This began a friendship by correspondence between Budé and Erasmus, a correspondence, however, that often contained sparring ambiguously humorous and serious jokes that were easily interpreted as jabs. Budé in his first letter to Erasmus promised to return somehow the favour Erasmus had done him in writing such a fine eulogy as Budé had found in the annotation. Erasmus waited in vain to see the promise fulfilled, and after Erasmus in 1528 had published his *Ciceronianus*, in which Budé had considered himself slighted, the friendship became inactive. Hence in the final edition of the New Testament Erasmus omitted entirely the effusive encomium he had so hopefully published in the first.[245] The annotation was virtually complete in *1516*; only a few minor changes and additions were made in subsequent editions.]

[**ASD VI 5 450–2** (apparatus criticus)] [AC 2] The printing of these annotations was already well advanced when [AC 6] my good friend Beatus Rhenanus of Sélestat[246] – who like a busy bee is eager to flit among accomplished writers of all sorts gathering whatever is helpful to the restoration of good literature – my Beatus opportunely pointed out what I had not noticed at that time[247] (that is, when I was preparing the first edition) that the preface to Luke[248] had also been turned into Latin by Guillaume Budé of Paris. I was indeed pleased that I had found (though almost too late, to my regret) confirmation of my understanding of the passage in a man so distinguished. It is a pleasure to agree with a friend so learned; in fact, so great is his authority as a literary man that if he disagreed with me at some point I would not hesitate to give up my own opinion and to adopt his.

Who is more diligent than Budé in research, more penetrating or more precise in judgment, fuller or richer in exposition, more correct in articulation, with language more Latinate and more polished? I am able to think of absolutely no one else north of the Alps who demonstrates so perfectly all the gifts and all the qualities of an educated man. He repeatedly demonstrates an ever greater excellence, a sort of noble self-conquest. When he gave us an example of his talent for translation in *The Sayings of the Philosophers* he left everyone

---

245 For Budé's life see CEBR I 212–17, also Ep 403 with the introduction.

246 Beatus Rhenanus (1485–1547) was in Basel from 1511 to 1527, where he worked closely with the Froben Press and with Erasmus. He was a devoted humanist who edited both classical and patristic texts, including the *editio princeps* of the works of Tertullian. His library, 'the Jewel of Sélestat … comprising 761 volumes containing more than a thousand works … is an almost unique example of the fully preserved library of a noted humanist' CEBR I 104–9. Erasmus' fine tribute to Beatus Rhenanus was omitted in *1535* along with the tribute to Budé.

247 [at that time … first edition)] Added in the second edition, *1519*.

248 Ie Luke 1:1–4.

else behind.[249] Then in his annotations on the *Pandects of Civil Law* it is simply marvellous just how very far he outstripped himself. Again, in his book on money,[250] good heavens! how much did he contribute in knowledge, in judgment, in eloquence, a man worthy to extend his years beyond a single lifetime for the cause of good literature, which owes the more to him from the very fact that he makes no charge for his contribution. Did I say, 'No charge'? Indeed, not only no charge, but on the contrary, at great cost to his own resources and health, and without any hint of vexation towards those who were constantly and annoyingly making demands upon him. [AC 60] For some, literary endeavours bring wealth, fame, and superior status. Budé was born into the upper class, possessed wealth, and now for some time has been held in honour for his outstanding royal service. He devotes the entire magnificent endowment of his family to support and enhance literature.

[AC 83] I shall not just now discuss whether the glory gained by wealth or war is true or false. The glory derived from literary fame honours even those whom people criticize and condemn. Long ago Italy had its Cicero and Virgil; more recently Theodore Gaza and Politian.[251] To both of these good literature, indeed the whole world, is in debt. Nevertheless these may perhaps because of the benefits gained owe as much to good literature as literature owes to them. To those who, like Budé, engage in literary activity at their own expense, put the public welfare before their own, and voluntarily spend their own fortune to promote and embellish literature, to these I doubt that any kind of thanks can be rendered that would equal their deserts. If only everyone would feel this way, and that we would be pleased to contend for this kind of glory with the Italians who challenge us with such signal examples. [AC 114] In this contest of literary glory the one who wins and the one who loses does so with good to all, harm to none. There are now people everywhere who gird themselves for this most splendid contest; for none, I think, has it turned out more successfully than for Budé. A former age gave to Italy such outstanding figures as

249 A reference to Budé's translation published in 1503 of Plutarch's *De placitis philosophorum*.

250 A reference to *De asse*.

251 Theodore Gaza (1400–76), born in Thessaloniki, spent much of his adult life in Italy as a teacher and translator. He enjoyed the patronage of Pope Nicholas V and later of king Alphonso I of Naples. Erasmus translated into Latin two of his four books of Greek grammar. Politian (1454–94) taught Greek and Latin in Florence and became famous for his book of *Miscellanies*. Erasmus admired his style and speaks of him frequently; cf *Adagia* II ix 1 CWE 34 89–91 and *Ciceronianus* CWE 28 443–5.

Ermolao Barbaro and Pico della Mirandola.[252] The present age seems to have given to France Budé.

(b) William Warham

From the annotation on 1 Thess 2:7 (***sed factus sumus parvuli*** 'but we became little ones [in the midst of you]' [DV]) [ASD VI-9 398–402:123–70, 178–202]

[A small scribal error has resulted in two readings for this short passage of Scripture: the witnesses divide between the reading *nepioi* 'infant' and *epioi* 'gentle.' The Vulgate represents the former reading, which Erasmus quotes as in the lemma above; Erasmus, following his Greek text of the Byzantine tradition read the latter, as does AV, RSV, and NRSV: 'But we were gentle among you.'

The image of Paul here as the gentle father provided the occasion for Erasmus to write this encomium on William Warham, whom Erasmus recognized as his 'Maecenas,' that is, his generous patron. Erasmus goes further and recognizes much more briefly others who had served him as patrons, Hendrik, bishop of Bergen (1449–1502) whom Erasmus names as the 'first patron of my studies,' and William Blount, Baron Mountjoy (1478–1534), another early patron of Erasmus whom Erasmus named as the inspiration for his first edition of the *Adages*' the *Collectanea*, published in 1500 (but cf CWE 30 8 n15). Erasmus concluded this annotation on 1 Thessalonians 2:7 with a lengthy review of the current distinguished humanists of Italy, France, Switzerland, and Germany, in doing so making a telling point: literature and the humanities will flourish where there are patrons to lend support. The annotation was virtually complete in *1516*, but in *1535* Erasmus omitted the entire concluding section (likewise omitted here). Among the names omitted in *1535* was that of Ulrich von Hutten, a brilliant humanist but impetuous religious/political reformer. The friendship between Erasmus and Hutten had come to an end before Hutten died of syphilis in 1523 at the age of 35 (cf CWE 78 1–29); this friendship broken was a likely factor in Erasmus' decision to omit the concluding section in 1535. In the *Ecclesiastes*, published in 1535, Erasmus once again wrote an

252 Ermolao Barbaro (1453–93) and Giovanni Pico della Mirandola (1463–94) are both spoken of in the *Ciceronianus* with admiration but not without criticism; cf CWE 28 415–16 with nn608, 609. Pico was famous as a humanist philosopher and also for his *Conclusiones*, some of which were regarded as heretical. He was the uncle of Alberto Pio with whom Erasmus engaged in a rather bitter quarrel; cf CWE 84 xvii–xix.

extensive encomium of Warham, 'a man who deserves to be remembered for all time' CWE 67 352–5. Cf also Erasmus' encomium of Warham in his letter to Cardinal Grimani (Ep 334:68–88).

William Warham (1456–1532), archbishop of Canterbury from 1503, and Lord Chancellor of England (1504–1515) was in a position to help Erasmus, whom he met in 1506 when the English humanist William Grocyn introduced him to the archbishop. In 1512 Warham presented Erasmus with the 'living' of Aldington, Kent; the archbishop also sent him money gifts from his private resources. Erasmus had originally intended to dedicate his New Testament to Warham, but in the end dedicated it to Pope Leo X, including, however, in the dedicatory letter an impressive laudation of Warham, 'to whom,' he writes, 'I owe all that I am' (Ep 384:85). There were thus good reasons for writing an encomium for Warham in this annotation on 1 Thessalonians 2:7.

Erasmus begins the encomium by pointing to Paul to whom belongs the highest praise because, though he excelled all the apostles in gifts and achievements, he seemed to ignore his apostolic office and became the greater in proportion to the degree to which he lowered himself to serve all. Erasmus continues:]

[**ASD VI-9 398–402**] [123] I know of no one in our day to whom this praise [bestowed upon Paul] is more appropriate than to William Warham, Archbishop of Canterbury, Maecenas not only to me but to all of Britain. This is a man whom you would judge to be a person not only of pre-eminent greatness but one who seems to be pre-eminent above all by the very fact that while he is the greatest in every way he alone is unaware of his greatness. Thus it is that while William Warham is superior even to the greatest in the other virtues, yet he is superior even to himself for the very reason that he does not regard himself as great. If anyone considers the high dignity of his office, the weight and magnitude of his responsibilities, his godlike judgment, the incomparable force of his natural capacities, his learning in every respect without a fault, the purity of his life, the splendour of his fortune, you would never find anyone even among the nobility to match him. Again, he is always open and available to all; in fact you will not find anyone who surpasses him in affability, courtesy, gentleness even in the midst of common folk, among the lowest class of people. And what a disposition! What an attitude of mind! truly worthy of an apostolic man: when you have exceeded human measure, then to reduce yourself to the common order, not even disdaining persons of the lowest social class.

[146] In a marvellous way he now undertakes for all of Britain a threefold service, serving as archbishop and primate, chancellor and

Maecenas as though he were a sort of triple-bodied Geryon.[253] [151] The archbishopric demands that he provides for all of Britain what the Roman pontiff owes to the whole world. The office of chancellor requires an uncorrupted judge, the highest in the whole kingdom, to whom all have access, laity and clergy alike, and from whom there is no appeal. What a massive heap of business! What a flood of cases! Do you suppose all this is sustained by one man? [160] Well, yes! In fact, this one man not only performs all the tasks of this kind that come his way, but even goes further: in the midst of such an enormous host of clamorous affairs he finds time for the obligations of religion, for friendships, for reading. [168] He devotes no portion of his time to dice, to pleasures, to banquets, to sleep, in fact he even neglects the demands of nature to contribute to the welfare of his native land. [178] Of his own free will he has assumed the character of a Maecenas, and now so faithfully fulfils the role that an island always rich in men and resources, from long ago celebrated for its devotion to religion, has, through his efforts especially, achieved such distinction in literature and academic studies that it need not yield to any country whether you are asking about expertise in both Greek and Latin literature or whether you are looking for eloquence, mathematical acumen, knowledge of other fields of philosophy or the mysteries of the sacred Scriptures. He himself nourishes many, advances most, honours many, enhances and keeps watch over all, not only those who excel, but even those modestly endowed, and not only his own people but foreigners as well, regardless of their native land – among whom his kindness included me in spite of my insignificance. To his generosity he adds a twin grace: he scarcely ever has to be reminded, never to be solicited. Indeed, he immediately interrupts anyone who is thanking him, as though it is beyond obligation that anyone who has received the greatest possible benefit should verbally acknowledge the gift. He thinks gratitude has been sufficiently shown if one advances in his pursuits, if the gift conferred in private turns out good for all. He does not boast if his kindness has a good result, and he pays no attention and seems not even to remember if it turns out otherwise. [201] If I had had this Maecenas in my early years, perhaps I would have been able to accomplish something significant in literature!'[254]

253 Geryon, in Greek mythology a triple headed monster, was slain by Hercules in the course of the latter's tenth 'labour' – the capture of Geryon's oxen. Warham fulfills three functions as though he had three bodies.

254 If Erasmus was born in 1466 he would have been about forty when he met Warham.

(1) The Royal Burgundian Family

From the annotation on Matt 1:5 (***de Rahab*** 'by Rahab') [ASD VI-5 68–70:80–90]

[This brief laudation of some of the members of the family of Charles V arises incidentally from a simple matter of spelling. Erasmus objects to the Vulgate spelling 'Rahab' and notes that the Hebrew is properly represented by the Greek *Rachab*. In early 1519 and later he had access in Mechelen to the Latin *Codex aureus* (cf 12 above and n257 just below) in the library of Margaret, aunt of Charles V, who at that time was regent of the Netherlands. Hence in the third edition he writes:]

[ASD VI-5 68–70] [80] 'Certainly I found the spelling "Rachab" in the library of the most illustrious Lady Margaret, a woman most abundantly endowed with every kind of virtue, quite beyond what is normally expected of her sex, a woman conspicuously worthy of her father, Maximilian, her brother Philip, and her nephews, the emperor Charles and Ferdinand.[255] Of these two the divine favour has raised the former to a felicity almost greater than anyone can possibly desire, while the latter is so embellished with heroic and truly regal gifts that no good fortune, however great, could befall anyone that would not seem inferior to his own particular and truly proper endowments.[256] How I wish that men, too, would follow the example of Margaret and spend their free time reading good books rather than wasting it in games or idle tales. The codex, kept at Mechelen, is quite extraordinary, the whole book written in golden letters.'[257]

---

255 Maximilian, emperor (1493–1518) and Mary of Burgundy had two children, Margaret, cited here, and Philip. Philip married Joanna, daughter of the Spanish monarchs Ferdinand II and Isabella. Between 1497 and 1506, when Philip died, the two had six children, three of whom figured largely in Erasmus' life: Charles, the emperor, and his brother Ferdinand, and Mary, wife of Louis II of Bohemia. After Margaret's death in 1530, Mary, in 1531, followed her aunt as regent of the Netherlands. After Louis II's death Erasmus wrote for Mary the *De vidua christiana* translated in CWE 66. For a convenient chart representing the relationships of this family see CWE 66 183.

256 Erasmus dedicated the *Paraphrase on John* to Ferdinand, where Ferdinand's gifts are extolled; cf Ep 1333.

257 It is probable that Erasmus saw this Latin codex of the Gospels for the first time when he was passing through Mechelen in March 1519. He seems to have explored it much more fully perhaps in the spring or summer of 1521 when he was more actively engaged in preparing his third edition of the New Testament. He greatly admired this codex and cited it extensively in the third edition. It is now in the

(2) Bruges and Marcus Laurinus

From the annotation on Matt 3:16 (***baptizatus autem Iesus*** '[when] Jesus [had been] baptized') [ASD VI-5 122:309–26]

[The brief but pleasing images here of Bruges and Marcus Laurinus are set in the context of a description of manuscripts Erasmus used for the text of his New Testament. We have just seen his admiration for the *Codex aureus*. Elsewhere also he offered vivid descriptions of codices he had found in the library of St Paul's cathedral London, used in the first edition (cf Ep 373:22–5), and those to which he had access through the services of John Botzheim of Constance for the fourth edition (cf the annotation on John 21:22 [*sic eum volo manere*] where Erasmus speaks of a manuscript of 'astonishing antiquity' at Constance). The excerpt that follows here describes the remarkable manuscripts he found in Bruges when he was with the court in 1521. This excerpt was added in the third edition (1522).]

[**ASD VI-5 122**] [309] The word 'Jesus' is absent from the *Codex aureus* and also in one of the Donatian codices. When I was recently in Bruges – and there is no other city today more flourishing or more productive of people of talent – at a most celebrated meeting of innumerable princes, especially the emperor Charles and the Reverend Lord Thomas Wolsey, Cardinal of York, I examined the library of that most ancient college, commonly called St Donatian; even today it retains traces of its ancient scholarship and erudition.[258] I found there several codices of the Gospels, the writing in several of which showed that they had been copied eight hundred years ago, one that contained the entire New Testament, another, the oldest and most worn of all, but mutilated and torn, that contained only the Epistle of Paul to the Romans and the Epistles of James, Peter, John, and Jude. I was given access to these by the Dean of the College, Marcus Laurinus, a man outstanding in every kind of virtue. The Library had also several other books of venerable

---

library of the Escorial, Spain (approximately 40 kilometers north-west of Madrid) – its golden letters are truly magnificent (cf 12 above).

258 In the early sixteenth century Bruges was an important centre of both commerce and diplomacy. Charles V and his court were in Bruges in the summer of 1520 and again in the summer of 1521. It is to the latter occasion that Erasmus refers here. He followed the court to Bruges as a councillor of Charles. See Epp 1106 introduction, 1233 introduction and 1233:1–17.

antiquity that had perished through the neglect of certain people – just as it is now the character of priests who devote themselves more to banquets than to books,[259] and have more interest in money than in letters. I wanted you to know this, reader, because I will frequently refer to the witness of these codices.'

(3) An Anonymous Critic

From the annotation on Matt 10:28 (***Gehenna*** 'hell'; in *1516* ***praedicate*** 'proclaim' [Matt 10:27]) [ASD VI-5 191–2:984–90 and 192–3:10–36]

[Although Erasmus claimed that in his *Annotations* he never named his critics, his comments are often so clearly directed that the critic intended can easily be identified. An exception is the critic bitterly attacked in this annotation, who has been identified both as Girolamo Aleandro and as Egidio Antonini (ie Giles of Viterbo). In any case the critic was the author of a stinging attack on Erasmus in an unpublished document with the title 'Racha' (cf Matt 5:22) that circulated anonymously in Rome. For the identity of the document's author see CEBR I 30 (Aleandro) and 65 (Egidio/Giles). See also Ep 1553:57–8 where Aleandro is called a 'flatterer to one's face but behind one's back ... quite a different person,' and n9 where Aleandro is considered the author of 'Racha'; cf also Ep 1717:38–48. Erasmus believed the author was Aleandro (cf Ep 1717:38–54 with n17 and 15 above).

While Erasmus' response to his critic in this annotation is not a 'portrait' it is included here as an illustration of Erasmus' exceptional ability to suggest arrogance, ignorance, spite, and violence in an opponent. 'Racha' was circulating in Rome in 1525; Erasmus responded in the 1527 (fourth) edition of the *Annotations* with the excerpt given here. The response arises out of Erasmus' effort in the 1516 edition to identify 'Gehenna' with the 'valley of Hinnom' as the Tophet.]

[ASD VI-5 191–2:984–90 and 192–3:10–36] [984] I have noted these references, good reader, to point to the rabid attack of a certain slanderer who is regarded by many people as incredibly learned, while he himself obviously regards himself as a god – though hatred and jealousy snatch away all judgment even from the learned. He writes that in this annotation I have stitched together almost as many lies as words. He calls it a

259 In Latin a pun: *patinis ... paginis* 'plates than pages.'

lie because, he says, [I misquote] 2 Kings 23 and Jeremiah 7.[260] [10] He throws in my face the fact that I wrote that parents used to sacrifice their children in the Tophet. [14] He picks away at my work, complaining that whereas Jerome wrote that Tophet was a place of delights, I said the word was especially hateful to the Jews – truly a strange delight to burn your children in sacrifice to an idol! [21] He throws in my face that I deny that I see any difference between 'Racha' and 'fool,' and the clever fellow deduces from this that I attribute injustice to Christ. [25] He casts up against me that I quote only one passage from the Psalms where 'Racha' is used in the sense of 'empty' or 'foolish,' drawing from this the heady conclusion that I had never read more than one or two psalms. [28] He casts up against me that others have doubts about 'Racha,' while I am the only one who definitely affirms. [32] He smears me with the charge of disparaging the perpetual virginity of the Virgin Mother, and the divinity of Christ, shamelessly lying, and besides all this he accuses me of having taught the Germans contempt for the papacy. The man thinks himself preserved by fate to uphold the church of God, bawling out that it is truly impudent for anyone to write books in this age in which such talent exists, and he writes this kind of blather on many other similar subjects as well.

260 To explain that the New Testament 'Gehenna' is the 'Valley of Hinnom,' also called the Tophet in the Old Testament, Erasmus had referred to Jer 7:31–2 and 2 Kings 23:10. In *1527* he not only referenced but for the sake of convincing evidence cited 2 Kings 23:10, 2 Chron 28:3, Jer 7:31–2, 19:6, and 32:35 (all citations omitted here).

CHAPTER EIGHT

Erasmus Reflects on His New Testament Projects

[Our understanding of Erasmus' work is greatly enhanced by comments from him that reveal his intent in undertaking his programme of New Testament scholarship, and that indicate at least partially the process and the principles that determined the development of his editions of the New Testament and his *Paraphrases*. We find such comments both in his Correspondence and in the formal defence of his work in the face of criticism whether friendly or hostile. It is appropriate, therefore, to conclude this study with selections in which we hear the voice of Erasmus as he attempts both to explain and to defend his work, a man whose memory sometimes failed and who inevitably presented his own necessarily slanted point of view. In spite, however, of ambiguities and perhaps some dubious claims found in such sources, Erasmus' general intent, his underlying presuppositions, and his approach to his work can fairly clearly be discerned from them. We begin (section I) with the lively discussions that focused upon the editions of his New Testament, then (section II) we listen to Erasmus speaking about his *Paraphrases*.]

I. ERASMUS' REFLECTIONS ON THE NATURE AND PURPOSE OF HIS NEW TESTAMENT

(1) Explanation and Description of the Project

Erasmus to Pope Leo X, February 1516 [Ep 384:31–70]

[Leo X (1475–1521) was christened Giovanni de Medici, the son of Lorenzo the Magnificent of Florence, famous for his wealth, power, and his support of humanism. Destined for an ecclesiastical career Giovanni was appointed cardinal in 1489, went to Rome in 1492 where he came to enjoy the favour of the 'warrior pope' Julius II (elected pope 1503), whose wars Giovanni supported. As cardinal the future Leo was 'particularly kind' to Erasmus when he was in Rome in 1509 (CEBR II 320, Ep 335:12–15). On the death of Julius II (1513) Giovanni de Medici was elected pope. Erasmus had originally intended to dedicate his edition of Jerome to Leo and his New Testament to Warham. Possibly after he had received the letter of Dorp, which spoke favourably of the Jerome enterprise but critically of the New Testament, Erasmus, recognizing the importance of some form of papal approval of the latter, decided to dedicate the New Testament to Leo and the Jerome edition to Warham. The letter offered Erasmus the customary opportunity to flatter the pope (a passage omitted here); but Erasmus takes the occasion to explain his work – a very humble kind of work, but of immense importance for the Europe of the sixteenth century, and he addresses Leo as the hope of Europe for a renewed and vital faith:]

[**Ep 384:31–70**] Since you do all you can to pursue your chosen purpose of rebuilding religion, it is right that Christians of all lands and all peoples should support, each of them to the best of his power, one who follows this most noble and most profitable aim. Already I see men of outstanding gifts, like great and wealthy kings, sending our Solomon their marbles, their ivory, their gold, their precious stones for the building of his Temple. We petty chieftains, we mere mortals, gladly bring what we can, timber perhaps or goatskins at any rate, rather than contribute nothing – an offering worth very little if measured by the help we actually give, but (unless I am all astray) likely to be of not a little use though not much beauty in the temple of Christ, especially if it win the approval of him whose yea or nay alone governs the whole sum of human things.[1]

For one thing I found crystal clear: our chiefest hope for the restoration and rebuilding of the Christian religion, our sheet-anchor as they call it, is that all those who profess the Christian philosophy the whole world over should above all absorb the principles laid down by their Founder from the writings of the evangelists and apostles, in which that heavenly Word which once came down to us from the heart of the Father still lives and breathes for us and acts and speaks with more immediate

1 'Marble … Temple … goatskins … temple': Perhaps an allusion to the building of St Peter's, but of greater significance is the allusion (carried here by conventional imagery) to the contrast between the contribution of biblical scholars concerned with the simple matters of grammar and text (timber, goatskins) and that of the grand theologians and ecclesiastical personages (gold, precious stones) towards the enhancement of Christian faith (temple, ie the church).

efficacy, in my opinion, than in any other way.[2] Besides which I perceived that that teaching which is our salvation was to be had in a much purer and more lively form if sought at the fountain-head and drawn from the actual sources rather than from pools and runnels. And so I have revised the whole New Testament against the standard of the Greek original, not unadvisedly or with little effort, but calling in the assistance of a number of manuscripts in both languages, and those not the first comers but both very old and very correct. And well knowing that sacred subjects demand equally scrupulous treatment, I was not content with that degree of care, but passed rapidly over all the works of the classical theologians, and ran to earth from their quotations or their comments what each of them had found or altered in his text.[3] I have added annotations of my own, in order, in the first place, to show the reader what changes I have made, and why; second, to disentangle and explain anything that may be complicated, ambiguous, or obscure; and lastly as a protection, that it might be less easy in future to corrupt what I have restored at the cost of scarcely credible exertions. Not but what, to speak frankly, this whole undertaking might be thought too lowly to be offered to one than whom the world can show nothing greater, were it not fitting that whatever contributes to the restoration of religion should be consecrated by choice to the supreme head of our religion who is its champion.

(2) Justification of the Project: The Correspondence with Maarten van Dorp – Epp 304 and 337

(a) Maarten van Dorp to Erasmus, September 1514 [Ep 304:95–156]

[Maarten van Dorp (1485–1525) matriculated at the University of Louvain in 1501, and progressed through the ranks to become eventually a member of

2 A succinct statement of the 'philosophy of Christ,' which is a fundamental image in Erasmus' biblical scholarship and articulated elsewhere eg the *Paraclesis*; cf 30, and 33–6 and 46–7 above.

3 To establish his Greek text Erasmus sent to the printers three manuscripts, all copied in the twelfth century (as it is now thought), one containing the Gospels, one Acts and the Epistles, and one that included the book of Revelation. He consulted other manuscripts as well, and the results of his collation of these is often noted in the annotations. Latin manuscripts provided important support inasmuch as they served as witnesses to omissions from and additions to the original Greek text. Likewise patristic writers (Erasmus here calls them the 'classical theologians'), both Greek and Latin, not only quoted Scripture in their commentaries, but explained passages, and in either case became a significant witness to the text of the New Testament as it was read in the early church. For the 'very old' manuscripts from the library of St Paul's cathedral see 286 above.

the faculty of arts, where he demonstrated his commitment to the humanist cause. He was introduced into the faculty of theology in 1510, and by 1515 was admitted to the council of the theological faculty as *magister noster*, ie as professor. In the summer of 1514 Erasmus met him in Louvain when he was on his way to Basel. In Louvain Erasmus evidently informed him in some manner of his 'notes' on the New Testament, and Dorp, representing no doubt the voice of the Louvain faculty of theology, wrote to Erasmus in September warning him against the publication of his notes (Ep 304). Erasmus did not receive the letter until May 1515, but then replied almost at once (Ep 337). Dorp begins his letter by questioning the wisdom of publishing the *Praise of Folly*, then briefly expresses appreciation for Erasmus' work on Jerome, finally approaches the subject of Erasmus' efforts to 'correct the Vulgate':]

[**Ep 304:95–156**] [95] I understand that you have also revised the New Testament and written notes on over a thousand passages, to the great profit of theologians. This raises another point on which I should like in the friendliest possible spirit to issue a warning. [102] What sort of an operation this is, to correct the Scriptures, and in particular to correct the Latin copies by means of the Greek,[4] requires careful thought. If I can show that the Latin version contains no admixture of falsehood or mistake, will you not have to confess that the labours of all those who try to correct it are superfluous, except for pointing out now and again places where the translator might have given the sense more fully? Now I differ from you on this question of truth and integrity, and claim that these are qualities of the Vulgate edition that we have in common use. For it is not reasonable that the whole church, which has always used this edition and still both approves and uses it, should for all these centuries have been wrong. [115] That councils of this kind duly constituted never err, in so far as they deal with the faith, is generally agreed among both theologians and lawyers. If some new necessity should arise and require a new general council, this beyond doubt is the text it would follow whenever a knotty problem arose touching the faith. We must confess therefore either that the Fathers were ill-advised and will be ill-advised in the future if they follow this text and this version, or that truth and integrity are on its side. In any case, do you believe the Greek copies to be freer from error than the Latin? Had the Greeks any greater concern than the Latins for preserving the Scriptures undamaged, when

4 In a lecture published in Sept 1519 Dorp retracted the implication here that the Vulgate should not be corrected by the Greek manuscripts.

you think of the blows Christianity has suffered among the Greeks,[5] [127] while among the Latins the Bride of Christ, the church, has continued always inviolate? And how can you be sure you have lighted on correct copies, assuming that in fact you have found several, however readily I may grant that the Greeks may possess some copies which are correct?

[146] But you will say 'I should not like you to change anything in your text, or to suppose that the Latin is in error; I merely display what I have found in the Greek manuscripts that differs from the Latin ones; and what harm will that do?' My dear Erasmus, it will do a great deal. For a great many people will discuss the integrity of the Scriptures, and many will have doubts about it, if the presence of the least scrap of falsehood in them becomes known, I will not say from your work, but simply from some man they have heard holding forth. Then we shall see what Augustine writes in a letter to Jerome: 'If falsehoods were admitted into Holy Scripture even to serve a useful purpose, what authority can they still retain?'[6]

(b) Erasmus to Maarten van Dorp, May 1515 Ep [Ep 337:750–947]

[Erasmus responds in order to the three subjects in Dorp's letter, coming in the third place to his work on the New Testament. He undermines the foundation on which Dorp establishes the authority of the Vulgate; he also addresses matters of textual criticism: he notes that the text he is producing is based not only on the authority of manuscripts, but on the evidence of quotations from the early Fathers, as well as on the proper use of conjecture based on a rational evaluation of context.]

[Ep 337:750–919] [750] Then again what you write in the third part about the New Testament makes me wonder what has happened to you, or what has beguiled for the moment your very clear-sighted mind. [767] One thing the facts cry out, and it can be clear, as they say, even to a blind man, that often through the translator's clumsiness or inattention the Greek has been wrongly rendered; often the true and genuine reading has been corrupted by ignorant scribes, which we see happen every day, or altered by scribes who are half-taught and half-asleep. Which man encourages falsehood more, he who corrects and restores these

5 The western church regarded the Greek church as schismatic after the separation in 1054.
6 Augustine Epistle 28.3.4.

passages, or he who would rather see an error added than removed? For it is of the nature of textual corruption that one error should generate another. And the changes I make are usually such as affect the overtones rather than the sense itself; though often the overtones convey a great part of the meaning. But not seldom the text has gone astray entirely.

[782] You say that in their day the Greek copies were more correct than the Latin ones, but that now it is the opposite, and we cannot trust the texts of men who have separated from the Roman church. [790] Now make me a list of all the heads under which the Greeks differ from the orthodox Latins; you will find nothing that arises from the words of the New Testament or has anything to do with this question. The whole controversy relates to the word *hypostasis*,[7] to the procession of the Holy Spirit,[8] to the ceremonies of consecration, to the poverty of the priesthood, to the powers of the Roman pontiff. For none of these questions do they lean on falsified texts. But what will you say when you see their interpretation followed by Origen, Chrysostom, Basil, Jerome? Had somebody falsified the Greek texts as long ago as that? Who has ever detected falsification in the Greek texts even in one passage? And finally, what could be the motive, since they do not defend their particular tenets from this source?

[806] Again, you say that one should not depart from a text that enjoys the approval of so many councils. [809] Pray produce me one synod in which this [Vulgate] version has been approved. But suppose that some synod has approved it? [812] Was it approved in such terms that it is absolutely forbidden to correct it by the Greek original? Were all the mistakes approved as well, which in various ways may have crept in? [829] What are we to say when we see that even copies of our Vulgate version do not agree? Surely these discrepancies were not approved by a synod. [860] Nor can there be any danger that everybody will forthwith abandon Christ if the news happens to get out that some passage has been found in Scripture which an ignorant or sleepy scribe has miscopied or some unknown translator has rendered inadequately. How much more truly Christian it would be to have done with quarrelling

7 The western church expressed the 'Threeness' of the Trinity with the word *personae* 'three persons,' while the Greeks adopted the word *hypostasis*, which the West tended to understand in the sense of 'substance.'

8 Cf the famous *filioque* phrase added (sixth century) to the Nicene Creed: 'I believe in the Holy Spirit who proceeds from the Father "and the Son"'; the Greek church insisted rather on 'proceeds from the Father through the Son.'

and for each man cheerfully to offer what he can to the common stock and to accept with good will what is offered, so that at the same time you learn in humility what you do not know and teach others ungrudgingly what you do know!

[905] I have translated the whole New Testament after comparison with the Greek copies, and have added the Greek on the facing pages, so that anyone may easily compare it. I have appended separate annotations in which, partly by argument and partly by the authority of the early Fathers, I show that my emendations are not haphazard alterations, for fear that my changes might not carry conviction and in the hope of preserving the corrected text from further damage. I only wish I had been man enough to perform what I so laboriously undertook! As far as the business of the church is concerned, I shall have no hesitation in presenting my labours, such as they are, to any bishop, any cardinal, any Roman pontiff even, provided it is such a one as we have at the moment. In the end I have no doubt that you too will be delighted with the book when it is published, although you now dissuade me from publishing it, once you have had even a brief taste of the studies without which no man can form a right judgment on these questions.[9]

[947] Farewell, Dorp, dearest of men.

(3) Preparation and Production of the Editions of the New Testament

(a) Erasmus to Guillaume Budé, June 1516 [Ep 421:47–80]

[On 1 May 1516 Budé had written to Erasmus describing his satisfaction in finding the eulogy to him in the annotation on Luke 1:4 (cf 279–82 above). In the letter he had also expressed 'astonishment' that Erasmus had used 'such eloquence and such intellectual gifts on trivialities' (Ep 403:134–5) or what Erasmus himself called *minutiae*.[10] This led Erasmus to a famous description of the unexpected turns in the development of his work and the hasty publication of the first edition.]

[Ep 421:47–80] [47] In this work (ie the *Novum instrumentum*) I have done what I usually do elsewhere. I had decided to treat the whole thing lightly, as I was to be concerned with minutiae,[11] and merely to

9 Ie the study of Greek; Dorp was yet to take up the study of Greek.
10 Budé had used a Greek word, translated in CWE as 'trivialities.'
11 Ie matters of text, grammar, and language in contrast to the grand issues of theology.

point a finger, as it were, at some passages in passing. Then, when the work was already due to be published, certain people encouraged me to change the Vulgate text by either correcting or explaining it.[12] This additional burden would, I thought, be very light; but in reality I found it by far the heaviest part. Then they pushed me into adding rather fuller annotations; and very soon, as you know, everything had to be done again. And there was a further task: I thought correct copies were available in Basel, and when this hope proved vain, I was obliged to correct in advance the texts the compositors were to use.[13] Besides which, two good scholars had been engaged, one a lawyer and the other a theologian who also knows Hebrew, who were to be in charge of correcting proofs;[14] but they had no experience of this and were unable to fulfil their undertaking, so it was necessary for me to take the final checking of the formes, as they call them,[15] upon myself. So the work was edited and printed simultaneously, one ternion (which is the modern word) being printed off every day: nor was I able all this time to devote myself entirely to the task. At the same time they were printing off Jerome, who claimed a large share of me;[16] and I had made up my mind either to work myself to death or to get myself free of that treadmill by Easter. On top of that we made a mistake about the size of the volume. The printer affirmed that it would run to thirty ternions[17] more or less, and it exceeded, if I mistake not, eighty-three. And so the greatest part of my

---

12 Cf the introduction (chapter 1) for a more extended account of the transformation in design that occurred when Erasmus consulted with Froben at the Press in Basel in 1515.

13 In fact Erasmus made relatively few 'corrections' to the manuscripts sent to the printers; cf n3 above.

14 The 'two good scholars' were Nikolaus Gerbel and Johannes Oecolampadius. Nikolaus Gerbel (1485–1560) had shown an interest in Erasmus' New Testament project in 1515 (Ep 352), and joined the Froben press later that year to work on the edition. A devoted humanist, he would later work as an editor and corrector for the Press of Matthias Schürer of Strasburg. Johannes Oecolampadius (1482–1521) had been ordained a priest and had studied Greek and Hebrew (1513–15). In 1515 he moved to Basel and joined the Froben firm as corrector. He later became the leader of the Reform movement in Basel.

15 Ie 'proofs.'

16 Erasmus went to Basel in 1514 with several texts to present to Froben for publication, including the Letters of Jerome that he had edited and annotated. These letters became the first four volumes of a nine-volume edition of the *Opera* of Jerome, a work Froben had already undertaken and which appeared in the summer of 1516.

17 'Ternion,' ie three sheets of paper folded in two to form a set of six leaves or twelve pages. In the 'table of ternions' at the end of the *1516* New Testament seventy nine ternions are listed and four quaternions.

time was spent on things that were not really my business or had been no part of the original plan; and I was already weary and well-nigh exhausted when I came to the annotations. As far as time and my state of health permitted, I did what I could. Some things I even passed over of set purpose; to many I knowingly closed my eyes, and then changed my opinion soon after publication. And so I prepare the second edition, wherein I beg you urgently to help a man who is trying hard. Let people like you rebuke if they must and I shall take it as a friendly act.

(b) Erasmus to Johann von Botzheim[18]
January 1523 [Ep 1341A:478–95]

[In 1523 Erasmus wrote at the request of his friend John Botzheim an account of his literary endeavours, an account he extended in 1524 to become almost a little book – 1844 lines in the CWE edition. His narrative included the brief statement here that suggests a radical change in the conception of the first edition after he had arrived at the Froben Press. He briefly refers to the three subsequent editions. Without question his enormous labours on the second edition virtually made a new work of his New Testament. The third edition (1522) offered significant new evidence for the text and some important additions to the *Annotations* but may have been rather hurriedly put together, and is not inappropriately described as a 'supplement' to the second, while the fourth edition, mentioned here in a 1524 addition, would not be published until 1527. It seems most probable that his work on the *Paraphrases* contributed substantially to the fourth edition, since, as the footnotes in the CWE volumes of *Paraphrases* have shown, in writing the *Paraphrases* Erasmus not only compared the Greek text with the Latin Vulgate but read through large quantities of the patristic authors. In the same letter (1341A:750–74) Erasmus briefly describes his progress in writing his *Paraphrases* (1517 to 1524).]

[Ep 1341A:478–95] After these preliminary exercises,[19] I addressed myself to the New Testament, in which I had made up my mind to be so sparing of words that my plan was to write notes in two or three

18 Johann von Botzheim (d1535), was canon from 1510 of the cathedral of Constance, Switzerland. His beautiful house and its setting is described at length by Erasmus (Ep 1342:369–500) after he had visited Botzheim on the latter's invitation in 1522. He provided Erasmus with important Latin manuscripts of the Gospels from the cathedral library, which Erasmus used extensively in the fourth edition (1527).

19 Ie translations and editions of classical texts.

words on every passage, especially as I had already issued Lorenzo's critical work,[20] which seemed to me more long-winded than the subject requires. None the less, when Froben was already set to print my work, scholarly friends, to whom I sometimes defer more than I should, moved me actually to alter the Vulgate text, and to be rather fuller in my annotations. This work of mine provoked a great many men to the study either of Greek or of a purer form of theology; but at the same time the reputation it earned me was leavened with much ill will. Here too I soon paid penalties that were by no means light, either for my audacity or for my undue readiness to follow my friends' wishes rather than my own judgment. With incredible labour I remade the whole work[21] and sent it again to the printer. Once again I have taken it in hand, for the third time, and supplemented it most carefully, in the year 1522, and this is the latest edition I have yet published. But I have a fourth ready, having discovered while writing the paraphrases many things that had previously escaped me.[22]

(4) Erasmus Responds to His Critics

[As we have seen, particularly in the portrait of Aleandro, Erasmus could create a devastatingly negative impression of his critics. But however impatiently Erasmus bore his critics, his response to their criticism often illuminates his intentions in pursuing his work with the New Testament. In this regard two responses are of special interest. The first is in the form of a letter to his friend Maarten Lips, who sent Erasmus a 'pamphlet' just before he left Louvain for Basel to see his second edition (March 1519) through the Press. The 'pamphlet,' written by a very hostile critic whose identity remains uncertain, was a sustained and pointed attack on Erasmus' New Testament project. Erasmus replied to Lips in a long letter of

---

20 Erasmus discovered and published (1505) the *Collatio* of the Italian Laurentius Valla (1400–54). The *Collatio* consisted of short notes comparing the text of the Vulgate with that of a few Greek and Latin manuscripts. In the title of his publication Erasmus designated the notes '*Annotations*'; cf 4 above.

21 A reference to the preparation of the second edition of his New Testament, which Erasmus promised even before the first was published (cf the preface to the annotations on Mark). The second edition was so greatly improved and enhanced that Erasmus justly describes it here as a work remade.

22 For a detailed and scholarly study of Erasmus' progress in preparing the first edition see Henk J. deJonge 'The Date and Purpose of Erasmus' *Castigatio Novi Testamenti*. A Note on the Origins of the *Novum Instrumentum*' in A.C.Dionisotti, Anthony Grafton, and Jill Kraye eds *The Uses of Greek and Latin. Historical Essays* (London 1988) 97–110.

ninety-five numbered paragraphs that answered the points raised in the pamphlet. The second was a more general response to all who had brought their criticism to bear on the first edition of the New Testament. Erasmus wrote his response in one hundred and eleven numbered paragraphs, and this he incorporated into the second edition of the New Testament as an additional preface with the rather prejudicial title, 'The Chief Points in the Arguments Answering Some Crabby and Ignorant Critics.' This response serves as a kind of 'catch-all' for the various objections to Erasmus' work and reflects the sometimes very significant differences between Erasmus and many of his sixteenth century contemporaries in their presuppositions about Scripture, to recognize which is to go far towards a better understanding of Erasmus' work on the New Testament. For both responses I retain the paragraph numbering as in CWE.]

(a) To Maarten Lips, May 1518 [Ep 843 paragraphs 2–76]

[Maarten Lips was an Augustinian canon and a faithful friend of Erasmus on whom Erasmus frequently called for help in his work. Shortly before Erasmus left Louvain to be present in Basel at the printing of the second edition of his New Testament Lips sent him a pamphlet whose author had attacked Erasmus' New Testament with serious criticisms apparently quite severely expressed, criticisms made fairly evident in Erasmus' reply. The excerpts below represent some of the more widespread criticisms. The editors of the letter for CWE suggest that Erasmus wrote his reply while 'on the Rhine' en route to Basel. The author of the 'pamphlet' has often been thought to be Edward Lee, but in fact his identity remains uncertain. For Lee see the introduction to the *Contra morosos* just below.]

2. [My critic] imagines that I publicly correct and alter the Vulgate text, whereas I leave that intact and untouched and have turned into Latin what is found in the Greek copies, pointing out as I go along the agreements or disagreements of our own text; not seldom preferring what is in these copies of ours, correcting anything corrupt, explaining ambiguities, elucidating obscurities, and changing anything that is notably barbarous in expression,[23] because I understand that very many people

23 'Barbarous in expression.' The Vulgate Latin Bible contained many expressions that were not used in standard classical Latin. Such expressions were jarring to the ears of Renaissance men and women educated in the more elegant Latin of the classics authored by the ancient Romans. Later in the letter (cf paragraph 33) Erasmus calls such expressions 'solecisms.'

are so disgusted by the prodigious errors (which however are nearly always the translator's work and not the authors') that they cannot bring themselves to read the Scriptures. Nor for that matter have all mortals such an iron digestion that they can endure the style of the Vulgate. But if we simplify our language for the benefit of ignorant and simple folk, should we not help educated readers too by purifying the language?[24]

13. He dreams up the idea that the Latin Translator produced what we now have under the inspiration of the Holy Spirit, though Jerome himself in his preface openly testifies that each translator renders to the best of his ability what he is capable of understanding.[25]

33. In fact, all through this argument the solecisms we find in our Latin New Testament, and even the errors that his old friends have introduced in no small number, are ascribed by him to the authority of the Holy Spirit – with barefaced impudence, for it would be improper to do such a thing even with the apostles.

54. The same wisdom is evident in his remark that the Greeks falsified their texts when they split off from the Roman church.[26] And what, pray, was the reason why they should corrupt them all? Moreover, their separation from the Roman church being quite recent, how comes it that their modern texts and their very ancient ones are in agreement? How comes it that Origen and Basil and Chrysostom – and Latin Fathers too, Ambrose, Jerome, Hilary, Cyprian – are in accord with their falsified texts and disagree with the Vulgate text? Did the Greeks falsify at one stroke the texts used by all these authors?

65. He instructs me that I ought to have sent my book to the supreme pontiff for him to decide whether it should be suppressed or published. On that argument every book ought to be sent to the supreme pontiff, for every book might contain matter of offence for someone. And furthermore, as I do not uproot the old version, but by publishing a revision of it make it easier for us not only to possess it in a purer form but to

---

24 Erasmus indicated on several occasions that his New Testament with its relatively refined translation and its annotations was intended for educated people reading it privately in their study; cf the annotation excerpted from John 1:1 on 'word' 214–16 above and the *Contra morosos* 305 with n37 below.

25 Cf Jerome's Preface to the Pentateuch. Underlying the critic's objection is a fundamental issue: what do we mean when we say that Scripture is inspired? That every word is dictated by the Holy Spirit? In the original or in translation, too? If Scripture is not inspired in every word how can we claim it to be trustworthy? If a translation is not inspired how can we trust it?

26 A reference to the schism of 1054; cf Dorp's letter to Erasmus 293 with n5.

understand it better, how could I suspect that there would be malignant critics like this man, ready to take offence at a work that would benefit everyone?

67. In any case, what does he mean by 'authorize'? Put through such tests that there is no error left? If that is the law, nothing we have is authorized outside the canonical Scriptures. Nor is that what I asked of Leo. I merely draw men's attention, leaving the decision to scholars, if they have found something more correct.

68. After these declamatory flights he spreads himself in a more agreeable field and portrays for us the gifts of a translator. He declares that no one can translate Scripture unless he is provided with the gift of the Holy Ghost. And yet St Jerome's view was different, though he is the translator of both Testaments.

69. Besides this, while there is, I suppose, no one today arrogant enough to claim that he has the gift of prophecy or of tongues, it is rash to pass judgment on the spirit of other men. I have striven to convey the very truth, following in the footsteps of the orthodox Fathers, nor have I set any goal before me save the reader's profit and Christ's glory. As I toiled, from time to time I sought the guidance of the Holy Spirit; at least there was no lack of good intentions.

70. He declares it unlawful for any man to teach without public authorization. Does it not satisfy him that I have the same authorization that Thomas had? (Not that I would compare myself with him.) Does it not satisfy him if I do it at the urgent request of the best of prelates and on encouragement from the pope himself?[27]

76. Then again, rejecting a remark of mine that in what I write I never reflect on any man's reputation, he objects that in a number of passages I dissent from Thomas, from Peter Lombard, from Lyra, from Hugo of St-Cher, as though no one could dissent without insulting or attacking the reputation of his opponent. And yet if I do dissent it is with a prior expression of respect for those to whom such respect is due, among whom I do not reckon Lyra or St Cher. And if some do accord them less weight than they used to, there was no reason why to preserve their authority we must always follow a false view.[28]

27 Erasmus had the permission of the bishop of Basel to publish his New Testament, and he regarded the pope's acceptance of the dedication of the New Testament as 'encouragement.' But the matter of authorization led Erasmus to seek a specific authorization from the pope for his second edition, a request the pope granted; cf Ep 864.

28 Erasmus often made the claim that he never mentioned specifically the name of any hostile critic to cast aspersions upon him; cf 287. This claim did not apply to

(b) The Contra morosos[29] *[CWE 41 799–855]*

[Erasmus might well have been surprised by the rapidity with which criticism of his New Testament arose, some of it notoriously hostile. The New Testament was published in March 1516; already in August he relayed to a friend a report from 'trustworthy witnesses' who said that one Cambridge College had 'provided by solemn resolution that no man bring the said volume [ie the New Testament] by horse, boat, wagon or porter within the curtilage of the College!' (Ep 456:11–15]. Few critics proved to be more annoying to Erasmus than Edward Lee, a young English Franciscan who had come to Louvain to improve his Greek (cf 10–11 above). Erasmus met Lee in the summer of 1517 and entered into a friendly relationship with him, in which he received 'notes' from Lee questioning comments made in the 1516 edition of the *Annotations*. Erasmus at first responded to these on sheets of paper more or less as they came from Lee, but he eventually tired of the young monk's intrusions, ceased to respond and let the friendship cool. If Lee, however, was the inaugurating motive for the *Contra morosos*, Erasmus was determined to use the occasion of a response to this impertinent young man to knock down all his critics in one sustained counter attack – one hundred and eleven paragraphs as I have noted above (cf 8 and 299), often reflecting criticism similar to that in Ep 843 excerpted immediately above. Although there were significant later additions all the excerpts below were printed in the second edition (1519) of the New Testament, answering the many criticisms that had arisen after only the first had been published.]

THE CHIEF POINTS IN THE ARGUMENTS ANSWERING SOME CRABBY AND IGNORANT CRITICS [Introduction and paragraphs 1–110]

---

the well-known exegetes of antiquity and the medieval world. Erasmus' attitude towards Thomas Aquinas was ambiguous. In the 1516 edition in particular he spoke highly of Thomas, 'on any account a great man' (annotation on Rom 1:4 CWE 56 10), but he also acknowledged Thomas' 'misunderstanding of Scripture,' blaming it on his ignorance of Greek. For Lyra and Hugh of St Cher Erasmus had little respect, calling them as exegetes mere 'stable boys.' But Erasmus' depreciation of medieval exegetes was not unrelated to his great respect for the exegetes of early Christianity. Cf *Ratio* 46 with n19, and 69–70.

29 Ie 'Against the Crabby Critics.' The *Contra morosos* 'Against the Crabby Critics' is the convenient short title frequently given to this work, taken from the longer title, 'The Chief Points in the Arguments Answering Some Crabby and Ignorant Critics.'

To respond to all the captions of all critics, my very esteemed reader, apart from the fact that it is an endless task, I neither consider to be at all suitable to the dignity of this undertaking nor believe to be worthwhile. Accordingly here I note only the chief points in arguments for the benefit of the readers who are either preoccupied or somewhat dull.

[1] First I testify that I have never intended to depart from the judgment of the Catholic church by so much as a hair's breadth. But if anyone catches anything anywhere of that sort that was not, however, deliberate but an oversight on my part (for I am only human), I now in fact wish it to be considered as disavowed.

[2] Nor do I pre-empt the judgment of the learned or prejudice the authority of the recognized universities. Everyone is free to make up his own mind. I write annotations, not laws, I propose points to be considered, not immediately to be taken as certain.

[6] [They say that] those who do not know Latin are offended [by the new translation] and they insist on having the old solecisms they are used to. Such people have the old edition,[30] which is whole and intact, for anything I have to do with it. I have known many who have been repelled by Holy Scripture because of the inelegance (not to say crudeness) of the language. Let the critics take it in good part that I wanted to accommodate these people also. In any case, I do not change Holy Scripture the slightest bit; I am dealing with translators and corrupters. And I do not remove the simplicity of Scripture; I restore it. Besides, it is a godly duty and a human kindness to entice the weak at first with some alluring pleasantness.

[7] God, they say, is not offended by solecisms. This indeed may be true, but neither is he delighted with them. Augustine excuses incorrectness in language; he does not recommend it. Moreover, he excuses it for the uneducated, not for theologians. But if a solecism renders the meaning ambiguous or inaccurate, as I have shown it does in some places, then Augustine hates the solecism.[31] In fact God hates the proud proponents of solecisms who assail those who speak correctly. [9] In any case, what Augustine writes about solecisms is no more pertinent to us than if he had admonished a preacher speaking French to Frenchmen that he should use French words known to the masses.

---

30 Ie the Vulgate.

31 For Augustine's position on solecisms see *De doctrina christiana* 2.13 and *De catechizandis rudibus* 9.13.

[15] Though I would not deny that the Greek of the apostles and Evangelists departs in some ways from ordinary grammar, there was still no reason for us[32] to add so many outrageous solecisms.

[16] And though it was perhaps advantageous in those times for the apostles to use uncultivated language, it might now be advantageous to change this, since nowadays bishops do not even dress as the apostles did; rather the church has grown more splendid in every sort of way. At that time it was helpful for the apostles to speak the language that was most widespread and was understood by both the literate and the illiterate, but that does not mean that those who have learned Latin should now learn a new way to babble because of the solecisms not of the apostles, but of the Translator.

[20] As I have often said already, I do not change a single syllable in the language of the apostles; instead I restore their language where it has been corrupted by scribes or in some other way. Accordingly, let no one cry out 'here he corrects the Gospel, here he emends the Lord's Prayer,'[33] but rather 'here he eliminates errors from the manuscripts of the Gospels.' I am no more to be rebuked than someone who uses a broom to sweep the filth out of the temple. For not everything that is in the temple is for that very reason holy.

[21] Now, if someone wants to attribute to the Holy Spirit whatever this translator[34] writes and if it is therefore a crime to change anything in it, why does Jerome dare to disparage its readings, now criticizing individual words, now a whole sentence, now removing something he asserts has been added. For he does this not infrequently, even in the books which he published long after he had published his translation of the Old and New Testaments.[35]

[27] Moreover, if the inspiration of the Holy Spirit is absolutely required in a translator, what is to prevent me also from having the

32 A reference to the translator(s), and indirectly the users, of the Vulgate.

33 Critics pointed especially to the Magnificat (Luke 1:46–55) and the Lord's Prayer (Matt 6:9–13), though in *1516* the changes in either were relatively minor. In the case of the Lord's Prayer Erasmus followed his Greek text in adding the doxology, absent from the Vulgate, and replaced the Vulgate's *dimittere* with the more classical *remittere* for 'forgive.'

34 Ie the unknown translator of the Vulgate.

35 Jerome revised the Old Latin translation of the Gospels, but not that of the Epistles, during his stay in Rome (382–5). He wrote commentaries on some of the Epistles in 386–7. Occasionally in his commentaries Jerome criticizes the Old Latin translation of the Epistles, which had become a part of the Vulgate Bible. Jerome had completed his translation of the Hebrew Scriptures by 406 and thereafter wrote numerous commentaries on the Old Testament.

Spirit common to all Christians, who ordinarily gives more abundant aid to those who also contribute their own industry?

[28] I hear that some are so superstitious that they will not allow a single word of the Gospels to be changed in translation, as if such rigidity would give a version and not a perversion. Discourse consists of two elements, language as its body and meaning as its soul. If both can be rendered, I have nothing against it; but if not, then it would be preposterous for a translator to cling to the words and diverge from the meaning. [29] Certainly, whenever possible, a translator should aim at expressing the meaning faithfully in the most suitable language.

[34] If someone should contend that we should never diverge from this translator at all, let him first justify the places where I show that he very clearly nodded or was mistaken. [35] Even if many errors are such that they were probably introduced by scribes, though the church may approve the Vulgate translation, she certainly does not approve the corruption.

[38] The authority of Holy Scripture is not shaken when errors are removed from manuscripts; actually it is shaken if it is clear that we are using corrupt copies; and that certainly cannot be denied.

[39] We must wish that Sacred Scripture contained no errors and we must strive to make it so, as much as possible. But this has not happened after 1300 years and perhaps it will never come to pass completely.

[41] Accordingly, I do not publish this edition as if I intended it to be completely free of errors. For I translated whatever I found most frequently and most uniformly in the Greek,[36] pointing out where our [Vulgate] version agrees or disagrees with it and indicating what seems to me to be the most correct.

[42] I know that sacred matters are to be treated with religious reverence; therefore, even though I was engaged in a minor task, I was as circumspect as I could be. I collated the most ancient and reliable manuscripts in both languages, and indeed no small number of them. I investigated the commentaries of ancients and moderns, both Greek and Latin. I noticed the various readings they furnished. I weighed the meaning of the passage and only then did I pronounce what I thought. No, I did not even pronounce; rather I informed the reader, leaving everyone free to make up his own mind.[37]

36 Since the Greek manuscripts Erasmus consulted all belonged to the Byzantine manuscript tradition, their general uniformity was more or less guaranteed. The Vulgate translation was based on a different manuscript tradition.

37 Ie in the annotations where Erasmus 'pronounces,' or rather, 'informs' the reader. For the claim made just below, that Erasmus wrote for 'the learned,' see 300 with n24.

[49] But I hear some of them saying: 'We accept the facts but the masses are scandalized if they perceive that there is anything corrupt or unintelligible in the codices which we have followed up till now.' First of all, these things are not written for the masses, but for the learned, especially students of theology. They should not be offended. And I do not call my task correction but rather annotation. I cause no trouble for anyone who wants to cite another version or to follow an old or even a corrupt version. Rather the scandal arises from those who scream that someone is correcting Sacred Scripture and the Lord's Prayer, crying out in sermons before the public, in drinking parties, in wagons and ships among illiterates and empty-headed women.

[55] 'No attempt [to correct the Scriptures] should be made,' they say, 'without the authorization of a synod.' Could they say anything more ridiculous than this? For me to show what seems to be corrupted by a scribe or what might have been better rendered by the Translator, especially drawing upon the judgment of the ancient Fathers, for this must an entire synod be assembled? Everyday new commentaries are written on Sacred Scripture, pronouncements are issued about the most serious matters, many articles are laid down, and all of this is done without requiring any synod.

[59] I have removed many errors; I have explained many passages badly translated; I have eliminated many outrageous solecisms; I have unravelled many knots that baffled even the ancient exegetes; I have pointed out many extraordinary lapses in writers; I have eliminated many ambiguities; I have reordered many transpositions;[38] (to come to an end) I have often illuminated the meaning of passages that before were obscure or cloudy; I have freely conferred much that is useful; and yet some people scream at me, though they are in my debt. If there is the slightest error, they raise tidal waves of protest. Benefits bestowed earn no gratitude.

[80] Now the fact that some scorn my efforts as lowly and elementary because my labours concern syllables and words does not disturb me very much. As for me, I consider whatever concerns the subject matter of theology to be great. And since I was not unaware of how much reverence is due to Sacred Scripture, I deliberately chose what might

38 'Transpositions': Latin *hyperbata*, a passage in which the order of the Greek words is unnatural and confusing. Erasmus shows in some cases how to reorder the words to provide the correct sense, eg in the annotation on Rom 1:4 ('from the resurrection of the dead of Jesus Christ').

seem most lowly in that profession. [81] Let them call it grammatical, elementary, trivial, as long as they confess it is necessary.

[83] But in fact it will seem all the more clear that such matters should not be neglected if anyone puts to the test how much labour they require or if someone undertakes to handle Holy Scripture and to investigate single details in it with the painstaking care they deserve. What is useful is perceived by continuous application, not by a helter-skelter reading. Finally, a person will cease to feel contempt if he considers not one or two annotations but the whole enterprise. At your ease and at leisure you pass judgment on me about this or that passage and you think you could have handled it with considerably more amplitude and learning. I could have done so too if I had had to analyze only ten places. But to provide the proper diligence in many thousands of places is very difficult indeed; at least it was so for me. I will not begrudge it if someone has a happier lot.[39]

[108] I hear that some bruit it about that I pass over many places that I ought to have annotated. First of all, I want the reader to be advised that I did not seek out every place in the New Testament that seems to call for annotation but only those places where a true reading was at stake; and of those also I had the good sense to omit many so as not to overburden the reader. If someone adds to what I have done, I will actually applaud his contribution to the public good. Indeed, if someone disagrees with me on some point, I will not be offended in the least, as long as he does so with arguments and not with insults (as any learned person ought to do).

[110] Against the poisonous hissing of my enemies I take comfort in a clean conscience and also in the judgment of many persons whom either holiness of life or extraordinary learning or very high status or the dignity of an ecclesiastical office or (for some) all of these together place beyond reproach. They thank me daily in letters sent from all over the world because my researches (whatever they may be worth) have inspired them to improve their minds and study Holy Scripture; persons who have never seen Erasmus know and love him from his writings. As I said, I have asked nothing of them and they have no reason to

39 Critics sometimes complained that Erasmus' work was somewhat carelessly done, and he himself recognized that he worked with too much haste, a fact he regretted in later life. Cf the letter from Wolfgang Capito commenting on Erasmus' first edition (Ep 459). When later in life he was encouraged by a young Spanish admirer to 'polish' his writings, he replied, 'It is my nature to write extemporaneously; when it comes to revision I am remarkably lazy!' (Allen Ep 3043:35–8).

flatter me. They have nothing to fear from me or to seek from me. I have gained their support because they have found useful what I have done and are grateful for it. Just as I have laboured for everyone in general, so too all who are fair and sound are grateful to me, from whatever country, from whatever class of people. I consider this a greater reward than the dignity of a bishopric.

II. ERASMUS' REFLECTIONS ON THE NATURE AND PURPOSE OF THE *PARAPHRASES*

[Just as Erasmus found many occasions over the years to reflect on the nature and purpose of his New Testament, so with the *Paraphrases* Erasmus offered, both on his own initiative and provoked by critics, abundant insights into his conception of his work. I present here a very small selection of many relevant comments. He speaks eloquently of his understanding of his endeavour in two dedicatory letters, while the insights of his critic Alberto Pio forced Erasmus to discuss some very important issues. The two dedicatory letters are those that prefaced his *Paraphrase on Romans*, first of the Epistles to be published, and his *Paraphrase on Matthew*, first of the Gospels to appear.

The dedicatory letter to the *Paraphrase on Romans* (1517) addresses the question of the nature of a paraphrase, particularly a paraphrase on Scripture. Erasmus indicates that he wishes to do in the *Paraphrase* what he had done in his New Testament translation – to clarify and to delight, but he recognizes that paraphrase goes further in this direction than translation: a paraphrase endeavours to say things differently without saying different things. It is not a commentary but can be used as a commentary. Although one will not actually hear the original author speaking (as one does in a translation), one may read the paraphrase as though the author were in fact speaking!

The dedicatory letter to the *Paraphrase on Matthew* (1522) likewise speaks of the paraphrase as a 'kind of commentary,' but without the freedom offered to the author by a commentary. At the same time there is a special problem for anyone who would paraphrase a Gospel, a problem that arises from the special respect owed to Christ: how would one dare to change his words? Indeed, as critics would point out, when the paraphrast puts his own words into the mouth of Christ, the authority of the paraphrast as commentator tends to assume, unacceptably, the authority of Christ. For a further general characterization of Erasmus' *Paraphrases* see 20 above.

While the *Paraphrases* were at first warmly welcomed, in 1525 under the watchful eye of Noël Béda at the University of Paris they began to receive severe criticism. Much of the criticism, particularly by the Paris theologians, but also by Spanish monks, was directed against statements in the *Paraphrases* that were perceived either as unorthodox or as offering support to unorthodox opinion. The criticism of Alberto Pio, however, addressed quite directly the claims Erasmus made for his work as a paraphrast. Thus the excerpts given below from *The Reply to the Letter of Alberto Pio* (*1529*) speak forcefully to the problems inherent in the Erasmian practice of paraphrasing.]

(1) The Dedicatory Letter to the *Paraphrase* on the Epistle to the Romans (Ep 710)

[Domenico Grimani (1461–1523) was a member of a distinguished Venetian family. He was created cardinal in 1493. Though addressed here as cardinal of St Mark's, he was in fact Cardinal-bishop of Porto (the designation 'St Mark's' perhaps deriving from his palace). He was a friend of Julius II, but was not in sympathy with Julius' successor, Leo X, and was in Rome very little after 1517, and Erasmus thereafter had little communication with the cardinal. Domenico may possibly have thanked Erasmus for this dedication, but no explicit acknowledgment of such has been found in Erasmus' correspondence (CEBR II 134). Domenico was a magnificent patron of arts and letters and an avid collector of antiquities. He had befriended Erasmus in Rome in 1509 and Erasmus later described his magnificent library (Ep 2465:5–60).]

TO THE MOST REVEREND FATHER IN CHRIST
MY LORD GRIMANI OF VENICE, CARDINAL OF ST MARK'S,
FROM ERASMUS OF ROTTERDAM, GREETING [Ep 710:4–53]

[4] Those who find it surprising, most reverend Father in God, that Paul the apostle, who was a good linguist,[40] should have written to the Romans in Greek rather than Latin, will wonder no more if they remember that at that date the use of the Greek language was almost as widespread as the Roman rule. [19] But now that Rome is entirely Christian, in fact the chief seat of the Christian religion, and Latin is spoken all the world over by everyone who acknowledges the authority of the Roman pontiff, I thought I should be doing something worthwhile if I could make Paul speak to men who are now pure Romans and adult Christians, not only in the Roman tongue but more intelligibly; if, in fact, he

40 Ie 'spoke several languages.'

could talk Latin in such a way that one would not recognize the Hebrew speaking but would recognize the Apostle.[41]

I will not set forth here how much this small work has cost me, such as it is, for I am sure that no one who has not made the experiment himself in similar subject-matter would find it easy to value or to believe the difficulty of bridging gaps, smoothing rough passages, bringing order out of confusion and simplicity out of complication, untying knots, throwing light on dark places, and giving Hebrew turns of speech a Roman dress – in fact, of altering the language of Paul, the heavenly spokesman, and so managing one's paraphrase that it does not become a *paraphronesis*, a caricature. One must say things differently without saying different things, especially on a subject which is not only difficult in many ways, but sacred, and very near the majesty of the Gospel; one works on slippery ground where a fall is very easy, and yet one cannot fall without grave peril.

[42] I shall think, however, that my efforts have been richly rewarded, if I can feel that as a result Paul has become somewhat more attractive and certainly more accessible to your Eminence, and through you to the rest of Rome, to whom it is right that he should be most attractive and most accessible. For I know well how many people have been deterred from reading him hitherto by the strangeness of the language, and how many more by the difficulty of disentangling and understanding what he says, wrong though it is that any inconvenience should deter men from such fruitful reading. It is the distaste or the despair of such people that I have tried to remedy by this enterprise of mine, so balancing my work that he who rejects any change in the letter of Holy Writ may use it as a commentary, while he who is free from such superstition may hear the voice of Paul himself.

(2) The Dedicatory Letter to the *Paraphrase* on Gospel of Matthew (Ep 1255)

[Charles V (1500–58) grandson of Emperor Maximilian I, was through Spanish descent heir to the throne of Castile and of Aragon, of which he became king in 1517. He was elected emperor in 1519, crowned king of the Romans in 1520, and crowned Holy Roman Emperor in 1530. His election as emperor aroused the jealousy of Francis I and in 1521 war broke out between the two of them. The antagonism continued for many years. This *Paraphrase*

41 Erasmus refers to the Hebraic idioms carried over into Paul's Greek, which was not the pure, standard Greek of classical authors.

was published in 1522 so that Erasmus understandably concludes the dedicatory letter with a plea (somewhat timidly expressed) for peace.]

TO THE INVINCIBLE EMPEROR CHARLES, FIFTH OF THAT NAME, FROM ERASMUS OF ROTTERDAM, GREETING [Ep 1255:3–92]

[3] Right well I know, invincible Emperor Charles, the great respect and reverence due to all the sacred literature which sainted Fathers put forth for our benefit under the inspiration of the Holy Spirit, and especially to those which give us a faithful account of all that our heavenly Father did or uttered in the person of his Son Jesus Christ for the salvation of the whole world; and I am well aware of my own unworthiness. When a few years ago I first set my hand to an exposition of the Pauline Epistles in the form of a paraphrase – it was an unprompted impulse that put the idea into my head – I felt myself to be undertaking an exceedingly bold and self-confident enterprise and one 'full of dangerous hazard' as the saying goes;[42] so much so that after trying the experiment with two or three chapters, I was minded to furl my sails and abandon my intended course, had not my learned friends with surprising unanimity urged me to continue. Nor would their importunity allow me any rest until I had finished all the apostolic Epistles that we possess, although I had not intended to deal with any except those which beyond all question were written by St Paul.[43]

[25] Having performed this task, I was not expecting thereafter to have anything more to do with this type of literature. But no: I went to pay my respects to his Eminence Matthäus, cardinal of Sion, when he was in Brussels on his way back from the Diet of Worms, and in our very first conversation, as though he had thought of this in advance, he began to urge me to do for St Matthew's Gospel what I had done for the apostolic Epistles.[44] I at once made numerous excuses. I had already

42 An expression recalling Horace *Odes* 2.1.6, where it is used of an author undertaking a risky literary task.

43 Erasmus published the *Paraphrase on Romans* in 1517, the *Paraphrases* on the Epistles whose Pauline authorship was then undisputed (1 Corinthians–Philemon) (1519–20), finally the *Paraphrases* on the Catholic Epistles and Hebrews (1520–1).

44 Matthäus Schiner (1465–1522), made cardinal of Sion in Switzerland in 1511, acted for both Julius II and the Hapsburgs. Erasmus may have met him as early as 1516, but it was probably in 1520 when Schiner was with the court of Charles V in November after Charles' coronation that Schiner urged Erasmus to paraphrase the Epistles of James and John. After the Diet of Worms in 1521 (immediately following which Luther was put under a ban of the empire) Schiner was in Brussels where he again met Erasmus and urged him to paraphrase the Gospel of Matthew. Cf John Bateman's brief but excellent account in CWE 44 132 n1 of Schiner's relations with Erasmus.

shown sufficient audacity, I said, in attempting this for the letters of the apostles. The apostles were of course inspired, but they were only human, while the majesty of Christ was too great for the same boldness to be permissible in respect of the words he uttered. If I were not deterred by the solemn nature of the task, yet the subject-matter was unsympathetic and did not admit of paraphrase; and not solely because in the gospel different characters appear, so that while the writer adapts his style to suit them (as he has to), his pen is constrained within very narrow limits and of course is debarred from the freedom allowed to other kinds of commentary. For a paraphrase is a kind of commentary. Besides that, since a great part of the gospel consists of a narrative of events in a simple and straightforward style, he who seeks to paraphrase such material will perhaps be thought to do no more than, as the Greek proverb has it, kindle a lamp at midday.[45]

Then again, since the ancients in expounding the allegories show great variation and sometimes behave, in my view, as though they were not wholly serious, nor will it prove possible to set them down except as one who reports the words either of Christ or of the evangelist, it is clear that I should be facing very great difficulties. I need not add that Christ sometimes spoke as though at the time he wished not to be understood; for instance, [54] in the discourse in which he foretells the destruction of Jerusalem, the end of this world, and the afflictions that will befall the apostles in the future,[46] Jesus so mixes and adapts what he has to say that he seems to me to have wished to remain obscure not only to the apostles but to us. Again, there are some passages which in my opinion are quite inexplicable, among them the phrase about the sin against the Holy Spirit which can never be forgiven, and the last day which only the Father knows and which is unknown even to the Son.[47] Faced with such places in a commentary, one can without peril report the differing views of different scholars, and even confess outright that one does not understand the passage. But the author of a paraphrase is not allowed the same freedom. Furthermore, some things are expressed in such a way that they refer equally to modern times, in which we see many things that conflict with the institutions of the apostolic age. Granted that the evangelists knew these things in advance by the spirit of prophecy, they cannot be recounted as if the evangelists themselves were speaking, except in a very unnatural and artificial way. My mind

45 Cf *Adagia* II v 6.

46 Cf Luke 21:5–33.

47 Cf Matt 12:31–2 (sin against the Holy Spirit), Mark 13:32 (last day).

was influenced also by the thought that if I undertook this task in Matthew only, some people would demand forthwith the same treatment for the other evangelists. If I were to comply with their wishes, I foresaw that I should often have to repeat the same words, wherever in fact the evangelists agree among themselves.

[80] With these arguments and many others like them I begged to be excused the task that was set before me, and thought I had a good case which must win the day. But the cardinal's eloquence and his authority were too much for me; he took the risk and hazard of the whole business on his own shoulders. I had not the face to stand out any longer against the advice of a man whose wisdom your Majesty is often happy to follow in matters of the greatest moment. At any rate, though I had not entirely accepted the burden, but had only promised that I would try sometime if it could be made to work, he went on to Milan,[48] and promised the Germans in my name that the work would come out this winter. Consequently on my return to Basel I was beset by my German friends, who can be very obstinate when they want something, so that to fulfil the promises he and I had made I finished the work in about a month.

(3) *Reply to the Letter of Alberto Pio* [CWE 84 74–84]

[Alberto Pio (1475–1531), nephew of the distinguished Italian humanist Pico della Mirandola, was a capable international diplomat, eventually becoming the ambassador of Francis I at Rome. In Rome he was a member of the humanist Roman Academy, where, according to reports, he attacked Erasmus. An initial correspondence with Erasmus led him to publish a work early in 1529 that accused Erasmus of aiding Luther by his attacks on the church. Erasmus responded with *The Reply to the Letter of Alberto Pio* from which a few excerpts are cited here. The excerpts reflect Pio's concern with the language of a sacred text, and the problem of distortion in any representation of it. I conclude this study of Erasmus' New Testament scholarship with this citation from Erasmus' response to Alberto Pio.]

[74] You say that many condemn my expounding Scripture more clearly and elegantly through paraphrase, because the Scriptures scarcely admit of commentary let alone of paraphrase. Now you know that Sacred Scripture consists above all of its mystic meaning rather than of

48 After leaving Brussels Schiner went first to Switzerland where he secured troops to lead against the French who held Milan; cf Ep 1248 n7 and 1250 n5.

words, and that it is situated in the languages in which it was handed down by its original writers. I have changed nothing in these languages.

[75] There are two types of translation, one that transfers a book from one language into another, a second that explains the meaning of Scripture under consideration.[49] If you decree that commentaries and all expositions must be banned, I will allow my *Paraphrases* also to be banned. [76] But if you allow those, then a paraphrase is nothing other than a type of commentary, one more suitable for the busy or fastidious reader. I have explained the content [of Scripture] in a somewhat more polished way than the apostles transmitted it, or than the Latin translator, whoever he or she was, rendered it. If you acknowledge the absolute truth of these statements, there is no room for the statements you declaim with a sort of Ciceronian amplification, namely that the Holy Spirit has no need of my polishing.

[78] Where, moreover, did you light upon those babblers who say, who declare, who suspect, that my goal is for my *Paraphrases* to be read in place of divine Scripture in the churches? Since this is so extraordinarily absurd I will not refute it, even though many things are read in churches that are less suited to the liturgy than my *Paraphrases*.

If the expounding of Sacred Scripture is in itself forbidden, then you must condemn along with me those who first dared to produce commentaries on it. Of course, there are different types of commentary. What Erasmus dared to do, Juvencus dared to do before him in verse, and he did not [79] fail to win his share of praise. His poem is in fact a paraphrase. After Juvencus, Arator dared to do the same thing to the Acts of the Apostles, and not so long ago Aegidius Delphius, a theologian from the Sorbonne, did this to the Psalms and a number of other books of Sacred Scripture.[50]

But you are scandalized by the fact that I present a *persona* speaking differently in paraphrase from the way he does in his own work.

49 Cf CWE 84 75 n371: 'Erasmus is not contrasting liberal [*sic*, literal?] and free translation … but translation and interpretive paraphrase; note eg Erasmus' words in Ep 1274:37–43: "In a version the sense is rendered literally; in paraphrase it is legitimate to add something of your own as well … a paraphrase is … a kind of commentary in which the writer and his author retain separate roles."'

50 Juvencus, a Spanish priest (fourth century), wrote in Latin verse a paraphrase on the Gospels. Arator (sixth century) wrote a poem 'based more or less on the Acts of the Apostles but with considerable allegorical and mystical interpretation' (Ferguson *Early Christianity* 99). Gillis van Delft (d 1524), theologian, for a number of years at the University of Paris, wrote paraphrases on the Psalms and on the Epistle to the Romans.

[80] And you say, 'In fact, you sometimes bring on the *persona* of Christ preaching in a very unsuitable style, as if he were a Cicero pleading a case in a studied language and artificial speech, and, what is even more revolting, saying a great many things not contained in Scripture, in words adapted to merely human wisdom.' To reply briefly: there are in my *Paraphrases* none of the trappings of declamation that you ascribe to them. Nowhere do I assign to Christ a speech that is studied and highly wrought, since there is no work of mine that I completed more extempore.[51]

[81] Now to your next point, that someone who has lapsed into error by following the authority of a commentator can readily be recalled to the right path by the assistance of the Scriptures, but there is no way to put right someone who has been misled by my paraphrase, I pray you, illustrious sir, did you write this as a joke or in earnest? [82] But what prevents one who has gone wrong from being corrected through the still extant Scripture? Indeed it was for this purpose that I made note of the chapters in the margins, so that the reader could more conveniently make comparisons.[52]

---

51 In the *Ratio* (cf 49–50 n35) Erasmus had spoken of *persona* in the sense of the characters in the narrative assuming certain roles; here he reports Pio as referring the word to the author assuming the voice of a person in the narrative: Pio complained that in paraphrasing Erasmus assumed 'the *persona* of the author, [tempering] the words of the Holy Spirit according to [his] pleasure' CWE 84 79 n393. Pio's complaint was not entirely without basis. The paraphrastic speech of the angel to Joseph in Matthew 1 has the character of a speech of Mercury bearing a message from Jupiter in the *Aeneid*.

52 Erasmus not only placed in the text of his paraphrases the chapter numbers traditional in the biblical text, but added in the margins 'catch-words' from the Vulgate so that the reader could identify the point in the Vulgate at which the paraphrase had arrived. Our system of verses did not yet exist, but the catch-words from the Vulgate, though relatively few, are effective markers for anyone who knows the Bible well.

Works Frequently Cited

Allen	*Opus epistolarum Des. Erasmi Roterodami* ed. P.S. Allen, H.M. Allen, and H.W. Garrod (Oxford 1906–58) 11 vols and Index
ASD	*Opera omnia Desiderii Erasmi Roterodami* (Amsterdam 1969–)
AV	*The Holy Bible, Authorized King James Version* (London 1611)
CEBR	*Contemporaries of Erasmus: A Biographical Register of the Renaissance and the Reformation* ed P.G. Bietenholz and T.B. Deutscher (Toronto 1985–7) 3 vols
CWE	*Collected Works of Erasmus* (Toronto, 1974–)
DV	*The Holy Bible, Douay-Rheims Version* rev by Bishop Richard Challoner (Baltimore 1899)
Ferguson *Early Christianity*	*Encyclopedia of Early Christianity* 2nd ed, ed Everett Ferguson et al (New York 1997)
Fitzgerald	*Augustine through the Ages: An Encyclopedia* ed Alan D. Fitzgerald O.S.A. et al (Grand Rapids MI 1999)
FOTC	*Fathers of the Church* (Washington DC 1947–)
NEB	*New English Bible* (Oxford and Cambridge 1970)
NRSV	*The Holy Bible: New Revised Standard Version* (New York 1989)
ODCC	*Oxford Dictionary of the Christian Church* ed F.L. Cross 3rd ed rev ed E.A. Livingstone (Oxford 2005)
PL	*Patrologiae cursus completus … series Latina* ed J.-P. Migne. *Patrologia Latina Database*, electronic version representing the first edition (Paris 1844–1865; ProQuest Learning Company 1996–2018)
RSV	*The Bible: Revised Standard Version* (New York 1973/1980)
TOB	*Traduction oecuménique de la Bible* (Paris 1988)

Suggestions for Further Reading

Works by Erasmus

Erasmus' voluminous work provides an important context for understanding his New Testament scholarship. The following list provides some contextual expressions of themes represented in the selections above.

Enchiridion CWE 27
Praise of Folly CWE 27
The *Adages* CWE 34 and 35:
'The Labours of Hercules III i 1,' 'The Sileni of Alcibiades III iii 1,' 'War is sweet to those who have not tried it' IV i 1 (also available in *The Adages of Erasmus selected by William Barker* [Toronto 2001])
The *Colloquies* CWE 39 and 40:
'The Godly Feast,' 'The Young Man and the Harlot,' 'A Pilgrimage for Religion's Sake,' 'A Fish Diet,' 'Cyclops, or The Gospel Bearer,' 'The Sermon'
Expositions of the Psalms CWE 63 and 64:
'Introduction' by D. Baker-Smith to CWE 63: 'Psalm 22' and 'Psalm 28 with "On the Turkish War"' CWE 64

Works about Erasmus

Listed below (in order of date of publication) are four biographies, each with a very distinctive perspective, and several studies on aspects of Erasmus' work on the New Testament.

R. Bainton *Erasmus of Christendom* (New York 1969)
G. Faludy *Erasmus of Rotterdam* (London 1970)
C. Augustijn *Erasmus: His Life, Work, and Influence* (Toronto 1991)
J.K. McConica *Erasmus* (Oxford 1991)

J. Bentley *Humanists and Holy Writ* (Princeton 1983)
E. Rummel *Erasmus' Annotations on the New Testament* (Toronto 1986)
A. Rabil *Erasmus and the New Testament: The Mind of a Christian Humanist* (Lanham MD 1993 [1972])
M. Hoffman *Rhetoric and Theology: The Hermeneutic of Erasmus* (Toronto 1994)
H.M. Pabel and M. Vessey *Holy Scripture Speaks … Erasmus' Paraphrases on the New Testament* (Toronto 2002) (Essays)
M. Wallraff, Silvana Seidel Menchi, and K. von Greyerz eds *Basel 1516: Erasmus' Edition of the New Testament* (Tubingen 2016) (Essays)
R.D. Sider ed *The New Testament Scholarship of Erasmus: An Introduction with the Prefaces and the Ancillary Writings* CWE 41 (Toronto 2019) (The 'Introduction' [pp 3–388] offers a historical account of the development of Erasmus' New Testament scholarship)

Index